PROGRESSIVE COMMUNITY ACTION: CRITICAL THEORY AND SOCIAL JUSTICE IN LIBRARY AND INFORMATION SCIENCE

PROGRESSIVE COMMUNITY ACTION: CRITICAL THEORY AND SOCIAL JUSTICE IN LIBRARY AND INFORMATION SCIENCE

Bharat Mehra and Kevin Rioux
Editors

LIBRARY JUICE PRESS
SACRAMENTO, CA

Published in 2016 by Library Juice Press

Library Juice Press
PO Box 188784
Sacramento, CA 95822

http://libraryjuicepress.com/

This book is printed on acid-free, sustainably-sourced paper.

Library of Congress Cataloging-in-Publication Data

Progressive community action : critical theory and social justice in
library and information science / edited by Bharat Mehra and Kevin Rioux.
    pages cm.
Includes bibliographical references and index.
ISBN 9781936117659 (acid-free paper)
1. Library science--Social aspects. 2. Information science--Social aspects.
3. Libraries and society. 4. Libraries and community. 5. Social justice. I. Mehra,
Bharat, editor. II. Rioux, Kevin, editor.
    Z665 .P96 2016
    020--dc23

                    2016011895

Contents

PREFACE

Clara M. Chu

"Books for librarians with a critical edge," this book publisher's tagline, is an intellectual space this edited volume aptly engages and fills. *Progressive Community Action: Critical Theory and Social Justice in Library and Information Science* (PCA) aims to examine the intersections of critical theory and social justice in library and information science (LIS) and how these are negotiated toward tangible actions that result in positive change in communities. PCA follows the 2009 article "Social Justice in Library and Information Science," written by co-editors Bharat Mehra and Kevin Rioux, and co-author Kendra Albright in the *Encyclopedia of Library and Information Sciences*[1]. A foundational treatise on social justice in the library and information field, the authors defined social justice by describing the ways that it has been conceptualized, and reviewed how social justice had been engaged in the library and information professions, especially in public libraries, and in LIS research. In order to provide the necessary context to understand how social justice has been and can be engaged in LIS, the authors needed

---

1. Bharat Mehra, Kevin Rioux, and Kendra S. Albright, "Social Justice in Library and Information Science," in *Encyclopedia of Library and Information Sciences*, edited by Marcia J. Bates and Mary N. Maack, 4820-4836. New York: Taylor and Francis, 2009.

to draw on the literature outside of LIS, including philosophy, ethics, sociology, education, critical studies, ethnic studies, women's studies, computer science, law, political science, and management.

Taking 2009 as a temporal reference, it is heartening to observe the growing number of publications and conference presentations on critical perspectives in LIS and the promotion of social justice. The LIS field has long had a commitment to social responsibility, which has been a core value of the American Library Association, and is expressed in the profession's service orientation, and from the civil rights era, in professional advocacy for equitable information access. However, we are now turning the corner and finding a voice that questions inequity and normativity, names the inequities, represents the oppressed, and speaks clearly and loudly of action that can be modeled or structural barriers that need to be eradicated. In one breath, when we utter diversity, we also now state or understand that it engages the work of inclusion, equity, and social justice. We are seeing in practice, policy, and research that this range of diversity/social justice activities comes from a genera-tion of library professionals, educators, and researchers who examine and undertake their practice from a critical perspective. Although the twenty-first century has brought much progress, the world continues to be rife with inequity, injustice, and conflict, with which the LIS field has to contend. The advocacy that is needed for these times is now conducted in the LIS field with a growing fluency in the language of critical studies and theory, and the use of information and communi-cation technologies (ICTs) for collective action. It is also heartening to see the growth in publication of critical theory and practice in LIS, which has lagged behind archival studies, a field which has a solid critical theoretical foundation that informs its practice and research.

PCA is surfacing at a time when I can confidently state that critical studies and social justice in our field have blossomed, as evidenced by publication productivity and professional discourse. For example, we have the volumes published by Library Juice Press; the recent book *Libraries, Human Rights, and Social Justice: Enabling Access and Promoting*

Inclusion, by Paul T. Jaeger; Natalie Greene Taylor, and Ursula Gorham;[2] and the last 2015 issue of *Library Trends,* edited by Bharat Mehra,[3] and the first 2016 issue of *Library Quarterly,* both focused on social justice. While we continue to have the journals *Progressive Librarian* and *Information for Social Change,* the publication of an open access journal, the *Journal of Inclusion and Diversity in Library & Information Science Education* (JIDLIS), has been announced by the University of Maryland's iSchool. In terms of professional discourse, to complement LIS conferences and personal professional blogs on diversity, we have the 2015 to 2017 annual conferences of the Association for Library and Information Science Education (ALISE) focusing on social justice themes, and Critlib (http://critlib. org/), short for "critical librarianship," which is "a movement of library workers dedicated to bringing social justice principles into our work in libraries." An international collective, Critlib promotes discussion about critical perspectives on library practice and recognizes that "we all work under regimes of white supremacy, capitalism, and a range of structural inequalities, [and asks] how can our work as librarians intervene in and disrupt those systems?" Twitter chats and conferences facilitate discussions, projects promote collective action, and recommended readings support intellectual growth.

Readers within and outside of LIS can benefit from reading PCA. As a work that presents critical theories in LIS, and cases of progressive community action which engage critical theory and social justice, LIS students, instructors, and researchers will learn about critical theory and practices in LIS that they can model or on which they can build. PCA covers social critical theory and social justice work in the context of libraries, classrooms, a library professional association, and a museum. The museum and archival field can use it to learn about comparable work

---

2. Paul T. Jaeger, Natalie Greene Taylor, and Ursula Gorham, *Libraries, Human Rights, and Social Justice: Enabling Access and Promoting Inclusion* (Lanham, MD: Rowman & Littlefield, 2015).

3. Bharat Mehra, "Introduction," *Library Trends: Social Justice in Library and Information Science & Services* 64, no. 2 (2015): 179-197.

in the library and information sector, and those in cognate fields such as education, ethnic studies, and sociology will understand critical theory and social justice work in the context of libraries and information work.

A specific focus of PCA and explicit in its title, which serves to distinguish it from other publications, is the term progressive. For Mehra and Rioux, progressive thinking addresses justice and fairness, and in turn the community action included in the book is necessarily progressive through its engagement of critical theory and furthering of social justice. This key word rings familiar to anyone paying attention to the current electoral discourse as the Democratic Party presidential candidates fight over the meaning of "progressive." I agree that to conduct social justice work, the action taken benefits individuals or a community positively and should be understood in critical terms. However, beyond such actions for the common good, progressive action needs to move beyond the immediate and situational toward sustainable community development. This means that, for long-term benefit, progressive action necessitates the eradication of systemic barriers that create structural inequities and unrecognized privileges. PCA accentuates libraries as a social good, and the library and information field as an intellectual and professional space addressing critical theory and social justice.

Bibliography

Mehra, Bharat. "Introduction." *Library Trends: Social Justice in Library and Information Science & Services* 64, no. 2 (2015): 179-197.

Mehra, Bharat, Kevin Rioux, and Kendra S. Albright. "Social Justice in Library and Information Science." In *Encyclopedia of Library and Information Sciences* (3rd ed.), edited by Marcia J. Bates and Mary N. Maack, 4820-4836. New York: Taylor and Francis, 2009.

Jaeger, Paul T., Natalie Greene Taylor, and Ursula Gorham. *Libraries, Human Rights, and Social Justice: Enabling Access and Promoting Inclusion.* Lanham, MD: Rowman & Littlefield, 2015.

INTRODUCTION

Kevin Rioux and Bharat Mehra

Along with like-minded colleagues interested in socially-relevant information work and research, we began discussing connections between social justice and information service over a barbeque lunch at the 2005 American Society for Information Science and Technology (ASIS&T) meeting in Austin, Texas. In many ways, we haven't stopped talking about this topic since.

Of course, over the past decade, our discussions have gone in several different directions, and together as well as with others we have written and spoken about social justice and library and information science (LIS) research and practice at various local, regional, national, and international venues.[1] Bharat's social justice path has led him to work with and study specific user groups and communities (e.g., "The

---

1. Kevin Rioux, Bharat Mehra, and Kendra Albright, "Conceptualizing Social Justice in the Information Sciences," *Proceedings of the American Society for Information Science and Technology* 44, no. 1 (January 1, 2007): 1–4, doi:10.1002/meet.1450440130; Bharat Mehra, Kendra S. Albright, and Kevin Rioux, "A Practical Framework for Social Justice Research in the Information Professions," *Proceedings of the American Society for Information Science and Technology* 43, no. 1 (January 1, 2006): 1–10, doi:10.1002/meet.14504301275; Bharat Mehra, Kevin S. Rioux, and Kendra S. Albright, "Social Justice in Library and Information Science," in *Encyclopedia of Library and Information Sciences*, 3rd ed. (Abingdon, UK: Taylor & Francis, 2009), 4820–36, http://www.tandfonline.com/doi/abs/10.1081/E-ELIS3-120044526.

Library-Community Convergence Framework:[2]) and Kevin's work has tended toward the conceptual (e.g., "Metatheory in Library and Information Science"[3]). Together we have kept a keen eye on LIS discourse and practice that both explicitly and implicitly connect information to social justice concepts. In addition to our scholarly activity and action research, we both teach LIS graduate courses that integrate social justice in the information professions at our respective universities.

We are gratified to see an increased interest in social justice among LIS researchers, students, and practitioners that is reflected both in the LIS literature and at professional conferences.[4] The social justice movement in LIS is indeed gaining momentum, and is identifying lacunae for new and expanded analysis and practice. Yet there are challenges due to the fact that social justice in LIS is still an emergent and amorphous construct. In many ways, social justice remains a loose, feel-good concept instead of a rigorous framework that can guide LIS efforts to bring about societal change for the better. This suggests that additional venues, such as this edited volume, are currently necessary for exploration, description, and sharing of examples of LIS-related social justice activities, and for developing social justice practice frameworks and research methods. It also seems that the time is right for LIS researchers, practitioners, and students to look for ways to demonstrate relevance by reporting on the outcomes of LIS activity associated with social justice ideas, and to create solid and precise articulations of social justice theory for the field.

---

2. Bharat Mehra and Ramesh Srinivasan, "The Library-Community Convergence Framework for Community Action: Libraries as Catalysts of Social Change," *Libri: International Journal of Libraries & Information Services* 57, no. 3 (September 2007): 123–39.

3. Kevin Rioux, "Metatheory in Library and Information Science: A Nascent Social Justice Approach," *Journal of Education for Library & Information Science* 51, no. 1 (2010): 9–17.

4. Paul T. Jaeger et al., "Library Research and What Libraries Actually Do Now: Education, Inclusion, Social Services, Public Spaces, Digital Literacy, Social Justice, Human Rights, and Other Community Needs," *Library Quarterly: Information, Community, Policy* 84, no. 4 (October 1, 2014): 491–93, doi:10.1086/677785; "ALISE 2015 Conference," accessed August 17, 2015, http://www.alise.org/2015-conference-2.

In response to these needs, we as editors sought for this book original, methodologically-varied scholarship that addressed the intersections of *progressive community action, critical theory,* and *social justice* in library and information science. The conceptual space provided by these intersections allows for broad exploration of a variety of topics, and provides an overall structure and scope for this edited collection. Using this frame of inquiry also allowed us to include examples from different types of libraries, museums, and other information settings that tell the stories of a wide range of social justice interests and concerns that exist in today's information landscape.

The reader will notice that the reflections and observations described in these chapters clearly demonstrate a *progressive* mindset on the part of LIS professionals that supports democracy, freedom, and individual liberty. Progressive thinking promotes elements of justice and fairness, and embraces the concepts of equality and equity. Overall, the positions described herein are those that work against discrimination based on race, ethnicity, national origin, geography, sex, gender, sexual orientation, age, education, income, disability, veteran status, and other variables of difference.

In recent years, the progressive mindset in LIS has been linked to *action*, and the organic relationship between social justice and library and information science has been characterized as action-oriented, socially-relevant outcomes via information works-in-progress.[5] Action elements are fundamental to a meaningful application of the social justice construct to LIS because they translate philosophical, legal, and intellectual discourse into substantive outcomes that change existing power imbalances, social inequities, and marginalized realities at all levels.[6]

---

5. Bharat Mehra, "What Is the Value of Social Justice in Pakistan's Library and Information Science Professions," *Pakistan Journal of Information Management & Libraries,* (December 31, 2014).

6. Bharat Mehra and Lisette Hernandez, "Libraries as Agents of Human Rights Protection and Social Change on Behalf of Sexual Minorities in India: An Action-Based Manifesto for Progressive Change.," in *Perspectives on Libraries as Institutions of Human Rights and Social Justice*, ed. Ursula Gorham, Natalie Greene Taylor, and Paul T. Jaeger, Advances in Librarianship Series (Bingley, UK: Emerald Group Publishing Limited, forthcoming).

This application can be achieved through a wide range of LIS-related experiences, which include social justice planning, conceptualization, and implementation integrated with all types of information work, including information creation, organization, management, and dissemination processes. Social justice actions provide tangible results that challenge the status quo[7] and change norms and existing modes of practice from what is to what should be.[8]

The *progressive community action* elements that distinguish these collected chapters are urgently important to LIS efforts in shaping public perception about the value of information work in everyday life and culture. The authors document their activities as information creators, organizers, educators, students, leaders, and facilitators in terms of the community-wide changes their projects achieved or have the potential to achieve. They suggest that social justice actions and positive changes attributable to information professionals will demonstrate relevance to the public, and empower them to play a more important and visible community leadership role. This includes interacting with political, economic, and policy leaders, and resisting power imbalances that negatively affect democracy, civil society, and individual freedom.[9]

The works in this collection also acknowledge (either implicitly or explicitly) that critical thinking and critical theory go hand-in-hand with a reflexive process that questions traditional understandings and scrutinizes existing values, practices, ideological frameworks, and processes.[10]

---

7. Mehra, Albright, and Rioux, "A Practical Framework for Social Justice Research in the Information Professions"; Rioux, Mehra, and Albright, "Conceptualizing Social Justice in the Information Sciences."

8. Bharat Mehra and Lisette Hernandez, "Rural and Urban Queering Alliances Out of the Library towards Legal Protection of Lesbian, Gay, Bisexual, Transgender, and Questioning People in India," in *Queer Library Alliance: Global Reflections and Imaginings*, ed. Rae-Anne Montague and Lucas McKeever (Sacramento, CA: Library Juice Press, forthcoming).

9. Bharat Mehra, "Introduction: Social Justice in Library and Information Science & Services," *Library Trends* 64, no. 2 (2015): 179-197.

10. A. Michael Froomkin, "Habermas@discourse.net: Toward a Critical Theory of Cyberspace," *Harvard Law Review* 116, no. 3 (January 2003): 749; Jurgen Habermas, *Justification and Application: Remarks on Discourse Ethics*,

With roots in service-based ethics, critical approaches to examining LIS theory and practice are appropriate, especially in relation to community contexts and progressive actions to make a societal difference.

The term *critical theory* originated in the Frankfurt School, a collaboration of social philosophers who studied societal development problems in Germany between the two twentieth century world wars. Included in this group were Herbert Marcuse, Theodor Adorno, Max Horkheimer, Walter Benjamin, Erich Fromm, and others. Since the 1960s, the second-generation scholars of the Frankfurt School (e.g., György Lukács, Antonio Gramsci, and especially Jürgen Habermas) took critical theory from its roots in German idealism and introduced elements of American pragmatism. Critical theory is today concerned with social foundations such as the forces and relations of production, employer-employee work conditions, division of labor, property relations, cultural institutions, political power structures, roles and rituals, and the nature of state control. The chapters in this collection explore the application of critical approaches in the context of the professional activities of LIS researchers, practitioners, and educators. The characteristics of critical theory are relevant here because they focus on the perspectives of all stakeholders in a given information context, and include the points of view of those on society's margins in order to do justice to a diversity of perspectives while providing a grounding for the evaluation of potentially divisive problems.[11] The integration of critical theory with the social justice and progressive community action foundations of this book is intentional, as these constructs are deeply intertwined, and their connections may serve as a guide for future theory-building in LIS.

Keeping all of the above in mind, we are pleased to present this collection of essays written by a mix of new and experienced doers, scholars, and observers of contemporary social justice in LIS. Readers

Studies in Contemporary German Social Thought (Cambridge, Mass: MIT Press, 1994); Douglas Kellner, "Boundaries and Borderlines: Reflections on Jean Baudrillard and Critical Theory," *Current Perspectives in Social Theory* 9, 1989.

11. Ben Endres, "Habermas and Critical Thinking," *Philosophy of Education Archive* (1996): 176.

of these chapters will learn about roles played by progressive LIS professionals in bringing about positive community changes, and will gain understanding of how social justice is evolving as a critical approach that can guide action in LIS research, education, policy, service design, and programming, among other areas.

Chapters are grouped into two sections, but readers may approach these essays in any order, according to their specific interests. The first section, "Emergent Conceptual Frameworks for Progressive Community Action in Library and Information Science," includes three chapters:

- While thoughtfully considering activist libraries such as the People's Library of Occupy Wall Street and urban community information spaces, **Zachary Loeb** argues that libraries are more than sites in which various groups encounter particular information technologies—that in fact, libraries can be conceptualized as a type of technology or tool that can support socially-just community action.

- Using a critical framework, **Gabriel Gomez** discusses emergent trends in behaviorist-oriented Big Data collection. He suggests that these trends are likely to shift the foci of human information behavior research to largely commercial ends, affecting libraries' core values, social justice goals, and community actions.

- **Jonathan Cope** discusses trends in the marketization of public goods, places, and services (such as those provided by libraries). In response to these trends, he introduces a critical framework based on his idea of "socially generated information." Cope then explores ways in which this framework can be used to support democracy, progressive community action, and community development.

The second section of the book, "Contextual Examinations of Progressive Community Action in Library and Information Science," features the following six chapters:

- Using Giroux's critical theories as a framework, **Wendy Highby** offers an auto-ethnographic case study that describes her efforts as an academic librarian in Colorado to lead colleagues at her university in a community action against a proposal to lease mineral rights to an energy corporation that plans to use fracking techniques on the campus. Her work suggests that librarians can indeed engage in the public political sphere and nurture environmental justice, progressive values, and community action.

- **Nicole Cooke**, an LIS researcher and educator, and **Joseph Minarik**, a social worker and educator, report on their collaboration in developing techniques and conceptual frameworks for teaching diversity, community action, and social justice topics to LIS graduate students. They present strategies to help a variety of learners understand the complexity of inequality and privilege, and give suggestions for discerning the difference between progressive and pseudo-progressive policies.

- **Laura-Edythe Coleman** argues that museums must develop a socially-inclusive curatorial voice in order to position themselves within a social justice advocacy role. She offers a curatorial voice gatekeeping framework that can generate and encourage progressive social action on the part of museum leaders.

- **Jeanie Austin** uses a queer theoretical lens to explore the concept of youth development. She questions the philosophy underpinning the 40 Development Assets for Adolescence used by the Young Adult Library Association (YALSA), and suggests that socially-just community action for youth service would be best served by working with youth rather than providing services to youth.

- **Kaurri Williams-Cockfield** explores how public library leaders can develop, implement, and advocate for progressive, socially-just library services in rural communities that collectively perceive no need to change. To address this issue, she takes novel approaches in using unstructured research techniques to study a sample of rural libraries.

- **Punit Dadlani** reports on an exploratory study of high school students engaged in a collaborative online project. Using context-specific methods, he provides insight on how young people in an information space construct notions of social justice, particularly around ideas of control, power, and fairness—useful to school teachers and librarians eager to support collaborative, socially-just pedagogical environments.

Despite a traditional reluctance toward taking activist stances in LIS, we know that many in our field are motivated by social justice thinking, and there are many implicit and explicit social justice elements that drive LIS practice and research. Yet working toward social justice is not trivial. We recognize that information workers face a number of challenges as agents of social justice, including an underdeveloped social justice theory base for LIS, overly-specialized and fragmented voices for social justice in LIS, and workplace and political pressures to maintain the status quo. We hope the chapters in this book help begin to address these issues for readers, and inspire LIS professionals to more fully explore, experiment, and integrate critical social justice theories, strategies, and practices in their work. We look forward to the continued discussion.

Bibliography

"ALISE 2015 Conference." Accessed August 17, 2015. http://www.alise.org/2015-conference-2.

Endres, Ben. "Habermas and Critical Thinking." *Philosophy of Education Archive* (1996): 176.

Froomkin, A. Michael. "Habermas@discourse.net: Toward a Critical Theory of Cyberspace." *Harvard Law Review* 116, no. 3 (January 2003): 749.

Habermas, Jurgen. *Justification and Application: Remarks on Discourse Ethics*. Studies in Contemporary German Social Thought. Cambridge, MA: MIT Press, 1994.

Jaeger, Paul T., Ursula Gorham, Natalie Greene Taylor, Karen Kettnich, Lindsay C. Sarin, and Kaitlin J. Peterson. "Library Research and What Libraries Actually Do Now: Education, Inclusion, Social Services, Public Spaces, Digital Literacy,

Social Justice, Human Rights, and Other Community Needs." *Library Quarterly: Information, Community, Policy* 84, no. 4 (October 1, 2014): 491–93. doi:10.1086/677785.

Kellner, D. "Boundaries and Borderlines: Reflections on Jean Baudrillard and Critical Theory." *Current Perspectives in Social Theory*, 9 (1989). https://pages.gseis.ucla.edu/faculty/kellner/essays/boundariesborderlines.pdf.

Mehra, Bharat. "Introduction: Social Justice in Library and Information Science & Services." *Library Trends* 64, no. 2 (2015): 179-197.

———. "What Is the Value of Social Justice in Pakistan's Library and Information Science Professions." *Pakistan Journal of Information Management & Libraries*, (December 31, 2014).

Mehra, Bharat, Kendra S. Albright, and Kevin Rioux. "A Practical Framework for Social Justice Research in the Information Professions." *Proceedings of the American Society for Information Science and Technology* 43, no. 1 (January 1, 2006): 1–10. doi:10.1002/meet.14504301275.

Mehra, Bharat, and Lisette Hernandez. "Libraries as Agents of Human Rights Protection and Social Change on Behalf of Sexual Minorities in India: An Action-Based Manifesto for Progressive Change." In *Perspectives on Libraries as Institutions of Human Rights and Social Justice*, edited by Ursula Gorham, Natalie Greene Taylor, and Paul T. Jaeger. Advances in Librarianship Series. Bingley, UK: Emerald Group Publishing Limited, forthcoming.

———. "Rural and Urban Queering Alliances Out of the Library towards Legal Protection of Lesbian, Gay, Bisexual, Transgender, and Questioning People in India." In *Queer Library Alliance: Global Reflections and Imaginings*, edited by Rae-Anne Montague and Lucas McKeever. Sacramento, CA: Library Juice Press, forthcoming.

Mehra, Bharat, Kevin S. Rioux, and Kendra S. Albright. "Social Justice in Library and Information Science." In *Encyclopedia*

of Library and Information Sciences, 3rd ed., 4820–36. Abingdon,
UK: Taylor & Francis, 2009. http://www.tandfonline.com/
doi/abs/10.1081/E-ELIS3-120044526.

Mehra, Bharat, and Ramesh Srinivasan. "The Library-Community
Convergence Framework for Community Action: Libraries
as Catalysts of Social Change." *Libri: International Journal of
Libraries & Information Services* 57, no. 3 (September 2007):
123–39.

Rioux, Kevin. "Metatheory in Library and Information Science: A
Nascent Social Justice Approach." *Journal of Education for
Library & Information Science* 51, no. 1 (Winter 2010): 9–17.

Rioux, Kevin, Bharat Mehra, and Kendra Albright. "Conceptualizing
Social Justice in the Information Sciences." *Proceedings of the
American Society for Information Science and Technology* 44, no. 1
(January 1, 2007): 1–4. doi:10.1002/meet.1450440130.

SECTION ONE:
EMERGENT CONCEPTUAL FRAMEWORKS FOR PROGRESSIVE COMMUNITY ACTION IN LIBRARY AND INFORMATION SCIENCE

Chapter 1

BEYOND THE PROTOTYPE: LIBRARIES AS CONVIVIAL TOOLS IN ACTION

Zachary Loeb

Introduction

When thinking about libraries, it is difficult not to think about technology.

From the special collection's rare tomes to the medical library's databases, and from the college library's shelves of scholarly monographs to the public library's paperbacks and public computers: different types of libraries may be filled with different types of technologies (books, computers, and so forth), but strip all the technology from a library and little worth calling a library is left. A library provides a space wherein technology is not simply encountered, as such, but in which technology is used within a culturally rich context. Thus a book becomes part of a larger collection, a database becomes an informational tool open to a community, a "personal computer" becomes a public access terminal – the library provides an atmosphere in which a given tool becomes part of a larger whole. It is due to this mutually shaping and reinforcing relationship with technological forms that libraries and librarians have a particular responsibility to critically approach technology.

Legion are the librarians who have heard the woebegone refrain that technological change will render libraries obsolete, but libraries have successfully adjusted to technological shifts for as long as there have been libraries.[1] If libraries (defined broadly) are to meet the informational needs of their patrons, they cannot ignore the role that new technologies play.[2] Nevertheless, since the tools used in libraries determine their shape and influence future development, a critical-minded approach to librarianship must include a rigorous consideration of technology.[3]

In this chapter I argue that a library is more than a site in which various user groups encounter particular tools, but that the library itself can be conceived of, and can represent, a type of tool. Insofar as every technology – and in particular large systems – represents a set of political, economic, and social biases, it is worth considering which sets of values are embodied in libraries, and by extension, what varieties of tools help and which hinder the actualization of this ethos.[4] In constructing this argument I aim to build a constructive bridge between elements of Science, Technology and Society (STS) scholarship and Library Science. In applying this argument at the practical level, this chapter will venture outside the sturdy walls of the classically established library to consider the library as a tool for community action by investigating the People's Library of Occupy Wall Street and the Tuli Kupferberg Library

---

1. Mark Y. Herring, *Are Libraries Obsolete? An Argument for Relevance in the Digital Age* (Jefferson, NC: McFarland, 2014).

2. Jesse Shera, "Daedalus, Icarus, and the Technological Revolution" in *The Compleat Librarian* (Cleveland, OH: Case Western Reserve University Press, 1971), 63-65. "If we sever irrevocably our ties with tradition, the risk is very great indeed. But no profession can stand still and survive" (64).

3. Chris Bourg, "Never Neutral: Libraries, Technology, and Inclusion," Feral Librarian blog, January 28, 2015. https://chrisbourg.wordpress.com /2015/01/28/never-neutral-libraries-technology-and-inclusion/ This is the text of a talk that was delivered at the OLA Super Conference. See also Mandy Henk, *Ecology, Economy, Equity: The Path to a Carbon-Neutral Library* (Chicago: ALA Editions, 2014) for a detailed discussion of the environmental implications of library use of technology.

4. Langdon Winner, *The Whale and the Reactor* (Chicago: University of Chicago Press, 1986), 19-39. The chapter "Do Artifacts Have Politics" is a careful analysis of the way in which "political, economic and social biases" influence the shape and impact of technologies. For a discussion of the ways this plays out in libraries see: Henk, *Ecology, Economy, Equity,* and Mark Y. Herring, *Are Libraries Obsolete? An Argument for Relevance in the Digital Age* (Jefferson, NC: McFarland, 2014).

at The Well (a community space in Astoria in Queens, New York). By applying a critical theoretical consideration of technological systems, and foregrounding the question of technology within libraries, I will argue that technological questions are tied to the very notion of what libraries are, what they should be, and what they can be.

Despite the technophobia that is occasionally – comically – attributed to librarians, it is not a matter of libraries resisting technological change, but of considering which technologies most effectively promote the values to which libraries hold fast.[5] As the cases of libraries in protest movements and community activism demonstrate, the library is not simply a site in which tools are used; rather, the library is *itself* a type of tool to further social justice.

"The Prototype of a Convivial Tool"

If "technology" is a broad category encompassing much, then so too is "library." While "technology" includes everything from metal keys to keyboards, "library" includes everything from the cloistered special collection to the protest library. Yet, though it is a space wherein much technology appears, it would be odd to characterize a library as itself being a technology. Instead, a library appears at a point of intersection: not itself a technology but heavily influenced by the presence of particular artifacts.

Therefore, it may be fruitful to consider a library as an example of a "technological system" wherein, as Ruth Schwartz Cowan has written, "each implement used...is part of a sequence of implements—a system in which each must be linked to others in order to function appropriately."[6] It is this linking of artifacts within the system that is

---

5. Herring, *Are Libraries Obsolete?* 189. "What new technologies exist now or are emerging that either influence what libraries will do, or are replacing what libraries are already doing?" Italics in original text.

6. Ruth Schwartz Cowan, *More Work for Mother: The Ironies of Household Technology from the Open Hearth to the Microwave* (New York: Basic Books, Inc., 1983), 13.

particularly important. As Judy Wajcman explains: "A technological system is never merely technical: its real-world functioning has technical, economic, organizational, political and even cultural elements,"[7] and thus, as Wajcman notes elsewhere, "technology must be understood as part of the social fabric that holds society together…technological change is a contingent and heterogeneous process in which technology and society are mutually constituted."[8]

Libraries appear in a variety of forms today – as they did in the past as well – and these forms bear the marks of forces beyond the technical, including "economic, organizational, political and…cultural" influences. What a visitor encounters in a "public" library, a "medical" library, or a "university" library has been "linked…in order to function appropriately" for that library's demographic.[9] At the same time, the library takes on a "constituting" role that in turn comes to reinforce who is and who is not considered to be a member of the patron base.[10]

This clearly raises the question, returning to Cowan's terminology, of what the "function" is, in pursuit of which the library attempts to exert a "linking" influence. In addressing this question – particularly in the way in which it interacts with the goals of librarianship – André Cossette paraphrased Jesse Shera's answer as: "Librarianship is the art

---

7. Judy Wajcman, *Techno Feminism* (Cambridge, UK: Polity Press, 2004), 35.

8. Ibid., 106.

9. Jesse H. Shera, *Libraries and the Organization of Knowledge* (Hamden, CT: Archon Books, 1965), 3-11. In the first chapter of this book, Shera traces the development of libraries – defined broadly – and notes the way in which the library has been brought "into intimate contact with a wide variety of social organizations and institutions" (9).

10. Such a case of this "constituting" function is particularly evident in the case of special collections libraries. In his article, "'You've Got to Be Carefully Taught': American Special Collections Library Education and the Inculcation of Exclusivity," *RBM: A Journal of Rare Books, Manuscripts and Cultural Heritage* 7 (2006): 55-63, Michael Garabedian makes this tension particularly clear as he discusses the way in which librarians in special collections often took on the function of "gatekeepers" whose main responsibility was to keep a very narrow gate closed to the majority of library users (58). This is a stark, but important example, of the way that libraries and librarians "constitute" their user base.

and science of the acquisition, preservation, organization, and retrieval of written and audiovisual records with the aim of *assuring a maximum of information access for the human community*"[11] (emphasis added). While "acquisition, preservation, organization, and retrieval" are important, it is the emphasis upon "assuring a maximum of information access for the human community" that speaks to the library's "function." Therefore, for the purposes of the present discussion, the "function" of the library as a "technological system" will be interpreted as the "assuring" functions of which Cossette wrote – though the "human community" will be defined, broadly or narrowly, depending on the library's setting.

The merit of treating libraries as technological systems, or "tools" themselves, is demonstrated in Ivan Illich's book *Tools for Conviviality*, wherein he wrote: "at its best the library is the prototype of a convivial tool."[12] This declaration comes after Illich has cast a withering gaze towards impersonal and large-scale technological systems. The "convivial tool" is not simply meant as a pleasant idea, but as an alternative to a world in which, with the increase in the "power of machines…the role of persons more and more decreases to that of mere consumers."[13] In opposition to this, Illich argued for "a convivial society" bolstered by "convivial tools" – such a society being one "designed to allow all its members the most autonomous action by means of tools least controlled by others."[14] And it is within this framework that Illich pronounced the library to be "the prototype of a convivial tool." It is clear that in Illich's thinking this status is owed to a similar recognition of the type of goals to which Cossette had alluded; for Illich it is not merely that a library contains books, but that "repositories of other learning tools can be organized on [the library's] model."[15]

---

11. André Cossettte, *Humanism and Libraries: An Essay on the Philosophy of Librarianship* (Duluth: Library Juice Press, 2009), 33.

12. Ivan Illich, *Tools for Conviviality* (New York: Harper & Row Publishers, 1973), 65.

13. Ibid., 11.

14. Ibid., 20.

15. Ibid., 65.

Though Illich saw tremendous potential in the library's "model," he remained concerned about the way in which the contents of a library could become the "specialized tool" of a few. Thus, there is an important difference between Illich's claim that the library "is the prototype" and a claim that the library simply is "a convivial tool." What the term "prototype" makes clear is that the library as tool (or technological system) is not automatically "convivial." For the library is "mutually constituted," and despite Cossette's emphasis on "assuring," it is quite possible for a library to put up barriers to informational resources, define its public in a way as to bar access, or put emphasis on a set of technological artifacts that represent value systems that may clash with the "function" of a library.

Thus, what becomes evident is not just a matter of technological systems, but also the problem of what types of political and economic biases are manifested in technological forms. That technologies cannot be viewed as existing in a vacuum should be evident; or, as Rosalind Williams has written, "just because technologies are constructed by humans does not mean they do not exert control over human life. In many cases, they are constructed precisely to exert such control."[16] Such insight provides an important reminder of the larger social context in which libraries exist – that context generally being the one against which Illich hoped to deploy "convivial tools" as a corrective.

In discussing the politics inherent in various technological forms, Langdon Winner notes that "the things we call 'technologies' are ways of building order in our world…consciously or unconsciously, deliberately or inadvertently, societies choose structures for technologies that influence how people are going to work, communicate, travel, consume, and so forth for a very long time."[17] To apply Winner's insight in line with Illich's optimistic trepidation shows that the technologies a library makes use of will shape the experience of users, and while

---

16. Rosalind Williams, *Retooling: A Historian Confronts Technological Change* (Cambridge, MA: MIT Press, 2003), 122.

17. Winner, *The Whale and the Reactor*, 28.

technologically-mediated alterations of user experience may be for the better, it should not be forgotten that such choices represent just that: choices. When a library favors one set of technologies over another, it is determining how patrons will access information.

To give an example: in the case of the book versus the e-book, a library must contend with different sets of biases and ethical issues, even as it attempts to pursue the goal of "assuring a maximum of information access." When a library lends a book, the item remains a part of the technological system of the library itself; however, when a library lends an e-book, it must compete with the technological system governing those devices upon which the e-book is read. After a book has been sold, the printing press retains little control over what is done with the book, but the same cannot be fully claimed of an e-reader. To continue with the previous example, while privacy is a value that libraries take quite seriously, such a value is somewhat at odds with the preferences of some device manufacturers who are routinely seeking more information on device users.[18]

Thus, as libraries come to make use of more complex technologies, what occurs is that the library must attempt to subsume new technological systems that are simultaneously attempting to subsume the library. As Ruth Schwartz Cowan notes, "Tools set limits on our work; we can use them in different ways, but not in an infinite number of ways."[19] A library can do much with a "tool," but not everything. Computers and other Internet connected devices have clearly become important ways for "assuring a maximum of information access," but they nevertheless represent a trade-off. While a library can seek to manage these trade-offs in line with the library's goals (through installing encryption software, anti-tracking plug-ins, and so forth), the basic point remains that the more complex a technology that a library seeks to bring within its own system, the more difficult it may be for the library to ensure that this technology matches the library's values.

---

18. Henk, *Ecology, Economy, Equity*, 66-67.

19. Cowan, *More Work for Mother*, 9.

This is not to argue an absolutist stance against particular technologies, however; it is to state that just because a given technology is being used in a library does not mean that the device accords fully with the library's values. As Winner noted, technological systems bring about a state wherein "without anyone having explicitly chosen it, dependency upon highly centralized organization has gradually become a dominant social form."[20] This applies as much to libraries as to society at large. Such recognition is a reminder of why a library is "the prototype" but not necessarily "a convivial tool" – for libraries exist within societies that are themselves shaped by technological forces. That libraries must balance a range of values has generally been true, but as libraries negotiate these choices they must remain cognizant of the values that are reified in certain technologies.

Thus, it is essential for a library (and its staff) to carefully consider the various technologies that are brought within its ambit. Here, those who take seriously the goals of libraries and the ways in which technologies shape them can benefit from taking a critical stance towards technology, even, and perhaps especially, for technologies that are well-liked. As Andrew Feenberg explains: "In choosing our technology we become what we are which in turn shapes our future choices."[21] What engaging critically with technology provides is a theoretical framework to better enable libraries to consider the technological choices they have made and that they are making. It allows libraries to see that the technologies they use are not "neutral." Rather, as Judy Wajcman notes, "technologies result from a series of specific decisions made by particular groups of people...technologies bear the imprint of the people and social context in which they develop."[22] Therefore, the technologies within a library are part of a discussion between the library and the public it serves, about the type of system that the library will represent: a convivial one

---

20. Winner, *The Whale and the Reactor*, 47.

21. Andrew Feenberg, *Critical Theory of Technology* (Oxford, UK: Oxford University Press, 1991), 14.

22. Judy Wajcman, *Pressed for Time: The Acceleration of Life in Digital Capitalism* (Chicago: University of Chicago Press, 2015), 29.

or a closed one, a space working towards community change or another space wherein users are subjected to surveillance and bombarded with advertisements.

Discussing the politics of technology, Langdon Winner noted: "We should try to imagine and seek to build technical regimes compatible with freedom, social justice, and other key political ends."[23] Such a sentiment aligns with Illich's observation that "at its best the library is the prototype of a convivial tool," for what emerges when these two comments are compared is a sense that we can use technological tools in such a way that accords with social justice oriented values.

That the library may be such a tool is something upon which many activists have seized.

Convivial Tools in Action

Libraries, and librarians, are familiar with the budgetary puzzle in which an ever-decreasing pool of finances must be distributed across staff, material acquisitions, maintenance, technological upgrades, and considerations of which new technologies to purchase. Should a library buy more computers? Is it worthwhile for the library to obtain and lend e-readers? Would a 3-D printer be useful?

Such technological purchasing decisions force libraries to consider how those technologies will be incorporated into the library. These choices can be seen in the context of a trade-off; after all, an investment in staff is quite different from an investment in new devices that will swiftly succumb to planned obsolescence. By choosing to purchase certain technologies a library may well find itself committed to repurchasing them continuously, as newer models become available. Indeed, it is enough to make one pine for the peculiar freedom that comes with having a budget so small that it might as well not exist.

Though the previous sentence is meant in jest, it may be that a way to consider the technological priorities of a library – and to see the

---

23. Winner, *The Whale and the Reactor*, 55.

library itself as a tool—is to consider what form a library takes when it is reduced to its core function. For such purposes, activist movement libraries can provide useful insight. Unburdened by the need to balance a host of budgetary priorities or satisfy a board of directors, such libraries gesture towards the library as a "prototype of a convivial tool." Furthermore, by placing the complex tool that is the library in a new social context, activist libraries are able to demonstrate how this tool can build community in a variety of situations.

The People's Library of Occupy Wall Street (OWSPL)[24] and the other protest libraries that appeared in various cities during the Occupy movement may represent one of the more visible examples in recent years of the activist library. Such libraries often had their origins in something as inauspicious as a "pile of books" over which a group of activists took responsibility, stewarding those piles into ordered collections that eventually contained thousands of volumes. While the People's Library had its own blog, a Twitter feed, and used the website LibraryThing to catalog its collection, the library's primary holdings were based almost entirely around books. Some members of the working group hoped to be able to offer Internet access, but the limited availability of electricity and unpredictable elements (including the actual elements) kept the People's Library decidedly "low-tech." The collection of the People's Library was the result of donations by thousands of individuals (including a few publishers and many authors), and books were, overwhelmingly, what people donated to the library (though a few laptops were also donated).[25] Indeed, the great technological advances for the People's Library were a waterproof tent and shelves.

---

24. The author of this piece was an active participant in the People's Library of Occupy Wall Street.

25. For a more detailed history of the People's Library see: Jaime Taylor and Zachary Loeb, "Librarian is My Occupation: A History of the People's Library of Occupy Wall Street," in *Informed Agitation*, ed. Melissa Morrone (Sacramento: Library Juice Press, 2013), 271-288. Also available online at: https://librarianshipwreck.wordpress.com/2014/04/16/librarian-is-my-occupation-a-history-of-the-peoples-library-of-occupy-wall-street/

After the various encampments of the Occupy movement were destroyed, the activists in these movements did not simply vanish, even if their visibility was greatly diminished. The tactic of setting up libraries within activist spaces continued. In the greater New York City area, to give two examples, the Brooklyn Base opened in Brooklyn which included the Lucy Parsons Library[26] and The Well in Astoria provided a home to the Tuli Kupferberg Library. Included in the collections of both of these spaces were remnants of the People's Library collection.

The Well, home to the Tuli Kupferberg Library,[27] was founded by activists in Queens, many of whom had been involved with Occupy Wall Street and/or Occupy Long Island City.[28] The library takes its name from the counterculture figure Tuli Kupferberg (known for books such as *1001 Ways to Beat the Draft* and his membership in the band The Fugs), whose personal library made up the original core of the library collection. This represented several thousand books, though the activists

---

26. For more information on the Lucy Parsons Library visit: http://the-basebk.org/the-lucy-parsons-library

27. The author of this piece was an active participant at The Well, particularly in terms of helping to organize and catalog the Tuli Kupferberg Library during the period in which the space seemed like a possibility. When the group of activists involved with The Well lost access to the space in May of 2015, they searched for a new site to which the books could be moved. After many months a new home for the books was found at the Astoria First Presbyterian Chruch (www.astoriafirstpcusa.org), whose building also provides space to the organization Art House Astoria. As Astoria First Presbyterian Church has become the host of many progressive events in Astoria, the activists affiliated with The Well felt it would be a fitting locale for the Tuli Kupferberg Library. As of this writing, activists from The Well (including the author of this chapter) are currently working on the physical labor of transporting and re-assembling the library.

28. The process of organizing and opening a community space can be quite difficult, as those involved in The Well discovered directly. The goal was for The Well to be open to the community by the Spring/Summer of 2015; however, after more than two years of work the activists involved with The Well were informed that they would no longer have access to the space. Please see the previous footnote for details on the new home of the Tuli Kupferberg Library. For a further explanation see "'Walking Makes the Road' and the Library," (May 14, 2015), LibrarianShipwreck, https://librarianshipwreck. wordpress.com/2015/05/14/unpacking-and-repacking-the-library/.

involved with The Well certainly hoped that in the future the library would grow with new donations of books from visitors.

While activists involved in creating The Well had envisioned a Spring/Summer 2015 opening, after more than two years of work preparing the space, this goal was unrealized. The Well had been made possible thanks to a community member making a building freely available for transformation into a community space. Unfortunately, this individual decided to no longer make the space available in May of 2015. And thus The Well ran dry. As The Well never came to genuine fruition, it remains impossible to definitively predict the various technologies that would have eventually been found there. However, as the rows upon rows of shelves attested, the focus of the Tuli Kupferberg Library (affectionately called Tuli's Library) had been books. It is a sad fact that The Well joins the list of community spaces that "could have been" instead of community spaces that "are." The presence of the library as a key feature of The Well, however, remains important. When envisioning the type of space that would ideally serve their community, those involved with The Well considered the presence of a library to be a key component.

Though the People's Library and Tuli's Library may have contained some of the same books, these libraries were very different. While the People's Library existed in the murky legal limbo of the festive occupation of Zuccotti Park, relying on a tent for shelter, Tuli's Library safely sat on shelves beneath an actual roof. While the People's Library existed in the midst of a chaotic and exciting created community, Tuli's Library was created to serve an already existing community. Though there are further differences that could be noted, it is more fruitful to focus on similarities, on the ways in which these libraries attempted to approximate being "the prototype of a convivial tool," regardless of whether or not any of those involved were actually thinking in precisely these terms.[29] And yet one feature that both libraries share is that they demonstrate

---

29. In the case of the People's Library and Tuli's Library there was at least one person involved who was drawn to library activism and librarianship directly as a result of Illich's comments regarding libraries as "convivial tools." Illich's *Tools for Conviviality* is the book that convinced me to become a librarian.

the degree to which library collections rely on access to actual physical space. Activists involved may be committed and well meaning, but if they do not ultimately have control of the space where their shelves are set up, then the future of the library remains uncertain. Alas, as The Well attests, sometimes even the promise of a well-meaning individual regarding access to a space proves insufficient.

The inviting edifices of "legitimate" libraries can be found a relatively short distance from the People's Library and Tuli's Library, as well as numerous other protest/activist libraries. The existence of activist libraries should not be interpreted as an affront to such institutions, but as a complement, and in this manner the choice of certain technological forms over others comes into sharper relief. When Langdon Winner notes the importance of "technical regimes compatible with freedom, social justice, and other key political ends,"[30] this claim does not refute the importance of traditional libraries. It does, however, leave space open in which other types of libraries can develop.

During and in the aftermath of the wave of protests in which Occupy emerged, one of the narratives that was regularly disseminated pointed to the important role played by smart phones and social media in allowing these movements to grow. The "tools" that were lauded as vital to these movements were portrayed as being decidedly high tech. This tension was captured eloquently by Manuel Castells in comments related to Occupy: "The movement was born on the Internet, diffused by the Internet, and maintained its presence on the Internet....Yet, at the same time, the movement's material form of existence was the *occupation of public space*. A space where the protestors could come together and form a community beyond their differences. A space of conviviality."[31] Even the most committed critic of technology would recognize that Castells is not off point – the Internet did play a major role in Occupy (and similar movements).

---

30. Winner, *The Whale and the Reactor*, 55.

31. Manuel Castells, *Networks of Outrage and Hope: Social Movements in the Internet Age* (Cambridge, UK: Polity Press, 2012), 168. Italics in original text.

The Internet and social networks served as important nodes for disseminating information, and such tools gave activists powerful means for sharing and amplifying messages. Yet, as Castells also captures, such technological outreach was still reliant upon what was happening "on the ground." Castells evokes "a space for conviviality" which echoes how elements like libraries helped construct the basic infrastructure that made these spaces "convivial." For the "conviviality" encountered in the parks was reliant upon more than just an assemblage of individuals. The encampments were not only masses of people; they were functional (albeit temporary and flawed) communities. What people encountered in the encampments (at their best) were real examples of people taking care of one another. If social media platforms such as Twitter and Facebook played an important role in getting people to the protests, it was the sociality of structures, including the libraries, which helped define what people got out of their time at the protests. The presence of libraries in these encampments attested to the ways in which libraries could be among the tactics and tools deployed by activists.

The contemporary library is a site wherein an individual will encounter much more than simply rows upon rows of shelves lined with carefully ordered books. Computers, e-readers, "maker spaces," video game consoles, and a host of material formats, have all become common features of libraries. Lacking access to certain essential elements of infrastructure – such as a reliable source for electricity – many of the protest libraries were unable to offer devices requiring electricity. Instead, what the libraries were able to offer were books. In some cases quite a lot of them, even if the books were not always carefully ordered and neatly arranged. What activist libraries like the People's Library and Tuli's Library point to are the ways in which breaking away from certain elements of the technological society (though they may still be used) can provide access to a "wide and genuine" space for action. This is not to deny the important role that social media such as Twitter and Facebook may play in promoting social justice movements (which may or may not include libraries), nor is it to idealize some problematic image of a pastoral time before smart phones. Nevertheless it is a reminder that, as Albert Borgmann put it, "social justice, understood as an equal level of affluence, will not be advanced merely by technological progress."[32] Granted, as Tuli's Library and the People's Library both discovered, lack of control over essential infrastructure can eventually prove to be an insurmountable obstacle.

When Ivan Illich describes libraries as being prototypical "convivial tools," one of the things he is pointing to is the way in which the values embodied by libraries, at their best, transcend the narrow technological and economic priorities of their time. Libraries in activist and protest movements, and libraries in general, emphasize a vision of "the good" that is at odds in many ways with an economic system that insists on placing a price upon every single thing.

As Naomi Klein writes, "if there is a reason for social movements to exist, it is not to accept dominant values as fixed and unchangeable but to offer other ways to live," and this "also means defending those parts of our societies that already express these values outside of capitalism, whether it's an embattled library, a public park, a student movement demanding free university tuition, or an immigrant rights movement fighting for dignity and open borders."[33] It is not accidental that libraries appear on Klein's list. At risk of evoking the lore of kindergarten over the denseness of critical theory, libraries foreground the value of sharing (or mutual aid to use activist terminology), and this value is clearly on display in activist libraries where people are encouraged to share of their own collections, that they may share from the larger collection. Thus it may be that the library, as a tool, functions as a technological system that runs on sharing.

Langdon Winner has observed that in "complex technological systems...Whatever claims one may wish to make on behalf of liberty, justice, or equality can be immediately neutralized when confronted with

---

32. Albert Borgmann, *Technology and the Character of Contemporary Life: A Philosophical Inquiry* (Chicago: University of Chicago Press, 1984), 112.

33. Naomi Klein, *This Changes Everything: Capitalism vs. The Climate* (New York: Simon and Schuster, 2014), 61.

arguments to the effect, 'Fine, but that's no way to run a railroad.'"[34] What libraries, at their best, and protest libraries demonstrate is that other "moral reasons" can still have a powerful impact. After all, it may be that some can say, "that's no way to run a railroad," but as the People's Library and Tuli's Library make quite apparent: that is a way to run a library.

Libraries come in many forms and are in no way bound to quiet locations. A library can function as well in the middle of a protest encampment as in the safety of a historical building, for the foundations of a successful library are not concrete and books, but ethical principles. A library is not simply a place that houses books. It is (or can be) a site where information access is extended to the whole "human community," a place where mutual aid in action is modeled and enacted on a daily basis.

Librarianship and Pre-Figurative Political Activism

A raucous protest filled with excited conversations, the pounding rhythm of drummers, shouted information, and numerous people converging in a relatively small space are, in all likelihood, not the types of images conjured up when the term "library" is used. Though some contemporary librarians may chafe at the lingering image of a library as a place where there are five hundred and seventy-three different words for "shush!" – the idea of a library still seems cozily nestled in the popular imagination as a quiet place filled with bookshelves. And yet, in recent years libraries have become a common feature of some particularly loud events wherein key library infrastructure may have been hard to come by.[35]

---

34. Winner, *The Whale and the Reactor*, 36.

35. This section is an outgrowth of the author's presentation delivered as part of "Informed Agitators: Librarian and Information Professionals in Social Justice." Panel with Shawn(ta) Smith, Maggie Schreiner, Amy Roberts, and Jaime Taylor, presented at Left Forum 2014. June 1, 2014. The text of that presentation was posted on the author's blog under the title "Modeling a Different World – The Library and Prefigurative Activism," (June 2, 2014) https://librarianshipwreck.wordpress.com/2014/06/02/modeling-a-different-world-the-library-and-prefigurative-activism/.

Ranging from Madrid's Puerta del Sol to Instanbul's Gezi Park to Occupy encampments across the USA and Canada to Egypt's Tahrir Square, Ukraine's Euromaidan protests in Kiev and the "Umbrella" protests in Hong Kong – these various public demonstrations have many differences, and yet at each one of them a library could be found. These libraries were of various shapes and sizes; their eccentricities reflecting the particular situation in which each library was couched. The role of the libraries in these locations had varying levels of importance to the narrative arc of the movements, and thus the history of the libraries played different roles in the after-lives of these movements. Amidst the violent repression of the protestors in Gezi Park, the fate of the library was but another sad incident, while the destruction of the People's Library of Occupy Wall Street was treated by some as a particularly egregious moment in the smashing of the Occupy movement. The presence of libraries in these various protests may have struck some as rather odd, particularly as the idea of a library seems, at least to some, to be rather at odds with the nature of the protests. Yet, the difficult question that lingers around these protest libraries is: "Why even set up a library at a protest?"

Libraries may have a reputation as being quiet places, but at their core they have a loud ethos. In some respects Shera's definition and Illich's declaration, cited earlier, suggest that undergirding libraries is a certain pre-figurative value. It is not that libraries are always successful in "assuring a maximum of information access for the human community" but it is that they can be treated as "a prototype" or a pre-figuration of this value. Illich's usage of the qualifier "at its best" is not a throwaway comment. They are institutions that value the free flow of information without such talk simply being a pleasant pablum for mining data or selling advertisements. What the presence of libraries in protest move-ments points to is a recognition that it is not enough for a library to wait for "the human community" to come to it, sometimes the library must leave the stacks and go to "the human community."

Insofar as libraries emerge in societies, it is inevitable that societal influences will shape and determine them. Therefore, it is unfortu-nately the case that libraries have at many junctures served to reinforce hierarchies and the narratives of dominant forces. The cataloging and classification languages one encounters in a library (the Dewey Decimal System, Library of Congress subject headings) cluster power in the hands of those who can "classify" instead of restoring power to those who are "classified," while many library collections display a bias towards the cultures and histories of only certain segments of the "human community." Too often, libraries can act as a barrier that in the name of providing "information access" for some winds up barring access to others.[36]

In protest movements the library is in many ways broken down to its "convivial" core; it ceases to strictly be a hallowed and storied institution and is treated as one among many "tools" that activists deploy. The library takes the form of a utopian seed, sprouting the roots from which a different world can grow. As Grace Lee Boggs writes, "the best community activism does not simply provide for others, but teaches them how to provide for themselves."[37] Boggs's comment echoes Illich and Shera – for in providing access to "the human community" (in being "the prototype of a convivial tool"), a library provides informational resources to the community but does so in a way that leaves much of the onus on the individual.

Even if the library is taken out of the stacks and put into the streets, and even if the individuals staffing it work tirelessly to help patrons find materials, it ultimately remains the choice of the patron to actually read what they borrow. Thus, a library can be considered as aligning with a broadly defined notion of freedom similar to the one put forth by Simone De Beauvoir: "to be free is not to have the power to do anything you like; it is to be able to surpass the given toward an open future."[38] By making a variety of resources available to the public, by

---

36. Cossette, *Humanism and Libraries*, 45-47.

37. Grace Lee Boggs, *The Next American Revolution: Sustainable Activism for the Twenty-First Century* (Berkeley, CA: The University of California Press, 2012), 120.

38. Simone De Beauvoir, *The Ethics of Ambiguity* (New York: Citadel Press, 1976), 91.

becoming "a convivial tool," a library "at its best" allows people "to surpass the given" and provides them with the tools with which they can work towards "an open future."

That books were the primary medium being disseminated by protest libraries is not strictly accidental. Indeed, the privileging of books itself says something about the libraries in protest movements. For it is not only that the library itself is a tool, but that the library is a larger system that makes use of other tools as well. Some of this sentiment around the rich value of books has been grounded in library thinking for decades. Indeed, the use value of books is central to the first three of S.R. Ranganathan's classic "Five Laws of Library Science," which are: 1. Books are for use, 2. Every reader his book, and 3. Every book its reader.[39] Of particular importance to the present discussion is the first law ("books are for use"), but beyond this it is the particular ways in which books can be used that makes them "convivial tools" that inform the way in which a library can be seen as such a prototype.

To put it simply, it is easy to pass a book from one person to another, and unless some type of careful recording is made and kept of this passage, it can be challenging for prying eyes to know all of the hands a given volume has passed through. While books come in many shapes and sizes, it is fairly simple for a person to take a book with them as they go about their daily affairs. A further noteworthy aspect of books is that they are usually rather sturdy and can take a fair bit of bumping without being rendered unusable; one can toss a book out of a third story window (this is not a suggestion that one should do so) and when the book hits the ground it will be relatively unscathed. Of how many digital devices can the same be said?

Along these same lines, physical books tend to be long-lasting; a book from fifty years ago will likely still be accessible and readable today – how many pieces of computerized technology could something similar be said regarding? Paper books are composed of a non-toxic, renewable

---

39. S.R. Ranganathan, *The Five Laws of Library Science* (Madras, India: The Madras Library Association, 1931). (Digitized by the Hathi Trust).

resource (paper) that is much easier to repurpose and recycle than many high technology elements we encounter in our daily lives. To use a book one need only be able to read (a teachable skill); no proprietary piece of hardware is required. Furthermore, it is easy for a person to donate their unwanted, or unneeded, books to an upstart protest library, where these books will move back from a "personal library" to a library that attempts to serve a broader community. Though these points may be obvious, particularly to librarians, they stand as important reminders of the ways in which certain "low tech" things can still serve high purposes. While the intention should not be to romanticize the book, it should not be ignored that in many ways books act as particularly useful "means" for pursuing the library's ends.

In approaching the library itself as a tool, it is also important to consider what role the librarian plays, as taking the library out of the stacks also requires taking the librarian out from behind the reference desk. In considering the role of the librarian in his "prototype," Illich emphasized that "we should learn to ask first what people need if they want to learn and provide these tools for them."[40] Regarding the role of the librarian, Illich lamented the way "the reference librarian placed himself between people and shelves".[41] Within the context of the protest library, the "reference librarian" is often placed between the patron and the shelves; however, the degree to which this happens is predominantly a reflection of the eccentric way in which the books had been organized. Though various protest libraries may still have had individuals who took care of the library and took on the title "librarian," these individuals were not separate from the movement but a part of it; working group members took on the title "librarian" with little concern for professional qualifications, thereby demonstrating that in serving "the human community," the first step is to remember that one is a part of that very community.

---

40. Illich, *Tools for Conviviality*, 65.
41. Ibid.

Protest movements make use of a range of tools and tactics: marches, occupations, hanging posters, writing articles, banner drops, handing out flyers, die-ins, blockades, etc. To this list should be added setting up libraries. When protestors build libraries, it does not merely reflect a love of books but a recognition that the library itself functions as a tool. Furthermore, it is the type of tool that demonstrates a particular value system: one based upon sharing instead of selling. In the midst of acrimonious debates about the goals of a given movement, what libraries in protests help show is that, as Lewis Mumford put it in discussing utopias, "We need not abandon the real world in order to enter these realizable worlds; for it is out of the first that the second are always coming."[42]

For librarians accustomed to mocking comments about coming obsolescence, the omnipresent specter of budget cuts, and the drudgery that becomes an element of any job, it may seem odd to think of the library as carrying a utopian seed. Yet what the presence of libraries in protest movements helps demonstrate is that sometimes a seed can lay dormant beneath the snow for a very long time and still have the potential to sprout into something wondrous.

Conclusion

While the library may appear to be a quiet locale, at its core is a loud and radical premise.

The history of libraries may emphasize large institutions, yet as basic tools and frameworks, libraries can appear as cornerstones for the development of alternative communities. In raising the question "What does bottom-up change look like?" – Grace Lee Boggs answers "our catastrophes are not acts of nature but the consequences of our own ideas and actions. Therefore, we can bring an end to them by transforming the way we have been thinking and living."[43] Yet this is

---

42. Lewis Mumford, *The Story of Utopias* (New York: BiblioBaaar, 2008), 29.
43. Boggs, *The Next American Revolution*, 167.

a challenge to which we need not look for answers in the darkness of space or the mysteries of our minds; rather, we can look at the aspects of our societies that have helped nurture certain values over time. The ethos which can be detected as foundational for libraries are not simply the foundations for successful libraries, they are foundational for any society that emphasizes "the good life" over "the goods life."[44]

When Shera invokes service to the "human community" as a core obligation of libraries, it is not suggested merely as a ploy to give an equitable gloss to a political, economic, or technological system that derives its power from inequity. Rather it is a statement of a powerful grounding ethos, an ethos that dares consider "the good" and then attempts to realize this in the actual world. That libraries have become a recurring feature of activist movements points to this radical core. And yet, to pause and consider the matter for a moment, it truly is quite significant that in the midst of a society yoked to a neoliberal economic viewpoint and in thrall to the shining promises of technology, libraries still represent a space that serves the "human community," based not upon how many Twitter followers a person has or how much they make annually, but by virtue of their being part of the human community. As Peter Kropotkin observed, noting the pre-figurative value of libraries in 1906, "When you go into a public library…the librarian does not ask what services you have rendered to society before giving you the book, or the fifty books which you require, and he comes to your assistance if you do not know how to manage the catalogue."[45] Similarly, Simone Weil once observed that "Where a real civic life exists, each one feels he has a personal ownership in the public monuments, gardens, ceremonial pomp and circumstance; and a display of sumptuousness, in which

44. While not a direct citation this comparison between the "good life" and the "goods life" is based upon the way Lewis Mumford would often describe his book *The Story of Utopias*.

45. Peter Kropotkin, *The Conquest of Bread* (Oakland, CA: AK Press, 2007), 76.

nearly all human beings seek fulfillment, is in this way placed within the reach of even the poorest."[46] It may well be that libraries belong on Weil's list between "public monuments" and "gardens" – that a library can be the "prototype of a convivial tool" flows from libraries being part of "a real civic life."

Libraries have always been filled with a variety of technological forms; however, as a critical reading of technology and activist praxis demonstrate, a library must be cognizant of the way it uses technology lest it wind up being used by that technology. Though many a library offers its patrons rows and rows of computers along with all manner of other technological accoutrements, what the People's Library and Tuli's Library help show is that there is still much to be said for something as seemingly mundane as sharing books. It is, as Grace Lee Boggs has written, that "activism can be the journey rather than the arrival; that struggle doesn't always have to be confrontational but can take the form of reaching out to find common ground with the many 'others' in our society who are also seeking ways out from alienation, isolation, privatization, and dehumanization by corporate governance."[47] What activist libraries such as The People's Library of Occupy Wall Street and The Tuli Kupferberg Library at The Well demonstrate is that using libraries as tools within activist movements allows them to "be the journey" and also "the arrival."

The tools we carry with us today are the tools we will have at hand to build a more just tomorrow. Clearly, the library is a tool worth holding onto.

---

46. Simone Weil, *The Need for Roots* (London: Routledge Classics, 2002), 35.
47. Boggs, *The Next American Revolution*, 48.

Bibliography

Boggs, Grace Lee. *The Next American Revolution: Sustainable Activism for the Twenty-First Century*. Berkeley, CA: The University of California Press, 2012.

Borgmann, Albert. *Technology and the Character of Contemporary Life: A Philosophical Inquiry*. Chicago: University of Chicago Press, 1984.

Bourg, Chris. "Never Neutral: Libraries, Technology, and Inclusion." January 28, 2015. https://chrisbourg.wordpress.com/2015/01/28/never-neutral-libraries-technology-and-inclusion/

Castells, Manuel. *Networks of Outrage and Hope: Social Movements in the Internet Age*. Cambridge, UK: Polity Press, 2012.

Cossettte, André. *Humanism and Libraries: An Essay on the Philosophy of Librarianship*. Duluth, MN: Library Juice Press, 2009.

De Beauvoir, Simone. *The Ethics of Ambiguity*. New York: Citadel Press, 1976.

Feenberg, Andrew. *Critical Theory of Technology*. Oxford, UK: Oxford University Press, 1991.

Garabedian, Michael. "'You've Got to Be Carefully Taught': American Special Collections Library Education and the Inculcation of Exclusivity." *RBM: A Journal of Rare Books, Manuscripts and Cultural Heritage* 7 (2006): 55-63.

Henk, Mandy. *Ecology, Economy, Equity: The Path to a Carbon-Neutral Library*. Chicago: ALA Editions, 2014.

Herring, Mark Y. *Are Libraries Obsolete? An Argument for Relevance in the Digital Age*. Jefferson, NC: McFarland, 2014.

Illich, Ivan. *Tools for Conviviality*. New York: Harper & Row, 1973.

Klein, Naomi. *This Changes Everything: Capitalism vs. The Climate.* New York: Simon and Schuster, 2014.

Kropotkin, Peter. *The Conquest of Bread.* Oakland, CA: AK Press, 2007.

Mumford, Lewis. *The Story of Utopias.* New York: BiblioBaaar, 2008.

Ranganathan, S.R. *The Five Laws of Library Science.* Madras, India: The Madras Library Association, 1931.

Schwartz Cowan, Ruth. *More Work for Mother: The Ironies of Household Technology from the Open Hearth to the Microwave.* New York: Basic Books, 1983.

Shera, Jesse H. *Libraries and the Organization of Knowledge.* Hamden, CT: Archon Books, 1965.

Shera, Jesse. "Daedalus, Icarus, and the Technological Revolution." In *The Compleat Librarian,* 63-65. Cleveland, OH: Case Western Reserve Press, 1971.

Taylor, Jaime and Zachary Loeb. "Librarian is My Occupation: A History of the People's Library of Occupy Wall Street." In *Informed Agitation,* edited by Melissa Morrone, 271-288. Sacramento, CA: Library Juice Press, 2013.

Wajcman, Judy. *Pressed for Time: The Acceleration of Life in Digital Capitalism.* Chicago: University of Chicago Press, 2015.

———. *Techno Feminism.* Cambridge, UK: Polity Press, 2004.

Weil, Simone. *The Need for Roots.* London: Routledge Classics, 2002.

Williams, Rosalind. *Retooling: A Historian Confronts Technological Change.* Cambridge, MA: MIT Press, 2003.

Winner, Langdon. *The Whale and the Reactor.* Chicago: University of Chicago Press, 1986.

Chapter 2

WILL BIG DATA'S INSTRUMENTALIST VIEW OF HUMAN BEHAVIOR CHANGE UNDERSTANDINGS OF INFORMATION BEHAVIOR AND DISRUPT THE EMPOWERMENT OF USERS THROUGH INFORMATION LITERACY?

Gabriel Gomez

> The amount of data in our world has been exploding. Companies capture trillions of bytes of information about their customers, suppliers, and operations, and millions of networked sensors are being embedded in the physical world in devices such as mobile phones and automobiles, sensing, creating, and communicating data. Multimedia and individuals with smartphones and on social network sites will continue to fuel exponential growth. Big data—large pools of data that can be captured, communicated, aggregated, stored, and analyzed—is now part of every sector and function of the global economy.[1]

Introduction

Big data is changing how we understand human behavior and human interaction with the physical world, a process that will inevitably change understandings of information seeking behavior and information searching behavior. These behaviors are a focus of study within LIS because they recognize the importance of understanding human beings

---

1. James Manyika, et al., *Big Data: The Next Frontier for Innovation, Competition, and Productivity* (New York: McKinsey Global Institute, 2011), 3.

as they access and use information sources.[2] While the access and use of information is of crucial importance to some LIS researchers and practitioners, few may be aware that big data is a challenge to the very nature of the means we use to understand behavior originating in social science across numerous fields. This is how the editor of *Wired*, Chris Anderson, put it in an editorial:

> Out with every theory of human behavior, from linguistics to sociology. Forget taxonomy, ontology, and psychology. Who knows why people do what they do? The point is they do it, and we can track and measure it with unprecedented fidelity.[3]

In this sweeping, sensational, statement Anderson dismisses, even if with a sense of irony, just about everything the social sciences use to understand human behavior. If these academic fields are no longer important for understanding human behavior, a fundamental concern at the heart of these enterprises may also be lost, namely, the expansion of knowledge. A recognition of this loss can be discerned in Anderson's oddly phrased question, a question that seems to denigrate anyone who might ask it, "Who knows why people do what they do?" While answering such a question is often part of theorizing in social science, in the new world of big data it seems that seeking to answer this question is now beside the "point." The expansion of knowledge that centers most academic disciplines may well conflict with the commercial aims often supporting big data use. Commercial use of big data is, at its core, part of an effort to monetize information and not necessarily a means to understand how or why people behave in certain ways. The commercialization of the social sciences through big data continues and facilitates an ever-greater positivistic impulse that focuses on behavior

---

2. Tom Wilson, "Human Information Behaviour," *Informing Science* 3, no. 2 (2000): 49.

3. Chris Anderson, "The End of Theory, Will the Data Deluge Make the Scientific Method Obsolete?" *Wired Magazine* 16.07 (2008), accessed November 28, 2014, http://archive.wired.com/science/discoveries/magazine/16-07/pb_theory.

at the expense of building knowledge. The advent of big data may, as a result, herald a shift from more academic and human-centered approaches for understanding behavior toward a more instrumental, mechanistic view of that behavior, one that is redolent of behaviorism. This could have a huge impact on the social sciences and also the study of information behavior.

In this chapter I want to explore some issues related to this change in social science: the study of information behavior and social justice aims. From the standpoint of social justice, the role of studying information-seeking behavior is situated in LIS both theoretically and historically within the article, "Social Justice in Library and Information Science," particularly within the section, Critique of Social Justice in LIS. There, Mehra, Rioux, and Albright describe a "user's learning of information systems and services as a complex mechanism where individuals go through a dynamic process in learning about a particular subject...."[4] The very concept of information seeking behavior is at the heart of how libraries can deliver information, but big data will forever change human interaction with information and the way such behavior is both studied and taught. Just as importantly, big data will not only change the study of behavior but also orient it towards commercial ends, since so much of the infrastructure that supports it is not built by governments or governmental institutions like libraries, but by private enterprise.

Human behavior has traditionally been of concern to many information researchers, so changes arising from big data may have important implications for those areas of LIS where human behavior is important. While this chapter seeks to explore, from a critical theory perspective, the impact of big data on understandings of human behavior, ultimately my concern at the end of this chapter must be smaller than the totality of social science or even LIS, though the implications of big data on research can have repercussions in numerous areas in LIS such as values

---

4. Bharat Mehra, et al., "Social Justice in Library and Information Science," in Encyclopedia of Library and Information Sciences, 3rd ed., ed. Marcia J. Bates and Mary Niles Maack (New York: Taylor and Francis, 2009), 4829.

and ethics, education, collection development, services, informatics, or information retrieval systems. In part, this chapter is about the potential for big data to disrupt current ideas about research on information behavior; consequently, I begin by examining a potential theoretical transformation of the social sciences by big data's foregrounding of instrumentalist or behaviorist frameworks. This is a change that also threatens social justice aims rooted in understanding human behavior for the sake of expanding knowledge and not just maximizing profit or improving economic efficiencies. Then, of all the possible areas of LIS that I could examine, I focus on information literacy as a practice used by librarians to empower users in order to find a path toward using big data for social justice aims.

In the subsequent section I begin by addressing the instrumentalist view of human behavior found in big data, something that leans toward behaviorism and conflicts with the altruistic stance found in some aspects of LIS. Then I discuss a critical stance against big data's trend toward behaviorism that I find in the work of Paul Virilio and Michel Foucault. The third section of this chapter describes how I became interested in big data and information literacy while considering the differences between knowledge and information societies. To facilitate a knowledge society, information literacy must balance evolving technology while helping users remain in control of their information use. This can be especially challenging as big data's transformation of social science affects the theoretical roots of information literacy. This idea leads to a quick look at how education itself could change as big data manages learners. Current information literacy problems, the future of education, and even contemporary academic work are already heavily impacted by IT use. The transformation of text into multimedia, new Web 2.0 applications, and patron driven acquisition are just some examples of how IT continues to transform some aspects of LIS or librarianship. IT's centrality in these areas, along with many other areas of contemporary life, has already led to widespread fears that machines work on us instead of for us, a problem that Virilio and Foucault anticipated. Tellingly, one author on big data sees a solution to this problem in big data itself, an idea that helps me articulate a solution. Ultimately, information literacy must be a tool to teach users both about the nature of big data and how to use it; that is, to master it. This is the source of my possible solution to the problem with big data's instrumentalist framework. Information literacy must be a tool in the library that empowers users in an evolving environment where big data is a chief source for understanding human behavior.

My conclusion focuses on the impact big data has on practitioners, especially those who work in user instruction and aim to help users find information for ends that they themselves define. User instruction is of importance for those who engage in information literacy in academic or public libraries. I believe big data could make the work of practitioners in these settings much more difficult. If that is the case, social justice aims and concomitant community action arising from the empowerment of information users, particularly through information literacy or other similar practices, will be adversely affected by an ever more sophisticated, mechanistic big data emphasis on past behavior, one that predicts and manages user behavior for largely commercial ends. To theorize how empowerment can remain a part of information literacy efforts in the era of big data is a difficult prospect. Ultimately, my hopes for the future are that big data can be a tool for social justice aims.

Big Data and the Drift Towards Behaviorism

The use of big data, which is data that accrues from nearly every digital information transaction one can imagine, will certainly be used, whenever possible, to judge and predict how people behave. Much of that information will arise from and feed into commercial aims, a view widely understood in most literature on the subject.[5] Changes in research methods caused by big data have already had an impact on library practitioners represented by the Association of College and Research Libraries (ACRL), who can get an idea of this change from

---

5. Manyika, *Big Data*, 68.

the ACRL website: "Librarians in all disciplines, in order to facilitate the research process, will need to be aware of how big data is used and where it can be found."[6] In addition, library practitioners who seek to provide evidence of relevance and accountability regarding the use of information resources will most likely need to come to terms with future big data means used to measure and predict basic library services or manage library resources when current, commercial big data efficiency practices trickle down from large corporations to ever smaller entities. In such a scenario it is easy to imagine big data applications that measure and predict how library services and resources are used. Such information, while potentially valuable for managing services and resources, could override ideas about services and resources that don't originate with data. For example, big data could show a great use of graphic novels but fail to buttress arguments made by librarians for useful and necessary but less popular materials. I will return to this idea of the greater availability of big data for libraries when I discuss user-driven collection development. Ultimately, if a trend such as this develops, it may well conflict with the social justice aims of any librarians trying to equalize the power differentials between those who produce commercial information and those who consume it.

Kevin Rioux addresses issues of power in his article "Metatheory in Library and Information Science: A Nascent Social Justice Approach" where he articulates "the long-held altruistic stances of LIS,"[7] and defines five assumptions of an LIS social justice metatheory. The fifth one is most explicit about the role of power: "Access, control, and mediation of information contain inherent power relationships. The act of distributing information is itself a political act."[8] Both the altruism and the

---

6. Association of College and Research Libraries (ACRL), "Keeping Up With... Big Data," accessed March 26, 2015, http://www.ala.org/acrl/publications/keeping_up_with/big_data.

7. Kevin Rioux, "Metatheory in Library and Information Science: A Nascent Social Justice Approach," *Journal of Education for Library and Information Science* 51, no. 1, (Winter 2010): 14.

8. Ibid., 13.

importance of the political act of distributing information articulated by Rioux in his metatheory may well become crowded out by the growth and use of big data for two reasons. First, there is the changed focus of research into human behavior inherent in the use of big data since it is often largely commercial. Big data is certainly projected to grow at an amazing "26.4% compound annual growth rate to $41.5 billion through 2018, or about six times the growth rate of the overall information technology market."[9] Second, there is the changed nature of research into human behavior, a change that promises to encompass all human behavior, not just some areas. As a consequence, any field concerned with human behavior will be changed by big data. If I extrapolate from Anderson's concern with what people do as opposed to why regarding information behavior, then we would see library services and resources in thrall to wants and desires over needs.

Big data is grounded in an understanding of human behavior that conflicts with many existing understandings currently underpinning and produced within social science that foreground understanding human behavior as opposed to merely channeling it. While there are resources and practices that fall outside commercial parameters in libraries, most commercial information resources in libraries (books, journals, and various media), are easily subject to the increasingly commercialized influence of big data, or will be as such influences increase. The changing nature of research arising from big data is harder to characterize but equally important, for that is where a drift to instrumentalism or behaviorism threatens the primacy of human agency.

In the book, *Social Physics: How Good Ideas Spread—The Lessons from a New Science*, Alex Pentland calls for a new science he calls social physics, in part because: "The scientific method as currently practiced in the social sciences is failing us and threatens to collapse in an era of big data.[10]

---

9. International Data Corporation, "Big Data & Analytics: An IDC Four Pillar Research Area," accessed April 5, 2015, https://www.idc.com/prodserv/4Pillars/bigdata.

10. Alex Pentland, *Social Physics: How Good Ideas Spread—The Lessons from a New Science* (New York: Penguin, 2014), 216.

Pentland describes the collection of big data through the creation of proposed living laboratories; his current use of a badge "that records a wearer's behavior" and "behavior measurement software" for smart phones[11] are technological developments that many find difficult to accept for a host of ethical, moral, or intellectual reasons. Intellectually, non-objective understandings of human behavior, including humanistic or qualitative approaches to human behavior, stand to lose ground to this instrumentalist use of the scientific method within the social sciences. On an ethical or moral basis, one might object that the highly personal and formerly private information generated by the people involved in such efforts as those outlined by Pentland, lose privacy to benefit not themselves, but rather those who study them. Ultimately, such an emphasis could easily conflict with the social justice ideals of a librarian seeking to distribute information for the benefit of the user. Just as importantly, the data generated in this way is excellent at recording what people have done, but not necessarily why. As Pentland writes of his new science, "The social physics I envision, though, acknowledges our human capacity for independent thought but does not need to try to account for it."[12] This loss of accounting for human behavior is in line with a drift towards behaviorism that seems to arise from social science research that relies primarily on big data.

Librarians who address power relations as they pursue the goal of making information available will inevitably confront just such a return to the form of behaviorism seemingly embodied in current understandings of the use of big data,[13] as the overwhelmingly commercial world of information displaces libraries as an information source. Morrone and Friedman, in their article "Radical Reference: Socially Responsible Librarianship Collaborating With Community," wrote that "library workers are in a state of constant adjustment to new technologies and

---

11. Ibid., 218.

12. Ibid., 189.

13. George Siemens and Phil Long, "Penetrating the Fog: Analytics in Learning and Education," *Educause Review* 46.5 (2011): 31-40, accessed November 26, 2014, https://net.educause.edu/ir/library/pdf/ERM1151.pdf.

techniques for finding relevant, useful information."[14] I would emphasize that this constant adjustment arises because the nature of information is not only complex, but also continually evolving due to the commercial transformation of information in the digital era. To that end, the development and promotion of information literacy has also played a central role because it is based on a key ideal: to help a community of information users define and meet their information needs, as well as become sophisticated users of information technology who are then fully aware of this technology's implications. Information professionals have often served as key allies in the battle for social justice because they promote information seeking and use by individuals for needs and purposes those individuals themselves define.

Today of course, information seeking behavior in the digital realm generates big data, but the economic imperative to use such data on human behavior doesn't necessarily facilitate understanding that behavior. As danah boyd and Kate Crawford write in their paper, "Six Provocations for Big Data": "Why people do things, write things, or make things is erased by the sheer volume of numerical repetition and large patterns."[15] As a result, I think big data poses an existential threat to the promotion of information literacy, which is a key way that information professionals work to facilitate information seeking behavior. It is a threat that was articulated early on in the development of big data by Chris Anderson when he wrote, as previously noted, "Out with every theory of human behavior..."

Chris Anderson's hyperbolic regard for big data, a tone often echoed in numerous works on the advent of big data, is well met by a question posed by Paul Virilio discussing contemporary science: "After the

14. Melissa Morrone and Lia Friedman, "Radical Reference: Socially Responsible Librarianship Collaborating with Community," *Reference Librarian* 50 (2009): 371.

15. danah boyd and Kate Crawford, "Six Provocations for Big Data," (paper presented at A Decade in Internet Time: Symposium on the Dynamics of the Internet and Society, Oxford, England, September 21-24, 2011), accessed November 10, 2013, http://papers.ssrn.com/sol3/papers.cfm?abstract_id=1926431.

authority of human beings over their history, are we going to yield, with the acceleration of the real, to the authority of machines and those who program them?"[16] While Virilio is writing about the overarching development of science since the Cold War and specific areas like robotics or genetic engineering, his chief concern is with a science that is instrumentalist in nature and not directed towards "truth;" that is, science is becoming "a knowledge which denies all objective reality."[17] Just to be clear, this objective reality becomes lost when science becomes overwhelmed by a drive towards instrumentalist goals or a drive to solve immediate problems from a specific view (usually commercial), instead of seeking answers to the larger questions that science can also address. If Anderson is happy to dispense with a concern regarding "why people do what they do," Virilio is particularly dismayed by a science with a seeming disregard for "any effort to discover a coherent truth useful to humanity."[18] Simply stated, Virilio sees looming disasters in a science that no longer seems bound to its ethical, humanist past, a past that was tied to the development of human knowledge, while Anderson's words crystalize an opposing laudatory understanding of big data's promise to dispense with such concerns. In this latter view, it will no longer be necessary to understand why people do what they do since big data doesn't seem to need the traditional social sciences dismissed by Anderson.

While these two views may represent extreme understandings of a science that becomes ever more automated, it is clear that technological developments characterized by the term big data will have a significant impact on the way science approaches human behavior. Today human behavior is finding a new life in recorded digital form, and that recorded form of behavior will be the raw material for examining how we live and work, though for commercial ends, not the larger altruistic or intellectual ends that have traditionally defined science.

---

16. Paul Virilio, trans. Chris Turner, Information Bomb (New York: Verso, 2000), 122.

17. Ibid., 3.

18. Ibid., 1.

At this point, it is useful to discuss how some technological changes and the use of big data may well change understandings of information seeking behavior in line with a more instrumentalist or behaviorist perspective and how this aim poses a challenge to information professionals who see literacy in our current information environment as central to any form of self-directed progress or growth. The basic understanding of Foucault's articulation of the panopticon is that humans willingly participate in the tracking and supervision of their own behavior and thereby both create and accept new forms of power relations.[19] Together with the threat Virilio finds in "techno-science," these understandings articulated by critical theory help describe current developments in science, which in turn will allow me to articulate the threat to the social justice aims inherent in some aspects of LIS, as well as the social action we can undertake in light of such developments. Social action in such an environment will inevitably depend on a greater call to self-empowerment through information and by understanding how information is collected, sold, and utilized. Ultimately, information users will have to become incredibly active, engaged, and committed to understanding and using information for their own purposes, even as systems develop that seek to use information about them for other, often unknown purposes.

Information Literacy, Learning Theory and Practice, and LIS or Education Institutions

I became aware of the need for social action by information professionals, given the development of big data, when I was invited to speak at a conference sponsored by the Department of Library and Information Science at North Eastern Hill University in Shillong, Meghalaya, India. The conference theme, Information Literacy in the Knowledge Society, forced me to confront how a geographic area traditionally seen as underdeveloped, the Indian state of Meghalaya, could approach the

---

19. Michel Foucault, trans. Alan Sheridan, *Discipline and Punish: the Birth of the Prison* (New York: Random House, 1995).

ever-growing technological sophistication of information and the challenges it poses to the role of LIS professionals in the realm of social
justice. In preparation for this talk, it became clear that confronting the
implications of the growth of big data is a global challenge. From a
worldwide perspective, UNESCO helps to define an opposition between
societies where information becomes ever more equitably distributed
and societies where economic imperatives govern information by promoting "the concept of knowledge societies, rather than that of (the)
global information society."[20] Knowledge societies would continue the
growth of culture across the globe, while the other is seen as an agent
of commercial globalization. Today, information use in the information
society not only facilitates the collection of big data, but also relies on
its commercial infrastructure.

In accordance with this understanding, Grassian and Kaplowitz,
in *Information Literacy Instruction,* recognize "the powerful and political nature of the information commodity" and so deplore "a fruitless
attempt to convince them (users) to start their search somewhere other
than Google."[21] The information commodity described here is easily
understood by the invocation of the brand name Google, but this type
of commodity is certainly not limited to Google or its products, as a
view of Grassian & Kaplowitz's chapter, "The Psychology of Learning"
from *Information Literacy Instruction* indicates. There, they also describe in
detail the use of learning theory in information literacy. Ultimately, within
information literacy strategies and curricula, there is a range of theory
that spans from behaviorist to cognitive, constructivist, and even humanist schema. There is also a preference for cognitive and constructivist
approaches, beginning with Kulthau, a preference further endorsed in

20. Abdul Waheed Kahn, preface to *UNESCO's Basic Texts on the Information Society,* ed. Jean-Gabriel Mastrangelo and Melika Loncarevic, (Paris:
UNESCO, 2004), 5, accessed November 16, 2013, http://unesdoc.unesco.
org/images/0013/001355/135527e.pdf.

21. Esther S. Grassian and Joan R. Kaplowitz, *Information Literacy Instruction:
Theory and Practice,* 2nd ed. (New York: Neal-Schuman, 2009), 8.

the UNESCO document, "Towards Information Literacy Indicators."[22] Based on these numerous approaches from various social science fields, Grassian and Kaplowitz further suggest librarians "formulate a defini- tion of information literacy that is personally meaningful and works in your specific environment."[23] This practical understanding neatly accepts that librarians should work with users as they find them, that is, in a world where the information commodity and the infrastructure that ensure their delivery are ever more common. Even if this seems a reasonable place to start with information literacy, the changing nature of the information commodity may well imperil the central aim of information literacy and its underlying altruistic impulse and desire to empower users. The nature of information commodities presents a host of problems that I can only briefly address here.

For example, teaching information literacy becomes ever more dif- ficult in a constantly evolving commercial information environment where change and innovation may be qualities that sell new products, even if those products have distinct disadvantages regarding informa- tion use. Apple's recent introduction of a new type of USB port on its laptops follows in their tradition of limiting options for users by forcing a transition away from existing technologies like jump drives, just as this firm had previously done with floppy drives and CD drives. In this case, Apple's new USB port requires the purchase of another adapter or a greater reliance on Apple products, particularly from the cloud; this is something that may be good for commerce, but not necessarily for the consumer.[24] However, countering such changes by teaching that new isn't always better when it comes to information and information technology may seem not just particularly old fashioned, but well nigh

---

22. Ralph Catts and Jesus Lau, *Towards Information Literacy Indicators* (Paris: UNESCO, Information Society Division Communication and Information Sector, 2008), 28, accessed November 21, 2013, https://dspace.stir.ac.uk/bit- stream/1893/2119/1/cattsandlau.pdf.

23. Grassian, *Information Literacy Instruction*, 8.

24. Stephen Shankland, "How Apple's Embrace of the New USB Points to World Without Wires," *Cnet* (2015), accessed April 24, 2015, http://www. cnet.com/news/how-apples-embrace-of-the-new-usb-points-to-world-with- out-wires/.

impossible in a world where the latest product release by Apple or other such companies are sensations unto themselves. In such a world, the information commodity and its supporting infrastructure seem destined to win out over the idea that users should have the options and flexibility in the information environment they themselves define, as opposed to the options sold to them.

More fundamentally, the very nature of education may change under the influence of big data, which could impact learning theories that have played a role in information literacy and library practice. Patrick Tucker examines some possible changes in learning because of big data in his book on the loss of privacy in the era of big data titled, *The Naked Future*. In one passage, Tucker recalls a conversation he had with Peter Norvig, a highly regarded artificial intelligence expert:

> We're going to make rapid advances in understanding what works and what doesn't on the basis of interaction statistics," he (Norvig) told me. I asked him if he believed every student would have access to a predictive model of their own learning style in the next five years; if, in effect, there was a naked future for education. "That's the hope," he answered.[25]

This conversation is part of the chapter, "Relearning How to Learn," that describes how the use of detailed data on even the most minute aspects of a student's academic performance, as opposed to summative grades or tests, would reveal areas of confusion, problems with self-esteem, and the role of group interaction as they affect learning. Sadly, all of this is quite possibly at the price of a student's privacy. That is why Tucker uses the word "naked" in his book's title, as it describes this loss of privacy. The resulting changes in education promise to be great, but for my purposes I'm most interested in what this means for learning theory, particularly as it relates to information literacy.

Like most examinations of big data, the results point to specific areas of learning; or, as Norvig puts it, "what works and what doesn't on the

---

25. Patrick Tucker, *The Naked Future: What Happens in a World That Anticipates Your Every Move?* (New York: Penguin, 2014), 139.

basis of interaction statistics."[26] This leaves larger questions unanswered; for example, learning theory goes largely unaddressed in this chapter in favor of an open-ended understanding that education will have to change. The overall impression that this chapter, and indeed this entire book, creates is that we must face big data despite the problems it presents, particularly in terms of privacy. Tucker, like most proponents of big data, is not primarily concerned with key questions like why learning should happen, which is a concern librarians teaching information literacy might have, but rather with specific questions of how to learn. Big data seems to always be about how things happen, and not why they should or shouldn't. Interestingly, though, Tucker does acknowledge that there are problems with big data, an acknowledgement that I will elaborate on more in my conclusion.

More specific to LIS, promoting information literacy in any environment, whether in India or the US, may well mean accepting that many users bypass libraries and ignore library practices and standards. For example, researching an article like this once required a set of activities physically located in an academic library, but I only went to the library to get hard copies of books and articles not available as downloads. Most research was accomplished at my home through the online services of the library at my workplace, Chicago State University, and a browser set to Google Scholar.

While this process foregrounds an academic library and its educational mission, it is equally dependent on numerous commercial enterprises, particularly in the delivery of information, and that commercial use generates big data for those commercial enterprises. While librarians in the future might find such big data useful for collection development, determining policies regarding access, or other areas and needs, etc., the commercial enterprises that collect and analyze big data will not use this information for the altruistic ideals described in Rioux's "Metatheory in Library and Information Science,"[27] nor will these commercial enterprises foreground the empowerment of the user.

---

26. Ibid., 139.
27. Rioux, "Metatheory," 14.

Further, the technological and international character of such a research effort is a common experience that ties together not just scholars in information or library science, but cultures, countries, and regions, and the scholars or individuals within them who seek information, thereby contributing to the global information society described by UNESCO. In the struggle to create the opposite, a more human-centered knowledge society, education is just one of four contexts listed as a key area for the practice of information literacy within the UNESCO document, "Towards Information Literacy Indicators," based on the work of Garner.[28] If elements of my research process provide an example that mixes commercial and public institutions, how might such information seeking look for non-academic users who make no provision for library use and concomitant LIS ideals in those other three contexts defined in the UNESCO document, that is, in the context of society, work, and well-being? Would such information use be subject solely to commercial ends and simply generate even more data for commercial institutions? Further, how far will information professionals go to accommodate the existing environment of users? Will such accommodation grow a process of data collection that seems ever more independent of the public institutions like libraries and the cultural impulses behind such institutions? And what about the various social science fields that are devoted to understanding human behavior underlying such public institutions' understanding of human behavior?

For these reasons, definitions of information literacy and related concepts like computer, IT, Internet, digital, or media literacy are vitally important, though it might be hard to agree on a single definition or term. A discussion of aspects of information literacy by the International Federation of Library Associations and Institution (IFLA) includes:

> ...user education, learning styles, the use of computers and media in teaching and learning, networked resources, partnerships with teaching faculty in the development of instructional programmes, distance

---

28. Catts and Lau, *Towards Information Literacy*, 9.

education, and the training of librarians in teaching information and technical skills.[29]

Such a definition, while not necessarily definitive or universal (despite its source), foregrounds education, but the possibilities big data offers in the development of information resources and the solutions it offers regarding the examination of records of human behavior can be independent of educational institutions and aims, even if utilized in partnership with educational or LIS institutions.

LIS Professionals and Some Current Challenges with Information Literacy and Information Seeking Behavior as They Face Big Data

Initially I planned to list numerous challenges librarians face as they promote information literacy or come to terms with contemporary information seeking behavior, but in this brief chapter I can only mention some. For example, changes in media technology have led to large-scale transformations in text. The results include digital books as well as a host of online media – everything from web pages to wikis, blogs, tweets, and other 2.0 applications like Facebook, LinkedIn, etc.

Knowing how to find, evaluate, and use these text media is a challenge that requires technical skills, as well as technical understanding of each text medium, along with an understanding of their social, political, and economic meaning. Of course there are fears that text may be losing its key role, since many of these media are in fact multi-media, where digital sound, images, and video have become ubiquitous. If the challenges posed today by text are complex, I wonder if librarians as a profession are prepared to instruct users, or that key subset of users, students, who use and make images, sound, and video. In fact, the use of such media for educational assessment is outlined in "Assessing Student

29. International Federation of Library Associations and Institutions (IFLA), Information Literacy Section, last modified March 5, 2009, http://archive.ifla.org/VII/s42/..

Learning Online," a presentation made at the International Association for Development of the Information Society meeting in 2012.[30] According to another paper from this conference, distance learning is growing in importance in the workplace.[31] Together, changes like these, often driven by commercial and technological developments, threaten to overwhelm anyone trying to define, use, or teach information literacy. Other challenging areas for information literacy instruction include interactive digital environments and games, and the building of online communities.

Just consider the problem of evaluation in Web 2.0 applications. Are Twitter, Wikipeda, or social sites like Facebook valid, reliable, or authoritative? They certainly aren't stable. In my research for this chapter, I read Susan McKnight's article, "A Futuristic View of Knowledge and Information Management;" in it, she cited the phrase: "Getting the right information to the right person at the right place at the right time."[32] While this reminded me of Ranganathan's third law, "Every book its reader,"[33] McKnight wasn't referring to Ranganathan, but to *Wikipedia*, via the link, http://en.wikipedia.org/wiki/Information_management. When this link is followed, however, the phrase is no longer there; it has been edited out of existence.

While I feel this demonstrates that a resource like Wikipedia is unreliable, and therefore not authoritative, Humrickhouse, in her paper,

30. Stephen D. Arnold, "Assessing Student Learning Online," (paper presented at the annual meeting for the International Association for Development of the Information Society, Madrid, Spain, October 19-21, 2012), accessed November 28, 2014, ERIC (ED542719).

31. Susan Bolt, "Professional Development: Then and Now," (paper presented at the annual International Conference on Cognition and Exploratory Learning in Digital Age (CELDA 2012), Madrid, Spain, October 19-21, 2012), accessed November 28, 2014, ERIC (ED542831).

32. Susan McKnight, "A Futuristic View of Knowledge and Information Management," *BiD: Textos Universitaris de Biblioteconomia i Documentació* 17 (2007), accessed November, 24, 2014, http://bid.ub.edu/19mcknig.htm.

33. Shiyali Ramamrita Ranganathan, *The Five Laws of Library Science* (London: Blunt, 1957), 456.

"Information Literacy Instruction in the Web 2.0 Library" wrote, "It is no longer acceptable to use or disregard information based upon the way it is presented – today a Twitter feed may be just as authoritative as a scholarly journal article."[34] I don't fully agree with this statement. For me, Twitter isn't even as authoritative as Wikipedia, where certain strategies like editing "to prevent disruption or vandalism"[35] are meant to foster some measure of authority. In addition:

> Several mechanisms are in place to help Wikipedia members carry out the important work of crafting a high-quality resource while maintaining civility. Editors are able to watch pages and techies can write editing programs to keep track of or rectify bad edits. Where there are disagreements on how to present facts, editors work together to arrive at an article that fairly represents current expert opinion on the subject.[36]

The very editorial interest in facts revealed in these policies distinguishes Wikipedia from Twitter. Of course, Wikipedia's editing policies are still not as reassuring as the traditional editing practices that create similar resources like published encyclopedias and dictionaries, even in their online versions. While opinions on such Web 2.0 media might vary among information professionals, the widespread and growing reliance on such media as information sources inevitably complicates information literacy and information seeking behavior, a trend already well documented in contemporary journalism.[37]

Web 2.0 certainly has a great ability to democratize information creation and elevate the importance of social networks, trends that

---

34. Elizabeth Humrickhouse, "Information Literacy Instruction in the Web 2.0 Library," (2011), accessed November 28, 2014, ERIC (ED520720).

35. "Wikipedia: About," ed. LethalFlower, Wikipedia, The Free Encyclopedia, accessed April 5, 2015 https://en.wikipedia.org/wiki/Wikipedia:About.

36. Ibid.

37. Dominic L. Lasorsa, et al., "Normalizing Twitter: Journalism Practice in an Emerging Communication Space," *Journalism Studies* 13, no. 1 (2012): 19-36.

many applaud. According to scholars like Herring[38] and Wai-yi,[39] such networks have become even more important information sources in the workplace. Alarmingly, however, according to UNESCO, even in education, "teachers made little use of information sources and relied primarily on their senior managers and on informal exchanges of ideas with peers."[40] In light of these ideas on Twitter, Wikipedia, and the value of social networks, perhaps information literacy must re-emphasize the meaning of authority and objectivity. But such concepts are tied to non-commercial ideals and may receive less emphasis in an ever more commercial information environment where, for librarians, just keeping up with change, much less managing it, is a continual problem.

I also examined the articles, "Give'Em What They Want: A One-Year Study of Unmediated Patron-Driven Acquisition of E-books,"[41] and "Giving the Users What They Want: Is Patron-Driven Acquisitions the Answer?" [42] where the acquisition of e-books is directly tied to library user requests. In these studies, librarians listed items in their online catalogs but the items were only purchased as patrons requested them. Fischer, et al., point out that such practices may affect collection development and preservation, even causing publishers to grow more skittish when considering whether or not to publish material they fear

---

38. James E. Herring, "From School to Work and from Work to School: Information Environments and Transferring Information Literacy Practices," *Information Research: An International Electronic Journal* 16, no. 2 (2011), accessed November, 26, 2014, ERIC (EJ935870).

39. B. Cheuk Wai-yi, "An Information Seeking and Using Process Model in the Workplace: A Constructivist Approach," *Asian Libraries* 7, no. 12 (1998): 375-390.

40. Catts and Lau, *Towards Information Literacy*, 28.

41. Karen s. Fischer, et al., "Give'Em What They Want: A One-year Study of Unmediated Patron-Driven Acquisition of E-Books," *College & Research Libraries* 73, no. 5 (2012): 469-492, accessed November 14, 2013, http://crl.acrl.org/content/73/5/469.full.pdf.

42. Buddy Pennington and Steve Alleman, "Giving the Users What They Want: Is Patron-Driven Acquisitions the Answer?" (paper presented at the annual meeting, Brick and Click Libraries: An Academic Library Symposium, Maryville, Missouri, October 26, 2012), accessed November 28, 2014, ERIC (ED537605).

won't sell. Currently, many libraries purchase materials regardless of their economic prospects in order to fill key collection needs, and this gives publishers an incentive to publish such works. If big data is added to this equation, and data regarding usage becomes more decisive in building a collection vis-à-vis librarian expertise, then practitioner expertise in shaping collections might only diminish further. Ultimately, if patron-assisted collection development grows, information literacy might well have to encompass collection policies so that library users understand how browsing and using a catalog will shape library collections. Again, such a change seems to me unlikely given the current difficulty of simply keeping up with technological change.

These seemingly unrelated examples of issues with information literacy in terms of changing and new media forms, their evaluation and use, as well as greater reliance on social networks from ordinary people in the creation and distribution of media, and even methods of collection, may seem to have little connection to the role of learning theory, despite a clear relationship to commercial and technological change. They do have a connection, however, because all these online interactions contribute to big data,[43] and as a result, "We have massive databases of materials used by scholars in the humanities and social sciences ranging from digitized books, newspapers, and music to transactional data like web searches, sensor data or cell phone records."[44] Siemens and Long clearly state the problem arising from this shift in focus among scholars who use big data, particularly for those who want to understand human beings and their relationship to the complex nature of learning. They write: "we risk a return to behaviorism as a learning theory if we confine analytics to behavioral data."[45] Though Merriam-Webster's online

43. Jeff Morris, "Top 10 Categories for Big Data Sources and Mining Technologies," *ZDNet,* July 16, 2012, accessed November 26, 2014, http://www.zdnet.com/top-10-categories-for-big-data-sources-and-mining-technologies-7000000926/.

44. Lev Manovich, "Trending: The Promises and the Challenges of Big Social Data." *Debates in the Digital Humanities* (2011): 460.

45. Siemens, "Penetrating the Fog," 38.

dictionary defines analytics as "the method of logical analysis,"[46] I think Wikipedia is more in line with contemporary, commercial understandings of this term: "Analytics is the discovery and communication of meaningful patterns in data."[47] This process upends the traditional scientific method where scholars propose a hypothesis and then devise a way to test it. Instead, examining behavioral data to discover patterns foregrounds facts over questions. Ultimately, all our online information use feeds big data, which simultaneously feeds an emphasis on the study of behavior and a corresponding tendency toward the learning theory of behaviorism.

Big Data's Behaviorist View of Information Use vs. Social Justice Aims and Community Action

Libraries have long been in an information environment in which people were shifting from traditional brick and mortar libraries to online enterprises, where commercial firms often play a central role, or at the very least a vital supporting role, through the development and provision of digital information infrastructure. The rise of big data within this changing information environment encapsulates a shift to a more mechanistic view of human behavior or even behaviorism, a view that can easily overtake research streams in information seeking behavior and information use. As commercial aims displace the important political and ethical aims that are often central to the missions espoused by libraries and the social sciences, the very altruism and power relations found in some areas of LIS are at risk.

In this brief chapter I've tried to examine how the social justice impulses of librarians regarding power and information might be challenged by big data, particularly as librarians understand user behavior and promote information literacy. It's a large, complex issue, one that

---

46. *Merriam-Webster.com*, s.v. "analytics," accessed November 26, 2014, http://www.merriam-webster.com/dictionary/analytics.

47. *Wikipedia*, s.v. "Analytics," accessed November 26, 2014, http://en.wikipedia.org/wiki/Analytics.

is perhaps best articulated by exposing the creeping behaviorist impulse inherent in the emphasis that big data places on specific solutions; that is, answers to questions that ask how things happen, as opposed to asking larger questions that hint at an understanding of why people learn or use information.

Together with the commercial nature of most big data, this existential threat can harm the social justice nature of librarianship. Indeed, the power of large institutions and the power of big data have led many to feel a generalized dread characterized by Patrick Tucker: "We feel we have arrived at an age in which our devices communicate about us in a language we cannot hear to parties we cannot see. Big data belongs to them, not us. We are its victims."[48] While Tucker focuses on the threat to privacy in his book, perhaps the larger threat we face is in the behaviorist future he articulates in this statement, one where solutions are indeed devised to channel humans rather than to help them realize who they are and what they want. As Tucker concludes in a jarring echo of Virilio: "The threat of creeping techno totalitarianism is real."[49]

Virilio joins his fears of a more instrumentalist, contemporary science that has lost touch with a humanist past, to Foucault's description of new power relations in a society where surveillance becomes ever more sophisticated and all encompassing:

> Building the space of the multimedia networks with the aid of the tele-technologies surely then requires a new 'optic', a new global optics, capable of helping a panoptical vision to appear, a vision which is indispensable if the 'market of the visible' is to be established. The much-vaunted globalization requires that we all observe each other and compare ourselves with one another on a continual basis.[50]

Virilio's "market of the visible" finds partial expression in the detailed records of human behavior that create big data. Now everything from

---

48. Tucker, *The Naked Future*, xiv.

49. Ibid., xvii.

50. Virilio, *Information Bomb*, 61.

conversations to shopping, working, and every type of human interaction can leave a visible record that can also be the basis for studying what we do. This recording of human behavior, which can lead to what Tucker calls creeping techno-totalitarianism, is indeed something about which many have expressed fear.

Fortunately, though there is much I disagree with in Tucker's book, he does articulate a small hope that may well fit within the altruistic impulses of librarianship and favor the possibility of tipping the balance of power towards individuals in regards to information use and literacy. He states, "…your data is yours first because you created it through your actions."[51] With this simple statement Tucker creates an opening to empowerment, but not one that can easily be articulated or put into practice. Simply stated, when Tucker introduces the idea that we need to grapple with the advent of big data as a tool about ourselves that we ourselves can use, he creates a challenge that not only changes what information literacy is, but also challenges anyone who would teach information literacy to dramatically expand what they do because of big data. Any LIS professional concerned with empowering users must now begin by teaching that contemporary information media emerge from fundamentally dynamic and complex systems that not only change as we interact with them, but track our use for purposes we may never suspect. If information literacy is a tool for empowerment, it must teach users that such information is no longer static, like a CD or printed book, but part of a process that can help them realize who they are and who they will become.

> Think of it not as a liability but as an asset you can take ownership of and use. In the naked future, your data will help you live much more healthily, to realize more of your own goals in less time, avoid inconvenience and danger, and, as detailed in the book, learn about yourself and your own future in a way that no generation in human history ever thought possible.[52]

---

51. Tucker, *The Naked Future*, xviii.
52. Ibid., xviii.

The tone of optimism that Tucker expresses can be difficult to share for many reasons, including the one idea central to his book, namely that we will trade much that has been private to gain the benefits he lists. In addition to this, I also wonder if the difficulty librarians encounter staying abreast of technological change, and bringing the best of this change to users, is another great threat we face specific to LIS. Most importantly, how can librarians help others understand that their data belongs to them when many aren't even aware that this data exists, or if they are aware that it does exist, it remains relatively opaque in terms of its importance. Despite such misgivings, it is at this early point in his book on big data that Tucker shows a real concern with the idea that individuals can, or even should, use big data to better themselves, an idea that does correspond to altruistic impulses and a concern with the relationship between information and power in librarianship. Ultimately, Tucker thinks that as big data grows, it will become not just more commonplace, but cheaper and logistically more usable for individuals and not just large institutions, an issue that could bring greater efficiency arising from big data use into common library practices, especially regarding resources and patrons; but how exactly this will look is hard to predict. As David Bollier and Charles M. Firestone write in their article, "The Promise and Peril of Big Data":

> But big data also presents many formidable challenges to government and citizens precisely because data technologies are becoming so pervasive, intrusive and difficult to understand. How shall society protect itself against those who would misuse or abuse large databases? What new regulatory systems, private-law innovations or social practices will be capable of controlling antisocial behaviors—and how should we even define what is socially and legally acceptable when the practices enabled by big data are so novel and often arcane?[53]

If big data is a challenge for government and citizens, groups that easily encompass publicly funded libraries and many library users respectively,

---

53. David Bollier and Charles M. Firestone, *The Promise and Peril of Big Data*, (Washington, DC: Aspen Institute, Communications and Society Program, 2010), 40.

the commercial world sees things utterly differently. Here are some ideas about how the publishing industry can change through big data, changes that could impact the customers of publishers like libraries:

> Big-data helps publishers understand their target audience base and thus optimize pricing based on location, categories, and underperforming sections. Also, don't forget that personalized pricing can be an ideal element in personalized marketing to spur sales, reward customer loyalty, and urge reluctant readers to try something new....Publishers can track tweet hashtags, Facebook likes, and book reviews to aggregate and track in real-time and to provide tailored customized offerings and interactions based on preferences and feedback.[54]

If I understand these recommendations for publishers, privacy is certainly not a concern, since they are urged to use data about users to create different levels of pricing and also track the use of materials to anticipate future use. How does this affect libraries? While I've already mentioned that the Association of College and Research Libraries (ACRL) expects their members to brace for changes in research, ACRL also makes recommendations more specific to collections and services:

> Your library could be gathering big data for analysis to help make data driven decisions. What types of big data could you use to make better decisions about collection development, updating public spaces, or tracking use of library materials through your learning management system? Or you could be the thought leader on big data curation at your institution by providing guidance to storing and making accessible big data sets.[55]

In the era of big data, libraries may not only have to grapple with how big data changes research, but how it allows them to manage resources

---

54. Venkat Viswanathan, "5 Ways Big-Data Can Save Publishing," *All Analytics: The Community for Data Management, Business Intelligence, and Analytics*, September 10, 2013, http://www.allanalytics.com/author. asp?section_id=3031&doc_id=267533&.

55. ACRL, "Keeping Up With... Big Data."

and services as big data becomes more economical to use. In the future, libraries will have to educate the public about how big data can be another tool for information use, and that last item could be extremely complex. That could encompass seeing big data sets as information sources available in libraries, with all the attendant needs of adding to or building collections, which highlights the problem of staying abreast of technological change in order to use it or help users deploy it.

My focus on information literacy in this chapter was strategic. Recognizing and articulating the information environment of users has long been a central part of librarianship, and transmitting that knowledge is now more vital than ever. If librarians recognize the behaviorist impulse in big data and seek to both inform users of this change in information and how to utilize this data to further the goals users themselves define, then we can at least arm users with the information they need to exist on their own terms in this new information environment. This is how I see librarians attempting to equalize access for the less powerful. It goes beyond simply gaining access, or more and better access, to information because any such expansion not only serves commercial interests, but also enlarges the commercial infrastructure that grows big data so that more users become subject to data collection. Library practitioners must understand the change in information, information behavior, and underlying social science, as well as research in general to change who they are.

> New types of data intermediaries are also likely to arise to help people make sense of an otherwise-bewildering flood of information. Indeed, data-intermediaries and interpreters could represent a burgeoning segment of the information technology sector in the years ahead.[56]

This is the new role for librarians who seek to remain true to impulses that make information work for users, instead of generating information about users. Put simply, encouraging information use not only challenges a user's privacy, but also turns each user into a subject of data collection

---

56. Bollier, *The Promise and Peril of Big Data*, 40.

that grows the behaviorist impulse which, in turn, drives the examination of such data. If some LIS professionals can, however, become the intermediaries that make big data understandable, then those professionals can help users understand this new reality as we help them to take charge of this potential asset, the data they generate through their own actions, and thereby give users power over their data. Progressive community action arising from libraries and information use will require a foregrounding of learning about "big data," its existence, collection, sale, and ultimately, its utilization. It is an aspect of LIS because we are talking about a new type of information that could conceivably reach into every aspect of life. Knowing about this type of information and teaching about it, becoming the intermediary between users and big data through an expanded information literacy, is how we can empower users and bring progressive action into this new era. The changes arising from big data, a propensity to a more positivist, behaviorist view of human action that could crowd out other more human-centered approaches to the social sciences, must be openly discussed from an LIS perspective. Just as importantly, the data users generate must be actively promoted as their property, the existence of which has serious implications for their privacy. If all this sounds difficult or far off, we can't forget that the growth of big data is amazingly fast and already impacts commercial distribution and resource management, a trend that will one day spread beyond commercial enterprises to institutions like publicly funded libraries. Conversely, the growth of commercial information sources and use has already challenged the role of libraries in information use, a challenge that can only grow as big data makes commercial information sources even larger and more powerful. Ultimately, all the issues raised by big data regarding information use are so large that libraries or librarians can't address them alone. Instead, we must partner with existing progressive movements to keep users abreast of how information is changing due to technology and commercial interests. Only then can we preserve the social justice aims inherent in LIS.

If all this could happen, then with librarians to guide them, users might use data themselves to pose and answer the kinds of questions that science, in the service of big data, seems to be losing sight of, questions like: why do I do what I do, or what do I want or need? Addressing this challenge offers a possibility that could bring social justice, community action, and librarianship into the era of big data.

Bibliography

Anderson, Chris. "The End of Theory, Will the Data Deluge Make the Scientific Method Obsolete?" *Wired Magazine* 16, no. 7 (2011) Accessed November 28, 2014. http://archive.wired.com/science/discoveries/magazine/16-07/pb_theory.

Arnold, Stephen D. "Assessing Student Learning Online." Paper presented at the annual meeting for the International Association for Development of the Information Society, Madrid, Spain, October 19-21, 2012. Accessed November 28, 2014. ERIC (ED542719).

Association of College and Research Libraries (ACRL). "Keeping Up With... Big Data." Accessed March 26 2015 from http://www.ala.org/acrl/publications/keeping_up_with/big_data.

Bindé, Jérôme. *Towards Knowledge Societies: UNESCO World Report.* UNESCO Reference Works Series. Paris: UNESCO, 2005. Accessed November 3, 2013. http://unesdoc.unesco.org/images/0014/001418/141843e.pdf.

Bollier, David, and Charles M. Firestone. *The Promise and Peril of Big Data.* Washington, DC: Aspen Institute, Communications and Society Program, 2010. Accessed August 24, 2015. http://www.emc.com/collateral/analyst-reports/10334-ar-promise-peril-of-big-data.pdf.

Bolt, Susan. "Professional Development: Then and Now." Paper presented at the annual International Conference on Cognition and Exploratory Learning in Digital Age (CELDA 2012), Madrid, Spain, October 19-21, 2012. Accessed November 28, 2014. ERIC (ED542831).

boyd, danah and Kate Crawford. "Six Provocations for Big Data." Paper presented at A Decade in Internet Time: Symposium on the Dynamics of the Internet and Society, Oxford, England, September 21-24, 2011. Accessed November 10, 2013. http://papers.ssrn.com/sol3/papers.cfm?abstract_id=1926431.

Catts, Ralph and Jesus Lau. *Towards Information Literacy Indicators*. Paris: UNESCO, Information Society Division Communication and Information Sector, 2008. Accessed November 21, 2013, https://dspace.stir.ac.uk/bitstream/1893/2119/1/cattsand-lau.pdf.

Fischer, Karen S., Michael Wright, Kathleen Clatanoff, Hope Barton and Edward Shreeves. "Give'Em What They Want: A One-year Study of Unmediated Patron-Driven Acquisition of E-Books." *College & Research Libraries* 73, no. 5 (2012): 469-492. Accessed November 14, 2013, http://crl.acrl.org/content/73/5/469.full.pdf.

Foucault, Michel. *Discipline and Punish: The Birth of the Prison*. Translated by Alan Sheridan. New York: Random House, 1995.

Grassian, Esther S., and Joan R. Kaplowitz. *Information Literacy Instruction: Theory and Practice*. 2nd. ed. New York: Neal-Schuman, 2009.

Herring, James E. "From School to Work and from Work to School: Information Environments and Transferring Information Literacy Practices." *Information Research: An International Electronic Journal* 16, no. 2 (2011). Accessed November, 26, 2014. ERIC (EJ935870).

Humrickhouse, Elizabeth. "Information Literacy Instruction in the Web 2.0 Library." (2011). Accessed November 28, 2014. ERIC (ED520720).

International Data Corporation. "Big Data & Analytics: An IDC Four Pillar Research Area." Accessed April 5, 2015. https://www.idc.com/prodserv/4Pillars/bigdata.

International Federation of Library Associations and Institutions (IFLA). "Information Literacy Section." Accessed November 28, 2014. http://archive.ifla.org/VII/s42/.

Kahn, Abdul Waheed. Preface to UNESCO's Basic Texts on the Information Society Edited by Jean-Gabriel Mastrangelo and Melika Loncarevic. Paris: UNESCO, 2004. Accessed November 16, 2013. http://unesdoc.unesco.org/images/0013/001355/135527e.pdf.

Lasorsa, Dominic L., Seth C. Lewis, and Avery E. Holton. "Normalizing Twitter: Journalism Practice in an Emerging Communication Space." *Journalism Studies* 13, no. 1 (2012): 19-36.

Manovich, Lev. "Trending: The Promises and the Challenges of Big Social Data." *Debates in the Digital Humanities* (2011): 460-75.

Manyika, James, Michael Chui, Brad Brown, Jacques Bughin, Richard Dobbs, Charles Roxburgh, and Angela Hung Byers. *Big Data: The Next Frontier for Innovation Competition, and Productivity*. New York: McKinsey Global Institute, 2011. Accessed November 28, 2014. http://www.mckinsey.com/insights/business_technology/big_data_the_next_frontier_for_innovation.

McKnight, Susan. "A Futuristic View of Knowledge and Information Management." *BiD: Textos Universitaris de Biblioteconomia i Documentació* 17 (2007). Accessed November, 24, 2014. http://bid.ub.edu/19mcknig.htm.

Mehra, Bharat, Kevin S. Rioux, and Kendra S. Albright. "Social Justice in Library and Information Science." In *Encyclopedia of Library and Information Sciences*. 3rd ed. Edited by Marcia J. Bates and Mary Niles Maack, 4820-36. New York: Taylor and Francis, 2009.

Morris, Jeff. "Top 10 Categories for Big Data Sources and Mining Technologies." ZDNet. July 16, 2012. Accessed November 26, 2014. http://www.zdnet.com/top-10-categories-for-big-data-sources-and-mining-technologies-7000000926/.

Morrone, Melissa and Lia Friedman. "Radical Reference: Socially Responsible Librarianship Collaborating With Community." *Reference Librarian* 50 (2009): 371–396.

Pennington, Buddy, and Steve Alleman. "Giving the Users What They Want: Is Patron-Driven Acquisitions the Answer?" Paper presented at the annual meeting, Brick and Click Libraries: An Academic Library Symposium, Maryville, Missouri, October 26, 2012. Accessed November 28, 2014. ERIC (ED537605).

Pentland, Alex. *Social Physics: How Good Ideas Spread—The Lessons from a New Science*. New York: Penguin, 2014.

Ranganathan, Shiyali Ramamrita. *The Five Laws of Library Science*. London: Blunt, 1957.

Rioux, Kevin. "Metatheory in Library and Information Science: A Nascent Social Justice Approach." *Journal of Education for Library and Information Science* 51, no. 1 (Winter 2010): 9-17.

Siemens, George and Phil Long. "Penetrating the Fog: Analytics in Learning and Education." *Educause Review* 46, no. 5 (2011): 31- 40. Accessed November 26, 2014. https://net.educause.edu/ir/library/pdf/ERM1151.pdf.

Shankland, Stephen. "How Apple's Embrace of the New USB Points to World Without Wires." *Cnet*. March 11, 2015. Accessed April 24, 2015. http://www.cnet.com/news/how-apples-embrace-of-the-new-usb-points-to-world-without-wires/.

Tucker, Patrick. *The Naked Future: What Happens in a World That Anticipates Your Every Move?* New York: Penguin, 2014.

Virilio, Paul. *Information Bomb*. Translated by Chris Turner. New York: Verso, 2000.

Viswanathan, Venkat, "5 Ways Big-Data Can Save Publishing." *All Analytics: The Community for Data Management, Business Intelligence, and Analytics*. September 10, 2013. Accessed August 24, 2015. http://www.allanalytics.com/author.asp?section_id=3031&doc_id=267533&.

Wai-yi, Cheuk. "An Information Seeking and Using Process Model in the Workplace: A Constructivist Approach." *Asian Libraries* 7, no. 12 (1998): 375-390.

Wilson, Tom. "Human Information Behaviour." *Informing Science* 3, no. 2 (2000): 49–55.

Chapter 3

THE LABOR OF INFORMATIONAL DEMOCRACY: A LIBRARY AND INFORMATION SCIENCE FRAMEWORK FOR EVALUATING THE DEMOCRATIC POTENTIAL IN SOCIALLY-GENERATED INFORMATION

Jonathan Cope

Beginning in the 1890s, the term *industrial democracy* was used in the United States by middle-class social reformers, radicals in the Industrial Workers of the World, and socialists to articulate the idea that in order for democracy to have any substantive meaning, its logic must extend beyond formal political institutions and into the realm of economic production.[1] As early as 1973, sociologists began speaking of a "post-industrial society,"[2] and in the 1990s the idea that the production, consumption, and manipulation of information constituted the central logic of the "information economy" became widespread.[3] Recently, the term "information democracy" has been used by Microsoft founder and CEO Bill Gates to describe the wealth of information that is currently

---

1. David Montgomery, "Industrial Democracy or Democracy in Industry?: The Theory and Practice of the Labor Movement, 1870-1925," in *Industrial Democracy in America: The Ambiguous Promise*, ed. Nelson Lichtenstein and John Harris Howell (Washington, D.C.: Woodrow Wilson Center Press, 1993), 20.

2. Daniel Bell, *The Coming Post-Industrial Society: A Venture in Social Forecasting*, (New York: Basic Books, 1976).

3. "Economy, New." *The SAGE Glossary of the Social and Behavioral Sciences*, edited by Larry E. Sullivan. Thousand Oaks, CA: SAGE Reference, 2009. 168. Gale Virtual Reference Library. Web. 15 Apr. 2015.

available to ordinary citizens.[4] The idea that the new "information society" is "democratic" is so clearly implied that adding a democratic qualifier may seem unnecessary.

Missing from such discussions is any examination of how markets can occlude the development of vital knowledge, culture, and information without a clear economic value. Also missing is an examination of how equal access to the Internet can be inhibited by pre-existing social inequalities and how the human labor needed to create the devices, knowledge, and culture that constitute the information society should be valued. Thomas Augst has said that "[t]o think about libraries is to think about the material forms that culture takes in a social landscape."[5] All too often, the supposed immateriality of digital technologies has obscured the material infrastructure and human labor required to create a digital commons. The idea that socially-generated information contains the potential to create more participatory forms of communication and knowledge has a popular resonance. The proliferation of systems of "socially" generated information production, dissemination, and consumption has elicited commentary in Library and Information Science (LIS).[6] However, as the Internet critic Astra Taylor observes, a funny thing happened on the way to the democratic digital revolution when just "a handful of enormous companies… profit off the creations and interactions of others"[7] and when forms of culture and knowledge that cannot be easily monetized find institutional support lacking.

---

4. Peters, Michael. "The Political Economy of Informational Democracy." *The International Journal of Learning* 14, no. 6 (2007) 29-36.

5. Thomas Augst, "American Libraries and Agencies of Culture," in *Libraries as Agencies of Culture*, ed. Thomas Augst and Wayne A. Wiegand (Madison, Wis: University of Wisconsin Press, 2001), 5.

6. Kang-Pyo Lee, Hong-Gee Kim, and Hyoung-Joo Kim, "A Social Inverted Index for Social-Tagging-Based Information Retrieval," *Journal of Information Science*. 38, no. 4 (2012); Jonathan Furner, "User Tagging of Library Resources: Toward a Framework for System Evaluation," *International Cataloging and Bibliographic Control* 37, no. 3 (2008).

7. Astra Taylor, *The People's Platform: Taking Back Power and Culture in the Digital Age* (New York: Metropolitan Books, 2014), 14.

Libraries and the discipline of LIS must respond to these developments with a more fully developed conception of the common good and the fundamental role that knowledge, culture, and information play in its constitution. The increasing neoliberal marketization of public goods and services means that a well defined conception of social justice must play a larger role in how librarianship views these economic and technological developments in order for libraries to survive. Libraries are perfectly situated institutionally to develop a more socially just infrastructure for a new knowledge commons, but only if they develop a theory of action that examines critical theory and the political economy of librarianship so that librarians can rethink the material forms that culture can take in a digital social landscape.

In this essay, I advance a framework that draws from the methods of normative political theory, critical theory, and William Birdsall's[8] call for the development of a political economy of librarianship. Birdsall observes that "[l]ibraries are the creation and instrument of public policy derived from political processes,"[9] and what he calls an "ideology of information technology" obscures power relations and suggests that "[i]n the knowledge-based economy only the marketplace should determine how information, its primary raw material, is generated, priced, and distributed."[10]

Although the ideal of democracy is frequently invoked in LIS, the more complicated questions of what exactly democracy entails are frequently avoided, and "the vast portion of this literature (on democracy in LIS) rehearses and repeats the basic ideas of Jefferson and Madison from 200 years ago."[11] John Buschman argues that in LIS democratic theory is an "unfinished, discontinued idea... (and that) there is a silence

---

8. William Birdsall, "A Political Economy of Librarianship?" *Hermes: Revue Critique* 6 (2000).

9. Ibid., 4.

10. Ibid., 5.

11. John Buschman, "Democratic Theory in Library Information Science: Toward an Emendation," *Journal of the American Society for Information Science and Technology* 58, no. 10 (2007): 1483.

maintained" [12] when difficult questions about specific democratic practices arise. This is not a trivial, recondite theoretical concern—as more information and knowledge are produced and consumed "socially" in digital environs that are embedded in complicated social and economic relations, it has become commonplace to suggest simply placing information online somehow makes liberal democratic societies more democratic. LIS must rise to the occasion and develop a democratic theoretical apparatus that can be used to promote information policy and practice in the public interest. LIS's historical, institutional, and normative democratic commitments leave the discipline well situated to develop such a program; however, the aposiopetic—to use Buschman's term—nature of democratic theory in LIS, and its inattention to political economy and social justice, leaves LIS with few tools to critically evaluate claims and to guide action.

What I will henceforth call *socially-generated information*—derived from Yochai Benkler's[13] concept of social production—entails a massive transformation of the information systems in which information is produced. This essay begins by outlining the characteristics of socially-generated information and by acknowledging Benkler's contention that the "change brought about by the networked information environment is deep."[14] However, these changes cannot be extricated from the political economy of early twenty-first century capitalism. As a result, this essay briefly examines the political economy of information for contextual purposes before outlining a framework that libraries can use to analyze socially-generated information within a larger discussion about democratic communication and the contemporary information environment.

The evaluative framework that I propose in this essay involves three democratic horizons of analysis: *the horizon of access, the horizon of production*, and the *horizon of communicative speech*. First, I use scholarship about

---

12. Ibid., 1484.

13. Yochai Benkler, *The Wealth of Networks: How Social Production Transforms Markets and Freedom* (New Haven, CT.: Yale University Press, 2006).

14. Ibid.,1.

the persistence of the digital divide,[15] copyright law,[16] and what has been called the emerging knowledge commons[17] to argue for a *horizon of access* that can evaluate the ability of social actors to access and to shape the communicative networks and material used to communicate and transmit information. I then examine some of the key ideas of autonomist Marxists[18] about immaterial labor to analyze a *horizon of production* that evaluates the labor of information production and the complicated questions that uncompensated labor—the labor upon which many of these systems are built—poses for those interested in social justice. I conclude by developing what I call a *horizon of communicative speech* that evaluates how speech communities utilize these technologies by engaging in the democratic theory of thinkers like Jürgen Habermas and Nancy Fraser[19] that predates their development. I will conclude by outlining potential policies that could be pursued by governments, libraries, and educational institutions acting in accordance with such a framework.

This framework is intended as a way to provoke debate and suggest action when thinking about proposed forms of progressive community action and development. A great example of this type of method is the philosopher Martha Nussbaum's capabilities approach to global development that, instead of focusing on a traditional concept of human rights historically associated with "negative liberty," focuses on positive

---

15. Sharon Strover, "The US Digital Divide: A Call for a New Philosophy," *Critical Studies in Media Communication.* 31:2, 114-122.

16. Lawrence Lessig, "Getting Our Values around Copyright Right," *Educause Review* March/April 2010; Siva Vaidhyanathan, *Copyrights and Copywrongs: The Rise of Intellectual Property and How It Threatens Creativity*, New York: New York University Press, 2001.

17. Charlotte Hess and Elinor Ostrom, "An Overview of the Knowledge Commons," in *Understanding Knowledge as a Commons: From Theory to Practice,* ed. Charlotte Hess and Elinor Ostrom. (Cambridge, MA: MIT Press, 2007), 9.

18. Søren Mørk Petersen, "Loser Generated Content: From Participation to Exploitation," *First Monday* 13, no. 3 (2008); Tiziana Terranova, *Network Culture: Politics for the Information Age* (London: Pluto Press, 2004).

19. Nancy Fraser, "Rethinking the Public Sphere: a Contribution to the Critique of Actually Existing Democracy," *Social Text,* (1990): 57; Jürgen Habermas, *The Philosophical Discourse of Modernity: Twelve Lectures* (Cambridge, MA: MIT Press, 1987), 296.

liberties such as human dignity and flourishing.[20] Systematic reflection and debate about goals is a necessary first step in the development of any community action plan, and the methods of normative political theory—Nussbaum's capabilities approach being an instructive example of this method—provide LIS with excellent tools to begin this analysis.

Methodology

The goal of this essay is to provide library policy makers and those who work in libraries with a general set of concepts and principles that can be used to guide action. The intellectual project of critical theory is methodologically perfectly suited for this task. While John Rawls's concept of "justice as fairness" is relevant to any discussion of social justice, critical theory's interests in the further democratization of capitalism and in human liberation inform this work's conception of social justice. Drawing from a set of thinkers associated with the Frankfurt School tradition (e.g., Theodor Adorno, Max Horkheimer), critical theory is fundamentally concerned with human emancipation. James Bohman argues that critical theory "must be explanatory, practical, and normative, all at the same time. That is, it must explain what is wrong with current social reality, identify the actors to change it, and provide both clear norms for criticism and achievable practical goals for social transformation."[21] The collection and analysis of data are fundamental aspects of research in LIS and the social sciences, but systematic normative analysis lies at the core of both the critical theoretical and post-Rawlsian philosophical projects.[22] Political economists have had to confront the objections of

20. Martha Nussbaum, "Promoting Women's Capabilities," in *Global Tensions: Challenges and Opportunities in the World Economy*, ed. Lourdes Benería and Savitri Bisnath (New York: Routledge, 2004).

21. James Bohman, "Critical Theory," in The Stanford Encyclopedia of Philosophy, ed. Edward N. Zalta last modified 2013, http://plato.stanford.edu/archives/spr2013/entries/critical-theory.

22. Andrea Sangivanni, "Normative Political Theory: A Flight from Reality?" in *Political Thought and International Relations: Variations on a Realist Theme*, ed. Duncan Bell (Oxford, UK: Oxford University Press, 2009).

classical and neoclassical economists who contend that "value neutrality... define[s]... the limits of the relationship between economics and moral philosophy."[23] In other words, economics should strive to be a hard science, and it should only examine values as "preferences registered by market choices."[24] Normative political theorists confront the objections of realists who claim that political reality is defined by power politics and that normative reflection is a distraction that insists on an ideal theory of justice instead of presenting and comparing feasible "course[s] of action, policies, and reforms available to us here and now."[25] Such objections to normative analysis and political economy are likely to persist; however, LIS's institutional commitment to democracy makes systematic reflection and debate about what these commitments entail all the more important. Although an ideal may not be feasibly achieved in the here and now, articulating and debating ideals and examining how they are put into action is praxis—the ultimate goal of critical theory.

Although there has been more work from a critical theoretical perspective in LIS in recent years, the discipline's aspirations to be viewed as a descriptive science have all too often minimized the importance of historical, theoretical, and normative questions.[26] Libraries are material institutions, but they only exist in the world because human actors decided that they should be built, maintained, and expanded. The democratic mission of libraries (particularly public and academic libraries) in the United States is so clearly embedded in the rationale for their existence that this failure to rigorously engage in normative questions is not merely an intellectual issue; it threatens the basis for libraries' continued importance in society. As John Budd argues, the perception that libraries are simply "businesses in a market" inhibits the development

23. Mosco, *The Political Economy of Communication* (London, UK: Sage Publications, 2009), 33.

24. Ibid., 33.

25. Sangivanni, "Normative Political Theory," 225.

26. Wayne Wiegand, "Tunnel Vision and Blind Spots: What the Past Tells Us about the Present; Reflections on the Twentieth-Century History of American Librarianship," *Library Quarterly* 69, no. 1 (1999).

of these democratic capacities.[27] Critical theory provides an ideal basis for systematic thinking about how libraries as institutional actors can work to democratize the production, consumption, and ownership of knowledge.

This work applies theories and research from outside of LIS in an examination of a new information development (what I call socially-generated information) that, for the most part, developed outside of the institutional context of libraries. It is vital that developments and theories from outside of LIS be explored so that libraries can respond to them. If Birdsall's "ideology of information technology" influences a substantial number of decision makers and the general public then the growing importance of socially-generated information must be addressed. The advent of the modern American public and academic library was the consequence of a convergence of historical, techno-logical, and ideological factors. The shape that libraries will take in the twenty-first century remains undetermined. Libraries can play a vital role in building the infrastructure of new digital knowledge com-mons, but only if they look beyond LIS's disciplinary boundaries. The implications of the proposed framework for future empirical research and for academic and public libraries will be most fully explored at the conclusion of this essay.

Socially-Generated Information

In *The Wealth of Networks* (2006), Yochi Benkler analyzes a process of production that he calls *social production*. Benkler finds that social produc-tion upends classical economics in that the communicative networks created by distributed computing allow for collaborations in which the incentives that are assumed to be at the core of classical and neoclas-sical economics—consumers acting rationally in response to market incentives—do not come into play. For instatnce, there is no individual

---

27. John Budd, "Public Library Leaders and Changing Society," *Public Library Quarterly* 26, no. 3/4: (2007).

economic incentive to add tags to a YouTube video that will make it more widely accessible if the agent that is adding that information does not gain monetarily from their labor. Much of the literature on this topic calls this type of information user-generated content, and in recent years it has become a fundamental aspect of the Internet. It can be as simple as commenting on a page (e.g., "I like this!") or as complex as analyzing massive tranches of data (e.g., a "crowd-sourced" piece of investigative journalism). The participatory and collaborative development of software that has been described as the Free and Open Source Software (FOSS) movement plays a large role in Benkler's analysis. The most successful commercial Internet ventures of the past decade (e.g., Google, Facebook) have been able to use content/information produced by billions of users to generate value for their owners and stockholders. Enormous amounts of information are created every day as citizens communicate their dreams, fears, and desires via heavily commercialized distributed computing networks. The disclosures of Edward Snowden in 2013 about the depth and scope of the US National Security Administration's collection of information has demonstrated the degree to which so much of contemporary culture and communication occurs in online distributed networks with a nebulous, contested, and evolving social contract between users, private/corporate power, and the state.

Clearly, economic production and the creation of information has always been a highly social activity. What differentiates what I call socially-generated information from past forms of information production is the sheer scale of information being collected and the peer-to-peer nature of how it is exchanged. Benkler[28] goes so far as to say that social production is a new mode of production, because it eliminates many of the barriers to bringing an idea to market that existed in the Industrial Age. Instead of creating discrete packets of information that consumers consider to be commodities of sufficient value to purchase outright, the largest new technology companies create services and spaces in which users contribute value as they use the products. A critical strand

28. Benkler, "The Wealth of Networks," 23.

of analysis has emerged that views these organizational forms as ways of extracting uncompensated value[29] from users who freely donate their time and labor to produce value for these firms. In this endeavor, Autonomist Marxists have been perceptive in identifying how affective and social forms of labor (i.e., labor that is not tied to the production of specific commodities, or "playbor") adds to the general value present in an economy/society that can then be "reterritorialized" by capital for the extraction of surplus value.[30] For the remainder of this essay, the term socially-generated information will be used to describe this process of information production.

In order to contextualize socially-generated information, a brief account of the political economy of information is essential, although an exhaustive review of the literature on the political economy of information is beyond the scope of the present inquiry. Within LIS there is an emerging literature on neoliberalism[31] and how the discourse surrounding public institutions has changed in the United States and United Kingdom since the political and economic philosophies associated with Thatcher/Reagan came to power in the late 1970s. Whatever one names these philosophies, arguments that see a broadly defined free market as a neutral arbiter of value and as the ultimate processor of information have resonated widely and remain integral to the current political debate.[32] When the concept of socially-generated informa-

---

29. Søren Mørk Petersen, "Loser Generated Content: From Participation to Exploitation," *First Monday* 13, no. 3 (2008).

30. Ronald Day, "Social Capital, Value, and Measure: Antonio Negri's Challenge to Capitalism," *Journal of the American Society for Information Science and Technology* 53, no. 12 (2002).

31. For a discussion of neoliberalism and LIS see Maura Seal, "The Neoliberal Library," in *Information Literacy and Social Justice: Radical Professional Praxis*, ed. Lua Gregory and Shana Higgins (Sacramento, CA: Library Juice Press, 2013); John Buschman, *Libraries, Classrooms, and the Interests of Democracy: Marking the Limits of Neoliberalism* (Lanham, MD: The Scarecrow Press, 2012); Karen P. Nicholson, "The McDonaldization of Academic Libraries and the Values of Transformational Change" *College and Research Libraries* 76, no. 3 (2015): 328-338.

32. Philip Mirowski, *Never Let a Serious Crisis Go to Waste: How Neoliberalism Survived the Financial Meltdown* (London, UK: Verso, 2013).

tion is situated within a discussion about the role of markets in liberal democracy, it becomes apparent that the concept of the "wisdom of the crowd" as being synonymous with democracy can fit neatly within an ideological framework that sees the "wisdom of the market" as being the ultimate expression of democracy. In certain ways, Benkler cuts against the contention that markets are the ultimate processor of information, because he argues that "nonmarket collaborations" facilitate more efficient participation than "traditional market mechanisms and corporations."[33] Despite this critique of neoclassical economics, what Benkler calls "non-market" production is firmly embedded within a market-based society. Surely, Benkler is aware of this reality, and he minimizes this to emphasize the epochal change that social production signifies and its importance to "individual freedom, a more genuinely participatory political system, a critical culture, and social justice."[34] Benkler does briefly comment on political economy when he observes that expanding workplace democracy and creating a more egalitarian distribution of wealth have historically had to confront the sheer efficiency of proprietary market-based production.

While market-based production is surely efficient, such an account ignores that the wealth of western liberal democracies during the postwar period was a result of a mixture of free markets, state funding, and regulated labor markets. After all, the precursor to the Internet was ARPANET, an endeavor entirely funded by the state. The state continues to play a large role in production, research, and development. The economist Mariana Mazzucato[35] recently found that many of the key technological developments of the last few years came about because the state invested in risky innovations before they demonstrated their profitability. Adjudicating what is and what is not neoliberal, or market liberal, is not important for LIS in developing a theory of socially-generated information; however, acknowledging that markets are always embedded

---

33. Benkler, *The Wealth of Networks,* 7.

34. Ibid., 8.

35. Mariana Mazzucato, *The Entrepreneurial State* (London: Demos 2011).

within a particular social and governmental structure is fundamental. The producers of socially-generated information continuously utilize resources (e.g., educational institutions, public infrastructure) that are embedded in specific sets of market relationships that are reliant on the state for particular informational commodities to exist at all (e.g., intellectual property). Benkler's indifference to these issues means he is of little use to libraries interested in building an infrastructure for a democratic knowledge commons.

Karl Polanyi's landmark work *The Great Transformation*[36] can serve as a helpful guide in this analytic endeavor. Polanyi argued that an idealized market separate from society has never existed; markets are always contingent on the social forces of the society in which they exist. As with any popular conceptual framework, or widely cited historical work, specific aspects of Polanyi's thought have been criticized,[37] and the strengths and limitations of his framework for knowledge have been explored.[38] Although Benkler is correct in asserting that social production opens up dramatic new collaborative opportunities for the production of information, to view it as being a form of "non-market" production is to ignore Polanyi's insight that markets are always embedded in society.

A Polanyian perspective fits well within the literature that Robert McChesney[39] calls the Political Economy of Communication (PEC) and Birdsall's political economy of librarianship. PEC "evaluates media and communication systems by determining how they affect political and social power in society and whether they are, on balance, forces for

36. Karl Polanyi, *The Great Transformation: The Political and Economic Origins of Our Time* (Boston, Mass: Beacon Press, 2001).

37. Charles Kindleberger, "*The Great Transformation* by Karl Polanyi," *Daedalus*, 103, no. 1 (1974); Nancy Fraser, "A Triple Movement?: Parsing the Politics of Crisis After Polanyi," *New Left Review*, 81, (2013).

38. Bob Jessop, "Knowledge as a Fictitious Commodity: Insights and Limits of a Polanyian Perspective," in *Reading Karl Polanyi for the Twenty-First Century: Market Economy as a Political Project*, ed. Ayse Buğra, and Kaan Ağartan (Basingstoke, UK: Macmillan, 2007).

39. Robert McChesney, *Digital Disconnect: How Capitalism is Turning the Internet Against Democracy* (New York: The New Press, 2013), 63.

or against democracy and successful self-government. This critical or explicit normative basis distinguishes it from related fields like media economics or media law."[40] In addition to examining the institutions and markets that shape communication systems, PEC emphasizes the essential role of government in the development and maintenance of these systems. A political economy of librarianship in the vein of Birdsall's proposal would surely adopt a similar perspective by focusing on how libraries are a force for democracy. A Polanyian perspective moves the debate away from one about an abstract "free market," or a "non-market" form of production; instead, it shifts the focus to a conversation about the kinds of market-based societies that can be built, the forms of information production that are the most socially just, and the resources needed to create a democratic knowledge commons.

LIS must develop a robust normative theory of democracy for socially-generated information so that an ideologically limited and deterministic discourse about information technology does not crowd out libraries and educational institutions' public mission and limit the potential ways in which this mission can pursue new democratic goals. Socially-generated information is a substantive new development, but its use can be shaped by public policy. LIS is well positioned to play a large role in using new forms of knowledge production to promote a more just and participatory communicative democracy. As more information is produced in distributed networks that have new and ambiguous relationships to the specific geographical communities that libraries traditionally serve, it is LIS's responsibility to articulate a vision of how new methods of information production can protect information as a public and common good, help in a small degree to decommodify the informational labor which is the value created by socially-generated information, and deepen participatory democracy. LIS and its institutions are well positioned to fill the informational gaps left by markets and deterministic conceptions of "the Internet," but only if it articulates

---

40. Ibid., 64.

a positive democratic vision that acknowledges the changing economic and communicative dynamics of information.

The Horizon of Access

In order for democratic participation to occur, the material infrastructure and physical networks that socially-generated information requires must be readily and easily available for use to all in society. Therefore, the material, social, and legal limitations that inhibit or prevent democratic access must be overcome. Despite the rhetoric about the immaterial and limitless nature of online communication, the Internet is a collection of physical networks and systems that consist of material resources that place restraints on the nature of access. To state that access for all must be guaranteed is simple enough—to unpack what exactly equal access means (and the allocation of resources that it would entail) requires further examination. The Oxford English Dictionary defines access as it relates to "entrance or approach" as "[t]he power, opportunity, permission, or right to come near or into contact with someone or something; admittance; admission."[41] This definition suggests that access be thought of as something more than material; concepts such as power and rights suggest a discursive framework in which institutions and social subjects instantiate how these abstract concepts are enacted as social practice. Institutions must define the nature and limits of access and social subjects must articulate an understanding of the importance of access (e.g., "as a citizen my right to access information is an essential part of democratic participation").

Article IV of the American Library Association's Bill of Rights states that "[l]ibraries should cooperate with all persons and groups concerned with resisting abridgment of free expression and free access to ideas."[42]

---

41. Oxford English Dictionary, "access, n," OED Online, March 2015, Oxford University Press, accessed April 24, 2015, http://www.oed.com/view/Entry/1028?rskey=LvkstP&result=1.

42. American Library Association, "Library Bill of Rights," January 23, 1996, http://www.ala.org/advocacy/intfreedom/librarybill.

Situated within the context of the other articles in the document, the "free access to ideas" means that libraries should not censoriously limit what users can access based on content; in other words, users should consume the broadest possible spectrum of culture, ideas, and opinions available via libraries. During the twentieth century, American media critics recognized that corporate media ownership limited the participatory potential of mediums such as print, radio, and television.[43] The participatory nature of the Internet has made it easier to access and respond to a wide range of media and culture; however, the capacities that such access entails remain vague. I argue that there are three constraints that inhibit equal access: material inhibitions, legal constraints, and exogenous factors that limit the capacity of all participants to act once material access is guaranteed. The literature on access to information is vast; therefore, the following discussion will be limited to libraries and their relevance to the proposed analytical framework.

Although the digital divide has diminished due to the expansion of information technology and networks since the 1990s, it remains a consistent feature of American society.[44] Internet inequality persists, even in a developed nation like the US, in the form of slower network speeds in many less prosperous communities, communities of color, and rural areas.[45] Communicative inequality persists in the form of limited access to the Internet outside of the home, and in diminishing leisure time within the context of a deep recession. This has meant that the most active and prominent Internet contributors tend to be middle/upper class, white, and male.[46] Public libraries have experienced an increased demand to provide basic services. Citizens who do not personally own

---

43. Ben H. Bagdikian, *The New Media Monopoly* (Boston: Beacon Press, 2004); Robert McChesney, *Rich Media, Poor Democracy: Communication Politics in Dubious Times* (Urbana: University of Illinois Press, 1999).

44. Strover, "The US Digital Divide."

45. Ibid.,115.

46. Linda Jackson, et al. "Race, Gender, and Information Technology Use: The New Digital Divide," *CyberPsychology & Behavior* 11, no. 4 (August 2008): 437-442.

communications technologies frequently rely on public libraries for access to the Internet while libraries struggle with declining budgets that are the result of austerity policies.[47] If access to newer technological and democratic forums is not cast in the light of democratic and universal access, the opportunities to participate for those without—or with less—access will be diminished. In the twenty-first century, universal and affordable access to the Internet must be viewed as a public good and right if socially-generated information is to be evaluated for its democratic potential.

The public policy debate surrounding material inhibitions to access must also examine the issues that surround the potentially monopolistic control of communications technology networks and infrastructure. These communications resources are maintained by large multinational corporations whose primary obligations are to their shareholders, not to the public or to a broadly defined public interest. For example, when home access to Internet services is controlled by a corporation that distributes television content, there is a clear interest on behalf of that corporation to try to limit new competing methods of delivering that content into homes. The public policy questions that surround these issues are complicated because they need to reconcile conflicting commercial and public interests; however, it is important that a broadly construed public/democratic interest be promoted. An issue like Net neutrality (the policy of Internet Service Providers not to discriminate amongst users) is a key public policy flashpoint in this instance, because it demonstrates that normative questions about how the Internet should be regulated are not the product of some abstract Internet that has a set of immutable characteristics, but are instead shaped by public debate about the type of democratic and communicative society that is most desirable. Despite the transformative power of the Internet, remarkably few corporations produce the content and own the platforms through which all of this communication takes place. It follows that, absent a

---

47. Ibid., 118-119.

public policy that strives for universal material access, these corporate and state actors lack incentives to make access universal.

Incumbent corporate actors have strong incentives to shape the regulatory framework in ways that limit competition and enhance their own profits. This power can accrue to very few actors due to what has been called Metcalfe's law, named for Bob Metcalfe who posited that "the usefulness of a network increases at an accelerating rate as you add each new person to it."[48] Minus regulation, the tendencies towards monopoly seem evident (e.g., the more searches Google processes, the more valuable it becomes and the greater the barriers to entry for new firms trying to develop a competing product) and provide LIS with a substantive opening to explore how libraries can act to fill the spaces left open by these market forces. PEC can help make these arguments, as well as the history of the state's involvement in the development of the Internet. Such logic leads to antitrust legislation and an awareness of the continual potential for monopolistic control of key aspects of information production and distribution.

Another key flashpoint in the information economy has been the debates about intellectual property and copyright that scholars/public intellectuals like Siva Vaidhyanathan and Lawrence Lessig have worked on since the 1990s.[49] These scholars find that litigious corporations or state actors can easily stifle creative activity by creating intellectual property regimes that do not allow for users to playfully reuse and create culture that has a minimal impact on the market for the product being used. Although Lessig finds that the prospects for amending U.S. copyright law are poor, he argues that projects such as the *Creative Commons* can provide cultural producers with the tools to "see more clearly the freedoms they have with the creative work and the restrictions that the creator continues to insist upon."[50] A workable balance

---

48. Cited in McChesney, *Digital Disconnect*, 132.

49. Lessig, "Getting Our Values around Copyright Right," Vaidhyanathan, *Copyrights and Copywrongs*.

50. Lessig, "Getting Our Values Around Copyright Right," 36.

between the interests of producers and consumers must be achieved through public debate.

Assuming that material and legal access is universally assured, the ability of social subjects to participate in socially generated information will be determined by a range of external social factors, such as familiarity and comfort with technology, education and training, and the time to spend on generating content. Although many non-profits have created grant-funded programs to improve computing and Internet skills, Sharon Stover found that these inconsistent funding mechanisms created a "feast-or-famine method of living from grant to grant" and that a serious and sustained investment in digital divide literacy efforts is needed.[51] A key technological development is the role that mobile communications are now playing. Although the availability of mobile technology provides connectivity to more people, mobile connectivity is slower, more expensive, and more difficult to use for certain purposes (e.g., job applications, longer writing). In short, access to tools is not sufficient. Sustained efforts to fund technology education and policies that allow for the time to participate in creating socially generated information are an important part of guaranteeing equal access.

Issues related to material inhibitions, legal constraints, and external factors that limit the capacity of all participants to equally participate coalesce in a strand of interdisciplinary inquiry that has sought to articulate the key aspects of a "knowledge" or "information commons" modeled on conceptions of traditional resource commons. Hess and Ostrom[52] argue that knowledge is a non-rival—or public—good because one "person's use of knowledge… (does) not subtract from another person's capacity to use it."[53] Nancy Kranich contends that powerful forces are acting to enclose an emerging knowledge commons and argues that this enclosure can be countered by creating open access to

---

51. Strover, "The US Digital Divide," 116.

52. Charlotte Hess and Elinor Ostrom, "An Overview of the Knowledge Commons," in *Understanding Knowledge As a Commons: From Theory to Practice*, ed. Charlotte Hess and Elinor Ostrom (Cambridge, MA: MIT Press, 2007), 9.

53. Hess and Ostrom, "An Overview of the Knowledge Commons," 9.

scholarship and digital repositories. Kranich explores the open access movement as a countervailing force to corporate publishers that have acted against public informational interests by charging high prices for serials and databases that users and scholars deem essential.[54] Librarians have been at the forefront of the open access movement, because as publishers consolidate into fewer firms they are able to ask for more money from libraries that are straining under already limited and shrinking budgets to purchase the serials and databases upon which users and scholars rely. As a result, the owners of the most widely cited scholarly journals can extract large rents through their ownership of intellectual property rights.[55] Many open access advocates have argued for making publicly financed research available for free to the general public as part of a knowledge commons—the existence of publicly financed research being inaccessible to libraries and the general public being an obvious case of enclosure of a public good.

Christine Borgman's observation that libraries form an "invisible information infrastructure" is a helpful way to think about the role that libraries can play in developing a new knowledge commons.[56] In order to develop, preserve, and sustain new forms of social information production, libraries are ideally positioned to create an infrastructure for these new forms. Because of libraries' historical commitments to democracy, their potential role in the development of a knowledge commons has been acknowledged by scholars.[57] If libraries are to achieve these goals, the invisible infrastructure of libraries must become more visible. The material limits to participating can be overcome as librarians partner with other actors to build this infrastructure.

---

54. Nancy Kranich, "Countering Enclosure: Reclaiming the Knowledge Commons," in *Understanding Knowledge as a Commons: From Theory to Practice*, ed. Charlotte Hess and Elinor Ostrom (Cambridge, MA: MIT Press, 2007).

55. Nancy Kranich, "Countering Enclosure."

56. Christine Borgman, "The Invisible Library: Paradox of the Global Information Infrastructure," *Library Trends* 51, no. 4 (2003): 652-74.

57. Nancy Kranich, "Countering Enclosure: Reclaiming the Knowledge Commons," in *Understanding Knowledge As a Commons: From Theory to Practice*, ed. Charlotte Hess and Elinor Ostrom (Cambridge, MA: MIT Press, 2007).

LIS must advocate for the resources to provide material access to all, to participate in the larger public debates about how to guarantee universal access to knowledge and culture, and how regulatory issues (such as intellectual property and Net Neutrality) have a large impact on access to information and democracy. However, a fully developed democratic analysis of socially-generated information requires an analysis that goes beyond questions of access and looks at the process of information production itself. Although mainstream economics has abandoned a quantitative labor theory of value, one could easily forget that it is through the application of human labor power that knowledge, culture, and information are produced. The material and affective characteristics of this production are unique to the digital age; however, no analysis of this production is complete without crossing into the realm of production.

The Horizon of Production

Socially-generated information is always the result of labor. This statement might strike many as odd, because most people do not consider, for example, adding content to social media "work." Laurel Ptak's Wages for Facebook campaign raises the issues of such information production in stark terms: "THEY SAY IT'S FRIENDSHIP. WE SAY IT'S UNWAGED WORK. WITH EVERY LIKE, CHAT, TAG OR POKE OUR SUBJECTIVITY TURNS THEM A PROFIT. THEY CALL IT SHARING. WE CALL IT STEALING. WE'VE BEEN BOUND BY THEIR TERMS OF SERVICE FAR TOO LONG—IT'S TIME FOR OUR TERMS [caps in original]."[58]

Ptak's campaign suggests that any democratic theory of socially-generated information must address the complicated questions surrounding informational labor. As economic production becomes informationalized, and as information becomes commodified in new ways, the labor

---

58. Laurel Ptak, "Wages for Facebook," accessed March 3, 2015, http://wagesforfacebook.com.

that produces information must be addressed if LIS is to have a substantive democratic theory of socially-generated information.

If the Wages For Facebook campaign is a political perspective—and not actually a specific demand as Ptak argues[59]—then libraries must think about how such a perspective can be enacted. Ptak's campaign borrows from the Wages for Housework campaign from the 1970s echoing the text of Silvia Federici's "Wages Against Housework."[60] Liberal democratic theory has traditionally focused on participation in the public realm and what political philosophers have called *negative freedoms*.[61] When it has turned its attention to economic inequality, it has focused on questions of distribution and incentives (i.e., Rawls' *difference principle*), not on the sphere of production.[62] This inattention is incompatible with critical theory's insistence that human emancipation inform everyday life and relationships. While the commodification of sociality by Facebook may strike one as a minor concern given the many grave challenges confronting the planet, inattention to these complicated new forms of knowledge production leaves LIS unable to provide guidance on how libraries can further democratize the production of socially-generated information. To analyze this we must shift our attention to what Karl Marx famously called the "hidden abode of production, on whose threshold there hangs the notice 'No admittance except on business.'"[63]

There is a vast economics and management literature on the role of knowledge and information within various organizational forms and

---

59. Laurel Ptak, "Wages for Facebook."

60. Alex Jung, "Wages for Facebook," *Dissent Magazine*, April 2014, 47-50; Silvia Federici, Wages against Housework, London: Power of Women Collective, https://caringlabor.wordpress.com/2010/09/15/silvia- federici-wages-against-housework/.

61. Isiah Berlin, *The Proper Study of Mankind: An Anthology of Essays*, ed. Henry Hardy, and Roger Hausheer (New York: Farrar, Straus and Giroux, 1998).

62. G.A. Cohen, *Rescuing Justice and Equality* (Cambridge, MA: Harvard University Press, 2008).

63. Karl Marx et al., *Capital: A Critique of Political Economy* (London: Penguin Books in association with *New Left Review*, 1990), 280.

firms.[64] A critique of informational labor in late capitalism has developed from within a strand of Marxist theory first developed by the Italian thinker Antonio Negri's reading of Marx. In *Capital*, Marx observed that "[t]he maintenance and reproduction of the working class remains a necessary condition for the reproduction of capital."[65] In the *Grundrisse* Marx argues that, as the capitalist mode of production becomes generalized throughout society, specific commodities start to bear less of a discernible relation to the specific forms of labor required to produce them.[66] Through this process capital accrues and becomes more concentrated in the hands of fewer capitalists while simultaneously being generalized throughout society in a pool of common knowledge—what Marx calls the *general intellect*—that can then be redeployed by capital for the production of more surplus value (or profit in classical and neo-classical economics).[67] Autonomist Marxism emerged from a reading of Marx that focused on this process of generalization—specifically stressing the importance of social reproduction in the process of capital accumulation. Capital could not generate profits if it were not for the unwaged labor and production that has historically occurred outside of formal work structures (e.g., housework, child care). This theoretical move places actors not traditionally included in Marxian class frameworks (e.g., students, housewives, the unemployed) in a central role in class struggle.[68]

The idea that production and consumption have blurred is not confined to Autonomist Marxist analysis. In 1980, the celebrated futurist

---

64. John Brown and Paul Duguid, *The Social Life of Information* (Boston: Harvard Business School Press, 2000); Ronald Day, "Social Capital, Value, and Measure: Antonio Negri's Challenge to Capitalism," *Journal of the American Society for Information Science and Technology* 53, no. 12 (2002): 1074-1082.

65. Marx, Capital, 718.

66. Peterson, "Loser Generated Content"; Nick Dyer-Withford, "Autonomist Marxism and the Information Society," https://libcom.org/library/nick-dyer-witheford-autonomist-marxism-and-the-information-society-treason-pamphlet.

67. Peterson, "Loser Generated Content."

68. Ronald Day, "Social Capital, Value, and Measure."

Alvin Toffler used the term "prosumer" to describe this process;[69] more recently, observers such as Ritzer, Dean, and Jurgenson have examined this blurring of production and consumption and argue that it is a fundamental aspect of capitalism.[70] A casual reader of the business press would find it difficult to avoid discussions of the concept of the "sharing economy" and new ventures such as Uber and Airbnb. Although such constructions create a compelling analytical lens, Tiziana Terranova cautions that the

> increasingly blurred territory between production and consumption, work and cultural expression… does not signal the recomposition of the alienated Marxist worker. The Internet does not automatically turn every user into an active producer, and every worker into a creative subject. The process whereby production and consumption are reconfigured within the category of free labour signals the unfolding of another logic of value, whose operations need careful analysis.[71]

Terranova finds that the autonomist "social factory" construct accounts for the numerous ways that the general intellect creates a resource pool for capital. Autonomist Marxist perspectives recognize that when knowledge becomes subsumed under a market-based regime of informationalized capital accumulation the distinctions between labor and consumption blur; they become increasingly generalized and dispersed and are then "reterritoralized" by capital for the generation of profit. This general process of knowledge consumption and production is crystallized in what Bob Jessop calls *fictive capital* (e.g., the securitization of intellectual property rights).[72] This begs the question: if social production is simply a "social factory" ceaselessly creating value for

---

69. George Ritzer and Nathan Jurgenson, "Production, Consumption, Prosumption: the Nature of Capitalism in the Age of the Digital 'Prosumer,'" *Journal of Consumer Culture* 10, no. 1 (2010): 17.

70. Ibid, 14.

71. Tiziana Terranova, *Network Culture: Politics for the Information Age* (London: Pluto Press, 2004), 75.

72. Bob Jessop, "Knowledge as a Fictitious Commodity."

capital, how can public institutions like libraries broaden democratic participation in the realm of socially-generated information production?

Commentators such as Christian Fuchs have gone so far as to argue that socially-generated resources like Wikipedia and the Diaspora Project are "communist cells entangled into antagonistic relations with capitalism" and that, although these projects have a "mystified character," they contain this revolutionary potential because "[c]ommunism needs spaces to materialize itself as a movement. Struggles can manifest themselves in the form of noncommercial Internet projects, watchdog projects, public search engines, the legalization of file sharing, or the introduction of a basic income."[73] Such statements highlight the difficulties of using the autonomist social factory concept to guide community action. By reintroducing class struggle as the sole fulcrum around which the Internet and socially-generated information will be made more egalitarian, theorists like Fuchs deemphasize the important role that state policy can play in shaping and defining the nature of information as a commodity. While using the social factory concept to inform thinking about the production of socially-generated information is a useful starting point, these ideas need to be balanced by Karl Polanyi's insights about the commodification of labor and by the political economy of communication/librarianship because they argue that institutions can create communicative spaces not subject to market forces. The messy political and economic questions that a political economy of librarianship and/or communication necessarily confronts examine how to craft policies that affect the institutions of capitalism that actually exist. Libraries and public institutions must conceptualize ways to further democratize the production of knowledge and to, as Polanyi argued, go beyond the market by using society to curb its power.[74] This perspective would move away from emphasizing a dialectal transcendence and shift analysis to

---

73. Christian Fuchs, "Class and exploitation on the Internet," in *Digital Labor: The Internet as Playground and Factory*, ed. Trebor Scholz (New York: Routledge, 2013), 222.

74. Margaret Somers and Fred Block, "The Return of Karl Polanyi," *Dissent Magazine*, April 2014, 33.

how libraries and librarianship confront these issues "on the ground," accepting that libraries are ambiguous and contested institutions.

Although socially-generated information can be considered to be the product of labor, much of this information is available to be treated as commodities because newer technological forms make legible a range of interactions that were once illegible and more difficult to commodify (e.g., talking to a friend on Facebook). Although this raises important questions about privacy (to be addressed in the communicative horizon section of this essay), it becomes apparent that an initial shift for libraries would be to see socially-generated information as a product of labor. On this subject, PEC "has tended to situate its object within the sphere of consumption."[75] When Mosco focuses PEC on the sphere of production, he uses the work of Harry Braverman to examine how "capital acts to *separate* conception from execution, (and) skill from the raw ability to carry out a task."[76] The scientific management of Frederick Winslow Taylor exemplified this process in the Industrial Era by reducing complex human labor processes to simple and repetitive tasks. Socially-generated information is produced under a different labor regime and in a distributed and generalized manner; therefore, an avenue for democratizing the production of this information would be to examine how these forms of production can act to separate, or merge, conception and execution.

In Yochai Benkler's description of social production, he finds that the "quintessential instance of commons-based production has been free software."[77] A collaborative form of production in which people freely associate to share knowledge and expertise to build a common project offers the promise of merging conception and execution; however, such forms of production occur within an institutional context. Libraries can exert influence over the types of socially-generated information that is

75. Mosco, *The Political Economy of Information*, 139-140.

76. Ibid., 139.

77. Yochai Benkler, *Wealth of Networks*, 63.

considered important, the nature of the information produced, and the content of the knowledge preserved and made available for the public. For many, the knowledge-based economy raised the hope that newer forms of industrial relations would supplant the hierarchy and impersonality of industrial production.[78] The emergence of social production is concomitant with increased precarity for workers in the global north and ever increasing levels of global inequality.[79] In a market-based economy, labor and other commodities are sold in a marketplace that prices the value of specific commodities for their perceived capacity to produce profit or utility or to fulfill necessity (e.g., food, shelter). By bracketing off a sphere of production to be "non-market," Benkler disembeds it from market exchange. With respect to labor and production, the insights of PEC can help LIS examine how a countervailing movement for the protection of society might develop. The Wages for Facebook political perspective can offer some guidance on this issue, but libraries' positions as public institutions can enable them to use their power to encourage the development of specific forms of social production and new ways to conceptualize and articulate that production as a public issue. Many libraries have hosted community "hackathons" or Wikipedia editing events that call on an ethic of civic volunteerism to add to the general knowledge. A new approach would be to acknowledge that this knowledge production adds value and may even be encouraged with compensation.

When United Kingdom Prime Minister David Cameron suggested that libraries be administered by uncompensated volunteers instead of librarians as a part of his "big society" initiative, the library world was quick to condemn this disregard for the professional status of library workers.[80] A similar spirit of volunteerism is called upon by libraries and

---

78. Benkler explores how "third way" industrial relations literature tried to move away from hierarchical production and how peer-to-peer production circumvents bureaucracy. *Wealth of Networks*, 138-139.

79. Thomas Piketty and Arthur Goldhammer, *Capital in the Twenty-First Century* (Cambridge, MA: The Belknap Press of Harvard University Press, 2014).

80. *The Guardian*, "Oxfordshire Cuts Test 'Big Society' as Librarians are

universities when it comes to socially-generated information projects. Peter Levine describes a civic engagement project developed at the University of Maryland that sought to involve economically disadvantaged adolescents in a valuable research project to produce a deliberative website to address the causes of obesity.[81] Levine admires "commons such as public libraries, community gardens, the Internet, and bodies of scholarly research because they encourage *voluntary*, diverse, creative activity."[82] LIS must add a horizon of analysis that can discuss the value of labor in the production of this kind of information commons. These considerations may not always imply that users can be compensated for the production of knowledge with a social value, but only by beginning with the premise that labor produces culture and knowledge can libraries think about how their own knowledge commons projects can become more socially just.

Libraries traditionally collected material produced by the large culture industries, smaller publishers, and other entities that produced records, documents, and information deemed potentially important by librarians working autonomously. The publishing industry, although mostly owned by large multinational firms, created a framework in which the labors of creators, editors, and numerous other actors were often compensated. The most used socially-generated information sites and platforms (e.g., Google, Facebook) are owned by corporations that create spaces and services that bring in users to produce the information that they then sell to other parties, or use to run advertisements. Enormous amounts of information are being created in these systems, and the thought of collecting even a fraction of this information and organizing it into an information commons of some kind faces myriad practical difficulties. What is worth collecting? Who owns the rights to this content? Could

---

Replaced with Volunteers," http://www.theguardian.com/society/2011/jun/02/oxfordshire-library-staff-replaced-volunteers.

81. Peter Levine, "Collective Action, Civic Engagement, and the Knowledge Commons," in *Understanding Knowledge As a Commons: From Theory to Practice*, ed. Charlotte Hess and Elinor Ostrom (Cambridge, Mass: MIT Press, 2007).

82. Ibid, 250 (emphasis added).

we imagine a public institution paying someone for creating a Wiki or community information portal?

Only by insisting that cultural/knowledge production should be valued as a newer form of labor can LIS examine questions of what is socially just and guide library policy and action. The Marxian tradition and PEC are well attuned to inequalities in the realm of production and have complicated the classical liberal democratic (e.g., Jefferson, Tocqueville, Mill) approach that focuses on communicative subjects in the public realm. Although this line of analysis has been able identify how the interests of capital are personified in newer communicative forms (such as socially-generated information), it does not provide libraries a positive normative account of how such forms could be used to broaden and deepen democracy.

The Horizon of Communicative Speech

When discussing the role of speech online, a great deal of commentary has focused on differentiating between what Richard Stallman, one of the founders of the FOSS movement, described as "free as in speech (ideas), not free beer (things)."[83] Although democracy is often discussed in formalistic terms (e.g., ballots, governmental structures) the work of thinkers such as John Rawls and Jürgen Habermas has created a widely shared understanding of democracy as being "government by discussion," and governance is inextricably concerned with both ideas and things. The stakes of such a connection are demonstrated in Amartya Sen's finding that no *functioning* democracy has ever experienced a major famine.[84] For Sen, this is because democracy creates incentives for elites (who would otherwise be insulated from the consequences of famine) to respond to popular demands. This is what Sen calls the "informational

---

83. Lawrence Lessig, "Free, as in Beer," *Wired*, September 2006, http://archive.wired.com/wired/archive/14.09/posts.html?pg=6.

84. Amartya Sen, *The Idea of Justice* (Cambridge, MA: Belknap Press of Harvard University Press, 2009).

role of democracy."[85] This informational role is a public, deliberative discussion about the consequences of policies, and it creates a space in which empirical questions of public importance can be debated, shared, and adjudicated. The normative imperatives of a democratic framework for evaluating socially-generated information must situate democratic deliberation as an important aspect of production and access; however, the creation and maintenance of a public sphere in which open discussion works towards mutual understanding is necessary.

Whatever one's opinion of a company like Facebook, the empirical reality is that socially-generated information platforms are spaces in which ample online public discussion occurs. One need not accept the idea of "Twitter revolutions" or be a technological determinist to concede the importance of these platforms and networks. Given that these are for-profit companies that have an economic incentive to shape the content and character of the information shared and spread, it raises important questions for LIS as it interacts with the information, knowledge, and culture produced by socially-generated platforms. A democratic theory of socially-generated information must embrace a normative theory of communicative rationality that articulates characteristics that would constitute a democratic public sphere. Such a perspective moves beyond the stasis that Buschman identified as plaguing LIS writing on democracy.[86]

Any discussion of the public sphere and communicative rationality must begin with the work of Jürgen Habermas. The scope of Habermas's work is vast and only key ideas related to the public sphere, communicative action, and LIS will be discussed here.[87] For Habermas "the performative attitude of participants in interaction, who coordinate their

---

85. Ibid, 344.

86. Buschman, *Democratic Theory in Library and Information Science*.

87. For a thorough treatment of the applicability of Habermas's ideas to LIS see Buschman's "'The Integrity and Obstinacy of Intellectual Creations': Jürgen Habermas and Librarianship's Theoretical Literature," *Library Quarterly*, 76, no.3 (2006): 270-299; Gloria J. Leckie, "Three Perspectives on Libraries as Public Space," *Feliciter* 50, no. 6 (December 2004): 233-236.

plans for action by coming to an understanding about something in the world"[88] is a key aspect of communicative reason. It is through speech acts and validity claims that the Habermasian lifeworld emerges as a situated entity. Habermas engages many of the key critiques of enlightenment that echo what Max Weber called purposive rationality—the idea that enlightenment rationality is a cold, impersonal, and oppressive "technique and calculation, of organization and administration" that leaves social subjects disenchanted.[89] This "cold" rationality has been the target of varied enlightenment critics such as Nietzsche, Adorno, Foucault, and Derrida. Habermas's theory is not focused on the "cold" questions of discovering the empirically true; instead, it sees "the dialectic of knowing and not knowing as embedded within the dialectic of successful and unsuccessful mutual understanding."[90] The development of situated spaces to facilitate a communicative exchange that works towards mutual understanding is of primary concern to Habermas and to any democratic theory of social-generated information.

It is Habermas's work on the public sphere that has cast a long shadow over democratic theory and is arguably his most important concept for LIS. The Habermasian public sphere is an entity that is not embedded in the economic sphere or formally in the state; it is "rather one of discursive relations, a theater for debating and deliberating rather than for buying and selling."[91] The public sphere is created "when private citizens form to create a public body."[92] In Nancy Fraser's examination of the public sphere she finds that, although "something like Habermas's idea of the public sphere is indispensable to critical social theory and to democratic practice,"[93] it requires a "critical interrogation" if it is to

---

88. Jürgen Habermas. *The Philosophical Discourse of Modernity*.

89. Thomas McCarthy, "Translator's Introduction," in Jürgen Habermas, *The Theory of Communicative Action: Vol 1* (Boston, MA: Beacon Press, 1984), xviii.

90. Habermas, *The Philosophical Discourse of Modernity*, 324.

91. Fraser, "Rethinking the Public Sphere."

92. Jürgen Habermas, Sara Lennox, and Frank Lennox, "The Public Sphere: An Encyclopedia Article (1964)," *New German Critique*, (1974): 49-55.

93. Fraser, "Rethinking the Public Sphere," 57.

successfully guide democratic discussion. For Fraser, the problem with Habermas's public sphere is its *bourgeois masculinist* conceptual baggage. The public sphere concept assumes a space that is open and accessible to all. Even if formal openness is guaranteed, excluding "social inequalities in deliberation means proceeding as if they don't exist when they do." For Fraser, "such bracketing usually works to the advantage of dominant groups in society and to the disadvantage of subordinates."[94] Fraser proposes the development of *subaltern counterpublics* drawing on the history of "subordinated social groups—women, workers, peoples of color, and gays and lesbians—(that) have repeatedly found it advantageous to constitute alternative publics."[95] For Fraser, these *subaltern counterpublics* have a dual character in that "they function as spaces of withdrawal and regroupment... [and *subaltern counterpublics*] also function as bases and training grounds for agitational activities directed towards wider publics."[96]

Fraser's observations about how supposedly open and participatory public spaces that assume formal equality can reproduce hierarchy clearly apply to recent findings about the degree to which white men tend to dominate discourse online.[97] The Internet can now easily be a site of harassment, leading popular authors to go so far as to declare that women are unwelcome online.[98] Importantly, Fraser's subaltern counterpublic sphere emphasizes the importance of deliberation and debate and Habermas's original stress on communication towards mutual understanding while insisting that such spaces are embedded in the web of social relations that make up late capitalist liberal democratic societies. In short, a democratic space that uses socially-generated information will have to address messy procedural realities to insure that the ideal

---

94. Ibid., 64.

95. Ibid., 67.

96. Ibid., 68.

97. Linda Jackson, et al. "Race, Gender, and Information Technology Use."

98. Amanda Hess, "Why Women Aren't Welcome on the Internet," *Pacific Standard*, accessed January 6, 2014, http://www.psmag.com/health-and-behavior/women-arent-welcome-internet-72170.

of communication towards mutual understanding is preserved while acknowledging how, in Fraser's words, "inequality affects relations among publics in late capitalist societies, how publics are differently empowered or segmented, and how some are involuntarily enclaved and subordinated to others."[99]

Embedded in the concept of the public sphere is the notion that there is a private sphere. A thorough examination of the issues related to privacy is beyond the scope of this essay; however, a communicative democracy would articulate a sense of where the line between the private and public realms should be drawn. Feminist theory has demonstrated how issues that are often considered "private" in the traditional male-dominated polis need to become part of the public debate in order to be addressed.[100] Socially-generated information blurs some of the traditional distinctions between the public and private realm in that it creates a record of a range of interactions that were once illegible to bosses, corporations, governments, and citizens. A public sphere that facilitates an ideal space for democratic communicative exchange would actively reinforce a normative commitment ensuring wide participation and a sanction-free space where ideas can be debated and explored in relation to one another. For thinkers like Richard Sennett and Hannah Arendt, the public realm is a space where strangers meet. This incomplete knowledge affords a degree of anonymity for communicative subjects to freely discuss and debate ideas.[101] Socially-generated information, or "big data," is frequently being used predictively by authorities and the state. This use raises important questions about privacy and civil liberties.[102] Any socially-generated information project within the library

---

99. Fraser, "Rethinking the Public Sphere," 77.

100. Ibid., 77.

101. Richard Sennet, "The Public Realm," Richard Sennet's Website, accessed April 11, 2015, http://www.richardsennett.com/site/senn/templates/general2.aspx?pageid=16&cc=gb; Hannah Arendt, *The Human Condition* (Chicago: University of Chicago Press, 1958).

102. Kate Crawford and Jason Schultz, "Big Data and Due Process: Toward a Framework to Redress Predictive Privacy Harms," *Boston College Law Review* 55, 1 (2014): 93-128.

must clearly articulate a privacy policy and inform users about how the information is being created, stored, and analyzed.

A refined theory of the public sphere and communicative action provides LIS with powerful normative tools to complicate discussions about democracy and to move beyond the eighteenth-century concepts and ideas that Buschman identified as continuing to predominate in LIS democratic theory.[103] The previous horizons of analysis demonstrate how, in an online environment, this kind of public sphere can only emerge if potential participants have the access, the time, and the capacity to participate in communicative exchange towards mutual understanding. The creation of socially-generated information involves both the materiality of information technology and the creative labor of communication.

The Framework as a Guide to Progressive Community Action and Community Development

In this essay I have argued that socially-generated information is a new phenomenon and in order to evaluate the democratic potential of a particular project the accessibility, the process of production, and the communicative terrain upon which the action occurs must be carefully considered. I have identified three key horizons of analysis and I have argued for their importance in thinking about how libraries can expand democratic participation and further democratize twenty-first century capitalism. Readers may well have their own considerations to add to those outlined here—any such list is necessarily limited and open to contestation. This framework should benefit libraries engaged in progressive community action projects by providing a set of democratic considerations specifically designed to examine socially-generated information. Some of the most important recent thinkers about global development (e.g., Sen, Nussbaum) have argued that normative frameworks that can be used to evaluate community development outcomes

---

103. Buschman, *Democratic Theory in Library Information Science*.

must be created so that conversations and empirically informed debate about what polices encourage human flourishing can be prioritized. Progressive community action on the part of libraries necessitates robust theoretical debate about normative goals and aims. I hope in some small measure to have contributed to such a debate here. I also hope that I have provided libraries and librarians a useful conceptual toolkit for thinking about issues related to progressive community action and for evaluating community development outcomes when using socially-generated information.

A key point of complexity arises when thinking about the role of the public sphere in relation to the role of information production. A key concept underlying the Habermasian public sphere is the idea that it is a space set apart from both the market and the private realm where social subjects "behave neither like business or professional people transacting private affairs" but come together to form a public body.[104] However, I have argued in this essay that the realm of production must be analyzed and that the labor that creates economic value in socially-generated information must be considered if a public communicative space/commons is to be developed as a part of progressive community action. In the 1960s, Habermas found that in a social welfare state mass democracy that groups have

> needs which can expect no satisfaction from a self-regulating market now tend towards a regulation by the state. The public sphere, which must now mediate these demands, becomes a field for the competition of interests... [resulting] in a more or less unconcealed manner to the compromise of conflicting private interests... With the interweaving of the public and private realm, not only do the political authorities assume certain functions in the sphere of commodity exchange and social labor, but conversely social powers now assume political functions.[105]

The post-World War II period mass democracy in the West required the further development of political interest groups to organize and express

---

104. Jürgen Habermas, "The Public Sphere: An Encyclopedia Article," *New German Critique*, No. 3 (1974): 49-55.

105. Ibid., 54.

public opinion (e.g., labor unions, political parties, non-governmental organizations), along with media and cultural institutions that maintained public-oriented missions (e.g., public broadcast media, libraries). The trends that communications scholars like McChesney and Mosco examine all point to the importance of subsidizing the production of information in the public interest. A twenty-first century public sphere requires open access to all participants, remuneration for labor that produces necessary resources, and a space that fosters a free communicative exchange. Libraries can play a large role in providing resources for all of these activities. Such action is a key way that libraries can participate in community development projects.

The Internet age has seen the decline of traditional journalistic outlets because the economic model that sustained them during the twentieth century has proven insufficient in the twenty-first. Robert McChesney and John Nichols argue that "[s]aving newspapers may be impossible. But we can save journalism. Step one is to begin debating ways for enlightened public subsidies to provide a competitive and independent digital news media."[106] Libraries can play a particularly important role in this broader conversation and could act to fill many of the spaces that commercial information interests no longer address. A way to apply this essay's democratic framework would be for libraries to support new socially-generated information forums and platforms for specific communities. Below, I list a few initial proposals that libraries could explore if they wished to place this perspective into action.

- Libraries could create employment programs that would pay unemployed/underemployed citizens to help build and create the content in a community information commons online. Librarians would assist these "reporters" in their research. These "reporters" would be paid the prevailing living wage to attend community functions, school board meetings, and city council

---

106. Robert McChesney and John Nichols, "Robert W. McChesney and John Nichols on Federal Subsidies for Journalism," *Washington Post*, October 30, 2009, accessed April 21, 2015, http://www.washingtonpost.com/wp-dyn/content/article/2009/10/22/AR2009102203960.html.

meetings. By creating and maintaining a community-generated information commons libraries could play a role in building this crucial aspect of the democratic information infrastructure that market forces are neglecting. Although the political culture of the United States is suspicious of public subsidy, a program of this sort could also address employment in many communities by updating the logic behind Franklin Delano Roosevelt's Works Project Administration in the 1930s or by acknowledging the role that public subsidy of the post office played in supporting the distribution of print media in the late eighteenth and early nineteenth century. The content of such a commons may well be very different from commercial news, but libraries' institutional histories and their location in specific geographical communities could greatly assist this process.

- Further research needs to be conducted into the ideal conditions for communicative rationality to occur. For example, there has been a great deal in the press about the vitriolic threats that women and people of color receive online when participating in public discourse. How can such threats be reduced? What external factors play a role? How to facilitate understanding across difference? What role could/should libraries play in trying to shape democratic participation and this type of civic engagement?
- Libraries must continue their role in storing and preserving vital public information and continue to collect the idiosyncratic and local forms of culture that may be lost to history if not preserved.
- Libraries should continue and expand public access to the Internet and provide training on how to use information technology.
- Librarians should advocate for a universal basic income, a reduced working day for greater leisure time, and other antipoverty measures. Social reforms like these could vastly improve the conditions necessary for broad public participation.
- This framework can be used by a library to evaluate the use of a particular new technology utilizing socially-generated

information. A number of attempts have been made by libraries to encourage civic engagement by using socially-generated technology. Libraries need to consider the accessibility of these projects. Libraries must think about the value of the labor embedded in the creation of these resources. Libraries must consider the kind of communicative public sphere they hope to create.

Industrial democracy is unlikely to return as a key concept in public debate, but concerns about how to democratize economic production should not be obscured by technological change; they should be at the center of such conversations. As more social scientists and economists speculate about rising inequality and the impact of technology replacing the need for human labor in market-based societies, it is notable that there is so little discussion of, as John Lanchester writes, an "alternative future... (of the) kind of world dreamed of by William Morris, full of humans engaged in meaningful and sanely remunerated labour. Except with added robots."[107]

Since their creation, libraries have continuously confronted the need to adapt to technological change. To move beyond what Birdsall called the "ideology of information technology" would be to reclaim and reorient the discourse that surrounds library innovation. Public investment and subsidy for public purposes is not antithetical to innovation—in fact, innovation would be impossible without infrastructure investments and, per the insights of Karl Polanyi, a market economy could not exist without the active intervention of the state and society. Libraries can act to fill the spaces that markets leave open in the public sphere, libraries can create meaningful, socially important employment opportunities, and libraries can provide access to a wide range of culture, knowledge, and information. In order to do so, they must guarantee access, acknowledge the role of labor in information production, and insure that a democratic communicative space is available to all.

---

107. John Lanchester, "The Robots are Coming," *London Review of Books* 37, no. 5 (2015), 8.

Bibliography

American Library Association, "Library Bill of Rights." Accessed April 14, 2015, http://www.ala.org/advocacy/intfreedom/librarybill.

Arendt, Hannah. *The Human Condition*. Chicago: University of Chicago Press, 1958.

Augst, Thomas, and Wayne A. Wiegand. *Libraries as Agencies of Culture*. Madison, WI: University of Wisconsin Press, 2001.

Berlin, Isiah. *The Proper Study of Mankind: An Anthology of Essays*. Edited by Henry Hardy and Roger Hausheer. New York: Farrar, Straus and Giroux, 1998.

Bagdikian, Ben H. *The New Media Monopoly*. Boston: Beacon Press, 2004.

Bell, Daniel. *The Coming Post-Industrial Society: A Venture in Social Forecasting*. New York: Basic Books, 1976.

Benkler, Yochai. *The Wealth of Networks: How Social Production Transforms Markets and Freedom*. New Haven, CT: Yale University Press, 2006.

Birdsall, William. "A Political Economy of Librarianship?" *Hermes: Revue Critique* 6 (2000). http://kimle1311.files.wordpress.com/2007/10/week3b_birdsall.pdf.

Borgman, Christine L. "The Invisible Library: Paradox of the Global Information Infrastructure." *Library Trends* 51, no. 4 (2003): 652-74.

Bohman, James. "Critical Theory." In *The Stanford Encyclopedia of Philosophy*. Spring 2013. Edited by Edward N. Zalta. Accessed October 14, 2014, http://plato.stanford.edu/archives/spr2013/entries/critical-theory/.

Brown, John and Paul Duguid. *The Social Life of Information*. Boston: Harvard Business School Press, 2000.

Budd, John. "Public Library Leaders and Changing Society." *Public Library Quarterly* 26, no. 3/4 (2007): 1-14.

Buschman, John. "The Integrity and Obstinacy of Intellectual Creations: Jügen Habermas and Librarianship's Theoretical Literature." *Library Quarterly* 76, no. 3 (2006): 270-99.

———. "Democratic Theory in Library Information Science: Toward an Emendation." *Journal of the American Society for Information Science and Technology* 58, no. 10 (2007): 1483-96.

———. *Libraries, Classrooms, and the Interests of Democracy: Marking the Limits of Neoliberalism.* Lanham, MD: The Scarecrow Press, 2012.

Cohen,G.A. *Rescuing Justice and Equality.* Cambridge, MA: Harvard University Press, 2008.

Crawford, Kate and Jason Schultz, "Big Data and Due Process: Toward a Framework to Redress Predictive Privacy Harms." *Boston College Law Review* 55, no. 1 (January 2014): 93-128.

Day, Ronald E. "Social Capital, Value, and Measure: Antonio Negri's Challenge to Capitalism." *Journal of the American Society for Information Science and Technology* 53, no. 12: (2002), 1074-82.

Dyer-Withford, Nick "Autonomist Marxism and the Information Society." Accessed May 19, 2015, https://libcom.org/library/nick-dyer-witheford-autonomist-marxism-and-the informationsociety-treason-pamphlet.

Federici, Silvia. *Wages against Housework.* London: Power of Women Collective, 1975. https://caringlabor.wordpress.com/2010/09/15/silvia-federici-wages-against housework/.

Fraser, Nancy. "Rethinking the Public Sphere: a Contribution to the Critique of Actually Existing Democracy." *Social Text*, 25/26 (1990): 56-80.

————. "A Triple Movement?: Parsing the Politics of Crisis After Polanyi." *New Left Review* 81 (2013), 119-32.

Fuchs, Christian. "Class and exploitation on the Internet." In *Digital Labor: The Internet as Playground and Factory*. Edited by Trebor Scholz. New York: Routledge, 2013.

Furner, J. "User Tagging of Library Resources: Toward a Framework for System Evaluation." *International Cataloging and Bibliographic Control* 37, no. 3 (2008): 47-51.

The Guardian, "Oxfordshire Cuts Test 'Big Society' as Librarians are Replaced with Volunteers." Accessed April 4, 2015. http:// www.theguardian.com/society/2011/jun/02/oxfordshireli- brary-staff-replaced-volunteers.

Habermas, Jürgen. "The Public Sphere: An Encyclopedia Article." *New German Critique* 4 (1974): 49-55.

————.. *The Philosophical Discourse of Modernity: Twelve Lectures*. Cam- bridge, MA: MIT Press, 1987.

Hess, Amanda "Why Women aren't Welcome on the Internet." *Pacific Standard*, Jan. 6, 2014. Accessed April 4, 2015, http://www. psmag.com/health-and-behavior/women-arentwelcome- internet-72170.

Hess, Charlotte and Elinor Ostrom. "An Overview of the Knowl- edge Commons." In *Understanding Knowledge as a Commons: From Theory to Practice*. Edited by Charlotte Hess and Elinor Ostrom. Cambridge, MA: MIT Press, 2007.

Jackson, Linda A., Yong Zhao, Anthony Kolenic III, Hiram E. Fitzgerald, Rena Harold, and Alexander von Eye. "Race, Gender, and Information Technology Use: The New Digital Divide." *CyberPsychology & Behavior* 11, no. 4 (August 2008): 437-442.

Jessop, Bob. "Knowledge as a Fictitious Commodity: Insights and Limits of a PolanyianPerspective." In *Reading Karl Polanyi for the Twenty-First Century: Market Economy as a Political Project*.

Edited by Ayse Buğra, and Kaan Ağartan. Basingstoke, UK: Macmillan, 2007.

Jung, Alex E. "Wages for Facebook." *Dissent Magazine*, April 2014.

Kindleberger, Charles. "*The Great Transformation* by Karl Polanyi." *Daedalus* 103, no. 1 (1974), 45-52.

Kranich, Nancy "Countering Enclosure: Reclaiming the Knowledge Commons." In *Understanding Knowledge As a Commons: From Theory to Practice*. Edited by Charlotte Hess and Elinor Ostrom. Cambridge, MA: MIT Press, 2007.

Leckie, Gloria J. "Three Perspectives on Libraries as Public Space." *Feliciter* 50, no. 6 (December 2004): 233-236.

Lee, Kang-Pyo, Hong-Gee Kim, and Hyoung-Joo Kim."A Social Inverted Index for Social Tagging-Based Information Retrieval." *Journal of Information Science* 38, no. 4 (2012): 313-32.

Levine, Peter. "Collective Action, Civic Engagement, and the Knowledge Commons." In *Understanding Knowledge As a Commons: From Theory to Practice*, edited by Charlotte Hess and Elinor Ostrom, 247-76. Cambridge, MA: MIT Press, 2007.

Lanchester, John. "The Robots are Coming." *London Review of Books* 37, no. 5 (2015), 3-8.

Lessig, Lawrence. "Getting Our Values around Copyright Right." *Educause Review* 45, no. 2 (March/April 2010), 26-42.

———. "Free, as in Beer." *Wired*, September, 2006. Accessed April 4, 2015, http://archive.wired.com/wired/archive/14.09/posts.html?pg=6.

Marx, Karl, Friedrich Engels, Ernest Mandel, Ben Fowkes, and David Fernbach. *Capital: A Critique of Political Economy*. London: Penguin Books in association with *New Left Review*, 1990.

Marx, Karl, and Martin Nicolaus. *Grundrisse: Foundations of the Critique of Political Economy*. London: Penguin Books, 1993, in association with *New Left Review*.

Mazzucato, Mariana. *The Entrepreneurial State*. London: Demos, 2011.

McCarthy, Thomas. "Translator's Introduction." In Jürgen Habermas, *The Theory of Communicative Action: Vol 1*. Boston, MA: Beacon Press, 1984.

McChesney, Robert and John Nichols. "Robert W. McChesney and John Nichols on Federal Subsidies for Journalism." *Washington Post*, October 30, 2009. http://www.washingtonpost.com/wp-dyn/content/article/2009/10/22/AR2009102203960.html,

McChesney, Robert. *Rich Media, Poor Democracy: Communication Politics in Dubious Times*. Urbana: University of Illinois Press, 1999.

———. *Digital Disconnect: How Capitalism is Turning the Internet Against Democracy.* The New Press: NY, 2013.

Mirowski, Philip. *Never Let a Serious Crisis Go to Waste: How Neoliberalism Survived the Financial Meltdown*. London: Vesrso, 2013.

Montgomery, David. "Industrial Democracy or Democracy in Industry?: The Theory and Practice of the Labor Movement, 1870-1925." In *Industrial Democracy in America: The Ambiguous Promise*, edited by Nelson Lichtenstein and John Harris Howell, 20-42. Washington, D.C.:Woodrow Wilson Center Press, 1993.

Mosco, Vincent. *The Political Economy of Communication*. London: Sage Publications, 2009.

Nicholson, K. P. "The McDonaldization of Academic Libraries and the Values of Transformational Change." *College and Research Libraries* 76, no. 3 (2015): 328-38.

Nussbaum, Martha. "Promoting Women's Capabilities." In *Global Tensions: Challenges and Opportunities in the World Economy*, edited by Lourdes Benería and Savitri Bisnath, 241-56. New York: Routledge, 2004.

Oxford English Dictionary. "access, n." OED Online. Accessed March 11, 2015. Oxford University Press, http://www.oed.com/view/Entry/1028?rskey=LvkstP&result=1.

Ptak, Laurel. *"Wages for Facebook." Accessed March 3, 2015, http://wagesforfacebook.com.*

Peters, Michael. "The Political Economy of Information Democracy." *The International Journal of Learning* 14, no. 6 (2007)29-36.

Petersen, Søren Mørk. "Loser Generated Content: From Participation to Exploitation." *First Monday* 13, no. 3 (2008). Accessed October 12, 2014, http://firstmonday.org/article/view/2141/1948.

Piketty, Thomas and Arthur Goldhammer. *Capital in the Twenty-First Century*. Cambridge, MA: The Belknap Press of Harvard University Press, 2014.

Polanyi, Karl. *The Great Transformation*. Boston: Beacon Press, 1957.

Ritzer, George, and Nathan Jurgenson. "Production, Consumption, Prosumption: The Nature of Capitalism in the Age of the Digital 'Prosumer.'" *Journal of Consumer Culture* 10, no. 1 (2010): 13-36.

The SAGE Glossary of the Social and Behavioral Sciences. "Economy, New." Edited by Larry E. Sullivan. Thousand Oaks, CA: SAGE Reference, 2009.

Sangivanni, Andrea. "Normative Poltical Theory: A Flight from Reality?" In *Political Thought and International Relations: Variations on a Realist Theme*, edited by Duncan Bell, 219-39. Oxford, UK: Oxford University Press, 2009.

Seal, Maura. "The Neoliberal Library." In *Information Literacy and Social Justice: Radical Professional Praxis*, edited by Lua Gregory and Shana Higgins, 39-62. Sacramento, CA: Library Juice Press, 2013.

Sen, Amartya. *The Idea of Justice.* Cambridge, MA: Belknap Press of Harvard University Press, 2009.

Sennet, Richard. "The Public Realm." Richard Sennet's Website. Accessed April 2, 2015, http://www.richardsennett.com/site/senn/templates/general2.aspx?pageid=16&cc=gb.

Somers, Margaret and Fred Block. "The Return of Karl Polanyi." *Dissent Magazine,* April 2014.

Strover,Sharon. The US Digital Divide: A Call for a New Philosophy. *Critical Studies in Media Communication* 31, no.2 (2014): 114-122.

Taylor, Astra. *The People's Platform: Taking Back Power and Culture in the Digital Age.* NewYork: Metropolitan Books, 2014.

Terranova, Tiziana. *Network Culture: Politics for the Information Age.* London: Pluto Press, 2004.

Vaidhyanathan, Siva. *Copyrights and Copywrongs: The Rise of Intellectual Property and How It Threatens Creativity.* New York: New York University Press, 2001.

Wiegand, Wayne A."Tunnel Vision and Blind Spots: What the Past Tells Us about the Present; Reflections on the Twentieth-Century History of American Librarianship." *Library Quarterly* 69, no. 1(1999): 1-32.

SECTION TWO:
CONTEXTUAL EXAMINATIONS OF PROGRESSIVE COMMUNITY ACTION IN LIBRARY AND INFORMATION SCIENCE

Chapter 4

BEYOND THE RECYCLING BIN: THE CREATION OF AN ENVIRONMENT OF EDUCATED HOPE ON A FRACKED CAMPUS IN A DISPOSABLE COMMUNITY

Wendy Highby[1]

Introduction: The Reluctant Provocateur

Can an academic library serve as cradle and crèche for community action, providing a place where progressive values are nurtured? What actions can academic librarians take to create environmental justice on their campuses and in their communities? Are tempered forms of activism adequate? In a world fast approaching the brink of inalterable climate change, how does one rouse communities to action? And what about communities that willingly cede to authorities the power to determine environmental quality of life and levels of risk exposure? Does critical theory provide any guidance?

These questions, when posed rhetorically, are potentially provocative. But in genuinely dire situations, tempered activism may be insufficient, and provocation may be merely a first step. In this case, crisis was a necessary goad, initially prodding the reluctant activist. Critical theorist Henry Giroux suggests that "educators need to become provocateurs;

---

1. The opinions expressed in this chapter are solely the author's and do not represent the views of the University of Northern Colorado.

they need to take a stand while refusing to be involved in . . . doctrinaire politics," and they must fight "against the imposed silence of normalized power" in situations that involve "material and symbolic violence."[2]

In November of 2011, I was faced with a situation at my university that I felt involved material violence to the environment and potential endangerment of public health. The Board of Trustees made the unanimous decision to lease the mineral rights under campus property to an oil and gas corporation. The company plans to use the controversial technique of hydrofracturing ("fracking") to extract the resources. Some scientists argue that the potential negative public health and environmental consequences of fracking are such that a precautionary approach is warranted.[3] Confronted with circumstances that I judged sufficiently serious to warrant action, I eventually escaped the inertia of well-informed futility, overcame my fear, and took a stand.

In September of 2013, I broke the twenty-one month campus-wide silence on this issue. With the support of two Faculty Senators, I made a presentation to the Faculty Senate of my university in which I openly questioned the Board of Trustees' decision to allow fracking beneath our campus. Subsequently, we formed a grassroots "Hydrofracturing Task Force" and produced our "Progress Report, Interim Findings, and Recommendations," with seventeen signers urging precautionary action.[4] The group now acts under the new name "Frack*ED@UNC"; we continue to educate and engage the campus and community about fracking, a fossil-free future, and other environmental justice-related issues. These collective and collaborative activities have created a microcosm of democratic participation.

---

2. Henry A. Giroux, *Youth in a Suspect Society: Democracy or Disposability?* (New York: Palgrave Macmillan, 2009), 140.

3. Robert W. Howarth, Anthony Ingraffea, and Terry Engelder, "Should Fracking Stop? Extracting Gas from Shale Increases the Availability of This Resource, But the Health and Environmental Risks May Be Too High," *Nature* 477, no. 7364 (September 15, 2011): 271-75, doi: 10.1038/477271a; Madelon L. Finkel and Jake Hays, "The Implications of Unconventional Drilling for Natural Gas: A Global Public Health Concern," *Public Health* 127 (2013), 889-93, doi: 10.1016/j.puhe.2013.07.005.

4. Frack*ED@UNC, née Hydrofracturing Task Force, "Progress Report, Interim Findings, and Recommendations," May 9, 2014.

My specialized knowledge as a librarian empowered me to proffer unique points of view and strengths to further the progress of Frack*ED@UNC. I offer this experience as an example to colleagues in the form of an autoethnographic case study. I am an academic librarian at a medium-size public university in northern Colorado, about sixty miles north of Denver. Historically, we were the State Normal School and we continue to be a center of teacher education. What place could be more ideal for embodying critical pedagogy and librarianship? I believe that academic libraries can and do serve as nurturing spaces for progressive values and community action, and that academic librarians and libraries are uniquely situated and equipped to work toward environmental justice on their campuses and in their respective communities. For example, most academic librarians are employed by institutions with investment portfolios that include fossil fuels and could organize political action to encourage divestment.[5] We each need to think globally and act locally; we can rouse those members of our local communities who have acquiesced to the hopelessness of their own or future generations' disposability.

The autoethnographic method is apt given this volume's tripart theme of action, critical theory, and social justice. The method employs self-critique or reflexivity, a cornerstone of critical theory. A probing analysis of one's role within a socially unjust system is a necessary precursor to changing that system. Too often, progressive scholars critique and issue calls to action and stop there. This chapter, through autoethnography, documents the full span of the process: the critique, the inner thoughts of the activist, the actual performance of the political action, and the consequences thereof. It models a reflexivity that was formerly rare but is beginning to emerge in the educational literature,[6] progressive

---

5. "Fossil Free: Divest from Fossil Fuels," 350.org, accessed April 27, 2015, http://gofossilfree.org/.

6. Dilys Schoorman, "Resisting the Unholy Alliance between a University and a Prison Company: Implications for Faculty Governance in a Neoliberal Context," *Cultural Studies – Critical Methodologies* 13, no.6 (2013): 510-9, doi: 10.1177/1532708613503777.

library publications,[7] mainstream library literature,[8] and documentary films.[9] Thus, I will toggle among first, second, and third persons as I converse with and confess to you my reader, interweaving reflexivity throughout this chapter.

The critical theories of Giroux provide a philosophical framework for academic librarians' effective engagement in the public political sphere. Librarians can apply Giroux's theories and become trans-formative intellectuals,[10] co-creating communities of fully-informed, well-educated, hope-filled citizens. Previous applications of Giroux's theories to academic librarianship can bolster our confidence. We can be nuanced and situational in our choices and still act ethically when we deliberately choose between neutrality and non-neutrality.[11] We can be well-versed on the tenets of social justice[12] and understand how activism around social justice issues relates to faculty governance.[13]

---

7. Ruth Mirtz, "Disintermediation and Resistance: Giroux and Radical Praxis in the Library," in *Critical Library Instruction: Theories and Methods*, edited by Toni Samek (Duluth, MN: Library Juice Press, 2010), 293-304; Patti Ryan and Lisa Sloniowski, "The Public Academic Library: Friction in the Teflon Funnel," in *Information Literacy and Social Justice: Radical Professional Praxis*, edited by Lua Gregory and Shana Higgins (Sacramento, CA: Library Juice Press, 2013), 275-96.

8. Bharat Mehra and Donna Braquet, "Marriage between Participatory Leadership and Action Research to Advocate Benefits Equality for Lesbian, Gay, Bisexual, and Transgendered People: An Extended Human Rights Role for Library and Information Science," in *Leadership in Academic Libraries Today: Connecting Theory to Practice*, ed. by Bradford Lee Eden and Jody Condit Fagan (Lanham, MD: Rowman & Littlefield, 2014), 185-211.

9. *Living Thinkers: An Autobiography of Black Women in the Ivory Tower*, directed by Roxana Walker-Canton (New York: Women Make Movies, 2013), presents an unflinchingly honest and compassionate picture of the challenges of being progressive, female, and African-American in academia.

10. Henry A. Giroux, *Teachers as Intellectuals: Toward a Critical Pedagogy of Learning* (Granby, MA: Bergin & Garvey, 1988).

11. Robert Jensen, "The Myth of the Neutral Professional," in *Questioning Library Neutrality: Essays from Progressive Librarian*, ed. Alison Lewis (Duluth, MN: Library Juice Press, 2008), 89-96.

12. Bharat Mehra, Kevin Rioux, and Kendra Albright, "Social Justice in Library and Information Science," in *Encyclopedia of Library and Information Sciences* 3rd ed. (New York: Taylor & Francis, 2010): 4820-36.

13. Dilys Schoorman and Michele Acker-Hocevar, "Viewing Faculty

A basic knowledge of the dynamics of climate change denial, inertia, fatalism, and realism sheds light on psychosocial aspects of information interpretation.[14] Our expertise in librarianship equips us to be effective information critics[15] and public intellectuals. With these strengths we can practice a public pedagogy that exposes the nexus of knowledge and power. In a community enlightened by such critical knowledge, socially just actions can follow, leading to positive change.

This primer is critical in approach and acknowledges the primacy of political economy in its interpretive framework. It is cognizant of the necessity for systemic reform with regard to climate change.[16] And finally, this primer is direct in its style. The time has passed for speaking in parables. The seriousness of climate change's threat to humanity's ecological survival[17] demands straightforward, decoded communication.

Critical Theory and the Trajectory of Giroux's Scholarship

The critical theories of Henry Giroux are a source of progressive ideas for academic librarians and provide a clarifying lens through which to view the educational system and librarians' roles within it. Giroux's concepts of the transformative intellectual, public pedagogy, and non-neutrality (the co-existing roles of teacher/citizen) are pertinent to a critical view of librarianship. On the systemic level, Giroux's concepts of the social construction of knowledge, neoliberalism, the corporatization

Governance within a Social Justice Framework: Struggles and Possibilities for Democratic Decision-Making in Higher Education," *Equity & Excellence in Education* 43, no. 3 (2010), 310-325, doi:10.1080/10665684.2010.494493.

14. Sandra Steingraber, *Raising Elijah: Protecting Our Children in an Age of Environmental Crisis* (Cambridge, MA: Da Capo Press: 2011).

15. Jack Andersen, "Information Criticism: Where Is It?, in *Questioning Library Neutrality: Essays from* Progressive Librarian, edited by Alison Lewis (Duluth, MN: Library Juice Press, 2008), 97-108.

16. Naomi Klein, *This Changes Everything: Capitalism vs. the Climate* (New York: Simon & Schuster, 2014).

17. United Nations, "UN and Climate Change," United Nations, accessed April 29, 2015, http://www.un.org/climatechange/.

of universities and privatization of the public educational sphere, the biopolitics of disposability, and the zombie politics of casino capitalism all offer meaningful philosophical perspectives. Giroux's theories are not sterile, but inherently creative and meant to be applied and encourage thought. They embolden the thinker to act, to question, and to change both self and system. Should Giroux's critical theory be your guiding philosophy? Try the ideas on for size. Do they provide clarity, comport with your values, and fit your situation?[18] Let's continue our test of Giroux's critical theory by examining the germination and trajectory of his scholarship.

Giroux is currently a Professor of English and Cultural Studies at McMaster University in Hamilton, Ontario. The contextualization of education in relation to sociopolitical issues is a continuous thread throughout his work. Giroux's doctoral dissertation explored curriculum theory and the sociology of education. He developed an interdisciplinary pedagogical model for the teaching of high school history within a sociopolitical and institutional context.[19] This interdisciplinary, contextual emphasis continues to the present day as shown in the research interests listed on his current university profile: "cultural studies, youth, critical pedagogy, democratic theory, public education, communication theory, social theory, and the politics of higher education."[20]

Critical theory is a way of seeing the world; it encourages consciousness of oppressive power structures and liberation therefrom. Critical theory "is not a theory proper but a set of complementary theoretical frames that examine structures of domination in society in order to open

---

18. Henry A. Giroux, interview by Bill Moyers, *Moyers & Company*, WNET, American Public Television, November 22, 2013, http://billmoyers.com/segment/henry-giroux-on-zombie-politics/. View Giroux's conversation with Bill Moyers to get a personal sense of his philosophy.

19. Henry A. Giroux, "Themes in Modern European History" (doctoral dissertation, Carnegie-Mellon University, 1977).

20. Henry A. Giroux, "Henry Giroux, PhD: Profile," McMaster University, accessed April 24, 2015, http://www.humanities.mcmaster.ca/~english/Faculty/girouxh.html.

possibilities for the emancipation of people, meanings, and values."[21] It was a neo-Marxist approach that emerged out of the Frankfurt School of Social Research in the 1930s. In the 1960s and forward, Jürgen Habermas influenced critical theory by adding the concepts of the public sphere and self-critique. He believed in the liberating power of critical knowledge. Habermas contended this knowledge enabled individuals to break away from forms of domination. The process of knowledge acquisition requires reflexivity, "the process of reflecting on one's participation in structures of domination." Habermas' influence caused critical theory to expand its scope to analyses of capitalism, culture industries, popular culture, and social institutions.[22]

Giroux incorporates the Frankfurt School's critical theory, Habermas' concept of the public sphere, and Paulo Freire's critical pedagogy[23] in his seminal 1988 work, *Teachers as Intellectuals: Toward a Critical Pedagogy of Learning.* By critical pedagogy, Giroux means that "rather than accept the notion that schools are vehicles of democracy and social mobility, educational critics make such an assumption problematic."[24] Giroux explains the critic's main task is to determine how schools reinforce and replicate the existing oppressive power structure in students' lives. In order to change this power structure, Giroux advises combining "the language of critique with the language of possibility." He defines schools as "democratic public spheres," christens teachers as "transformative intellectuals," and insists "they must speak out against economic, political and social injustices both within and outside of schools."[25] Social justice is integral to and figures prominently in Giroux's critical theory.

He is also concerned about the issue of neutrality in the workplace. He is cognizant of the power of the system to squelch political action

---

21. Sara L. McKinnon, "Critical Theory," in *Encyclopedia of Communication Theory* (Thousand Oaks, CA: Sage Reference, 2009, 237.

22. Ibid., 237-8.

23. Giroux, *Teachers as Intellectuals*, 100-2.

24. Ibid., xxix.

25. Ibid., 128.

by narrowly defining roles, thus inhibiting the educator from perform-
ing as a citizen:

> Lacking a self-consciously democratic political focus, teachers are often
> reduced to the role of a technician or functionary engaged in formalistic
> rituals, unconcerned with the disturbing and urgent problems that con-
> front the larger society or the consequences of one's pedagogical and
> research undertakings. In opposition to this model, with its claims to and
> conceit of political neutrality, I argue that academics should combine the
> mutually interdependent roles of critical educator and active citizen.[26]

Giroux's philosophy easily transfers from the realm of the classroom
professor to that of the academic librarian, given the similarity of roles
and workload and the shared sociopolitical context. Giroux strives to
liberate the teacher and student to confront their situations, to be fully
conscious of the sociopolitical context: "Such an intellectual does not
train students solely for jobs but also educates them to question critically
the institutions, policies, and values that shape their lives, relationships to
others, and connections to the larger world."[27] Giroux's ideas are highly
pragmatic without being prescriptive. They are profoundly holistic and
universal in their belief in both the individual and collective potential
for change. But Giroux can be challenging to librarians, since he encourages the integration of active citizenship into one's professional life;
such a practice does not allow the automatic assumption of a stance
of neutrality in all situations.

The topic of neutrality warrants extended discussion because of its
sometimes unquestioned enshrinement within librarianship. To further
apply Giroux's non-neutrality philosophy, we can self-reflexively examine our professional ethics. Such discernment can be accomplished by
clarifying our values. Toward that end, I have found the following two
authors helpful. In his essay in *Questioning Library Neutrality*, Robert
Jensen debunks the myth of the neutral professional. The myth keeps

---

26. Henry A. Giroux, *Neoliberalism's War on Higher Education* (Chicago: Haymarket, 2014), 143-4.

27. Ibid., 144.

us under control in a neoliberal society, seemingly benignly (in contrast to more brutal repression in totalitarian states). Yet, where there is unequal distribution of power, there is no such thing as neutrality. If we claim professional neutrality, we are accepting the status quo.[28] In his autobiography, *You Can't Be Neutral on a Moving Train*, Howard Zinn explains the context of his titular statement regarding neutrality. He says it applies in situations in which "events are already moving in certain deadly directions, and to be neutral means to accept that."[29] I contend that fossil fuel induced global warming and the public health implications of fracking constitute movements in certain deadly directions. I am arguing for the selective and situation-dependent employment of non-neutrality. This does not change my belief that neutrality should remain a central tenet of the ethics of librarianship. Good situational examples are collection development and reference service provision. Stances of neutrality and non-neutrality may be chosen when deemed appropriate for a given situation, but we should not be complacent and use neutrality as our fallback position when confronted with issues that should be processed within the democratic structure provided by faculty governance, or issues that demand a stance because of inherent social injustices.[30]

Giroux applies this principle of non-neutrality not only to professional roles, but also to the construction of knowledge. He views knowledge as "neither neutral nor objective," but as a "social construction embodying

---

28. Jensen, "The Myth of the Neutral Professional," in *Questioning Library Neutrality: Essays from* Progressive Librarian, ed. Alison Lewis (Duluth, MN: Library Juice Press, 2008), 91.

29 . Howard Zinn, *You Can't Be Neutral on a Moving Train: A Personal History of Our Times* (Boston, MA: Beacon Press, 2002), 8.

30. Anthony Ingraffea and Patty Limerick, "The Return of FrackingSENSE with Dr. Anthony Ingraffea," The Center of the American West, University of Colorado at Boulder, accessed April 27, 2015, http://www.centerwest.org/podcast/mp3/4-8-15ingraffea.mp3. A fine model of reflexivity is provided by this public conversation between Dr. Anthony Ingraffea (Cornell University engineer and environmental activist) and Dr. Patty Limerick (University of Colorado at Boulder historian). They frankly discuss the pros and cons of their respective stances of advocacy and neutrality in the academic context.

particular interests and assumptions." And here is the core idea: "Knowledge must be linked to the issue of power. . ." This epistemology sheds light on the practice of librarianship, adding a much needed sociopolitical dimension to typical conceptions of the scholarly communication system by illuminating the power structure underlying the system. "Knowledge becomes important to the degree that it helps human beings understand not only the assumptions embedded in its form and content, but also the processes whereby knowledge is produced, appropriated, and transformed within specific social and historical settings."[31] Even when defining a potentially abstract concept such as epistemology, Giroux is consistently situational, dependably grounded, and contextual. That is, knowledge embodies "particular interests," has "form and content," and emerges out of a process that is sociohistorical. Ultimately, Giroux's view of the world is hopeful, because a constructed reality can be deconstructed and reformed in a socially just manner.

From 2002 to current (the post 9/11 era that coincides with a solidification of both the civil liberties incursions by the U.S. government and the personhood of corporations), the deleterious effects of neoliberalism are emphasized in Giroux's writing. He turns his attention toward the corporatization of higher education and privatization of the public educational sphere in a 2002 article in the *Harvard Educational Review*, wherein he describes neoliberalism's single-minded, market-driven influence on politics, society, and culture; he contends that participatory democracy is undermined by market values. As this corporate influence deepens, basic civic institutions are eroded and "there is a simultaneous diminishing of noncommodified public spheres." He specifically names libraries as one of the spheres where information essential to participatory democracy is presented, and where issues are discussed and debated.[32]

---

31. Giroux, *Teachers as Intellectuals*, 7-8.

32. Henry A. Giroux, "Neoliberalism, Corporate Culture, and the Promise of Higher Education: The University as a Democratic Public Sphere," *Harvard Educational Review* 72, no. 4 (2002), 427-428, http://hepg.metapress.com/content/0515nr62324n71p1/fulltext.pdf.

In the last decade, Giroux has increased the fervor of his criticism; he perceives a burgeoning authoritarianism, deterioration of social conditions, the rise of a new gilded age, and the incessant neoliberal movement toward commodification and disposability of youth. These ideas are built upon Foucault's concept of biopolitical power of the state. Giroux initially applies the concept of "biopolitics of disposability" to the events surrounding Hurricane Katrina in 2005. He deems the failed U.S. government response to be the result of deliberately racist and classist policies that purposefully abandoned the African American poor and working class in New Orleans. Giroux extends his critical philosophy to explicitly include environmental issues; the ecosphere is featured as one of the public spheres threatened by neoliberalism's destructive bent. He contends that: "Waste, growing inequality, global warming, the rise in world sea levels, the decline of ecosystems on earth, and the extinction of many plant and animal species appear to the Bush administration to be a small price to pay for promoting the logic and reaping the rewards of market fundamentalism."[33] Giroux's analysis of the economics of ecocide is scathing. In the neoliberal scheme, externalities (the price of long-term consequences) are not included in the cost-benefit calculus.

In 2011, Giroux continued the ecological theme, critiquing neoliberal energy and economic policies and the resulting environmental degradation. He decried the Gulf Coast deep-sea oil spills as "casino capitalism's most treasured formula of short-term investments for quick profits" that ignore "the possibility of deadly social costs."[34] Giroux then connected the neoliberal economic juggernaut's ascendancy to higher education's demise: "What is unique and particularly disturbing about this hyper-market-driven notion of economics is that it makes undemocratic modes of education central to its politics and employs a mode of pedagogy aimed at displacing and shutting down all vestiges of the public

---

33. Henry A. Giroux, *Stormy Weather: Katrina and the Politics of Disposability* (Boulder: Paradigm, 2006), 89.

34. Henry A. Giroux, *Zombie Politics and Culture in the Age of Casino Capitalism* (New York: Peter Lang, 2011), 68.

sphere that cannot be commodified, privatized, and commercialized."[35] Giroux found similarities between the policies that despoil the planet and those that dismantle the public sphere of higher education. He worried that education had become a "form of commerce and nothing more," and that higher education "only matters to the extent that it promotes national prosperity and drives economic growth, technical innovation, and market transformation."[36]

Giroux's trenchant critique could have been directly aimed at my university, which leased its subsurface mineral rights, the very earth beneath our campus, in an apparent bid for short-term economic growth and in concert with national energy policy.[37] The attractiveness of the lease is not surprising given the dramatic decline of higher education funding in the State of Colorado. The American Council on Education reported in 2012 that "public higher education is gradually being privatized." Its statistics showed Colorado leading the nation toward this nadir with its plummeting 69.4 percent drop in higher education funding from 1980 to 2011.[38] Giroux warned of a time of crisis for universities. Financially vulnerable, they are "conscripted to serve as corporate power's apprentice." Giroux cautioned that corporate apprenticeships weaken institutions' ability to foster "critical inquiry, public debate, human acts of justice, and common deliberation."[39] The stress of financial exigency facing higher education permeates its governing bodies and erodes the democratic process. On my campus, this lack of participatory

---

35. Ibid., 68.

36. Giroux, *Neoliberalism's War*, 191.

37. U.S. White House, President Barack Obama, "Energy, Climate Change, and Our Environment," accessed April 29, 2015, https://www.whitehouse.gov/energy/climate-change.

38. Thomas G. Mortenson, "Budget and Appropriations: State Funding: A Race to the Bottom," *American Council on Education*, Winter 2012, http://www.acenet.edu/the-presidency/columns-and-features/Pages/state-funding-a-race-to-the-bottom.aspx. This was a change from $10.52 in fiscal 1980 to $3.22 by fiscal 2011 (the dollar amounts represent the amount spent on higher education per $1,000 of state personal income).

39. Henry A. Giroux, *On Critical Pedagogy* (New York: Continuum, 2011), 11.

deliberation not only characterized the decision-making process around leases, but also the initial and continuing apathetic response of a large portion of the campus and community, who appear to have acquiesced to the top-down decision and accepted the resulting negative consequences to their health and environmental quality of life, along with the implicit judgment of their own disposability.

The Neoliberal Narrative and the Critical Alternative

There are fundamental differences between the official narrative of oil and gas development in the Greeley/Weld County community and the critical narrative I present herein. The Minutes of the Board of Trustees' Meeting reflect the dominant view; they dispassionately describe the mineral rights leasing transaction in entirely economic terms: "UNC has a positive financial opportunity. Over the past year there have been discussions regarding oil and gas on UNC's property. After the negotiation of terms, market rate and the reputations of potential Lessees we are recommending to the Board that we lease these rights . . . There will be no surface oil and gas activity on our property, the drilling is horizontal. The return for us is in the royalty."[40] This narrative is classically neo-liberal in that it is entirely market-driven. In contrast, the critical view of the lease is holistic, addressing more than short-term economic consequences. It sees the extraction of fossil fuels as a process potentially exposing the community to an array of public health and environmental risks, such as those described by public health scientists Drs. Adgate, Goldstein, and McKenzie in a 2014 study.[41] Unfortunately, the Board of Trustees did not have access to the Adgate study in

40. University of Northern Colorado, Board of Trustees, Minutes, September 30, 2011, *University of Northern Colorado*, http://www.unco.edu/trustees/minutes_agendas/minutes_2011-2012/11-18-11%20BOT%20mtg%20minutes%20approved.pdf.

41. John L. Adgate, Bernard D. Goldstein, Lisa M. McKenzie, "Potential Public Health Hazards, Exposures and Health Effects from Unconventional Natural Gas Development," *Environmental Science & Technology* 48, no. 15 (2014), 8307-8320. doi: 10.1021/es404621d.

2010-2011. The decisive deliberations regarding the lease took place behind closed doors over the period of a year, and the public record does not evidence any overt consideration of the community members' rights to approve or disapprove. It appears that it was accomplished without any inclusive discourse or participatory process.

The Encyclopedia of Communication defines social injustice as "the exclusion of under-resourced and marginalized people, groups, organizations, and/or communities from important discourses affecting them."[42] Under the terms of the lease, there would be no surface activities on campus property. The subsurface nature of parts of the extraction process seems to reinforce the tendency to disregard rights of the affected community members. But in reality, there are intensely industrial surface operations associated with fracking.[43] What of the community members who live and work in locations proximate to off-campus surface activities? Of the two surface operation sites tied to the lease, one was proposed to be located in a densely populated working class neighborhood just a couple of blocks from student rental housing, while the second site was to be located less than 500 feet from an elementary school playground. Yet neither campus nor community members living and/or working in proximity to the proposed surface activities were consulted about these locations prior to the announcement of the decision. Those living closest (within 500 feet) were not officially notified until two years later when municipal planning processes required same.

Nancy Carre writes in the *Journal of Social Change* about an analogous situation in Delta County, Colorado involving fracking, environmental justice, and the grassroots participation of community members. She advises that such situations warrant a high level of community involvement: "When developmental policy can adversely affect a community's natural environment and health, it is a matter of social justice and, as such, must be subject to the community members' review and

---

42. Lawrence R. Frey, "Social Justice," in *Encyclopedia of Communication Theory* (Thousand Oaks, CA: Sage Reference, 2009), 908.

43. Adgate, "Potential Public Health Hazards," 8307-08.

approval."[44] But such a process would take time and the dominant market-driven, neoliberal narrative champions an economic agenda of unlimited, unstoppable growth that requires a frenzied pace of oil and gas development. The political backers of the dominant narrative claimed in local newspaper reports that proposed regulations resulting from participatory processes would result in economic catastrophe.[45]

The oil and gas boom began in Weld County, Colorado soon after October of 2009, when a well named "Jake," owned by Enron-spinoff EOG Resources, began producing at impressive rates.[46] As this became more widely known, the number of wells increased exponentially. The following narrative on the Weld County government web page is representative of the dominant viewpoint; it touts the economic benefits and mentions public library districts as beneficiaries of the largesse: "Horizontal drilling has brought new life to the energy industry in Weld County, and today, Weld has more oil and gas wells than any other county in the state; approximately 20,000. The positive economic impact oil and gas has had on the county has been tremendous. Schools, fire districts, libraries as well as county and municipal governments all benefit from this recent oil boom."[47] It is challenging to counter this rhetoric of "tremendous" positive economic impact, with its almost hypnotic mantra of unlimited growth.

Another feature of the dominant narrative is its claim to normalcy. The *Denver Post* provides a record of same:

> Selling mineral rights is no different than other public-private partnerships, such as the Marriott hotel on the Metropolitan State University of Denver campus or the University of Colorado Denver's J.P. Morgan

44. Nancy C. Carre, "Environmental Justice and Hydraulic Fracturing: The Ascendancy of Grassroots Populism in Policy Determination," *Journal of Social Change* 4, no.1 (2012): 1, doi: 10.5590/JOSC.2012.04.1.01.

45. Analisa Romano, "Setback Pushback," *Greeley Tribune*, January 10, 2013.

46. Peggy Williams, "Niobrara Oil Play Heats Up in the Rockies," *Oil and Gas Investor*, February 1, 2010, http://www.oilandgasinvestor.com/peggy/2010/02/01/niobrara-oil-play-heats-up-in-the-rockies.

47. Weld County, Colorado, "Discover Weld County Colorado," *Weld County, Colorado*, accessed November, 2014, http://www.discoverweld.com/about-weldcounty.html.

Center for Commodities, as far as the colleges are concerned. "We've all been forced to be more entrepreneurial in our operations," said UNC president Kay Norton. "We're all maximizing revenues. Certainly, I wouldn't say what we're doing is more extreme than anyone else."[48]

While one may have strong convictions that a situation is ecologically off-balance and socially unjust, it can be difficult to conceive the contrary position and consistently communicate it when one is isolated, constantly bombarded by corporate commercials, and/or living in a community or state where politicians are practiced at parroting Chamber of Commerce talking points that typically cleave to the narrow, market-obsessed neoliberal view.[49] The application of Giroux's critical theory clears away the confusion and exposes the core issues and imbalances of power. In the education literature, I discovered a case analogous to my local situation, and by example it helped me construct a counter-narrative.

Dr. Dilys Schoorman's autoethnographic case study is not environmental in nature, but it involves social justice, activism, and an educator openly challenging an administrative decision. She provides a reflexive, self-revealing account of her experiences as a faculty member and former faculty senator at a university that had decided to name its football stadium after a private prison company.[50] She found this prospect ethically untenable and a matter of social injustice. She offers her account of resistance and critical response as an invitation to fellow faculty to imagine what they would do if faced with a similar situation in their own academic workplace. Schoorman's activism puts into practice the

---

48. Anthony Cotton, "Weld County Schools Use Oil, Gas Leases to Tap into Revenue Streams," *Denver Post*, March 24, 2013, http://www.denverpost.com/ci_22857558/weld-county-schools-use-gas-leases-tap.

49. "Vital for Colorado," *Vital for Colorado*, accessed April 29, 2015, http://www.vitalforcolorado.com/. Unlike the political leadership in the States of New York and Vermont, a majority of the political leaders in the State of Colorado have ignored or actively opposed the grassroots movements for local and statewide banning of fracking; a strong bipartisan coalition supportive of fracking has emerged. Officials from local branches of the Chambers of Commerce are among the leaders of the "Vital for Colorado" pledge-signing coalition.

50. Schoorman, "Resisting the Unholy Alliance," page 510-9.

transformative pedagogy that "relentlessly questions the kinds of labor, practices, and forms of production that are enacted in public and higher education" and her analysis is "relational and contextual, as well as self–reflective and theoretically rigorous." She is engaging in what Giroux describes as "dangerous" critical pedagogy that "must always be contextually defined, allowing it to respond specifically to the ethical and political conditions, social issues formations, and economic problems that arise in various sites in which education takes place."[51]

Schoorman was troubled by the public silence of the faculty. She felt it imperative to safeguard "the role of universities as public spheres for democratic engagement." She frames her response as a critical endeavor. She borrows the rhetoric of Giroux when she says that "engaging proactively against the influences of neoliberalism . . . will require faculty (and students) to reclaim their ability to question in order to subvert 'attempts to eliminate an engaged critique'[52] about neoliberalism's most basic principles and social consequences." Schoorman writes: "Challenging corporatization requires that we develop the critical capacity to see through the charade of corporate rhetoric to ask the basic questions we encourage our students to pose: Whose perspective is being presented? For whose benefit and/or whose loss? What perspectives are excluded? How would their inclusion alter our perspective?"[53] Schoorman champions the social justice principle of inclusion. In her situation, many important perspectives were excluded as only the financial aspects were presented with regard to the decision-making scenario. The short-term economic benefit was touted. Schoorman uses Giroux as a frame for viewing the decision "within the broader context of the increasing corporatization of universities."[54] Her incisive formulation of questions

---

51 . Henry A. Giroux, *America's Education Deficit and the War on Youth* (New York: Monthly Review Press, 2013), 191-2.

52. Schoorman, "Resisting the Unholy Alliance," 515. Schoorman is quoting Giroux's "attempts to eliminate an engaged critique" phrase from his *Harvard Educational Review* article, previously cited in Note 30 above.

53. Ibid., 515.

54. Ibid., 511.

underscores the political value of insisting on responsiveness to those probing questions.

Schoorman's example helped me create a critical, Girouxian reading of the untenable situation at my campus. I refused to acquiesce to the normalcy of the narrow neoliberal agenda. I instead examined the sociopolitical context in a panoramic manner and asked: 1) How could it have been accomplished differently?[55] Who was excluded? In harmony with an egalitarian concept of power, the decision whether to frack could have been made in a participatory, democratic manner, with the full participation of university employees and community stakeholders; 2) Then, believing in political possibilities, I pondered, how could the situation be deconstructed? Because ideas and events reflect socially-constructed reality, even though the decision was made in a non-participatory manner and a contract was signed, the entirety of the process and policy should be subject to question, intervention, and restorative justice; 3) Third, I queried, what kind of environment would be conducive to open-mindedness and change? Ideally, universities are non-commodified public spheres and debate and discussion about fracking should be copious and fear-free. The options are plentiful and apparent when we approach the debate with an open mind: changing the severance tax structure, kick-starting alternative energy, reconsidering our economic priorities, and so on; 4) Finally, I asked, what information was excluded? Externalities such as long-term environmental damage and public health impacts were not considered; it appears to have been a purely market-driven decision. When perceived through a critical lens, the limitations of the decision-making process become apparent: the process precluded debate, excluded information, lacked connection with the community, and was structured to be politically non-responsive.

---

55. Bousson Advisory Group, "The Bousson Advisory Group," *Allegheny College*, accessed April 27, 2015, http://sites.allegheny.edu/boussonadvisorygroup/. The example of Allegheny College is instructive. Faced with a similar conundrum regarding fracking beneath their campus, they reacted in an entirely different manner than UNC, implementing a process that was democratically participatory in nature.

Giroux in the Library Literature

Let's further test Giroux. How have librarians applied his theories to date? Giroux appears only sporadically in the library literature within the last thirty years, and at first in relatively broad, conceptual applications of critical theory. In a 1994 critique of libraries' acquiescence to neoliberalism, John Buschman highlighted Giroux's demarcation and defense of the public sphere and its democracy-enhancing capabilities. Buschman criticized libraries' rush toward electronic formats, technologization, and entrepreneurship; he damned the aggressively servile attitude toward the dominant economic and technical agenda. He lambasted the failure "to promote an ethic of civic responsibility" and decried the lack of protection afforded critical democratic public spaces. He argued that "Libraries should be among the critical public spaces which fundamentally support and advance democracy" rather than bolster the market economy.[56]

A decade later, in 2004, Ryan Gage advocated for a critical approach toward librarianship: "Giroux's work is highly translatable and applicable to librarians" because it addresses "how and why public institutions such as schools, higher education, and libraries should be boldly fought for and why their value as sites of struggle and contestation requires further diagnosis, critique, and engaged participation."[57] Gage posited that libraries and LIS schools fall short of upholding their lofty ideals of "democracy, human emancipation, intellectual freedom and quality living standards" and instead merely preserve "the interests and legitimacy of class, commerce and professional stagnation."[58] Gage concluded with

---

56. John Buschman, "Taking a Hard Look at Technology and Librarianship: Compliance, Complicity, and the Intellectual Independence of the Profession," *Argus* 23, no. 2 (1994), 14.

57. Ryan A. Gage, "Henry Giroux's Abandoned Generation & Critical Librarianship: A Review Article," *Progressive Librarian* 23 (2004), 67 http://progressivelibrariansguild.org/PL_Jnl/pdf/PL23_spring2004.pdf.

58. Ibid., 73-4.

a straightforward plea to the profession to become self-reflexive, move out of complacency, and shake up the status quo.

In contrast to the conceptual approach of the foregoing articles, more recent scholars are concerned with praxis. Writing about critical theory and library instruction in 2010, Ruth Mirtz personalizes Giroux's philosophy, describing how she altered her teaching practice. She applied Giroux's philosophies to the topic of disintermediated learning, critically analyzing the do-it-yourself nature of Google-empowered research. On its face, independent learning may seem to be in harmony with an anti-authoritarian approach such as critical pedagogy. But Mirtz explains that the situation is not so simple. She confronts the commodification of education, querying, "In what ways do students 'buy' their education at the university, especially at the library? …Our answers depend on whether we primarily see the library as a service to students or … as an approach to lifelong learning."[59] She applies critical pedagogic theory in several scenarios, noting how librarians can empower students. Ultimately, she concludes that more mediation at the most opportune time provides a better educational experience for student and teacher. Mirtz does not shirk from difficult, nuanced questions about the broader political context: "Librarians have to ask if their fears of disintermediation are about their feelings of professional isolation, or insulation from other disciplines on campus, or their marginality in faculty governance, or economic exploitation by the university, or their fears of being pushed out of their socioeconomic and intellectual status in the community."[60] Mirtz conducts a thoughtful, rigorous, and self-reflective analysis. She is asking a psychologically difficult but seminal question: Are librarians disposable in the neoliberal schema?

Critical theory figures prominently in the text *Information Literacy and Social Justice*. Toni Samek boldly states in the foreword: "This is not your average information literacy text; thank goodness for that. It is high time we acknowledged openly how information literacy has been co-opted

---

59. Mirtz, "Disintermediation and Resistance," 297.
60. Ibid., 303.

by corporatist efficiencies and risk management." The book's goal is "to provide concrete examples of our labor as social justice work . . . to recognize our being in our doing."[61] In a chapter about the public academic library, Patti Ryan and Lisa Sloniowski cite Giroux and ask probing, reflexive questions: "How does one engage in a radical pedagogical praxis when constrained by a growing awareness of the ways in which academic libraries and librarians have become institutions of hegemonic order and often serve the imperatives of neoliberal capitalism that have dominated political and social discourse for the last thirty years?"[62] The co-authors demonstrate their simultaneous performance of dual roles as educators and citizens. They manifest the creativity and hopefulness characteristic of Giroux's critical theory when they ask: "How might we develop an alternate vision of libraries as imaginative and conceptual spaces of resistance?"[63] Ryan and Sloniowski describe the risk they took in teaching workshops on two controversial issues—the Iraq War and the Occupy Movement. They shunned hierarchy when they actively sought "to build solidarity" with their communities "as allies and equals, rather than as servants, information gatekeepers, and/ or pedagogues."[64] Ryan and Sloniowski express genuinely counterhegemonic ideas, document the performance of same, and analyze the results in a self-reflexive manner.

Schroeder and Hollister's 2014 article explored the relevance of critical theory and social justice to quotidian, everyday librarianship. The co-authors surveyed librarians' actual understanding and use of critical theory. A majority of the librarians surveyed were aware of critical theory (two thirds of the 369 librarians who took the survey were somewhat familiar with critical theory and theorists, while one-third had no familiarity with critical theory). When the group with familiarity was asked

61. Toni Samek, Foreword to *Information Literacy and Social Justice*, edited by Lua Gregory and Shana Higgins, Sacramento, CA: Library Juice Press, 2013), viii-ix.

62. Ryan and Sloniowski, "The Public Academic Library," 275.

63. Ibid., 275.

64. Ibid., 294.

"What keywords or theorists would you associate with critical theory," forty-one responses named the discipline of education, and Giroux was among the sixteen theorists named within that discipline. The surveyors found that "many librarians are concerned with social justice issues as they relate to the library, and many of them act upon these issues in their professional practices."[65] When asked, "to what extent does critical theory play a role in your professional life as a librarian," more than half of the respondents indicated that critical theory played a role in their professional lives to some extent, and many gave specific examples of how they applied a concept of critical theory to their practice.

Bales and Engle's 2012 piece is an interesting hybrid;[66] it is primarily conceptual, although a great portion of the article consists of an annotated bibliography intended to support strategic counterhegemonic actions.[67] It is replete with rousing rhetoric in which the authors challenge fellow academic librarians to become counterhegemonic intellectuals. They question the professional neutrality that is codified in the ALA Code of Ethics and ask: "When does a social justice issue become mainstream enough for the library to promote it?"[68] They cite Stanley Aronowitz and Henry Giroux's concept of the "accommodating

---

65. Robert Schroeder and Christopher V. Hollister, "Librarian's Views on Critical Theories and Critical Practices," *Behavioral & Social Sciences Librarian* 33, no.2 (2014): 113, doi: 10:1080/01639269.2014.912104.

66. Stephen E. Bales and Lea S. Engle, "The Counterhegemonic Academic Librarian: A Call to Action," *Progressive Librarian* 40, 16-40 (2012), 16-40, http://progressivelibrariansguild.org/PL_Jnl/pdf/PL_40.pdf.

67. Stephen E. Bales and Lea S. Engle, "The Counterhegemonic Academic Librarian," 30; J. K. Gibson-Graham and Gerda Roelvink, "An Economic Ethics for the Anthropocene," *Antipode* 41, S1 (2009), 320-346. The most pertinent and interestingly subversive of the annotations in Bales and Engle's article is Gibson-Graham's "An Economic Ethics for the Anthropocene." It concerns the innovative concepts of "hybrid research collectives" and "research as activism." If one delves into the full-text Antipode article, one discovers that this innovation is precipitated by humanity-threatening global climate change.

68. Stephen E. Bales and Lea S. Engle, "The Counterhegemonic Academic Librarian," 20.

intellectual" whose politics "further the interests of the dominant classes."[69] Bales and Engle call on academic librarians to "act politically . . . in consciously transformative ways that address inequities in society and the institutions that reproduce society."[70]

Critical library literature regarding environmental justice is elusive. Rachel Longstaff describes her development of cross-curricular environmental justice programming at her university's annual *Focus the Nation* event regarding climate change: "The strength of the interdisciplinary nature of the Social Justice program at Saint Leo University lies in the opportunity to work together in drawing connections between the disciplines."[71] In the library literature, environmentally-themed articles typically address recycling, conservation, and green building design. George Aulisio goes a step further in his article about sustainable academic libraries. He encourages academic librarians to work across campus inter-departmentally, both educating students and actively promoting library sustainability initiatives. He concludes that "Simply through education, leading by example, and outreach, librarians can make their library a 'green library.'"[72] While both of these authors' topics are laudable, they were not critical in their analysis and political activism was not their concern.

While the following articles do not mention Giroux, they are part of a noticeable upsurge in recent library literature concerning social justice and academic libraries. Myrna Morales and her co-authors have a two-pronged suggestion for academic libraries: first, diversify the library profession, and second, actively pursue social justice. They call on academicians to transform their "practices and standards in ways that

---

69. Stanley Aronowitz and Henry A. Giroux, *Education Still Under Siege* (Westport, CT: Bergin & Garvey, 1993).

70. Stephen E. Bales and Lea S. Engle, "The Counterhegemonic Academic Librarian," 23.

71. Longstaff, Rachel, "Social Justice across the Curriculum: Librarians as Campus Leaders," *Catholic Library World* 81, no. 4 (June 2011), 289.

72. George J. Aulisio, "Green Libraries Are More than Just Buildings," *Electronic Green Journal* 1, no. 35 (2013), 8, https://escholarship.org/uc/item/3x11862z.

leverage the power, expertise, and responsibility of academic librarians and libraries as forces for social justice."[73] A groundbreaking and thorough case study of social justice advocacy by library and information science (LIS) academics appeared in 2014. Bharat Mehra and Donna Braquet describe their participatory leadership and action research at the University of Tennessee-Knoxville (UTK). They document their extended, multi-year advocacy for a social justice/human rights issue—the implementation of LGBT partnership benefits at UTK. The authors conceive of their study as an illustration of extended social justice-related roles for academic librarians and other LIS professionals, aiding them in ". . . becoming active supporters of human rights by strongly affirming their commitment, via concrete and tangible actions, to diversity of all forms and by developing a socially progressive community based on democratic ideals of equality, justice, and fairness for all human beings." Complete with flowchart and a list of eight recommended directions to guide information professionals in advocating for marginalized groups, the chapter serves as both a useful handbook, inspiring exemplar, and richly instructive case study.[74]

The trending subject of social justice within academic libraries continues to rise with these two items that appeared in the April 2015 issue of *College & Research Libraries News*. In her "call to microactivism," Rachel Lockman urges academic librarians to begin practicing small-scale activism so their work "can be in dialogue with larger movements" and lead to progressive change. She urges us to form community "in the face of change-averse academic administrations and the behemoth of systemic oppression."[75] Another article in the same issue is a call to action with regard to the "Black Lives Matter" movement. The author advocates for

73. Myrna Morales, Em Claire Knowles, and Chris Bourg, "Diversity, Social Justice, and the Future of Libraries," *portal: Libraries and the Academy* 14, no. 3 (July 2014), 439-51. 448, doi: 10.1353/pla.2014.0017.

74. Bharat Mehra and Donna Braquet, "Marriage between Participatory Leadership and Action Research," 191.

75. Rachel Lockman, "The Way I See It: Academic Librarians and Social Justice: A Call to Microactivism," *College & Research Libraries News* 76, no. 4 (April 2015), 194.

"interrogating the oppressive structures at the heart of what remains a very white librarianship."[76] These two articles are forthright in their clarion calls, and will hopefully inspire a resurgence of activism. The scholarly communication of idealism can be a precursor to activism, but can also be a terminus. This is understandable as the actual leap from concept to action can be daunting.

Standing on the Ledge: Overcoming Well-Informed Futility and Fear with Collegiality as Catalyst and Conscience as Guide

Most situations will be quotidian and may call for micro-activism. The micro-activism that Lockman recommends could become a habit, and one that involves no indecisive angst, but fighting social justice incursions with real involvement demands soul-searching. The real-life application of progressive principles is unruly. The philosophical foundations of critical librarianship provide an essential framework for discussion and analysis; but they also project an illusion of logic and order. When such ideas are applied and fleshed out in real life, their embodiment is individual and messy. Here are some questions to help you critique and decide when to go public with information activism and when to deviate from neutrality: 1) Does your heart tell you to pursue this particular issue? 2) Are you motivated enough to overcome any fear? 3) Do you have an adequate support system? 4) Does the situation rise to a level that justifies taking on the risk of public non-neutrality?

I return to the rousing rhetoric of the Bales and Engle article because it urges such risk-taking, challenging academic librarians to create a counterculture of material support necessary to effect social change: "Counter-hegemonic academic librarians need not rely on the master's house for support but need to make themselves visible through action

---

76. Nicole Pagowsky and Niamh Wallace, "Black Lives Matter! Shedding Library Neutrality Rhetoric for Social Justice," *College & Research Libraries News* 76, no. 4 (April 2015), 200.

and scholarship to create networks of best practices and support."[77] While I laud their enthusiastic encouragement of librarians to take the leap into action, this lofty rhetoric glosses over the fact that academic librarians do rely on the master's house for economic support—their salaries. In counterpoint, Giroux warns that dissent is dangerous in academia: "Increasingly, as universities are shaped by a culture of fear in which dissent is equated with treason, the call to be objective and impartial, whatever one's intentions, can easily echo what George Orwell called the official truth or the establishment point of view."[78] Per Giroux, scholars now confront an environment with no mere paucity of democracy; it is a frightening, heavily-censored sphere. No wonder there is a hesitation to leap into action. Even if one successfully parses when neutrality is apt and when not, there is obvious tension between the need for academic activism and Giroux's perception of academia as an Orwellian culture full of fear. How can these two factors be resolved in order to discern an ethical but non-martyring course of action? Are we prepared to be public intellectuals, to be openly and publicly frank regarding counter-hegemonic positions? The growing trends in our profession toward proactive outreach, embedded instruction, and community engagement[79] are pushing many of us into more extroverted roles, similar to that of the public intellectual. But do the boosters of community and civic engagement conceive of these activities as including opposition to the neoliberal agenda and the open critique of decision-makers in one's campus and community? Nancy Kranich enthusiastically advises academic librarians to seize the day: "Now is the time for academic libraries to assume their rightful role in creating a new generation of informed citizens capable of acting to address complex, urgent social problems." Kranich's agenda is ambitious and progressive, but less confrontational

---

77. Stephen E. Bales and Lea S. Engle, "The Counterhegemonic Academic Librarian," 32.

78. Giroux, *Youth in a Suspect Society*, 137.

79. Nancy Kranich, Michele Reid, and Taylor Willingham, "Civic Engagement in Academic Libraries: Encouraging Active Citizenship," *College & Research Libraries News* 65, no. 7 (July/August 2004), 380-400.

than the critical points of view documented herein: "By sponsoring and promoting deliberative forums, librarians can foster student learning and faculty research while expanding linkages between the campus and its various communities."[80] It may be a matter of degree, stage, and philosophical approach. I argue that critical theory and direct political action are necessary to address human rights violations and other social injustices. The more conciliatory, corrective, and connective approach advocated by Kranich is viable once rights protections and remedies are in place. And the level of responsiveness or non-responsiveness of those in power is a factor as well.[81]

Critical theory, by definition, confronts and interrogates the power structure inherent in institutions. The critical theory of Giroux ventures boldly into an activist realm. "If educators are to function as public intellectuals . . ." Giroux says they must engage in "a practice of freedom that points to new and radical forms of pedagogies that have a direct link to building social movements in and out of colleges and universities."[82] I've demonstrated that Giroux's theories are apt for academic librarianship. The review of Giroux's appearances in the library literature provided a confirmation of same. The literature needs more case studies of location- and context-specific critical, counterhegemonic librarianship or professorship (such as Schoorman and Mehra/Braquet within). While Mirtz' and Ryan's articles concerned critical practice of librarianship (critical pedagogy specifically applied in teaching or programming situations), they are not directly analogous to the case study herein. Librarians need more examples along the entire continuum of

---

80. Ibid., 383.

81. Toni Samek, *Librarianship and Human Rights: A Twenty-First Century Guide* (Oxford: Chandos: 2007): xxv-xxvi. Samek "portrays library and information workers as participants and interventionists in social conflict"; she champions the global information justice movement, xxv-xxvi; Nancy Kranich, "Reviews: Review of Toni Samek's Librarianship and Human Rights: A Twenty-First Century Guide," Library Quarterly 78, no. 3 (July 2008): 343-5. Kranich praises Samek's passion for human rights but criticizes her for preaching to the choir; Kranich would prefer a more focused, traditional approach to the subject matter.

82. Giroux, *Neoliberalism's War on Higher Education*, 145-6.

counterhegemony—from mild to wild acts of critical librarianship/
professorship. Schoorman's experience appears to be a rare success story.
The AK Press anthology, *Academic Repression: Reflections from the Academic-
Industrial Complex*, tells the stories of professors variously punished and
martyred for their views and actions.[83]

I am willing to be provocative, but I don't want to endanger or
martyr myself when I engage in the "dangerous" critical pedagogy that
is "contextually defined" and "responsive" to the "ethical and political conditions, social issues formations, and economic problems"[84] on
my campus. And in all honesty, my decision to act was not an elegant,
erudite application of critical theory or an easy exercise in discernment,
nor was it based on the measured perusal of a literature review. I had
waited for twenty-one months for someone else to come forward and
go public, but no one else on campus stood up. I became the one for
whom I waited, eventually.[85] But at first I was mired in fear and well-
informed futility. The hardest questions for me were: Was I willing to
act? How effective would my action be?

Fortunately, well-informed futility is merely learned helplessness, so it
can be unlearned. Environmental writer Sandra Steingraber explains that
the term was used by psychologist Gerhart Wiebe in 1973 to describe
the reaction of Americans to the barrage of television coverage about
the protracted Vietnam War: "Wiebe noticed that a steady onslaught
of information about a problem over which people feel little sense of
personal agency gives rise to futility. Ironically, the more knowledgeable
we are about a problem, the more we are filled with paralyzing futility.
Futility, in turn, forestalls action. But action is exactly what is necessary
to overcome futility."[86] Several factors converged to help jolt me out of

---

83. Anthony J. Nocella II, Steven Best, and Peter McLaren, editors, *Academic Repression: Reflections from the Academic-Industrial Complex* (Oakland, CA:
AK Press, 2010).

84. Giroux, *America's Education Deficit and the War on Youth*, 191-2.

85. Alice Walker, *We Are the Ones We Have Been Waiting For: Inner Light in a
Time of Darkness* (New York: New Press, 2007).

86. Steingraber, *Raising Elijah*, 46.

my futility. The obvious factor was geographic proximity. The climate change crisis manifested in my community as an upsurge in oil and gas activity. While not literally in my back yard, it's in my community, as we are literally surrounded by more than 22,000 active wells.[87] This is the proverbial NIMBYism.

Part of the dynamic is highly personal, involving age and health. As a younger adult, I would not have been able to engage to the level at which I'm involved. My personality is partly conducive to activism and partly not (my idealism and sense of fairness are in direct conflict with my people-pleasing nature, and oft-times the fearful people-pleaser is ascendant); I don't know if I would have had the confidence as a younger person. But I'm middle-aged—fifty-five, I have Parkinson's disease, and time is very precious to me. Age and illness have given me a sense of urgency and confidence I did not possess when younger and healthier. I was moving closer to willingness, to overcoming my fear. In January of 2013 I did start a community group. But I still was not ready to be an on-campus activist, to be political in the pedagogical sphere.

Even though I was highly motivated when I started my community group, I did not hold out much hope for change. But I reached out to a community organizer who had experience working on oil and gas issues. Because of his political experience and acumen, he saw the potential for positive activism to accomplish political gain and compromise in situations where I saw none. I learned something life-changing from this experience. It infused hopefulness in situations that seemed past help. Looking at circumstances through a political lens was a new experience for me. There were things that could be changed, negotiated, and mitigated. Laws, regulations, and contracts could be amended; alliances could be made, compromises arranged. Influence could be wielded, power leveraged. I did have a belief in possibilities. I didn't know if my

87. Colorado Oil and Gas Conservation Commission, "Number of Active Colorado Oil & Gas Wells by County," *State of Colorado*, accessed April 29, 2015, https://cogcc.state.co.us/Library/Statistics/CoWklyMnthlyOGStats. pdf. Twenty-two thousand, three hundred eighteen active wells, to be exact, as of April 2, 2015.

actions would be effective, but I now believed it was possible that they could make a difference.

In my application essay for LIS graduate school in 1990, I recall reciting the tired truism, "information is power." By conveniently limiting my belief in the equivalence of information to power, I managed to avoid taking action. Twenty-five years later, I know that truism was insufficient; it left out the intervening, inactive stage of well-informed futility. I'd been drifting in and out of this stage for most of my adult life. But having had the experience of transcending futility, and subsequently discovering and applying Giroux, I would now change the truism from "information is power" to say, "transformational action is power." My activism was a leap of faith into the unknown, beyond futility and fear. At that juncture, the alternative community became a lifeline and agent for change.

The social network became the final aspect that pushed me out of inaction into activism. I would not have made the leap without the catalyzing collegiality of one person, and that happened somewhat serendipitously. I had been active for about six months in the grassroots community environmental group Weld Air and Water and was interviewed by the *New York Times*.[88] A colleague saw this and contacted me. She was interested in raising the issue of the non-democratic nature of the leasing process in the Faculty Senate. It was ironic that she became aware of me through national media rather than locally. But this serendipitous connection brought forth all the encouragement I needed. Solidarity with one or two others was enough. Meaningful personal interaction and collaboration were the catalysts that moved me out of inertia.

Was it wise to take action? This is where the support systems that guarantee academic and intellectual freedom come into play. To avoid martyrdom, it is important to be part of a tenure system that affords some amount of protection. And as time went on, it was helpful that we

---

88. Jack Healy, "Supporting Oil and Gas, but Resisting Encroachment," *New York Times*, June 9, 2013, http://www.nytimes.com/2013/06/10/us/supporting-oil-and-gas-but-resisting-encroachment.html.

grew from a group of three to a group of seventeen. There was safety and solidarity in numbers. While I hope my personal, specific example is helpful to the reader, I must emphasize—the key was collective action. Alone, I was unable to break out of the Orwellian prison of neoliberally and self-imposed silence. The beginning of discourse and our continuing collective action is still for me a miraculous turn of events.

Regarding the level of activism, was direct, albeit mild, provocation the way to go? Why not try the tempered, more moderate activism of professional development (e.g., mentoring, organizing forums, and utilizing existing networks)?[89] In this situation, some tempered activism had been ongoing. After the deal was inked on November 23, 2011, the immediate reaction of faculty was swift but noncommittal. A fairly low-key informational meeting was called and a mailing list formed, but no subsequent activity emerged at that time. Some tempered activism took place, very much under the radar (mentoring students, etc.). The most visible event was the appearance of activist filmmaker Josh Fox[90] on campus as a grant-funded guest speaker, and the co-sponsorship of two League of Women Voters community discussion roundtables. I co-created a pro/con research Libguide.[91] During 2012, I approached the local AAUP chapter and suggested action, but was declined. I was directed toward the more appropriate venue, the Faculty Senate, but did not have the heart or courage to approach it by myself at that time. That courage did not come for another year.

While collegiality was the catalyst, it was consciousness of the environmental justice aspects that gnawed at my conscience and fueled my desire for provocative political action. This was my workplace, my institution that had signed the lease, thus enabling what I deemed to

89. Adrianna Kezar, Tricia B. Gallant, and Jaime Lester, "Everyday People Making a Difference on College Campuses: The Tempered Grassroots Leadership Tactics of Faculty and Staff," *Studies in Higher Education* 36, no. 2 (2011), 129-151, doi: 10.1080/03075070903532304.

90. *Gasland*, directed by Josh Fox (New Video, 2010), DVD.

91. Wendy Highby and Bette Rathe, "Hydraulic Fracturing or Fracking Information," (Research Guide), *University of Northern Colorado*, accessed April 30, 2015, http://libguides.unco.edu/fracking.

be a dangerous practice. I felt responsible. By remaining silent, I was acquiescing. I felt the circumstances rose to a level that justified direct political action, given the public health and environmental danger. The biopolitical power of the neoliberal state was being used in my backyard to contribute to irreversible climate change. A powerful corporate-governmental alliance chose who was to be subjected to risks and at what level. And climate change impacts are felt most severely by the poorest of the poor.[92]

Breaking the Neoliberal Norm of Silence and Using the Strengths of Librarianship

The well-informed futility due to information overload can be less problematic than neoliberalism's "unassailable appeal of to common sense" and its "attempts to eliminate an engaged critique."[93] This formidable, untouchable stance of neoliberalism effectively dampens critical inquiry. It is accomplished in great part through self-censorship. Schoorman delineates the reason to overcome these fears and go public: "The ability to present these analyses succinctly and clearly to public audiences is central to a faculty's ability to engage as public intellectuals, especially when countering specific neoliberal assaults on the academy."[94] It is important to be as open and clear as possible. In some situations, for reasons of self-protection, you must speak in parables. But don't use them as the default. Giroux advocates for ". . . inventing a language that can create democratic public spheres in which new subjects and identities can be produced that are capable of recognizing and addressing the plight of the other and struggling collectively to expand and deepen the ongoing struggle for justice, freedom and democratization."[95]

---

92. United Nations, "UN and Climate Change," accessed April 29, 2015.

93. Giroux, "Neoliberalism, Corporate Culture, and the Promise of Higher Education," 428.

94. Schoorman, "Resisting the Unholy Alliance," 515.

95. Giroux, *Neoliberalism's War on Higher Education*, 204.

In September of 2013, twenty-one months after the lease was signed, I presented my PowerPoint plea for an investigative task force to the Faculty Senate.[96] This was my opportunity to help my colleagues recognize the "plight of the other," to understand that some economically-driven decisions have environmentally unjust consequences. I was anxious, but I soldiered through. I focused on my PowerPoint and didn't make much eye contact with the audience. I was highly conscious that I was breaking protocol, shattering the silent norm. In hindsight, I'm amazed that I did it. I am by no means a charismatic speaker, and I am truly poor at improvisational speaking. I am introverted and not practiced in building political alliances. But I had these things going for me: the courage of my convictions, the collegiality of two allies, and the relative safety of tenure as an associate professor. Additionally, and most importantly, I had my librarianship: *I knew my information.* I had chosen the best evidence and analyzed it logically and succinctly. I brought forward the public health and environmental science that had been ignored by the neoliberal narrative. I framed our concerns diplomatically, noting that some critical public health and environmental science information had not yet been published at the time the Board of Trustees made its decision. It was a perfect storm, a convergence of information and action. My training and varied experiences as an information professional gave me enough of an edge to counter my weaknesses. I was the conduit of crucial information on that difficult day—as an intellectual attempting to transform my campus and community, I was an unlikely and reluctant performer.

Essentially, I functioned as an information critic that day. I pointed out serious information gaps and the fact that impact science had been overlooked.[97] I attempted to intervene in the process because certain

---

96. Wendy Highby, Mark Anderson, and Marilyn Welsh, Hydro-fracturing PowerPoint Presentation to Faculty Senate, September 30, 2013, *University of Northern Colorado,* http://www.unco.edu/facultysenate/Campus%20Health%20and%20Safety%20Concerns%20Related%20to%20Hydrofracturing%2009302013PP-Highby.pptx.

97. Aaron McCright, Katherine Dentzman, Meghan Charters, and Thomas Dietz, "The Influence of Political Ideology on Trust in Science," *Environmental Research Letters* 8 (2013), doi: 10.1088/1748-9326/8/4/044029.

crucial pieces of information had not been considered in the decision-making phase. Librarians have so much to bring to the table: awareness of the knowledge production system and its sociopolitical context; comfort with multi-disciplinary approaches; a perspective and cognitive approach that is holistic; an ability to toggle between detailed micro-level analysis and the macro-sociopolitical level; a high consciousness of the limits of our knowledge with the humility to admit same; and general resourcefulness.

Librarians are well qualified and positioned to become public intellectuals and to publicly criticize information organization, production, and application. Jack Andersen uses the philosophy of Habermas and critical theory to encourage librarians to become information critics. He cites Habermas' generative theory of the social organization of society, which includes the production and organization of knowledge emanating from the various disciplines.[98] Especially noteworthy is Andersen's concern about the service of democracy: "Information critics can make an important contribution to the public's understanding of how the many knowledge organization activities going on in society operate and how these, in the long run, serve or suppress democratic purposes."[99] He suggests that librarians publicize and promote discussion of knowledge organization problems and place them within a social and cultural context.[100] Authors Mehra and Braquet are similar to Andersen in their desire to see librarians stretch themselves and increase their involvement in a broader range of knowledge-related activities. But with the added dimension of human rights, they affirm the dignity of both the LGBT community and library professionals. In their case study, they advocate for the highest potential of all parties. In the self-study of policy-making, leadership, and social justice advocacy by LIS professionals in an academic setting, the authors list in detail eight recommended and very transferable directions in which LIS leaders can extend their

98. Andersen, "Information Criticism, Where Is It?" 102-3.
99. Ibid.,104.
100. Ibid.,104-5.

professional influence for the purposes of advocacy. Each of these directions encompasses skills, expertise, and talents that information professionals can employ to empower a marginalized group and realize a socially just world. As an example, their first direction, "Strategize Your LIS Role in Meeting the Needs of Marginalized Populations In Your Community," includes, and then goes beyond the traditional role of information access provision to encompass power, prestige, resources, and social acceptance. Strategic planning (and subsequent implementation) requires excellent analytical skills, emotional intelligence, and sociopolitical awareness.[101] The pragmatic, humanitarian, and affirming nature of the project makes it a standout example of transformative pedagogy within the library literature.

The Collective Action of Frack*ED: Community and Visibility

Frack*ED@UNC, née The Hydrofracturing Task Force, has taken on the unending quest that Giroux describes as "transformative pedagogy." This sometimes quixotic activism "relentlessly questions the kinds of labor, practices, and forms of production that are enacted in public and higher education. Such an analysis should be relational and contextual, as well as self–reflective and theoretically rigorous."[102] And relentlessness has been necessary, given the turn of events. Our request for the formation of an official task force was denied, but we were given pseudo-legitimacy by this limited sanction and a small degree of official recognition by the body: if we chose to form on an ad hoc/independent basis, they would grant us two official representatives from the Senate.[103] What does this say about the state of governance on our

---

101. Bharat Mehra and Donna Braquet, "Marriage between Participatory Leadership and Action Research," 197-8.

102. Giroux, *America's Education Deficit and the War on Youth*, 191.

103. University of Northern Colorado, Faculty Senate Forum, "Minutes of the September 30, 2013 Senate Meeting," *University of Northern Colorado*, accessed April 29, 2015, http://www.unco.edu/facultysenate/September%20 30,%202013%20sen%20min.pdf.

campus? Perhaps it was not progressive, independent, or strong enough to handle such a neoliberal hot potato. But we were not privy to their strategic plans, so the following is conjectural. Their rationale was not clear, cloaked as it was in a brief but complicated discussion of rules of order. We're not sure why we were given this limbo-like pseudo status. Perhaps it was a deflective, self-protective and conflict-avoidant move, or it could have been a friendly gesture intended to give us more tactical freedom as a non-official group, able to set our own rules. Or maybe it should be taken at face value, as a procedurally expedient tactic.

There were pros and cons to this pseudo-legitimacy. Set adrift in this limbo of pseudo-status with no budget and little time to spare (as typically busy academics), we were now a group of four—myself and three fellow faculty members, two of whom were senators. We spent the next month and a half crafting our official charge and seeking representatives from each college and each campus group. In this task we were mostly successful, securing representatives from many of the scholarly divisions (all but two) and representative groups on campus (we had difficulties retaining classified staff representatives). Our first meeting was with University Counsel; he provided us a copy of the mineral rights lease and answered our questions regarding due diligence. Initially, our plans were much too ambitious; we imagined that each member of the Hydrofracturing Task Force would have the time and energy to become at least fundamentally expert on an aspect of fracking-related knowledge. No one was able to dedicate this amount of time to a volunteer, pseudo-sanctioned endeavor. With no money, limited access to campus resources (we used on-campus meeting space and communicated via campus email, but communication proved to be a challenge at times, because we were denied access to the bulk mail features of campus listservs), we secured volunteer guest speakers and hosted several information fora: a State regulatory agency representative, oil company representatives, a community activist, a retired corporate risk manager, and an occupational health expert. We toured an active well site. We created a web presence on Facebook[104] and opened a Gmail account. We co-sponsored a CU-Boulder think tank's informational series of expert panels, grateful that they brought their educational road show (called "FrackingSense") to northern Colorado. The content covered the basics of fracking, and the public health and policy aspects of same.[105]

In May, we issued our "Progress Report, Interim Findings, and Recommendations," distributing them to the Board of Trustees, University administrators and deans, and to colleagues. The Hydrofracturing Task Force refused to consider the process final and beyond mitigation. We presented two findings: first, we contended that extraction of oil and gas is a heavily industrial process that poses environmental risks; and second, we found our university was facing a potential public relations problem. We recommended a precautionary moratorium, further transparent dialogue, economic analysis that includes externalities and the repair of our public image by setting an environmentally-conscious example by joining the "Fossil Free" divestment initiative"[106] [see **Table 1**]. In the cover email for the "Progress Report," we announced our plans to go to the media; but then we began to have second thoughts about the timing of this action.

We backtracked and asked for a meeting with university administration prior to releasing our findings to the media. We had communicated indirectly via University Counsel and the Environmental Health & Safety Office, but never directly with the university president. We decided to make the first overture and asked for a meeting. We met with support staff initially and then got a direct meeting in midsummer. Although it was cordial, it was apparent that there was no movement on the basic

---

104. Frack*ED@UNC, née UNC Hydrofracturing Task Force. Facebook page, *Hydrofracturing Task Force*, accessed April 29, 2015, https://www.facebook.com/UNCHydrofracturing.

105. Center for the American West, "Events: FrackingSENSE: Greeley," Center for the American West. University of Colorado at Boulder, accessed April 27, 2015, https://centerwest.org/events/frackingsense-greeley.

106. Frack*ED@UNC, nee UNC Hydrofracturing Task Force, "Progress Report, Interim Findings." 2014. The Report was accompanied by an Appendix with 34 items.

Table 1: UNC Hydrofracturing Task Force. "Progress Report,
Interim Findings, and Recommendations." May 9, 2014

Finding 1: Unconventional natural gas (UNG) production is a multi-stage, potentially hazardous, heavily industrial process. The proposed UNC production locations pose substantial health and safety risks to our campus and community. These negative externalities were not considered in the financial analysis of the decision.	Recommendation 1: We recommend a moratorium on development of the above-noted locations until: (1) critical knowledge gaps are filled regarding cumulative risk and public health stressors; (2) the specific location-related concerns, as iterated above, are addressed; and (3) we raise the awareness level about the planned UNG production, engage in transparent dialogue about this decision, and work to repair our public image.
Finding 2: UNC has a potential public relations problem that we fear will impact our university's public image, student enrollment, and faculty and staff retention.	Recommendation 2: UNC can work to repair our public image by setting an environmentally-conscious example. First, we can mitigate our current carbon footprint by joining the "Go Fossil Free" divestment initiative. Second, we can conduct and make public an economic analysis of the true costs and benefits of UNG development, one that takes the negative externalities into consideration.

positions of each party regarding the lease and energy issues. Around that
same time, the oil and gas company (lessee) leaked to the press that the
proposed surface operations site closest to the University dorms might
be relocated farther east and thus farther from the densely populated
location.[107] This was a very significant development, as the Hydrofracturing Task Force had deep concerns about two issues: 1) the public health
implications of the close proximity of North Campus, residences, and
small businesses, and 2) the lack of notification to student renters and

107. Sharon Dunn, "East Greeley Drilling Site May Move to Another Location," *Greeley Tribune*, June 21, 2014.

others in the neighborhood. By the end of the summer, the permits to drill had indeed been withdrawn from the permitting process, so we did not release our findings to the media.

While we'll never know what happened behind closed doors, we feel our activism likely played a part in the relocation of the problematic site. The site contiguous to the elementary school playground has also been relocated so that it is now further away from the playground (more than 1,000 feet), though still too close to comfort many of the parents. It is still in the midst of municipal zoning processes. Though one location-related crisis was averted, we are still confronting massive oil and gas development in our community. We met again with University administration at the end of the summer to discuss co-sponsorship of future educational programs, but no plans have jelled. University leadership continues to respect our academic and intellectual freedom to pursue our fracking-related research and service activities. And while it is obvious that all parties care deeply about our students and educational mission, it appears there will be no meeting of the minds. Administration's interests veer toward development of new business incubation opportunities related to oil and gas and helping students seize oil and gas career opportunities. Frack*ED's members' propensity is toward mentoring of students and supporting research that studies the impacts of oil and gas development upon our community and the environment.

The collective action continues and we are now "branded" as Frack*ED, but not co-opted. We are pursuing our goal of increasing awareness about oil and gas development and its community impact. We still fight to be visible in a community that, while it says it desires dialogue, dislikes what we have to say and seems unable to see beyond the neoliberal narrative of unlimited economic growth and fossil fuel dependence. The dominant narrative is tenacious, as evidenced in a recent newspaper article and editorial.[108] Frack*ED presented a poster at an Engaged Community Symposium in November 2014, making new

---

108. Tyler Silvy, "Industry, Environmental Groups Clash as Weld Schools Cash in on Oil and Gas Activity, *Greeley Tribune*, November 7, 2014, http://www.greeleytribune.com/news/local/13660975-113/synergy-district-gas-oil.

friends and contacts.[109] We are supportive of energy-related student research and we encourage colleagues' research projects with regard to the impacts of energy development in the area. We successfully applied for a grant to fund an environmental writer's campus visit and speaking engagement. We have networked with researchers at Indiana University of Pennsylvania, a sister school similarly situated in a shale boom community. Oil and gas activity has slowed somewhat because of the temporary bust in prices, but no doubt it will boom again. We are vigilantly waiting. Administrative rulemaking at the state level will ensue this summer. A federal settlement related to ozone pollution awaits public comment. A recent oil tank conflagration is still being investigated as of this writing.[110] The fossil free divestment movement simmers on our agenda and may be moved to the front burner. There is no rest for the weary and no shortage of fodder for environmental advocates and activists. Though we were not successful and no moratorium was declared, I am still grateful that we got even this far. We produced an important report. We documented our minority opinion. And we will continue as Frack*ED. We are attempting to create a thriving counter-culture, radically changing the existing culture at the systemic level, both locally and globally. Business as usual cannot continue because of the potentially catastrophic consequences of climate change.

Was my leap into activism worth it? It has taken a significant amount of time and energy. The experience of breaking the silence on that day before the Faculty Senate was both terrifying and wonderful, but not magical—never underestimate the tenacity of bureaucracy, entrenched power, and the neoliberal status quo. Then again, never underestimate the power of visibility: showing up, requiring recognition that you exist, and refusing to disappear. At the end of the day, we can say we made a

---

109. Frack*ED@UNC, Poster presentation and flyer, Engaged Community Symposium, *University of Northern Colorado*, November 11, 2014.

110. James Redmond, "Greeley Firefighters Extiguish Blaze near Greeley-Weld County Airport," *Greeley Tribune*, April 17, 2015, http://www.greeleytribune.com/news/15948232-113/greeley-firefighters-battling-blaze-near-greeley-weld-county-airport.

good faith attempt at engaged critique. One cannot speak the "language of possibility" without the breaking of silence. The communication breakthrough was critical, and while personally meaningful to me, it is more important on a social level; it resulted in the creation of a cohesive group. I was not the only one who felt the need for participatory democracy and to express concerns about the environmental consequences of fracking. There is solace and security in our solidarity. We know we had some effect. In this pro-oil and gas, neoliberal community, I continue to feel grateful and often remind myself it is a minor miracle that we carry on. Our challenges are immense and formidable. Our community members, surrounded by more than 22,000 active wells, continue to be participants in a de facto public health experiment. We are guinea pigs, as there are significant data gaps regarding the cumulative effects on public health of such a concentration of oil and gas activity.[111] We produce approximately 200,000 barrels of oil a day out of our Wattenberg Field,[112] and thus continue to contribute significantly to the fossil fuel load that furthers climate change. We have so much yet to accomplish, so much we need to change.

Systemic Change for Social Justice: Changing Faculty Governance and Community Values

Libraries are ideal cradles and crucibles for change. Librarians tend to have a holistic, perceptive view of the political and economic landscape. Because they see the big picture as well as the details, they understand the need for systemic change. Canadian journalist Naomi Klein challenges readers to change our failed economic system in order to save the planet: "Fundamentally, the task is to articulate not just an alternative set of policy proposals but an alternative worldview to rival the one

111. John L. Adgate, Bernard D. Goldstein, Lisa M. McKenzie, "Potential Public Health Hazards," page h-i.

112. Sharon Dunn, "Weld County Oil Production on Pace to Break Records," *Greeley Tribune*, October 25, 2014, http://www.greeleytribune.com/news/13493110-113/oi-production-weld-bedard.

at the heart of the ecological crisis—embedded in interdependence rather than hyper-individualism, reciprocity rather than dominance, and cooperation rather than hierarchy."[113] Klein recognizes that libraries are exemplary, because they are grounded in human rights,[114] based on the "idea that real equality means equal access to the basic services that create a dignified life."[115] Our profession is grounded in part on socially just practices, and we can build upon this strength. We should continue to do what we do so well—the equitable provision of information—and step up our public criticism, interpretation, and communication of information.

We are working somewhat outside of the system with Frack*ED, creating a culture that operates on the margins. But it is important to work within the system as well. Obviously, something is awry and dysfunctional in the faculty governance system at my University, as evidenced by the lack of discussion about fracking and the twenty-one months of deafening silence preceding my Faculty Senate request. What can we do to strengthen the faculty governance and democratic decision-making systems on our campuses? We need systems in place that will enhance our democratic participation, harmonize with our values, and promote social justice in our communities, rather than thwarting them. Mehra, Rioux, and Albright survey the history of social justice in U.S. libraries in the *Encyclopedia of Library and Information Sciences*. They conclude that libraries and LIS research have effected only "moderate socially progressive changes" in communities due to three constraints: 1) permitted roles within the fabric of the social structure; 2) community values; and 3) academic streams of thought. They do perceive the beginning stages of development of a social justice theory in specific areas, such as community engagement.[116] I agree that social justice may be the correct

---

113. Klein, *This Changes Everything*, 462.

114. Toni Samek, *Librarianship and Human Rights: A Twenty-First Century Guide* (Oxford: Chandos: 2007).

115. Klein, *This Changes Everything*, 458.

116. Bharat Mehra, Kevin Rioux, and Kendra Albright, "Social Justice in Library and Information Science," 4829.

turnkey to solve this tripart, puzzling problem of structure, values, and academic thought.

Dilys Schoorman and co-author Michele Acker-Hocevar have some answers regarding the first constraint—the permitted roles within the university's social structure. They reconceptualized faculty governance by "integrating social justice principles into the ordinary work of professors."[117] They engaged in a radical experiment and altered the very fabric of the social structure of their College Faculty Assembly over the course of a year. In place of a top-down autocratic model of decision making, they created critically-aware shared governance by asking the representatives to become conscious of the political dynamics of decision-making. As in critical pedagogy, they inquired about power relations and asked "who was making which decisions, on behalf of whom, and for whose benefit?" This critique helped to generate a "bottom-up representative governance/decision-making structure." They summarize the non-hierarchical model: "the democratization of faculty governance entailed openness to all perspectives, an obligation to listen to and build consensus from this diversity, transparency in the decision-making process and leadership accountability through listening and action." The outcome of the research, expressed in qualitative terms, was increased willingness of faculty to participate and increased effectiveness. But there were challenges as well. They perceived "tensions between traditional values of deliberative decision-making typically valued by advocates for diversity and social justice and the values of expediency, efficiency, and market driven definitions of effectiveness."[118]

Schoorman's radical reformation of faculty governance mirrors the principles espoused by Naomi Klein in her prescription that systemic changes are needed to solve our ecological crisis ("interdependence rather than hyper-individualism, reciprocity rather than dominance, and cooperation rather than hierarchy"). Power must be shared in order to

---

117. Dilys Schoorman and Michele Acker-Hocevar, "Viewing Faculty Governance within a Social Justice Framework," 322.

118. Ibid., 322.

make room for social justice. And moving forward to community values, Mehra's second constraint: how can they be changed so that environmental justice takes precedence in a community? Sociologist Aaron McCright's research indicates that attitudes toward environmental science are value-based. He found that those who value the current economic order are also apt to trust certain types of science. McCright differentiates between science that serves economic production ("production science") and science that supports the understanding of human impacts on the environment and human health ("impact science"). Examples of production science would be physical and engineering sciences, such as polymer chemistry, nuclear physics, and petroleum geology. Examples of impact science would be environmental science, technology assessment, and conservation biology.[119]

McCright and his co-authors asked: "How do conservatives and liberals vary in their trust in both production and impact science?" They discovered that "conservatives report much less trust in impact scientists but greater trust in production scientists than their liberal counterparts."[120] The McCright study incorporates critical theory's principle of reflexivity in an interesting way. He explains the phenomenon of the "Anti-Reflexivity Thesis," which was developed to explain ". . . how certain sectors of society mobilize to defend the industrial capitalist order from the claims of environmentalists and some environmental scientists that the current economic system causes serious ecological and health problems." Reflexivity is defined as a "form of critical self-evaluation—a self-confrontation with the unintended and unanticipated consequences of modernity's industrial capitalist order."[121] McCright relates these differences in values to views of economics and environmentalism: "Much research on public scientific and technical controversies finds that what often appears at first glance to be a conflict over science is more accurately defined as a conflict over competing values. . . Our

---

119. McCright, "The Influence of Political Ideology on Trust in Science," 2.
120. Ibid., 2, 6-7.
121. Ibid., 2.

study here supports this finding. We find that political ideology aligns closely—but not perfectly—along a fault line between views defending the current economic order and views promoting reform of the current economic order to protect environmental and human health."[122] These economic views dovetail with the neoliberalism excoriated by Giroux --the devotion to the rewards of market fundamentalism at the cost of human rights and degradation of the ecosphere.

Differing perceptions of what constitutes environmental risk become an important influence upon community values when one connects the dots between legal theory and sociological research. Attorney Felicity Millner explains that key components of the definition of environmental justice are the recognition, minimization, and fair distribution of eco- logical risk.[123] Yet, turning to another of Aaron McCright's sociological studies, we find skewed risk perception in a key demographic group: conservative white males residing in the U.S. McCright finds that this par- ticular segment of society, conservative white males, have "significantly lower worry about environmental problems than do other Americans." This is due to "identity-protective cognition and their system-justifying tendencies." And McCright also discovered that conservative white males in the general public are "likely to deny that environmental problems pose a challenge to the continued functioning of the industrial capitalist economic system that historically has served them well—at least relative to other segments of society."[124] McCright's data seems to lend some support to Klein's contention that changing the overarching power structure (in this case, the privilege of conservative white males) is a linchpin. And it appears to be a possible key to understanding how we might begin to change community values as well.

---

122. Ibid., 7.

123. Felicity Millner, "Access to Environmental Justice," *Deakin Law Review* 16 (2011): 190.

124. Aaron M. McCright and Riley E. Dunlap, "Bringing Ideology in: The Conservative White Male Effect on Worry about Environmental Problems in the USA," *Journal of Risk Research* 16, no. 2 (2014):211, 222, doi:10.1080/136 69877.2012.726242.

As for academic streams of thought, the third factor influencing social justice's implementation, I agree with Mehra, et al., that the growing body of research regarding community informatics and engagement is a hopeful trend. The body of literature regarding progressive librarianship is also growing. I concur with Schoorman, who emphasizes that more studies are needed regarding "enhancing communities of practice governed by the principles of social justice in higher education . . . in the current context of mounting market-driven pressures on universities . . . where taken-for-granted notions of academic freedom, faculty voice and democratic governance could be subverted."[125] The implication is that the value systems are markedly polarized, to the point of subverting one another. We live in contentious times. Changing demographics may eventually be of help, as a recent Gallup poll indicates younger voters are more likely to believe in the seriousness of global warming: "Americans younger than 65 are much more likely than senior citizens to believe global warming will seriously threaten their way of life. Whereas 18% of seniors say global warming will be a threat to the way they live, roughly four in 10 of those in younger age groups do."[126]

Conclusion: Hope-Filled Pedagogy and Librarianship

The United Nations and Bill McKibben provide sobering assessments of our future in a world facing climate change.[127] Giroux's scathing critique compares our economic system to a casino and labels our universities as Orwellian. But Giroux also provides a common language of hope and a license for liberation. Social justice principles demarcate the ethical boundaries. It was my goal in this self-revelatory case study to

---

125. Schoorman, "Viewing Faculty Governance within a Social Justice Framework," 323.

126. Jeffrey M. Jones, "In U.S. Most Do Not See Global Warming as a Serious Threat," *Gallup*, March 13, 2014, http://www.gallup.com/poll/167879/not-global-warming-serious-threat-aspx.

127. United Nations, "UN and Climate Change," accessed April 29, 2015; Bill McKibben, "Do the Math Tour," 350.org, accessed 2014, http://math.350.org/.

suggest how academic librarians might answer the call to counterhege-monic action (in Bales and Engle's article above) and begin to develop "networks of best practices and support" in order to move their communities beyond the stasis of well-informed futility into an active state of educated hope and toward a fossil-free future. This is just a beginning; we need many more case studies to critically examine librarians' roles, the social construction of knowledge, the neoliberal system, and the potential for positive changes in librarianship and our bureaucratic institutions. There may be as many ways to practice as there are people. And there may be as many ways to form supportive networks as there are possible combinations of people. While we librarians bring numerous strengths to these endeavors, some of us may need more training in areas such as political organizing, strategizing, and group facilitation. If I speak the unvarnished truth, it is this: I couldn't let this environmental degradation happen on my campus without a response; future generations deserve a better legacy than this. I thank Henry Giroux, Dilys Schoorman, and the other academics cited herein for modeling academic language that rationally and reasonably expresses what we feel in our hearts. They've helped me to break the neoliberal norm of silence and to leave the most positive legacy possible.

In an interview in 2014, Giroux said we need to "think in terms of what it means to create the formative cultures necessary to fight racism, celebrity culture, the culture and institutions of casino capitalism, the assault on the environment, and the growing inequality in wealth and income . . . ."[128] When we formed Frack*ED@UNC née UNC Hydro-fracturing Task Force, we were creating a new faculty/staff culture on campus. Giroux says that "a viable politics in the present has to take seriously the premise that knowledge must be meaningful in order to be critical, in order to be transformative." When we presented our initial request for a task force, and then subsequently produced our "Progress Report," we carefully chose the information. Giroux champions "a language of hope, one that is realistic rather than romantic about the

---

128. Giroux, *Neoliberalism's War on Higher Education*, 204.

challenges the planet is facing and yet electrified by a realization that things can be different, that possibilities can not only be imagined but engaged, fought for, and realized in collective struggles." When we broke the silence, we were afraid, but hopeful. We refused to accept the status quo. But along with the opposition and antipathy, we also need to be constructive and creative. Giroux says that opposition to domination, while important, must be accompanied by "a language that moves forward with the knowledge, skills, and social relations necessary for the creation of new modes of agency, social movements, and democratic economic and social policies." He "fervently believe[s] in the need for both critique and hope."[129]

In so many ways we are just at the beginning, struggling to learn this new language and experimenting with our semi-legitimate status, which represents a new mode of agency. The formation and duration of Frack*ED still seems to me a miracle, given the dysfunction of our deafening twenty-one month silence. We continue to exist and persist, and to learn how to be participatory. Some of us remember the first Earth Day. And some were not yet born. But anyone born today inherits the terrifying countdown clock of climate change. So this is a renewed call to all academic librarians for counterhegemonic action, especially those boomers who came of age in the era of the Apollo space program, saw the beautiful and fragile blue-marble Earth, and believed in Earth Day from the beginning. We must leave a better legacy for those born today.

Think of your academic library as crucible and crèche for progressive community action, providing a place where progressive values are nurtured, for the sake of those children who call today their day of birth. You have been given the gift of academic freedom to pursue scholarship and service initiatives. Share that gift generously. Make your library a place of civic engagement. You could start with a discussion group. The library needs to be revitalized as a public sphere, a place of community engagement. We support the student research into all sides and aspects of controversial issues, as we should. But can we not

---

129. Ibid.

discuss and deliberate as well, when situationally appropriate? Remember, there are no "dumb" questions (as we librarians encouragingly tell our patrons). Vigilantly guard against self-censorship and the neglect of non-responsiveness. You can take creative action to secure social justice, especially environmental justice, on your campuses and in your communities. Perhaps you can begin with the fossil free divestment movement, or you may choose another cause. The list of injustices is unfortunately long. My creative action took the form of not accepting the status quo—and on this campus of dysfunctional, deafening silence, imagining the alternative took a significant amount of creativity!

What are your creative programming and research ideas? My story as a case study contained much oppositional energy—that of critique. Constructive energy is also needed. In a world fast approaching the brink of inalterable climate change, how does one rouse communities to action? This truly gargantuan problem will require our collective charisma, intellect, and creativity. And what about communities that appear to willingly cede to authorities the power to determine environmental quality of life and levels of risk exposure? This is perhaps the most difficult question. It is baffling that some act against their own interests, their own ecological survival. How do we understand people with whom we differ dramatically? The sociological studies of McCright provide some insight.[130] We all work with politically diverse patrons and communities; we need the benefit of each other's insight and creative strategies to bridge these seemingly unbridgeable differences.[131] In this case study I confessed that, for me, crisis was the necessary goad that initially provoked the reluctant provocateur. Don't wait for a local crisis. Act now. I'll repeat the full Giroux quote:

---

130. McCright, "The Influence of Political Ideology on Trust in Science."

131. Jonathan Haidt, *The Righteous Mind: Why Good People Are Divided by Politics and Religion* (New York: Vintage Books, 2013). A social psychologist, Haidt explains that people favor their intuitions over strategic reasoning and our morality is a nuanced mix of factors. He is a proponent of civil discussion of differing views, www.civilpolitics.org.

I have suggested that educators need to become provocateurs; they need to take a stand while refusing to be involved in either a cynical relativism or doctrinaire politics. This suggests that central to intellectual life is the pedagogical and political imperative that academics engage in rigorous social criticism while becoming a stubborn force for challenging false prophets, fighting against the imposed silence of normalized power, and critically engaging all those social relations that promote material and symbolic violence.[132]

I was a reluctant provocateur. I went beyond the recycling bin and advocated a precautionary stance toward fracking. I refused to stand by, to be complacent and comfortable in my moderately progressive, neutrality-cloaked library. And yes, it was only a first step. I have miles more to go. I collegially invite you to walk forward with me, taking steps toward progressive action in your own community. You, too, can go beyond the recycling bin. The survival of life on our planet depends on you.

Bibliography

Adgate, John L., Bernard D. Goldstein, and Lisa M. McKenzie. "Potential Public Health Hazards, Exposures and Health Effects from Unconventional Natural Gas Development." *Environmental Science & Technology* 48, no. 15 (2014): 8307-20. doi:10.1021/es404621d.

Allegheny College. "The Bousson Advisory Group." *Allegheny College.* Accessed April 27, 2015. http://sites.allegheny.edu/boussonadvisorygroup/.

Andersen, John. "Information Criticism: Where Is It?" In *Questioning Library Neutrality: Essays from Progressive Librarian,* edited by Alison Lewis, 97-108. Duluth, MN: Library Juice Press, 2008.

Aronowitz, Stanley and Henry A. Giroux. *Education Still Under Siege.* Westport, CT: Bergin & Garvey, 1993.

---

132. Giroux, *Youth in a Suspect Society,* 140.

Aulisio, George J. "Green Libraries Are More than Just Buildings." *Electronic Green Journal* 1, no. 35 (2013). https://escholarship. org/uc/item/3x11862z.

Bales, Stephen E. and Lea Susan Engle. "The Counterhegemonic Academic Librarian: A Call to Action." *Progressive Librarian* 40 (Fall/Winter 2012): 16-40. http://progressivelibrariansguild. org/PL_Jnl/pdf/PL_40.pdf.

Buschman, John. "Taking a Hard Look at Technology and Librarianship." *Argus* 23, no. 2 (1994): 13-20.

Carre, Nancy C. "Environmental Justice and Hydraulic Fracturing: The Ascendancy of Grassroots Populism in Policy Determination." *Journal of Social Change* 4, no. 1 (2012): 1-13. doi: 10.5590/JOSC.2012.04.1.01.

Center for the American West. "Events: FrackingSENSE: Greeley." *Center for the American West. University of Colorado at Boulder.* Accessed April 27, 2015. https://centerwest.org/events/ frackingsense-greeley.

Colorado Oil and Gas Conservation Commission. "Number of Active Colorado Oil & Gas Wells by County." *State of Colorado.* Accessed April 29, 2015. https://cogcc.state.co.us/Library/ Statistics/CoWklyMnthlyOGStats.pdf [site will be migrating to: http://cogccuat.state.co.us].

Cotton, Anthony. "Weld County Schools Use Oil, Gas Leases to Tap into Revenue Streams." *Denver Post.* March 24, 2013. http:// www.denverpost.com/ci_22857558/weld-county-schools-use-oil-gas-leases-tap.

Dunn, Sharon. "East Greeley Drilling Site May Move to Another Location." *Greeley Tribune* (Greeley, CO), June 21, 2014. http:// www.greeleytribune.com/news/11879587-113/greeley-site-project-drilling.

———. "Weld County Oil Production on Pace to Break Records." *Greeley Tribune* (Greeley, CO), October 25, 2014. http://www. greeleytribune.com/news/13493110-113/oil-production-weld-bedard.

Finkel, Madelon L. and Jake Hays. "The Implications of Unconventional Drilling for Natural Gas: A Global Public Health Concern." *Public Health* 127 (2013): 889-893. http://dx.doi.org/10.1016/j.puhe.2013.07.005.

"Fossil Free: Divest from Fossil Fuels." *350.org*. Accessed April 27, 2015. http://gofossilfree.org/.

Frack*ED@UNC, née UNC Hydrofracturing Task Force. Facebook page. *Hydrofracturing Task Force*. Accessed April 29, 2015. https://www.facebook.com/UNCHydrofracturing.

Frack*ED@UNC. Poster Presentation, Engaged Community Symposium. *University of Northern Colorado*, November 11, 2014.

Frack*ED@UNC, née UNC Hydrofracturing Task Force. "Progress Report, Interim Findings, and Recommendations." May 9, 2014.

Frey, Lawrence R. "Social Justice." In *Encyclopedia of Communication Theory*, 908-11. Thousand Oaks, CA: Sage Reference, 2009.

Gage, Ryan A. "Henry Giroux's 'Abandoned Generation' & Critical Librarianship: A Review Article." *Progressive Librarian* 23 (Spring 2004): 65-74. http://progressivelibrariansguild.org/PL_Jnl/pdf/PL23_spring2004.pdf.

Gasland. Directed by Josh Fox. New Video, 2010. DVD.

Gibson-Graham, J.K. and Gerda Roelvink. "An Economic Ethics for the Anthropocene." *Antipode* 41, no. S1 (January 2010): 320-346. doi:10.1111/j.1467-8330.2009.00728.x.

Giroux, Henry A. *America's Education Deficit and the War on Youth*. New York: Monthly Review Press, 2013.

———. "Henry Giroux, PhD: Profile." *McMaster University*. Accessed April 27, 2015. http://www.humanities.mcmaster.ca/~english/Faculty/girouxh.html.

———. *Moyers & Company*. By Bill Moyers. WNET, American Public Television. November 22, 2013. http://billmoyers.com/segment/henry-giroux-on-zombie-politics/.

———. "Neoliberalism, Corporate Culture, and the Promise of Higher Education: The University as a Democratic Public Sphere." *Harvard Educational Review* 72, no. 4 (2002): 425-63. Accessed April 27, 2015. http://hepg.metapress.com/content/0515nr62324n71p1/fulltext.pdf.

———. *Neoliberalism's War on Higher Education.* Chicago: Haymarket, 2014.

———. *On Critical Pedagogy.* New York: Continuum, 2011.

———. *Stormy Weather: Katrina and the Politics of Disposability.* Boulder, CO: Paradigm, 2006.

———. *Teachers as Intellectuals: Toward a Critical Pedagogy of Learning.* Granby, MA.: Bergin & Garvey, 1988.

———. "Themes in Modern European History." Doctoral dissertation, Carnegie–Mellon University, 1977.

———. *Youth in a Suspect Society: Democracy or Disposability?* New York: Palgrave Macmillan, 2009.

———. *Zombie Politics and Culture in the Age of Casino Capitalism.* New York: Peter Lang, 2011.

Gregory, Lua and Shana Higgins, editors. *Information Literacy and Social Justice: Radical Professional Practice.* Sacramento, CA: Library Juice Press, 2013.

Haidt, Jonathan, *The Righteous Mind: Why Good People Are Divided by Politics and Religion.* New York: Vintage Books, 2013.

Healy, Jack. "Supporting Oil and Gas, but Resisting Encroachment." *New York Times.* June 9, 2013. http://www.nytimes.com/2013/06/10/us/supporting-oil-and-gas-but-resisting-encroachment.html.

Highby, Wendy, Mark Anderson, and Marilyn Welsh. "Hydrofracturing Power Point Presentation to Faculty Senate. September 30, 2013." Accessed April 29, 2015. http://www.unco.edu/facultysenate/Campus%20Health%20and%20Safety%20Concerns%20Related%20to%20Hydrofracturing%2009302013PP-Highby.pptx.

Highby, Wendy and Bette Rathe. "Hydraulic Fracturing or Frack-
    ing Information." [Research guide]. *University of Northern
    Colorado*. Accessed May 1, 2015. http://libguides.unco.edu/
    fracking.

Howarth, Robert W., Anthony Ingraffea, and Terry Engelder.
    "Should Fracking Stop? Extracting Gas from Shale Increases
    the Availability of this Resource, But the Health and Envi-
    ronmental Risks May Be Too High." *Nature* 477, no. 7364
    (2011): 271–275. doi:10.1038/477271a.

Ingraffea, Anthony and Patty Limerick. "The Return of Frack-
    ingSENSE with Dr. Anthony Ingraffea." *The Center of the
    American West, University of Colorado at Boulder*. Accessed April
    27, 2015. http://www.centerwest.org/podcast/mp3/4-
    8-15ingraffea.mp3.

Jensen, Robert. "The Myth of the Neutral Professional." In *Question-
    ing Library Neutrality: Essays from Progressive Librarian*, edited by
    Alison Lewis, 89-96. Duluth, MN: Library Juice Press, 2008.

Jones, Jeffrey M. "In U.S. Most Do Not See Global Warming as a
    Serious Threat." *Gallup*. March 13, 2014. Retrieved from:
    http://www.gallup.com/poll/167879/not-global-warming-
    serious-threat.aspx.

Kezar, Adrianna, Tricia Bertram Gallant, and Jaime Lester. "Every-
    day People Making a Difference on College Campuses: The
    Tempered Grassroots Leadership Tactics of Faculty and
    Staff." *Studies in Higher Education* 36, no. 2 (2011): 129-151.
    doi: 10.1080/03075070903532304.

Klein, Naomi. *This Changes Everything: Capitalism vs. the Climate*. New
    York: Simon & Schuster, 2014.

Kranich, Nancy, Michele Reid, and Taylor Willingham. "Civic En-
    gagement in Academic Libraries: Encouraging Active
    Citizenship." *College & Research Libraries News* 65, no. 7 (July/
    August 2004): 380-4. http://crln.acrl.org/content/65/7/380.
    full.pdf+html. http://crln.acrl.org/content/65/7.toc.

————.. "Reviews: Review of Toni Samek's *Librarianship and Human Rights: A Twenty-First Century Guide.*" *Library Quarterly* 78, no. 3 (July 2008): 343-5.

Living Thinkers: An Autobiography of Black Women in the Ivory Tower. Directed by Roxana Walker-Canton, New York: Women Make Movies, 2013, DVD.

Lockman, Rachel, "The Way I See It: Academic Librarians and Social Justice: A Call to Microactivism," *College & Research Libraries News* 76, no. 4 (April 2015): 193-194

Longstaff, Rachel, "Social Justice across the Curriculum: Librarians as Campus Leaders," *Catholic Library World 81*, no. 4 (June 2011), 285-9.

McCright, Aaron M. and Riley E. Dunlap. "Bringing Ideology in: The Conservative White Male Effect on Worry about Environmental Problems in the USA." *Journal of Risk Research 16*, no. 2 (2014): 211-26. doi:10.1080/13669877.2012.726242.

McCright, Aaron, Katherine Dentzman, Meghan Charters, and Thomas Dietz. "The Influence of Political Ideology on Trust in Science." *Environmental Research Letters* 8 (2013). doi:10.1088/1748-9326/8/4/044029.

McKibben, Bill. "Do the Math Tour." *350.org.* Accessed April 27, 2015. http://math.350.org/.

McKinnon, Sara L. "Critical Theory." In *Encyclopedia of Communication Theory*, 237-43. Thousand Oaks, CA: SAGE Reference, 2009.

Mehra, Bharat, Kevin Rioux, and Kendra Albright. "Social Justice in Library and Information Science." In E*ncyclopedia of Library and Information Sciences.* 3rd ed.New York: Taylor & Francis: 2010.

Mehra, Bharat, and Donna Braquet. "Marriage between Participatory Leadership and Action Research to Advocate Benefits Equality for Lesbian, Gay, Bisexual, and Transgendered People: An Extended Human Rights Role for Library and Information

Science." In *Leadership in Academic Libraries Today: Connecting Theory to Practice*, edited by Bradford Lee Eden and Jody Condit Fagan, 185-211. Lanham, MD: Rowman & Littlefield, 2014.

Millner, Felicity. "Access to Environmental Justice." *Deakin Law Review* 16 (2011): 189-207.

Mirtz, Ruth. "Disintermediation and Resistance: Giroux and Radical Praxis in the Library." In *Critical Library Instruction: Theories and Methods*, edited by Toni Samek, 293-304. Duluth, MN: Library Juice Press, 2010.

Morales, Myrna, Em Claire Knowles, and Chris Bourg. "Diversity, Social Justice, and the Future of Libraries." *portal: Libraries and the Academy 14*, no. 3 (July 2014), 439-51. doi: 10.1353/pla.2014.0017.

Mortenson, Thomas G. "Budget and Appropriations: State Funding: A Race to the Bottom." *American Council on Education*. Winter 2012. Accessed April 29, 2015. http://www.acenet.edu/the-presidency/columns-and-features/Pages/state-funding-a-race-to-the-bottom.aspx.

Nocella II, Anthony J., Steven Best, and Peter McLaren, editors. *Academic Repression: Reflections from the Academic-Industrial Complex*. Oakland, CA: AK Press, 2010.

Pagowsky, Nicole and Niamh Wallace, "Black Lives Matter! Shedding Library Neutrality Rhetoric for Social Justice," *College & Research Libraries News* 76, no. 4 (April 2015): 196-214.

Redmond, James. "Greeley Firefighters Extinguish Blaze near Greeley-Weld County Airport." *Greeley Tribune* (April 17, 2015). http://www.greeleytribune.com/news/15948232-113/greeley-firefighters-battling-blaze-near-greeley-weld-county-airport.

Romano, Analisa. "Setback Pushback." *Greeley Tribune* (Greeley, CO), January 10, 2013. Page 1.

Ryan, Patti and Lisa Sloniowski. "The Public Academic Library: Friction in the Teflon Funnel." In *Information Literacy and Social Justice: Radical Professional Praxis*, edited by Lua Gregory and Shana Higgins, 275-96. Sacramento: Library Juice Press, 2013.

Samek, Toni. Foreword to *Critical Library Instruction: Theories and Methods*, edited by Toni Samek, viii-ix. Duluth, MN: Library Juice Press, 2010.

———. *Librarianship and Human Rights: A Twenty-First Century Guide*. Oxford: Chandos: 2007.

Schoorman, Dilys. "Resisting the Unholy Alliance between a University and a Prison Company: Implications for Faculty Governance in a Neoliberal Context." *Cultural Studies Critical Methodologies* 13, no. 6 (2013): 510-9. doi:10.1177/1532708613503777.

Schoorman, Dilys and Michele Acker-Hocevar. "Viewing Faculty Governance within a Social Justice Framework: Struggles and Possibilities for Democratic Decision-Making in Higher Education." *Equity & Excellence in Education* 43, no. 3 (2010): 310-25. doi:10.1080/10665684.2010.494493.

Schroeder, Robert and Christopher V. Hollister. "Librarians' Views on Critical Theories and Critical Practices." *Behavioral & Social Sciences Librarian* 33, no. 2 (2014): 91-119. doi:10:1080/0 1639269.2014.912104.

Silvy, Tyler. "Industry, Environmental Groups Clash as Weld Schools Cash in on Oil and Gas Activity." *Greeley Tribune* (Greeley, CO), November 7, 2014. http://www.greeleytribune.com/news/local/13660975-113/synergy-district-gas-oil.

Steingraber, Sandra. *Raising Elijah: Protecting our Children in an Age of Environmental Crisis*. Cambridge, MA: Da Capo Press, 2011.

United Nations. "United Nations and Climate Change." *United Nations*. Accessed April 29, 2015. http://www.un.org/climatechange/.

U.S. White House, President Barack Obama. "Energy, Climate Change, and Our Environment." *United States White House.* Accessed April 29, 2015. http://www.whitehouse.gov/energy.

University of Northern Colorado, Board of Trustees. "Minutes, Board of Trustees Meeting, November 18, 2011." *University of Northern Colorado.* Accessed April 29, 2015. http://www.unco.edu/trustees/minutes_agendas/minutes_2011-2012/11-18-11%20BOT%20mtg%20minutes%20approved.pdf.

University of Northern Colorado, Faculty Senate Forum. "Minutes of the September 30, 2013 Senate Meeting." *University of Northern Colorado.* Accessed April 29, 2015. http://www.unco.edu/facultysenate/September%2030,%202013%20sen%20min.pdf.

Vital for Colorado. "Vital for Colorado." *Vital for Colorado.* April 29, 2015. http://www.vitalforcolorado.com/.

Walker, Alice. *We Are the Ones We Have Been Waiting For: Inner Light in a Time of Darkness.* New York: New Press, 2007.

Weld County, Colorado. "Discover Weld County Colorado." *Weld County, Colorado.* Accessed November, 2014. http://www.discoverweld.com/aboutweldcounty.html.

Williams, Peggy. "Niobrara Oil Play Heats Up in the Rockies." *Oil and Gas Investor.* February 1, 2010. http://www.oilandgasinvestor.com/peggy/2010/02/01/niobrara-oil-play-heats-up-in-the-rockies.

Zinn, Howard. *You Can't Be Neutral on a Moving Train: A Personal History of Our Times.* Boston: Beacon Press, 2002.

Chapter 5

LINKING LIS GRADUATE STUDY AND SOCIAL IDENTITY AS A SOCIAL JUSTICE ISSUE: PREPARING STUDENTS FOR CRITICALLY CONSCIOUS PRACTICE

Nicole A. Cooke and Joseph D. Minarik

Introduction

This chapter describes the successful interdepartmental collaboration at the University of Illinois at Urbana-Champaign between a library and information science (LIS) faculty member (the first author, Cooke), who has developed courses in diversity and social justice explicitly for graduate students at the Graduate School of Library and Information Science, and a social worker attempting to promote social justice and intergroup relations.

The collaboration, which was initiated with the knowledge that students need skills and perspectives from outside the LIS spectrum, involved helping Master's and Ph.D.-level LIS graduate students learn an integrative, conceptual framework (created by the second author, Minarik) designed to make the complexity of inequality more comprehensible and accessible to various learners, including postsecondary and graduate students, faculty, professional staff, and community members. In particular, the form of inequality of interest is that which is based on social identity group memberships, including race, gender, sexual orientation, ability status, etc.

Following the presentation of the primary tenets related to privileging and how privileging relates to other key constructs related to social justice education, the chapter presents a detailed examination of an assortment of mechanisms used by pseudo-progressive organizations that maintain the privileging status quo through conditional inclusion, while appearing to reflect organizational change and fairness. Examples are included that illustrate how well-intentioned individuals and organizations seeking to do the right thing can create results that, instead of promoting equality, actually generate subtle forms of marginalization and inequality.

Background

Inequality in communities and organizations stemming from differences in social identity-based status is an exceedingly complex issue.[1] That is, individual inequalities do not necessarily stem from individual differences, but instead arise when others place individuals into artificial, socially-constructed groups, such as race, ethnicity, gender, sexual orientation, etc. Even though these social identity groups are inventions, they can still affect individual life chances and outcomes, because one is treated differently by others, based on which groups one has been categorized into. So, if one is being categorized as male by others, one will be treated differently by them than if one had been categorized female. Moreover, this categorization process serves as the first step in processes of inequality based on social identity.[2] Additionally, individuals seeking to promote fairness by altering the ways people treat each other cannot do so without understanding positionality, which includes

1. Bryan Hopkins, *Cultural Differences and Improving Performance: How Values and Beliefs Influence Organizational Performance* (Burlington, VT: Gower Publishing, 2009).

2. Bruce G. Link and Jo C. Phelan, "Conceptualizing Stigma," *Annual Review of Sociology* (2001): 363-385.

acknowledgement that everyone is gendered, raced, and classed,[3] that positionality informs our relations to others, and that it signals different degrees of status in social hierarchies.

Some scholars situate the problem of inequality as stemming from individual prejudice and corresponding discriminatory actions, contending that individual cognition and disposition should be the target of interventions. Others argue that the problem lies within the individual, but at the level of unconscious cognition.[4] From the organizational sciences literature, scholars argue that manifestations of differential, unintentional, and deleterious actions in organizations based on racial, gender, and other social identities reflect a "selective" form of incivility between individuals.[5] Such incivility is affected by situational factors, such as social norms[6] and leadership within the organization.[7] Others contend that inequality arises from interactions at multiple levels, including policy. Sexism, for example, can be seen as an interplay of individual action (and inactions) between women and men, and processes operating at institutional levels (like policies and practices) support the domination of women by men in patriarchal societies and organizations.[8]

Understanding inequality is further complicated by the number and variety of terms used by educators and others who seek to help people, including graduate students and professionals, devise ways

---

3. Renée J. Martin and Dawn M. Van Gunten, "Reflected Identities Applying Positionality and Multicultural Social Reconstructionism in Teacher Education," *Journal of Teacher Education* 53, no. 1 (2002):44-54.

4. Derald Wing Sue, et al., "Racial Microaggressions in Everyday Life: Implications for Clinical Practice," *American Psychologist* 62, no. 4 (2007): 271-286.

5. Lilia M. Cortina, "Unseen Injustice: Incivility as Modern Discrimination in Organizations," *Academy of Management Review* 33, no. 1 (2008): 55-75.

6. Linda Hamilton Krieger and Susan T. Fiske, "Behavioral Realism in Employment Discrimination Law: Implicit Bias and Disparate Treatment," *California Law Review* 94, no.4 (2006):997-1062, doi: 10.2307/20439058.

7. C.M. Harold and B. C. Holtz, "The Effects of Passive Leadership on Workplace Incivility," *Journal of Organizational Behavior* 36, no. 1 (2015):16-38, doi: 10.1002/job.1926.

8. Allan G. Johnson, *Privilege, Power, and Difference* (Boston: McGraw-Hill, 2001).

to help promote fairness. For example, the concept of privilege is often conflated with that of power.[9] While a rich body of literature has emerged describing unintentional actions which offend, called microaggressions,[10] empirical findings concerning workplace incivility predates the microaggression literature, even though it explores the same form of unconscious, unintentional actions.[11] The incivility literature, initially examining general forms of deviant behaviors in the workplace characterized by ambiguous intent, has been extended to examine the role of race, gender, and other types of social identity on these types of actions.[12] Moreover, the diversity of cultures, values, and beliefs adds even greater complexity to the issue of addressing inequality in organizations.[13] This same diversity of beliefs and values can affect both the way the problem of inequality is defined[14] and the types of alternate solutions that might stem from each problem definition. Problem definition is part of a complex process of setting explicit goals, whether one is referring to an individual, a group, or an organization.[15] Also, how a

9. Peggy McIntosh, "White Privilege and Male Privilege: A Personal Account of Coming to See Correspondences through Work in Women's Studies," paper presented at Virginia Women's Studies Association Conference, Richmond, VA, April 1986.

10. Derald Wing Sue, *Microaggressions in Everyday Life: Race, Gender, and Sexual Orientation* (Hoboken, NJ: John Wiley & Sons, 2010); Sue, et al., "Racial Microaggressions in Everyday Life."

11. Lynne M. Andersson and Christine M. Pearson, "Tit for Tat? The Spiraling Effect of Incivility in the Workplace," *Academy of Management Review* 24, no. 3 (1999): 452-471, doi: 10.2307/259136; Lilia M. Cortina, et al., "Incivility in the Workplace: Incidence and Impact," *Journal of Occupational Health Psychology* 6, no. 1 (2001):64-80, doi: 10.1037/1076-8998.6.1.64.

12. Lilia M. Cortina, "Unseen Injustice: Incivility as Modern Discrimination in Organizations," *Academy of Management Review* 33, no. 1 (2008): 55-75; Lilia M. Cortina, et al., "Selective Incivility as Modern Discrimination in Organizations: Evidence and Impact," *Journal of Management* 39, no. 6 (2013): 1579-1605, doi: 10.1177/0149206311418835.

13. Bryan Hopkins, *Cultural Differences and Improving Performance.*

14. Fae L. Korsmo, "Problem Definition and the Alaska Natives: Ethnic Identity and Policy Formation," *Review of Policy Research* 9, no. 2 (1989): 294-306.

15. Colin Eden and Fran Ackermann, "Problem Structuring: On The Nature of, and Reaching Agreement About, Goals," *EURO Journal on Decision Processes* (2013):1-22.

problem is defined determines the actions individuals, like managers, will likely take in solving the problem.[16] Problem definition also involves power and affects the quality of problem-solving actions and decisions.[17] Without embracing and understanding such complexity, individuals in organizations seeking solutions to injustice could inadvertently choose strategies that affect superficial manifestations of unfairness, while leaving fundamental mechanisms intact.

For example, in the case of race, some White people (and others) have defined the problem of racism as stemming from noticing or "seeing race," and so will adopt a stance of racial colorblindness.[18] Racial colorblind ideology asserts that if we don't pay attention to or acknowledge racial identity, then racism will be eliminated. According to racial colorblindness, everyone should see and treat each other as "human." The corollary to this idea is that anytime someone brings up the issue of race, then they are the ones causing racism. Given the role that cognitive biases play in doubting claims of ill treatment, including discrimination,[19] it could be uncomfortable for that White person to hear about an incident of racial discrimination shared by a person of color. It probably would be equally difficult to affirm the validity of the person's story, given the belief that race doesn't matter. But responding with incredulity to such a claim made by a person of color can easily feel invalidating. Such minimizations and dismissals are seen as a particular form of microaggression, that of microinvalidation.[20] Organizations and their leaders are also susceptible to the traps inherent in oversimplification of social identity-based inequality. For example, leaders in an organization might be well-meaning and well-intentioned when they

---

16. Paul C. Nutt, "The Formulation Processes and Tactics Used in Organizational Decision Making," *Organization Science* 4, no 2 (1993):226-251.

17. Paul C. Nutt, "Surprising but True: Half the Decisions in Organizations Fail," *Academy of Management Executive* 13, no. 4 (1999):75-90.

18. Eduardo Benilla-Silva, *Racism without Racists: Color-Blind Racism and the Persistence of Racial Inequality in the United States* (Lanham, MD: Rowman & Littlefield, 2006).

19. Faye Crosby, et al., "Cognitive Biases in the Perception of Discrimination: The Importance of Format," Sex Roles 14, no. 11-12 (1986): 637-646.

20. Sue, *Microaggressions in Everyday Life.*

review the demographics of their staff or volunteers, and decide that the organization looks "too White," "too male," etc. These leaders might frame such staff homogeneity as a problem of "not appearing diverse." The problem thus defined, the solution becomes one of figuring out how to "appear more diverse." Taking academia as an example, substantive empirical literature exists that attests in part to the form and effects of this approach to inequality, including underrepresentation and differences in career outcomes. Research exploring the experiences of women faculty in STEM find that women in STEM (science, technology, engineering, and mathematics)—and ethnic minority faculty in general—have more negative experiences in the workplace than White male faculty.[21] Across the literature, faculty of color report a sense of isolation and a lack of institutional support, often being expected to serve as representatives of their racial/ethnic group. The experience of tokenism, among other factors, can affect their performance and longevity.[22] Even where a university desires greater participation of minorities in decision-making bodies, like search committees, the underrepresentation in those colleges of faculty of color results in some feeling compelled to take on additional service responsibilities, which can lead to increased levels of stress.[23]

Unfortunately, libraries (and related information organizations) are as susceptible as any other organization to these kinds of challenges. Librarianship is at heart a service profession, one that is historically and characteristically White and female. As part of that service, librarians are in the position of serving those who do not look, act, think, or behave

---

21. L.V. Blackwell, L.A. Snyder, and C. Mavriplis, "Diverse Faculty in STEM Fields: Attitudes, Performance, and Fair Treatment," *Journal of Diversity in Higher Education* 2, no. 4 (2009): 195-205, doi: http://dx.doi.org/10.1037/a0016974; Caroline Sotello Viernes Turner, Juan Carlos González, and J. Luke Wood, "Faculty of Color in Academe: What 20 Years of Literature Tells Us," Journal of Diversity in Higher Education 1, no. 3 (2008):139-168, doi: 10.1037/a001283

22. Ibid.; Caroline Sotello Viernes Turner, Samuel L. Myers, Jr., and John W. Creswell. "Exploring Underrepresentation: The Case of Faculty of Color in the Midwest." *Journal of Higher Education* 70, no. 1 (1999): 27-59. doi: 10.2307/2649117.

23. Ibid.

as they do.[24] Successfully serving racially and otherwise socially diverse individuals and groups is an issue of fairness and/or social justice, and requires skills of empathy and perspective-taking, as well as the knowledge needed for critically conscious and culturally competent practice.[25] However, this type of empathic, culturally competent, and socially just service is not always intuitive.

In spite of successful LIS programs, such as the Spectrum Initiative and Knowledge River, that recruit outstanding candidates from diverse and underrepresented backgrounds,[26] the field remains woefully homogeneous and underprepared to deal with the increasingly diverse clientele that patronize libraries. Such efforts are laudable, but if these diverse candidates are not properly trained or retained, information organizations will continue to have the aforementioned diversity gaps and subsequent internal and external problems.

Libraries in general, and public libraries in particular, have long been noted in American history for social justice participation and activism, including the progressive librarianship occurring before World War I, library activism in the 1950s and 1960s, the radical library work that hallmarked the 1970s and 1980s, and a renewed enthusiasm for participatory actions that emerged in the 1990s and early 2000s.[27] Most recently, the

24. American Library Association, *Diversity Counts*, ALA Office for Research and Statistics and ALA Office for Diversity, last modified September 28, 2012, http://www.ala.org/offices/diversity/diversitycounts/divcounts; American Library Association, *American Library Association Releases New Data to Update Diversity Counts Report*, ALA Office for Research and Statistics and ALA Office for Diversity, last modified September 28, 2012, http://www.ala.org/news/2012/09/american-library-association-releases-new-data-update-diversity-counts-report.

25. Clara M. Chu, "Transformative Information Services: Uprooting Race Politics," *Black Caucus of the American Library Association Conference*, Las Vegas, July 19-22, 1999; Ghada El Turk, "Diversity and Cultural Competency," *Colorado Libraries* 29, no. 4 (2003): 5-7; Patricia Montiel Overall, "Cultural Competence: A Conceptual Framework for Library and Information Science Professionals," *The Library Quarterly* 79, no. 2 (2009): 175-204.

26. N.A. Cooke, "The Spectrum Doctoral Fellowship Program: Enhancing the LIS Professoriate," *InterActions: UCLA Journal of Education and Information Studies* 10, no. 1 (2014).

27. John Pateman and John Vincent, Public Libraries and Social Justice (Farnham, UK: Ashgate, 2012).

Occupy movement that began in 2012 saw the development of grass-roots libraries at the sites of protest, and librarians actively engaged in the cause while working with their communities. Indeed, libraries have played a significant, yet understated role in the development of the culture and collective knowledge of the United States.[28]

Despite the involvement of libraries in the social justice fabric of the United States, discussions and explicit instruction in areas of diversity and social justice in the LIS curriculum have been reactive (instead of proactive), temporary, and not as consistent and semantically direct as they should be.[29] LIS education and research have shied away from explicit discussions of race, prejudice, privilege, and other potentially inflammatory, yet critical, topics.[30] There are classes and curricular efforts in the LIS education landscape that include these topics in courses and in research, but such classes are the exception rather than the rule.[31]

---

28. Michael Fultz, "Black Public Libraries in the South in the Era of De Jure Segregation," *Libraries & The Cultural Record* 41, no. 3 (2006): 337-359; Cheryl Knott Malone, "Toward a Multicultural American Public Library History," *Libraries & Culture* (2000): 77-87; E.J. Josey, "Diversity: Political and Societal Barriers," *Journal of Library Administration* 27, no.1-2 (1999): 191-202; Wayne A. Wiegand, "The Development of Librarianship in the United States, *Libraries & Culture* 24, no. 1 (1989): 99-109; Rosemary Ruhig Dumont, "The Educating of Black Librarians: A Historical Perspective," *Journal of Education for Library and Information Science* (1986): 233-249.

29. Todd Honma, "Trippin' Over the Color Line: The Invisibility of Race in Library and Information Studies," *InterActions: UCLA Journal of Education and Information Studies* 1, no. 2 (2005); Lorna Peterson, "The Definition of Diversity: Two Views. A More Specific Definition," *Journal of Library Administration* 27, no. 1-2 (1999): 17-26.

30. Christine Pawley, "Unequal Legacies: Race and Multiculturalism in the LIS Curriculum," *Library Quarterly* 76, no. 2 (2006): 149-168.

31. Denice Adkins and Isabel Espinal, "The Diversity Mandate," *Library Journal* 129, no. 7 (2004): 52-54; Nicole A. Cooke, Miriam E. Sweeney, & Safiya U. Noble, "Social Justice as Topic And Tool: An Attempt to Transform a LIS Curriculum and Culture," *Library Quarterly* 86, no. 1 (2016):107-124; Paul T. Jaeger, John Carlo Bertot, and Renée E. Franklin, "Diversity, Inclusion, and Underrepresented Populations in LIS Research," *Library Quarterly* 80, no. 2 (2010): 175-181; Paul T. Jaeger, et al., "Diversity and LIS Education: Inclusion and the Age of Information," *Journal of Education for Library and Information Science* (2011): 166-183; Paul T. Jaeger and Renee E. Franklin, "The Virtuous Circle: Increasing Diversity in LIS Faculties to Create More Inclusive Library Services and Outreach," *Education Libraries* 30, no. 1 (2007): 20-26.

The strong and consistent bridging of theory (classes) and practice (the librarians on the ground) is necessary to keep the professional LIS workforce viable, culturally competent, and socially just. It should be part of the mission of library and information science graduate programs to educate and produce library and information professionals who are not only culturally competent, but as well are willing, able, and eager to serve dynamic communities. Teaching issues of social justice in the LIS classroom is a delicate yet potentially profound endeavor. This chapter highlights such an endeavor, an effort to revise and invigorate a graduate level course about the history and importance of social justice in libraries. The collaboration represented in the course *Social Justice in the Information Professions* has proven successful, most notably in the students' immediate realizations of their own privilege. The authors hope and presume that the students' realizations and growth continued beyond the immersive workshop that introduced complicated issues of privilege and inequality.

The Privileging and Marginalization Integrative Framework

The PMIF[32] focuses on the centrality of privilege and privileging as the primary mechanism perpetuating unfairness in contemporary society. This unfairness is based on social identity group differences and results in members of high-status groups (e.g., males, heterosexuals, White people, those who are not disabled, and others) being perceived more positively by people in decision-making positions, such as police officers, employers, and faculty teachers in a college classroom. This positive regard means high-status group members are permitted closer proximity to opportunities and increased likelihood to ascend within organizational hierarchies. The framework places privileging in relation to individual- and collective-level actions by low-status group members

---

32. Joseph D. Minarik, "Connecting the Dots of Oppression: The Privileging and Marginalization Integrative Framework (PMIF)," unpublished manuscript, last modified March 3, 2015.

who seek to circumvent barriers that privileging allows high-status group members to avoid. Different types of microaggressions are then placed in the context of privileging on the one hand, and collective efforts by low-status groups on the other, to illustrate their role in maintaining the privileging status quo. The PMIF culminates by explicating several categories of actions taken by some organizations that include low-status group members, but into a zone of conditional inclusion rather than full, progressive inclusion. **Figure 1** offers a graphical representation of the PMIF, adapted from Minarik.[33]

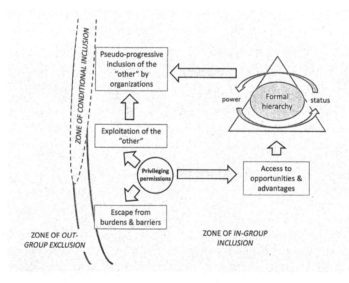

Figure 1: The PMIF Framework Privileging

Social identity-based privilege (and more accurately, *privileging)* is the centerpiece of how oppression is operationalized within the integrative framework used with GSLIS students and others. The following represents only an overview of how privileging is addressed among students and others within an instructional process.[34] Based on a careful reading

33. Ibid.

34. For a complete and detailed description of privileging, including how it is used with concept mapping in a workshop or classroom setting, see Joseph D. Minarik, "Privilege as Privileging: Making the Dynamic and Complex Nature

of the working paper on privilege written by McIntosh,[35] two concurrent processes emerged as critical elements of privilege: a high-status social identity group member is given permission to access certain advantages as well as to escape certain burdens, barriers, and disadvantages. Stemming from McIntosh and elsewhere, examples of advantages include being given: the benefit of the doubt, access to opportunities, a sense of belonging, and information. Disadvantages that high-status group members are permitted to escape include: proving one belongs or is competent, not being heard or visible, and having accurate knowledge about the low-status group "other,"[36] including their perspectives and life experiences. Without accurate knowledge about the "other," high status group members will rely on unfounded beliefs (stereotypes) to explain and justify the struggles of the "other" as individual failings.[37] This lack of accurate knowledge about the low-status "other" is a central source of high-status group member cultural incompetence, according to the PMIF, and is further exacerbated by a lack of awareness of the role that power plays in life chances and outcomes.

Privileging permits high-status group members to escape having critical knowledge of themselves as members of high-status social groups, including the ways that decision makers (such as teachers, employers conducting interviews, supervisors—even store clerks) have perceived them over time. Without knowledge about the privileging phenomenon, and its likely role in their own lives, high-status group members are also permitted to maintain a belief in the ideology of meritocracy, or

---

of Privilege and Marginalization Accessible," *Journal of Social Work Education* (in press).

35. Peggy McIntosh, "White Privilege and Male Privilege: A Personal Account of Coming to See Correspondences through Work in Women's Studies," Paper presented at Virginia Women's Studies Association Conference, Richmond, VA, April 1986.

36. Allan G. Johnson, *Privilege, Power, and Difference* (Boston: McGraw-Hill, 2001).

37. Craig McGarty, Vincent Y. Yzerbyt, and Russell Spears, eds., *Stereotypes as Explanations: The Formation of Meaningful Beliefs about Social Groups* (Cambridge, UK: Cambridge University Press, 2002).

attribute their own successes to hard work and personal effort, rather than the generally positive perceptions of them held by decision makers throughout their lives, all else being equal.

This treatment of privileging entails explicitly pointing out that high-status group members are not necessarily handed achievements of power and status within the classroom or places of employment, but instead will likely have to work in order to achieve these outcomes. This is not to deny that some White males in the US achieve wealth, status, and power, or are placed within elite positions, simply or solely because of who they know. Rather, the focus on privileging in the PMIF places these examples as exceptions to the rule. Most others perceived in high-status groups will have to exert effort in relation to opportunities they are permitted to access. That is, they will have to study and prepare (rather than play video games) in order to answer a challenging question in class, perform well on the test, or complete a difficult assignment given them by a supervisor (all of which are examples of "opportunities" in the PMIF).

Status, Hierarchy, and Power

This exploration of privileging can inadvertently leave an impression that the phenomenon only involves individual instances of a decision maker deciding to give an opportunity to a high-status group member, and not to an "other." Rather, the PMIF draws attention to the fact that privileging is an accumulation of such individual instances. The decision maker's belief about the potential for competence of the high-status group member can increase, and the person might then be given even more opportunities, tests, or challenges.

As a result of these decisions over time, the outcomes of successive accomplishments can result in the accumulation of various assets, such as social, human, and economic capital. In terms of social capital,[38] the

---

38. Alejandro Portes, "Social Capital: Its Origins and Applications in Modern Sociology," *Annual Review of Sociology* 24 (1998): 1-24; James S. Coleman, "Social Capital in the Creation of Human Capital," *American Journal of Sociology* (1988): S95-S120.

decision maker may sing the high-status group member's praises to others, including fellow managers. As he learns and grows, his knowledge, skills, and capabilities increase, resulting in increased human capital. If he chooses to record his accomplishments (for example, by including the projects he has completed on his resume), he can also signal his human capital when seeking promotions or growth opportunities elsewhere. The result of such signaling can result in commanding greater monetary compensation, as well as being considered for positions of greater responsibility and power within organizations. The accumulation of assets, which can take place over decades, reflects the dynamic process of cumulative advantage,[39] and is seen as a key element in inequality. Such inequality is an outcome of privileging and marginalization, from the perspective of the PMIF.

Privileging can result in high-status group members being promoted to positions of higher rank within both formal and informal hierarchies. Much of the proceeding discussion on hierarchy, status, and power stems from the work of Magee and Galinsky (2008).[40] The rank ordering of individuals within hierarchies may be either explicit or implicit, and involves relationships of subordination. According to those researchers, informal hierarchies develop spontaneously within groups, based on stereotypes and instant judgments about others' competence and power. Status can be reflected by a status hierarchy within a group and is related to the amount of respect one receives from others. Such respect can be based on direct observation, reputation, or stereotypes, according to those authors. From their perspective, power is defined as "asymmetric control over valued resources in social relations".[41] From that conceptualization, attention is drawn to the idea that those with

---

39. Thomas A. DiPrete and Gregory M. Eirich, "Cumulative Advantage as a Mechanism for Inequality: A Review of Theoretical and Empirical Developments," *Annual Review of Sociology* (2006): 271-297.

40. Joe C. Magee and Adam D. Galinsky, "Social Hierarchy: The Self-Reinforcing Nature of Power and Status," *Academy of Management Annals* 2, no. 1 (2008): 351-398.

41. Ibid., 361.

higher rank can certainly control the distribution of valued resources in relation to others. But where subordinates possess resources like expertise, they too may have power in relations with superiors.

The Power of the "Other" and Social Identity Theory

While the PMIF centers attention on the privileging of high-status group members, it also invites learners to think more about options available to low-status group members in light of such privileging. The work of Brown (2000)[42] helps outline the ways the "other" as outsider may use either individual or collective strategies to alter her low-status position. Individual strategies can include increasing her ability to signal competence as a way to challenge being stereotyped by decision makers. Such signals can include possessing and listing more degrees and certifications of her expertise on resumes. She might also seek to dampen down signals of being seen as "other." So, if she wanted to make her disability less visible to a potential employer, she might choose not to disclose it during a job interview. During facilitation of the PMIF, learners are asked to list the various individual strategies low-status group members might use to circumvent the barriers they face that those with privilege may avoid.

Individual strategies, according to Brown's theory, are more likely to be used under certain circumstances than others. These circumstances include the extent to which a low-status group member perceives: the boundary between the in-group and the out-group as permeable, the system as legitimate, and the system as stable. When individual strategies to exit one's low status are met with insurmountable barriers, or low-status group members perceive the status quo as being unfair and illegitimate, or it appears the system is in a state of flux, then collective strategies are seen as necessary. These include low-status group members finding and giving voice to their own experiences and challenging the

---

42. Rupert Brown, "Social Identity Theory: Past Achievements, Current Problems and Future Challenges," *European Journal of Social Psychology* 30, no. 6 (2000): 745-778.

exploitive and denigrating ways their group is treated or represented by others.

Relationship of Privileging and the PMIF to Microaggressions

Even if groups of people who have been marginalized and excluded choose to critique and collectively challenge the status quo of privileging, this does not necessarily mean that the status quo will be altered and transformed toward fairness. The PMIF invites learners to notice how those who believe the status quo is fair and legitimate will likely treat those who are excluded and give voice to their discontent by way of criticism.

Specifically, in-group members or others can confront low-status group member criticisms in ways that challenge the validity of their claims of unfairness and inequality. The out-group member may be portrayed as someone who is overly sensitive, misinterpreting the motives or the good intentions of others (including organizations), or just a malcontent who can never be satisfied no matter what sort of remediation is offered. This type of reaction has been categorized as one type of microaggression, that of microinvalidation.[43] According to those researchers, however, microaggressions are framed primarily in terms of interpersonal slights and indignities. But the PMIF seeks to help learners frame statements like microinvalidations not just as slights and indignities, but also as indicators of efforts aimed at maintaining the privileging status quo. In particular, microinvalidations serve to silence the legitimate critique of the status quo, and through such silence, the dual processes of privileging and marginalization may continue to be seen as fair and legitimate.

The significance of another category of microaggression, namely microinsult, is also enhanced when taken in the context of the PMIF.

---

43. Derald Wing Sue, *Microaggressions in Everyday Life*; Derald Wing Sue, et al., "Racial Microaggressions in Everyday Life."

Microinsults are another form of slights or indignities that are unintentionally insulting. These can include statements that, on the surface, might sound like compliments, making them difficult to grasp. For example, a microinsult concerning gender is embedded in the comment that might be made by a male to a female, when he states, "You are really good at math, for a girl." The statement sounds like it is complimenting the woman for her competence in mathematics. But it is (ostensibly unintentionally) insulting, because it is based on the speaker's unspoken assumption and belief in the stereotype that "girls are bad at math."

But from the PMIF, this same statement can also be seen as stemming from male privileging. Males are permitted to avoid developing accurate, robust knowledge about women, and so do not have to rethink or reexamine their beliefs about women and their intellectual competencies. Nor do males in a sexist society need to learn about the effects of gender stereotypes, the impact of stereotype threat on task performance, and the pervasiveness and persistence of gender stereotypes in STEM fields. Hence, according to the PMIF, microinsults are not only insults and indignities, but can also be traced back to gender-based male privileging and seen as a reflection of (in this case, gendered) cultural incompetence. Additionally, the solution to microinsults from the vantage of the PMIF is not for the male to just stop being insulting, but also to replace his bogus beliefs and ideas about women, based as it is on stereotypes, with accurate knowledge of women and their experiences, especially from their diverse perspectives.

Privileging, Conditional Inclusion, and Pseudo-Progressive Organizations

As argued earlier, microinsults could be reflecting high-status group member privileging, and manifest even when the person is motivated to treat members of low-status groups kindly and respectfully. Likewise, without addressing the process or effects of privileging, organizations seeking to promote fairness can instead end up promoting particularly subtle forms of inequality, while not necessarily even knowing it. These organizations, labeled here as "pseudo-progressive," include those comprised of high-status group members who believe the issue of fairness and social identity diversity can simply be fixed by including low-status group members into the organization. But without addressing the processes underlying the persistence of demographic homogeneity, including privileging and marginalization, those outsiders invited into such organizations can easily experience a limited kind of inclusion, one that is predicated upon their compliance with certain (usually implicit) conditions.

Ravaud and Stiker (2001)[44] elaborate on the bifurcated concepts of inclusion and exclusion by identifying several types of each and exploring their interrelationships. One type of inclusion, "conditional inclusion," is especially useful here. Conditional inclusion draws attention to ways that individuals who are otherwise excluded from mainstream society and organizations may be offered inclusion, but only to the extent that they comply with certain conditions. From the perspectives of Ravaud and Stiker, and applied to people with disabilities being included within an able-ist society and its organizations, people with disabilities would need to comply with expectations, such as being able to submit themselves to verification of their disability status by "experts" such as medical practitioners. This condition would need to be met to the satisfaction of those in decision making positions before the person with the disability would be granted access to services, protections from violators of legal rights, and so forth. Such verification does not necessarily mean inclusion in all the same systems as everyone else without a disability, such as the labor market, however. And as long as relevant conditions are met, the person with the disability will be permitted such limited inclusion. A person's lack of compliance with conditions and expectations held by high-status group members could also result in loss of inclusion.

---

44. Jean Francois Ravaud and Henri-Jacques Stiker, "Inclusion/Exclusion: An Analysis of Historical and Cultural Meanings," in *Handbook of Disability Studies*, ed., G. Albrecht, K. Seelman and M. Bury (Thousand Oaks, CA: SAGE Publications, 2001), 490-512.

Various individuals might be recruited into an organization, or drawn from within, to spearhead diversity-related issues. They might be given various titles, such as Diversity Director, or Chief Diversity Officer,[45] but no matter the title, these diversity workers are expected to play a leadership role in the organization. In her research on diversity workers within higher education in Australia and the United Kingdom, Ahmed[46] draws attention to a number of practices that appear to reflect efforts toward equality, but instead appear to be promoting something else. In the PMIF, these are called diversity as "happy talk"; diversity as documentation; casualization of diversity commitment; and institutional passing. Minarik, the second author, adds "diversity as commodification" to this list. Each will be described briefly.

Diversity as "Happy Talk"

According to Ahmed,[47] acts of racism can be seen by pseudo-progressive organizations not as issues of inequality, but instead as events that tarnish the reputation of excellence the organization is seeking to maintain. This serves to silence those who are targeted by such violations and anyone else who wishes to speak out as connected to larger processes of exploitation, such as white supremacy. Individuals who persist in drawing attention to these manifestations will also become seen as "sore points" themselves, according to Ahmed, framed as the real problem,[48] and may be individually silenced in response.

---

45. Caroline Sotello Viernes Turner, Juan Carlos González, and J. Luke Wood, "Faculty of Color in Academe: What 20 Years of literature Tells Us," *Journal of Diversity in Higher Education* 1, no. 3 (2008):139-168, doi: 10.1037/a0012837.

46. Sara Ahmed, *On Being Included: Racism and Diversity in Institutional Life* (Durham, NC: Duke University Press, 2012).

47. Ibid.

48. Problematizing, according to Philomena Essed, *Everyday Racism: Reports from Women of Two Cultures* (Alameda, CA: Hunter House, 1990).

Diversity as Documentation

Extraordinary changes have taken place over the last several decades in an effort to eliminate employment inequality, including affirmative action policies and making discrimination illegal. Since John F. Kennedy's Executive Order 10925, concerning affirmative action, human resource managers throughout the country have worked to develop policies and procedures for ensuring fair labor practices. Unfortunately, complying with these policies can substitute for actual changes in organizational practices, drastically limiting their effectiveness.[49] That is, offices charged with ensuring fair employment practices can sometimes focus the bulk of their attention on documenting that they have followed the letter of anti-discrimination laws, without realizing the spirit of those laws. In such organizations, it is likely the primary concern is demonstrating due diligence, thereby dampening the likelihood that the organization can be found guilty of discrimination in future litigation. Such documentation can also take the form of bringing groups of people together in committees, with the charge of devising the organization's diversity definition, the diversity statement, and so forth. According to Ahmed, years can be wasted creating documents about diversity rather than addressing inequality.

Casualization of Commitment

According to Ahmed,[50] diversity workers indicated that universities often would make statements proclaiming that "diversity is the business of everyone," as if stating such would translate into actions. What was discovered, however, is that by making diversity the business of *everyone*, it could become the duty of *no one*. Alternately, organizations could proclaim diversity as an imperative, but then delegate responsibility for promoting it within the organization to a single individual or

---

49. Ahmed, *On Being Included*.
50. Ibid.

group. Both approaches reflect a casual orientation to issues of equality that stem from social identity differences. Each also represents a way to hold off allocating adequate resources to addressing mechanisms that perpetuate inequality, while allowing the organization to appear committed to change.

Institutional Passing

According to Ahmed,[51] institutional passing is another phenomenon that has been discerned by those seeking to challenge inequality within higher education organizations. Similar to super-surveillance,[52] institutional passing takes place when those who are permitted inclusion into the organization must monitor themselves continuously, to make certain they do not violate the organization's informal rules, cultural expectations, or otherwise appear to in-group members like they do not belong. Such passing likely requires such low-status group members to maintain a posture of being "nice" toward high-status in-group members when the latter utter privilege-based microinsults.

Commodification

The last manifestation operating within the PMIF's zone of conditional inclusion is that of commodification. Low-status group members can be commodified when they are hired as "diversity hires." That is, organization leaders perceive the demographic homogeneity of their employees as a problem, and correct the problem by recruiting and hiring individuals from the missing low-status group. This form of participation, also known as tokenism, is seen as the most superficial form of inclusion, representing a symbolic gesture at best.[53] Those employees

---

51. Ibid.

52. Nirmal Puwar, *Space Invaders* (Oxford, UK: Berg Publishers, 2004).

53. Sherry R. Arnstein, "A Ladder of Citizen Participation," *Journal of the American Institute of Planners* 35, no. 4 (1969): 216-224.

can also be placed in highly visible positions within the organization, in order to create an impression that the organization is committed to diversity and hence equality. Moreover, low-status group members will likely be in high demand to "represent diversity" throughout the organization. So, they will be given additional tasks, including assignment to hiring committees (in support of documenting diversity), having their images printed on documents and brochures, and having them address any and all issues associated by leaders as having to do with "diversity," such as organizing cultural potlucks (casualization of commitment).

Members, including leaders, of pseudo-progressive organizations might actually value critical comments and points made by out-group members in the organization related to fairness, social identity, and inequality. A White supervisor might genuinely appreciate having his racist statement or assumption brought to his attention by the one person of color he has hired to be on his team. Unfortunately, it is also possible that the same supervisor uses the expertise of his subordinate as a substitute for developing his own critical knowledge and awareness of his white supremacist beliefs and actions. Instead, he relies upon his subordinate to "keep him honest," using her as his personal diversity consultant, and preserving his ability to escape developing accurate knowledge for himself. What's more, he probably doesn't even consider paying his subordinate for her expertise, assuming instead she should be grateful he is interested in her perspective and feedback. His privilege-based permission to escape knowing about the "other" is preserved. Meanwhile his subordinate's expertise has been commodified for his convenience, and simultaneously exploited as free labor.

Such complex thoughts and reflections are invaluable and should be standard practice in the LIS curriculum.

The Class

The authors had the opportunity to experience the discomfort and enlightenment that is possible when teaching a stand-alone social justice course in a graduate LIS program.[54] *Social Justice in the Information Professions* was an 8-week class that was taught synchronously in an online setting. In its first offering in 2014, the class of twelve consisted primarily of White students (eight White females, one Latina, two White males, and one Latino, in addition to an African-American female instructor), and when offered in 2015, the class of sixteen again consisted primarily of White students (ten White females, one African-American female, one Latina, one African-American male, two White males, and one Latino, in addition to an African-American female instructor). The course content is intense and covers material and topics unfamiliar and challenging (i.e., white privilege, racism, etc.) to students, who themselves come from homogeneous communities and are sometimes unaware, or minimally aware of their own privilege or the oppression experienced by others. And for some students, it was their first time having an African-American female as a professor. With these things in mind, the class is explicitly set up and expectations set during the first course meeting. Students are alerted to the fact that hard topics will be discussed and they are challenged to be comfortable with being uncomfortable. Students are also advised that because of the self-reflection and self-assessment required, this class may not be appropriate for them—if they need to drop the class they are encouraged to do so with absolutely no ill will or penalties. The goal is to prepare students for an intense eight-week journey of self-discovery.

In addition to carefully framing the course in the opening session and creating an environment of "comfortable discomfort," risk-taking, and respect, the course benefited from collaboration with the University's Office of Inclusion and Intercultural Relations, Program on Intergroup Relations. During an intensive three-hour session, students were introduced to the "Privileging and Marginalization Integrative Framework"

---

54. Nicole A. Cooke, "Creating Opportunities for Empathy and Cultural Competence in the LIS Curriculum," *SRRT Newsletter* 187, (2014), http://libr.org/srrt/news/srrt187.php#9; Paul T. Jaeger, et al., "The Virtuous Circle Revisited: Injecting Diversity, Inclusion, Rights, Justice, and Equity into LIS from Education to Advocacy," *Library Quarterly* 85, no. 2 (2015): 150-171.

(PMIF),[55] initially developed and used extensively as a way to guide the training of staff and graduate student facilitators of intergroup dialogue classes. The framework offers a way for learners to see the interconnections of a number of social justice education concepts and theories. These include: oppression, privilege, status, social identity, ideology, stereotypes, and microaggressions. The framework also draws attention to linkages between micro- and macro-level phenomena, including decision making, and the mechanisms that maintain the privileging status quo.

Learners were invited to share their knowledge and experiences of privilege, and their concealed stories of navigating systems where they have occupied positions of less power.[56] Attention was drawn to the complex interplay of social identity group categorization, resultant positionality, and the likelihood of corresponding advantages available, and disadvantages avoided or escaped, based on perceived high-status group membership. As an experiential exercise, learners were invited to specify what appear to be the subtlest forms of marginalization. And in a step-wise exploration of the PMIF, learners were encouraged to adopt a more complex understanding of unfairness within systems, but without being overwhelmed by such complexity. Learners were also obliged to raise their expectations of how fairness, justice, and inclusion or integration should be pursued within systems and organizations.

Implementing the PMIF with LIS students

The PMIF was presented by Cooke, facilitated by Minarik, to students in the *Social Justice in the Information Professions* classes near the end of the eight-week term when students came to campus for a short-in person

---

55. Joseph D. Minarik, "Connecting the Dots of Oppression: The Privileging and Marginalization Integrative Framework (PIMF)," unpublished manuscript, last modified March 3, 2015.

56. Lee Bell and Rosemarie Roberts, "The Storytelling Project Model: A Theoretical Framework for Critical Examination of Racism through the Arts," *Teachers College Record* 112, no. 9 (2010): 2295–2319.

residency.[57] The one day allotted for face-to-face interaction was valuable and enabled the PMIF to be presented to students in a comprehensive and unrushed way during the first three hours of the class. The timing of the face-to-face residency also allowed for sufficient lead-in time; by this point in the semester students had participated in many discussions and readings about the history of social justice in the LIS profession and become familiar with several social justice issues and underserved populations they might expect to work with in the field (i.e., the incarcerated, the homeless, those affected by the digital divide).

Class content and discussions also revolved around Critical Race Theory,[58] cultural competence,[59] segregation in libraries, radical organizing, microaggressions,[60] and social justice as seen in more typical aspects of LIS, such as cataloging and library instruction. Once the PMIF was presented in a session entitled "Power, Influence, Oppression, and Privilege," students were presumably open, engaged, and ready to accept the additional challenge this workshop presented. Students were asked to embrace a complex understanding of unfairness within systems and challenged to think about how they, as information professionals, will fit into, and perhaps fight back, within these systems.

Applying the PMIF in an LIS classroom can be a transformative experience for students and enlightening for the instructors as well. Students' discomfort is sometimes palpable, and their cognitive dissonance

---

57. GSLIS' online Masters of Science program is called LEEP, and LEEP students were required to come to campus once a semester and spend one day face-to-face for every course in which they were enrolled.

58. Richard Delgado and Jean Stefancic, *Critical Race Theory: An Introduction* (New York: New York University Press, 2012); Tracie D. Hall, "The Black Body at the Reference Desk: Critical Race Theory and Black Librarianship," in *The 21st-Century Black Librarian in America: Issues and Challenges*, ed. Andrew P. Jackson, Julius C. Jefferson, Jr. and Akilah S. Nosakhere (Lanham, MD: Scarecrow Press, 2012), 197-203; Derrick A. Bell, *Faces at the Bottom of the Well: The Permanence of Racism* (New York: Basic Books, 1993).

59. Ghada El Turk, "Diversity and Cultural Competency," Colorado Libraries 29, no. 4 (2003): 5-7; Patricia Montiel Overall, "Cultural Competence: A Conceptual Framework for Library and Information Science Professionals," Library Quarterly 79, no. 2 (2009): 175-204.

60. Derald Wing Sue, *Microaggressions in Everyday Life*.

is clearly manifested in their expressions, questions, discussions, and also in their silence. However, by the end of the session, it is also obvious that there is new understanding and even more openness and desire to become a socially just and culturally competent information professional. One student in particular was unusually silent after the session, and when questioned, she responded, "I'm really uncomfortable, but I know that's OK".[61] This comment was an acknowledgment of the difficulty of the initial class session, during which students were asked to take risks in an effort to grow and hopefully begin a process of transformation. Other reactions from students (in both 2014 and 2015) included the feeling that their experiences had been validated (this was especially true for the students of color). The workshop had named circumstances in their lives that they had not realized existed (privilege, for example). Most importantly, perhaps, the PMIF workshop gave students the "language" they needed to engage in further reflection and conversations in relation to advocacy initiatives.

Conclusion

The risk to libraries seeking to address inequality is that the types of mechanisms decision makers might be able to imagine can easily fall into the category of pseudo-progressivism if the fundamental components of addressing privileging and continuous cognizance of exploitation are not prioritized. Librarians, as activists and seekers of fairness and equality, can learn to question day-to-day practices within these organizations, looking for ways that opportunity hoarding,[62] for example in the form of routine communications practices, might in fact be serving to privilege some, adding to their cumulative advantage,[63] while disad-

---

61. Student, in discussion with first author Cooke, March 2014.

62. Charles Tilly, *Durable Inequality* (Berkeley, CA: University of California Press, 1999; Nancy DiTomaso, *The American Non-Dilemma: Racial Inequality Without Racism* (New York: Russell Sage Foundation, 2013).

63. Thomas A. DiPrete and Gregory M. Eirich, "Cumulative Advantage as a Mechanism for Inequality: A Review of Theoretical and Empirical Developments," *Annual Review of Sociology* (2006): 271-297.

vantaging others who are out of the loop. The activist can then seek to create mechanisms that bring outsiders "into the loop" of information flows, communication channels, and in closer proximity to opportunities.

Through persistent examination of processes that look progressive, but inadvertently promote unfairness, and by discerning mechanisms that allow the privileging status quo to continue, the mechanisms of fairness may be discovered, created, and perpetuated instead. Social justice may be achieved and sustained as part of the interplay of individuals and systems that make resource distribution decisions from within a critically conscious framework, one that is supported and nurtured by systems featuring organizational cultures that challenge the dominant discourse, but also draw unrelenting critical attention to individual actions and the aggregated effects of those actions over time. In such organizations, libraries included, everyone is expected to develop fluency in their ability to critically think and talk about privileging and marginalization, making it easier to diagnose inequality. Working as a group, individuals in such an organization can then develop dynamic prescriptions and solutions for the problems thus defined.

It was argued earlier that cultural incompetence is one of the many results emanating from the privileging process. But it is precisely in those organizations which place an emphasis on all its members developing their capacity for critical understanding that the interplay between social identity-based differences, categorization processes, in-group out-group dynamics, and the role of power imbalances that will likely lead to collective cultural competence. That is, especially when those in high status groups, like heterosexuals, White people, and the temporarily able-bodied, spend time, energy, and attention in developing trustworthy knowledge bases about those whom they have been able to escape knowing about, cultural competence is able to emerge.

Moreover, such competence takes on a radical or fundamentally critical nature when such knowledge includes understanding of oneself from a socially critical perspective. Libraries, which can be considered microcosms of the larger society, suffer from ingrained privilege and wrestle with the necessity to overcome homogeneous knowledge bases. It is the argument of this chapter that a key way to combat these issues is to shine a light on them in the LIS classroom.

So, in a hypothetical, radically culturally competent library, by focusing specifically on addressing race-based inequality, White librarians in leadership and/or management positions make decisions based on accurate knowledge about the lives and perspectives of people of color, and others whom they are serving through services, collections, and programs. These same White library leaders also have a critical understanding of how power generally operates between White people and people of color within white supremacist systems. These White people are also committed to challenging imbalances and abuse of that power, however subtle or distal the expression or effects of such might be, on a moment-to-moment basis, and over time. Moreover, the challenge to unfair uses of power occurs both individually and collectively.

At the level of social networks, old networks, such as what has existed in the library profession, should be stretched and new networks created that increase the connections between individuals within the library and individual members of marginalized communities. These new networks can be introduced and discussed, in part, in the LIS curriculum. In these and other ways, libraries can complement recruitment efforts with capacity building plans, and place both processes within longer-term, substantive, inclusion strategies based on strong relationships of mutual trust, respect, and reciprocity. That is, libraries comprised of socially just and culturally competent staff can make it their business to establish strong, enduring relationships.

Bibliography

Adkins, Denice, and Isabel Espinal. "The Diversity Mandate." *Library Journal* 129, no. 7 (2004): 52-54.

Ahmed, Sara. *On Being Included: Racism and Diversity in Institutional Life.* Durham, NC: Duke University Press, 2012.

Andersson, Lynne M., and Christine M. Pearson. "Tit for Tat? The Spiraling Effect of Incivility in the Workplace." *Academy of Management Review* 24, no. 3 (1999):452-471. doi: 10.2307/259136.

American Library Association. *Diversity Counts*. Chicago: ALA Office for Research and Statistics and ALA Office for Diversity, 2012. Last modified September 28, 2012. http://www.ala.org/offices/diversity/diversitycounts/divcounts.

American Library Association. *American Library Association Releases New Data to Update Diversity Counts Report*. Chicago: ALA Office for Research and Statistics and ALA Office for Diversity, 2012. Last modified September 28, 2012. http://www.ala.org/news/2012/09/american-library-association-releases-new-data-update-diversity-counts-report.

Arnstein, Sherry R. "A Ladder of Citizen Participation." *Journal of the American Institute of Planners* 35, no. 4 (1969): 216-224.

Bell, Derrick A. *Faces at the Bottom of the Well: The Permanence of Racism*. New York: Basic Books, 1993.

Bell, Lee, and Rosemarie Roberts. "The Storytelling Project Model: A theoretical Framework for Critical Examination of Racism Through the Arts." *Teachers College Record* 112, no. 9 (2010): 2295–2319.

Blackwell, L. V., Snyder, L. A., & Mavriplis, C. "Diverse Faculty in STEM Fields: Attitudes, Performance, and Fair Treatment." *Journal of Diversity in Higher Education* 2, no. 4 (2009): 195-205. doi:10.1037/a0016974.

Bonilla-Silva, Eduardo. *Racism Without Racists: Color-Blind Racism and the Persistence of Racial Inequality in the United States*. Lanham, MD: Rowman & Littlefield, 2006.

Brown, Rupert. "Social Identity Theory: Past Achievements, Current Problems and Future Challenges." *European Journal of Social Psychology* 30, no. 6 (2000): 745-778.

Chu, Clara M. "Transformative Information Services: Uprooting Race Politics." *Black Caucus of the American Library Association Conference,* Las Vegas, July 19-22, 1999.

Coleman, James S. "Social Capital in the Creation of Human Capital." *American Journal of Sociology* (1988): S95-S120.

Cooke, Nicole A. "Creating Opportunities for Empathy and Cultural Competence in the LIS Curriculum." *SRRT Newsletter* 187, (2014a). http://libr.org/srrt/news/srrt187.php#9.

———. "The Spectrum Doctoral Fellowship Program: Enhancing the LIS Professoriate." *InterActions: UCLA Journal of Education and Information Studies* 10, no. 1 (2014).

Cooke, Nicole A., Miriam E. Sweeney, and Safiya U. Noble. "Social Justice as Topic And Tool: An Attempt to Transform an LIS Curriculum and Culture." *Library Quarterly* 86, no. 1 (2016).

Cortina, Lilia M. "Unseen Injustice: Incivility as Modern Discrimination in Organizations." *Academy of Management Review* 33, no. 1 (2008): 55-75.

Cortina, Lilia M., Dana Kabat-Farr, Emily A. Leskinen, Marisela Huerta, and Vicki J. Magley. "Selective Incivility as Modern Discrimination in Organizations: Evidence and Impact." *Journal of Management* 39, no. 6 (2013): 1579-1605. doi: 10.1177/0149206311418835.

Cortina, Lilia M., Vicki J. Magley, Jill Hunter Williams, and Regina Day Langhout. "Incivility in the Workplace: Incidence and Impact." *Journal of Occupational Health Psychology* 6, no. 1 (2001):64-80. doi: 10.1037/1076-8998.6.1.64.

Crosby, Faye, Susan Clayton, Olaf Alksnis, and Kathryn Hemker. "Cognitive Biases in the Perception of Discrimination: The Importance of Format." *Sex Roles* 14, no. 11-12 (1986): 637-646.

Delgado, Richard, and Jean Stefancic. *Critical Race Theory: An Introduction.* New York: New York University Press, 2012.

DiPrete, Thomas A., and Gregory M. Eirich. "Cumulative Advantage as a Mechanism for Inequality: A Review of Theoretical and Empirical Developments." *Annual Review of Sociology* (2006): 271-297.

DiTomaso, Nancy. *The American Non-Dilemma: Racial Inequality Without Racism*. New York: Russell Sage Foundation, 2013.

Dobbin, Frank. *Inventing Equal Opportunity*. Princeton, NJ: Princeton University Press, 2009.

Dumont, Rosemary Ruhig. "The Educating of Black Librarians: A Historical Perspective." *Journal of Education for Library and Information Science* (1986): 233-249.

Ebbin, Syma Alexi. "The Problem with Problem Definition: Mapping the Discursive Terrain of Conservation in Two Pacific Salmon Management Regimes." *Society and Natural Resources* 24, no. 2 (2011):148-164.

Eden, Colin, and Fran Ackermann. "Problem Structuring: On The Nature of, and Reaching Agreement About, Goals." *EURO Journal on Decision Processes* (2013):1-22.

El Turk, Ghada. "Diversity and Cultural Competency." *Colorado Libraries* 29, no. 4 (2003): 5-7.

Essed, Philomena. *Everyday Racism: Reports from Women of Two Cultures*. Alameda, CA: Hunter House, 1990.

Fultz, Michael. "Black Public Libraries in the South in the Era of De Jure Segregation." *Libraries & The Cultural Record* 41, no. 3 (2006): 337-359.

Hall, Tracie D. "The Black Body at the Reference Desk: Critical Race Theory and Black Librarianship." In *The 21st-Century Black Librarian in America: Issues and Challenges*, edited by Andrew P. Jackson, Julius C. Jefferson, Jr. and Akilah S. Nosakhere, 197-203. Lanham, MD: Scarecrow Press, 2012..

Hamilton Krieger, Linda, and Susan T. Fiske. "Behavioral Realism in Employment Discrimination Law: Implicit Bias and Disparate Treatment." *California Law Review* 94, no.4 (2006):997-1062. doi: 10.2307/20439058.

Harold, C. M., and B. C. Holtz. "The Effects of Passive Leadership on Workplace Incivility." *Journal of Organizational Behavior* 36, no. 1 (2015):16-38. doi: 10.1002/job.1926.

Honma, Todd. "Trippin' Over the Color Line: The Invisibility of Race in Library and Information Studies." *InterActions: UCLA Journal of Education and Information Studies* 1, no. 2 (2005).

Hopkins, Bryan. *Cultural Differences and Improving Performance: How Values and Beliefs Influence Organizational Performance*. Burlington, VT: Gower Publishing. 2009.

Jaeger, Paul T., Nicole A. Cooke, Cecilia Feltis, Michelle Hamiel, Fiona Jardine, and Katie Shilton. "The Virtuous Circle Revisited: Injecting Diversity, Inclusion, Rights, Justice, and Equity into LIS from Education to Advocacy." *Library Quarterly* 85, no. 2 (2015): 150-171.

Jaeger, Paul T., John Carlo Bertot, and Renée E. Franklin. "Diversity, Inclusion, and Underrepresented Populations in LIS Research." *Library Quarterly* 80, no. 2 (2010): 175-181.

Jaeger, Paul T., Mega M. Subramaniam, Cassandra B. Jones, and John Carlo Bertot. "Diversity and LIS Education: Inclusion and the Age of Information." *Journal of Education for Library and Information Science* (2011): 166-183.

Jaeger, Paul T., and Renée E. Franklin. "The Virtuous Circle: Increasing Diversity in LIS Faculties to Create More Inclusive Library Services and Outreach." *Education Libraries* 30, no. 1 (2007): 20-26.

Johnson, Allan G. *Privilege, Power, and Difference*. Boston: McGraw-Hill, 2001.

Josey, E. J. "Diversity: Political and Societal Barriers." *Journal of Library Administration* 27, no. 1-2 (1999): 191-202.

Korsmo, Fae L. "Problem Definition and the Alaska Natives: Ethnic Identity and Policy Formation." *Review of Policy Research* 9, no. 2 (1989): 294-306.

Link, Bruce G, and Jo C. Phelan. "Conceptualizing Stigma." *Annual Review of Sociology (2001)*: 363-385.

Magee, Joe C., and Adam D. Galinsky. "Social Hierarchy: The Self-Reinforcing Nature of Power and Status." *Academy of Management Annals* 2, no. 1 (2008): 351-398.

Malone, Cheryl Knott. "Toward a Multicultural American Public Library History." *Libraries & Culture* (2000): 77-87.

Martin, Renée J. and Dawn M. Van Gunten. "Reflected Identities Applying Positionality and Multicultural Social Reconstructionism in Teacher Education." *Journal of Teacher Education* 53, no. 1 (2002):44-54.

McGarty, Craig, Vincent Y. Yzerbyt, and Russell Spears, Eds. *Stereotypes as Explanations: The Formation of Meaningful Beliefs About Social Groups*. Cambridge, UK: Cambridge University Press, 2002.

McIntosh, Peggy. "White Privilege and Male Privilege: A Personal Account of Coming to See Correspondences through Work in Women's Studies." Paper presented at Virginia Women's Studies Association Conference, Richmond, VA, April 1986.

Minarik, Joseph D. "Privilege as Privileging: Making the Dynamic and Complex Nature of Privilege and Marginalization Accessible." *Journal of Social Work Education* (forthcoming).

———. "Connecting the Dots of Oppression: The Privileging and Marginalization Integrative Framework (PMIFF)." Unpublished manuscript, last modified March 3, 2015.

Nutt, Paul C. "Surprising but True: Half the Decisions in Organizations Fail." *Academy of Management Executive* 13, no. 4
(1999):75-90.

———. "The formulation processes and tactics used in organizational decision making." *Organization Science* 4, no 2
(1993):226-251.

Overall, Patricia Montiel. "Cultural Competence: A Conceptual
Framework for Library and Information Science Professionals." *Library Quarterly* 79, no. 2 (2009): 175-204.

Pateman, John, and John Vincent. *Public Libraries and Social Justice.*
Farnham, UK: Ashgate, 2012.

Pawley, Christine. "Unequal Legacies: Race and Multiculturalism in
the LIS Curriculum." *Library Quarterly* 76, no. 2 (2006): 149-
168.

Peterson, Lorna. "The Definition of Diversity: Two Views. A More
Specific Definition." *Journal of Library Administration* 27, no.
1-2 (1999): 17-26.

Portes, Alejandro. "Social Capital: Its Origins and Applications in
Modern Sociology." *Annual Review of Sociology* 24 (1998):
1-24.

Puwar, Nirmal. *Space Invaders.* Oxford, UK: Berg Publishers, 2004.

Ravaud, Jean Francois, and Henri-Jacques Stiker. "Inclusion/Exclu-
sion: An Analysis of Historical and Cultural Meanings. "
In *Handbook of Disability Studies*, edited by G. Albrecht, K.
Seelman and M. Bury, 490-512. Thousand Oaks, CA: SAGE
Publications, 2001.

Stone, Deborah. *Policy Paradox: The Art of Political Decision Making.* 3rd
ed. New York: W. W. Norton, 2012.

Sue, Derald Wing. *Microaggressions in Everyday Life: Race, Gender, and
Sexual Orientation.* Hoboken, NJ: John Wiley & Sons, 2010.

Sue, Derald Wing, Christina M. Capodilupo, Gina C. Torino, Jennifer M. Bucceri, Aisha Holder, Kevin L. Nadal, and Marta Esquilin. "Racial Microaggressions in Everyday Life: Implications for Clinical Practice." *American Psychologist* 62, no. 4 (2007): 271-286.

Tilly, Charles. "Past and Future Inequalities." *International Social Science Review* 2, no. 1 (2001): 5-18.

————.. *Durable Inequality*. Berkeley, CA: University of California Press, 1999.

Turner, Caroline, Sotello Viernes, Juan Carlos González, and J. Luke Wood. "Faculty of Color in Academe: What 20 Years of Literature Tells Us." *Journal of Diversity in Higher Education* 1, no. 3 (2008):139-168. doi: 10.1037/a0012837.

Turner, Caroline, Sotello Viernes, Samuel L. Myers, Jr., and John W. Creswell. "Exploring Underrepresentation: The Case of Faculty of Color in the Midwest." *Journal of Higher Education* 70, no. 1 (1999):27-59. doi: 10.2307/2649117.

Wiegand, Wayne A. "The Development of Librarianship in the United States." *Libraries & Culture* 24, no. 1 (1989): 99-109.

Chapter 6

SOCIAL INCLUSION AND THE GATEKEEPING MECHANISMS OF CURATORIAL VOICE: ARE MUSEUMS READY TO BE AGENTS OF SOCIAL JUSTICE?

Laura-Edythe Coleman

Introduction

Information plays a key role in the construction of both individual and collective identities. It is understood that without access to cultural information, individuals and communities are barred from constructing a holistic identity.[1] Indeed, in order for people to generate more just societies, they must first have access to the cultural information necessary to construct their identity.[2] In societies around the globe, we have institutionalized culture within a museum format, and we rely upon museums and museum professionals to provide authoritative representations of culture.[3] As they are in service to humanity,[4] museums must preserve

---

1. Andrew Newman and Fiona McLean, "The Impact of Museums upon Identity," *International Journal of Heritage Studies* 12, no. 1 (January 2006): 49–68.

2. John H. Falk, *Learning from Museums: Visitor Experiences and the Making of Meaning*, American Association for State and Local History Book Series (Walnut Creek, CA: AltaMira Press, 2000), 217.

3. Tony Bennett, *The Birth of the Museum: History, Theory, Politics, Culture: Policies and Politics* (London; New York: Routledge, 1995), 28.

4. Stephen E. Weil, *Making Museums Matter* (Washington, DC: Smithsonian Institute Press, 2002), 30; Robert Janes, *Museums in a Troubled World: Renewal, Irrelevance or Collapse?* (London; New York: Routledge, 2009), 13-14.

and provide access to those objects that convey information for this necessary identity construction. In so doing, museums exemplify their status as socially inclusive institutions.[5]

It is the premise of this chapter that museums must first fortify their position as the proponents of *social inclusion* (within their collections, their exhibits, and their policies) prior to assuming an advocacy role for justice within society. The author of this chapter asserts that museums are rarely prepared to be the engines of progressive community action, and that exemplar museums are those originally formed through a community-based model for the purpose of localized social justice, such as the "Community-Based Exhibition" model of the Wing Luke Museum of the Asian Pacific American Experience.[6] She also argues that the first true step toward increased museum-generated social justice is *equity of access to cultural information through the socially inclusive role of curatorial voice.*[7]

To this end, this chapter provides an outline of the following themes: the use of social inclusion theory in libraries and museums; an example of applying the Library and Information Sciences (LIS) gatekeeping theory to illustrate the notion of social inclusion in museums; and suggestions for future research of museum curator roles. In this chapter, the author proposes a *Curatorial Voice Gatekeeping Mechanisms Chart* (Table 1) to be employed in the articulation of curatorial roles. This chart, designed by the author, is built upon LIS theories of gatekeeping, has been refined by curator participants of a 2014 pilot study, and is currently being vetted by curator participants of a research study in museums throughout the United States. The proposed use of gatekeeping theory in a museum context is extremely practical: museums have the ability to physically display only a small portion of their collection, and it is inevitable that

---

5. Richard Sandell, "Social Inclusion, the Museum and the Dynamics of Sectoral Change," *Museums and Society* 1, no. 1 (2003): 45–62.

6. Cassie Chinn, "Community–Based Exhibition Model," (Seattle, Washington: Wing Luke Museum of the Asian Pacific American Experience, 2006), http://www.wingluke.org/community–process.

7. Sandell, "Social Inclusion," 45-46.

certain objects must be withheld from exhibit display.[8] Readers are challenged to relate the *Curatorial Voice Gatekeeping Mechanisms Chart proposed within this chapter* to their own collections and exhibitions, and to view their work anew through the lens of LIS gatekeeping theory. Researchers are further challenged to investigate notions of museums as places of holistic identity construction. The chapter concludes with a challenge to museum informatics researchers to fill gaps within researcher and practitioner knowledge concerning curatorial roles, and to aid in the development of socially inclusive museums.

The Use of Social Inclusion Theory in Libraries and Museums

What is Social Inclusion Theory?

Provocative in nature, *social exclusion* became a tenet of Western European social studies during the 1970s.[9] The flashpoint for these studies was the French expansion of welfare systems, which groaned under the growing weight of a pluralistic society.[10] "Social exclusion" became the title of numerous economic and social injustices, but was essentially limited to naming the problem without offering practical solutions.[11]

The ability to name societal woes granted authority to several decades of politicians who were self-appointed champions for social justice.[12] Social exclusion has come to represent a broad variety of problems not limited to welfare benefits, and not localized to France.[13] By the mid-

---

8. Paul F. Marty and Katherine Burton Jones, eds., *Museum Informatics: People, Information, and Technology in Museums* (New York: Routledge, 2008), 81.

9. Hilary Silver, "Social Exclusion and Social Solidarity: Three Paradigms," *International Labour Review* 133, no. 5,6 (1994): 531–578.

10. Silver, "Social Exclusion," 532-533.

11. Ibid., 533.

12. Ibid.

13. Jocelyn Dodd and Richard Sandell, *Including Museums: Perspectives on Museums, Galleries and Social Inclusion* (Leicester, UK: Research Centre for Museums and Galleries, 2001), 8-9.

1990s the term *social exclusion* had become an essential part of western European political rhetoric and a part of museum studies literature.[14] In completing the circle of political rhetoric, Western European policy makers proposed solutions to exclusion under the term *social inclusion*.[15]

Social inclusion is often the "assumed corollary" to exclusion, being conceptualized solely in relation to exclusion.[16] In this perspective, social inclusion and exclusion are "inseparable sides of the same coin."[17] The term "social inclusion" has been attached to social and economic theories. It has become, since the 1970s, enmeshed in the government policies of Western Europe and the United Kingdom (UK).[18] The ambiguous discourse on social inclusion often contains descriptors such as 'combating' and 'mitigating' social exclusion, yet it rarely stands alone as its own term, and it is often explained in terms of being a response to social exclusion.[19] The conceptual framework of social inclusion provides a foundation for museums to address difficult social exclusion issues that hinder the advocacy of social justice.

----

14. Richard Sandell, "Museums as Agents of Social Inclusion," *Museum Management and Curatorship* 17, no.4 (1998): 401–18; "Museums and Social Inclusion: The GLLAM Report," Group for Large Local Authority Museums (Leicester, UK: Research Centre for Museums and Galleries, 2000), 5-6, 9; Dodd and Sandell, *Including Museums*, 8-9; Jocelyn Dodd et al., *A Catalyst for Change: The Social Impact of the Open Museum* (RCMG Leicester, 2002), 6; Richard Sandell and Eithne Nightingale, eds., "Museums, Equality, and Social Justice," *Museum Meanings* (Abingdon, Oxon; New York, NY: Routledge, 2012), 1-8; Richard Sandell, "Museums, Society, Inequality," *Museum Meanings* (London; New York: Routledge, 2002), 3-20; Sandell, "Social Inclusion," 45-62.

15. A. Tlili, "Behind the Policy Mantra of the Inclusive Museum: Receptions of Social Exclusion and Inclusion in Museums and Science Centres," *Cultural Sociology* 2, no. 1 (March 1, 2008): 123–47.

16. Nabin Rawal, "Social Inclusion and Exclusion: A Review," *Dhaulagiri Journal of Sociology and Anthropology* 2, (October 2, 2008):161–80.

17. Ibid., 171.

18. Stefan Bernhard, "Beyond Constructivism: The Political Sociology of an EU Policy Field," *International Political Sociology* 5, no. 4 (December 1, 2011): 426–45; Dodd and Sandell, *Including Museums*, 8-9; Newman and McLean, "The Impact of Museums," 49-50.

19. Rawal, "Social Inclusion and Exclusion," 171-172.

How has Library and Information Science Research Engaged Social Inclusion Theory?

In recent years the topic of social inclusivity has been broached in several library and information science (LIS) contexts: the socially-exclusive nature of Library of Congress Subject Headings, the role of local libraries in the cultural assimilation of immigrants, the local library as an agent of social inclusion for homeless persons, and the social purpose of libraries in reaching those marginalized by information poverty.[20] These discussions are not unique within professional discourse. In fact, quite the opposite is true: librarians have long been linked with social justice and the creation of more just societies through access to information.

Museum professionals, now tasked with similar social initiatives, can benefit from the development of the social role of librarians by acknowledging relevant links and walls between libraries and museums. Information professionals, regardless of context, museologist or librarian, are participants in dialogue:[21] we exist to assist individuals and communities in the process of identity negotiation through the provision of cultural information. This chapter proposes that LIS research and the example of LIS practitioners can bring several benefits to the expanding social role of museums today.

---

20. Nadia Caidi and Daniel Allard, "Social Inclusion of Newcomers to Canada: An Information Problem?" *Library & Information Science Research* 27, no. 3 (June 2005): 302–24; J.D. Hendry, "Social Inclusion and the Information Poor," *Library Review* 49, no. 7 (2000): 331–36, doi:10.1108/00242530010344192; Darrin Hodgetts et al., "A Trip to the Library: Homelessness and Social Inclusion," *Social and Cultural Geography* 9, no. 8 (December 2008): 933–53.

21. Marty and Jones, Museum Informatics, 3; Paul Marty, "The Changing Nature of Information Work in Museums," *Journal of the American Society for Information Science and Technology* 58, no. 1 (January 1, 2007): 97–107.

How can Museums Benefit from an LIS Perspective of Social Inclusion?

First, library and information science (LIS) and librarians have a long-standing relationship with social justice that should serve as a model for museums.[22] The philosophical fervor that has characterized the LIS profession, as evidenced by the promotion of libraries as "institutionalized organizers of world knowledge and service providers of information to meet the needs of all members in society,"[23] is an ideal that aligns well with the vision of museums through the International Council of Museums (ICOM).[24] Historically, librarians and information professionals embody their service-oriented philosophy, connecting themselves directly to the communities in which they serve.[25] Not only have librarians maintained a practical relationship with marginalized and excluded communities, LIS researchers have also focused on the needs of society. Rioux notes the work of Elfreda Chatman and others:

---

22. Bharat Mehra, Kendra S. Albright, and Kevin Rioux, "A Practical Framework for Social Justice Research in the Information Professions," *Proceedings of the American Society for Information Science and Technology* 43, no. 1 (October 10, 2007): 1–10; TJ Froehlich, "Ethical Considerations of Information Professionals," *Annual Review of Information Science and Technology* 27 (1992): 291–394; J. Shera, *Introduction to Library Service: Basic Elements of Library Service* (Littleton, CO: Libraries Unlimited), 1976, 7; Robert Schroeder and Christopher V. Hollister, "Librarians' Views on Critical Theories and Critical Practices," *Behavioral & Social Sciences Librarian* 33, no. 2 (April 3, 2014): 91–119; Kevin Rioux, "Metatheory in Library and Information Science: A Nascent Social Justice Approach," *Journal of Education for Library & Information Science* 51, no. 1 (2010): 9–17; S. Stauffer, "'She Speaks as One Having Authority': Mary E. Downey's Use of Libraries as a Means to Public Power," *Libraries and Culture* 40, no. 1 (2005): 38–62; Bharat Mehra, Kevin Rioux, and Kendra Albright, "Social Justice in Library and Information Science," In *Encyclopedia of Library and Information Sciences*, 3rd ed., (New York, NY: Taylor and Francis, 2009), 4820–36; American Library Association, "Core Values of Librarianship," American Library Association, 2004, http://www.ala.org/advocacy/intfreedom/statementspols/corevalues.

23. Mehra, Rioux, and Albright, "Social Justice," 4822.

24. "ICOM," *The ICOM Code of Professional Ethics*, 2013, http://icom.museum/the–vision/code–of–ethics/.

25. Shera, *Introduction to Library Service*, 42-59; Froehlich, "Ethical Considerations," 291-324; Mehra, Albright, and Rioux, "A Practical Framework," 2.

"…information professions have long been associated with inclusive-ness, civic-mindedness, and concern for the poor and under-served."[26] This heartfelt concern for marginalized communities is a characteristic of LIS that should serve as a model for museum professionals and researchers seeking to expand their social role.

Second, LIS research has expanded our understanding of the role of librarian as information provider, and the role of patron as informa-tion seeker.[27] Library and information science researchers, informed by museological history and LIS theory, may play a role in social inclusion evaluation of museums and museum community impact assessment, especially if the assessments clearly link back to local communities. In this way, LIS researchers reiterate the "importance of outcome-based, socially relevant evaluation methods in assessing library services,"[28] but within the museum context. LIS researchers also have specialized experience, expertise that transcends the library context, and may use their unique skills to assist local communities with the formalization of their cultural representation.[29]

Third, LIS has a theoretical area devoted to exploring the role of information in museums. Formally characterized as "Museum Infor-matics," this theory stream specifically addresses the overlap between

26. E.A. Chatman, "A Theory of Life in the Round," *Journal of the Ameri-can Society for Information Science & Technology* 50, no. 3 (1999): 207–17; E.A. Chatman, "The Impoverished Life–World of Outsiders," *Journal of the Ameri-can Society for Information Science &Technology* 47, no. 3 (1996): 193–2006; E.A. Chatman, "The Information World of Retired Women," *New Directions in Information Management*, no. 29 (New York: Greenwood Press, 1992), 23; Kevin Rioux, "Metatheory in Library and Information Science: A Nascent Social Justice Approach," Journal of Education for Library & Information Science 51, no. 1 (2010), 9.

27. M.J. Bates, "Toward an Integrated Model of Information Seeking and Searching," In *The New Review of Information Behaviour Research* 3 (2002): 1–15.

28. Mehra, Rioux, and Albright, "Social Justice," 4824.

29. John Agada, "Inner–City Gatekeepers: An Exploratory Survey of Their Information Use Environment," *Journal of the American Society for Information Science* 50, no. 1 (January 1999): 74–85; B. Hjorland, "Social and Cultural Awareness and Responsibility in Library, Information and Documentation Studies," In *Aware and Responsible*, eds. B. Rayward, J. Hansson, and V. Suom-inen, (Lanham, MD: Scarecrow Press, 2003), 71–91.

libraries and museums.[30] As library and information science researchers, we may provide key insights into the social role of museums by balancing the knowledge of museological history with LIS theory. Museology asserts that modern Western museums were forged by the desires of governments to civilize the masses through "cultural governance of the populace."[31] Informed by museological history, LIS researchers in the area of museum informatics position themselves at the apex of the connection between museums, information, people, and technology.[32] From this LIS vantage point, museum informaticists have the ability to provide foundational models of social inclusion, with the expressed intention of promoting social justice through museums.

How has Museum Research Used Social Inclusion Theory?

The idea of a *socially inclusive museum* as a proposed agent of social change first appeared in museum literature circa 1998.[33] Research into social inclusion in museums followed the publication of Richard Sandell's 1998 seminal article, "Museums as Agents of Social Inclusion."[34,35] Sandell proposed the identification of the social inclusivity of any museum in a new typology, defining the scope of museum responsibilities. His article reframed the social purpose of the museum within the context of social inclusion and proposed that museums have both the *responsibility* and the *ability* to combat the multi-faceted problems of social exclusion.[36] Of the varied manifestations of social exclusion, perhaps

---

30. Marty and Jones, *Museum Informatics*, 3; Marty, "The Changing Nature," 97.

31. Bennett, *The Birth of the Museum*, 21.

32. Marty, "The Changing Nature," 97.

33. Sandell, "Museums as Agents," 401-418.

34. Ibid.

35. Sandell, "Social Inclusion," 45; "The GLLAM Report," 9; Dodd et al., *A Catalyst for Change*, 6.

36. Sandell, "Museums as Agents," 408.

the most obviously museum-related is cultural exclusion. How museums represent cultures and ask cultures to participate in the making of exhibits directly impacts the inclusivity or exclusivity of a museum.[37] It is the assertion of this chapter, and a suggestion of Sandell's typology, that cultural inclusivity is the first step necessary for museums to become agents of social justice.[38]

Richard Sandell promoted museums as agents of social change, and combatants of social exclusion, a relatively new role for museums. Unlike the long history of community embeddedness demonstrated by the library, the museum has often been associated with the dominant elite within society.[39] To this end, Sandell's socially inclusive museum is not a simple solution to the problems of social exclusion, but a graduated, scaffolded approach. Within his typology, Sandell describes a spectrum of museums in three main categories: "the inclusive museum," "the museum as agent of social regeneration," and "the museum as vehicle for broad social change."[40] Each of these types of museums has different goals, methods, and levels of transparency. For the inclusive museum, the goal is to represent marginalized groups in exhibits and to provide access for those who would be excluded due to lack of transportation or wealth. The socially inclusive museum will prioritize the inclusion of objects and exhibits that represent the marginalized portions of their society. An example scenario of economic exclusion is readily available in the charge of admission to museums: an individual lacking the economic means to buy admission to a museum is unlikely to visit. Thus, the individual who does not visit the museum does not receive cultural information necessary for the construction of identity. It should be noted that an individual is rarely faced with an admission charge to a library; hence, the economic issues of exclusion are more

---

37. Ibid.

38. Ibid.; Sandell, "Social Inclusion," 45-46.

39. Weil, *Making Museums Matter*, 28-36; Bennett, *The Birth of the Museum*, 21; Janes, *Museums in a Troubled World*, 17.

40. Sandell, "Museums as Agents," 416.

easily tackled within libraries, and librarians can be more actively involved in social justice issues within their communities. As in libraries, the socially inclusive museum may engage those disenfranchised groups in participatory, collaborative ways and assure that access to cultural information is provided.[41]

Sandell proposes that as a community responds to the museum's socially inclusive overtures, the museum moves into a more active social justice role. This second category of museum is the museum as agent of social regeneration. This type of museum connects with the community on more than the just the cultural level. A museum functioning as an agent of social regeneration integrates cultural exhibits with social, economic, and political aspects of communities. A possible scenario for this type of museum would be an exhibit on health in collaboration with the local health department. In this museum type exists the presence of obvious initiatives to better the lives of the individuals within a community.

The museum as vehicle for broad social change is the third museum type in Sandell's typology. This museum acknowledges publicly its societal role and is determined to change society for the better. As a vehicle for broad social change, this museum type influences society in accordance with an articulated social inclusion agenda.[42]

Perhaps the most telling aspect of the social inclusion movement within museums is the awareness, even by the museum community in 1998, that many museums were not ready to become socially inclusive. According to Sandell, "Those museums which clearly articulate their purpose in relation to society and which purposefully seek to position themselves as organizations with a part to play in multi-agency solutions for tackling social exclusion, are nevertheless still rare."[43] This was noticeable in discussions of inclusive museums by 2003: "Evidence of

---

41. Nina Simon, *The Participatory Museum* (Santa Cruz, CA: Museum 2.0, 2010), i-iv; Sandell, "Museums as Agents," 408; Sandell, "Social Inclusion," 45.

42. Sandell, "Museums as Agents," 414-416.

43. Ibid., 415.

more widespread change within the sector (museums) remains elusive and many suspect that, though it is not always publicly voiced, internal resistance to change is high."[44] Along with the charge to become more socially inclusive in the late 1990s, a call for greater research into the social role of museums was issued, with primary examples based within the UK.[45] Recent policy and funding initiatives for museum research acknowledge that museums must first create a socially inclusive cultural foundation before embarking on strong social justice programs.[46]

By 2000, social inclusion theory began to strongly inform research in Western European and UK museums. In 1999–2000, Professors Eilean Hooper-Greenhil, Richard Sandell, Theano Moussouri, and Helen O'Rain led a team of researchers to study twenty-two UK museums, resulting in the Group for Large Local Authority Museums (GLLAM) report, *Museums and Social Inclusion*.[47] *The GLLAM Report* acknowledged that museums "have not been in the forefront of social inclusion work."[48] Following *The GLLAM Report*, the University of Leicester sponsored another study, *Small Museums and Social Inclusion: What Contribution Can Small Museums Make to Social Inclusion?* This report, a study of smaller museums and social inclusion, was also supported by the Museums, Library, and Archives Council and led to the publication of *Including Museums: Perspectives on Museums, Galleries and Social Inclusion*. The latter of these publications included the voices of many different museum practitioners, and sparked the interest within the museum community to pursue the social inclusion agenda.[49]

In 2008, Anwar Tlili investigated the ambiguous nature of social inclusion theory terminology found throughout the layers of society,

44. Sandell, "Social Inclusion," 46.

45. Ibid., 46.

46. Ibid., 45-46.

47. "The GLLAM Report," 1-59.

48. Ibid., 5.

49. Dodd and Sandell, *Including Museums*, i.

including the many levels of museum professionals.[50] Tlili conducted a series of interviews with museum professionals at four UK institutions. A cross-section of the staff was interviewed concerning their own perceptions of social inclusion and the role of museums in social inclusion.[51] Tlili determined that within those four UK museums, "Social inclusion has redefined the organizational priorities and the organizational identity of the museum, thus causing a ripple effect on the professional cultures and identities within the museum, and the balance of power between these."[52] He refers to social inclusion as "generic" and complex, since it is an "object of struggle as it lends itself to multiple and conflicting social ontologies and causal explanations." [53] In interviewing museum curators concerning their definitions of social inclusion, they predominately referred to social inclusion as an accessibility issue. Curator interpretation of social inclusion policy centered on making the museum accessible to marginalized community groups. Upon deeper examination, it became apparent that under New Labour government in the UK, museum accessibility was necessary to increase museum attendance among underrepresented groups. Under New Labour, museums became government funded and entrance fees per visitor were no longer collected. In turn, museums were expected to increase museum attendance in a way that would reflect the demographics of the population of Britain. For the museum professionals interviewed by Tlili, social inclusion was no longer a concept concerning broad social change, but a label for museum attendance quotas.

In the UK, social inclusion theory has had unintended consequences on policy, and in turn, an impact on museum professional identity. Museum professionals interviewed by Tlili reported a perceived threat to their professional identity due to the emphasis placed by policy makers

---

50. Tlili, "Behind the Policy Mantra," 123-124.

51. Ibid., 123-147.

52. Ibid., 142.

53. Ibid., 123–124.

on proving the numerical changes.[54] Tlili contends that the strength of social inclusion theory is countered by the weakness introduced to museum professional identity.[55] Tlili further states that UK-based museum professionals have changed the nature of social inclusion in museums such that "the organizational 'construct' of social inclusion is to a great extent governed by a numerical logic."[56]

Social inclusion theory has recently begun to appear in American museum practitioner discourse, as evidenced by the 2014 American Alliance of Museums (AAM) policy on "Diversity and Inclusion."[57] This chapter asserts that social inclusion theory, based on the past twenty years of research, meets museums at their current place within society and provides a key pathway to implementing a social justice agenda. Despite the trending professional discussions of social inclusion in museums as evidenced in museum conferences (Museum Next, The Inclusive Museum, AAM),[58] research into US-based inclusive museums remains limited. The lack of US-based research may be a result of several factors, including the small number of US museums articulating social inclusion within their mission statements, or confusion within the museum profession about social inclusion terminology.

Although a limited number of US-based museums articulate a social inclusion mission, the few examples are vivid cases. One such example is the Museum of Tolerance in Los Angeles, California, formed from the visionary leadership of Simon Wiesenthal, a Holocaust survivor. The articulated purpose of the Museum of Tolerance is, "To create an experience that would challenge people of all backgrounds to confront their most closely-held assumptions and assume responsibility for

---

54. Tlili, "Behind the Policy Mantra," 143.

55. Ibid., 142.

56. Ibid., 143.

57. "Diversity and Inclusion Policy," 2014, http://www.aam–us.org/about–us/who–we–are/strategic–plan/diversity–and–inclusion–policy.

58. "Museum Next," *Museum Next*, 2014, http://www.museumnext.com; "The Inclusive Museum," *The Inclusive Museum*, 2014, httt://onmuseums.com/the–conference.

change."[59] Although the Museum of Tolerance began with addressing the social issues that predated the Holocaust, it has expanded the scope of work to include modern-day issues of tolerance and prejudice. "The decision was made to create a museum – but not an ordinary museum of artifacts and documents. As Simon Wiesenthal expressed, it must not only remind us of the past, but remind us to act."[60] The Museum of Tolerance, and its associated educational programs, are strongly socially inclusive and push the visiting public to take responsibility for social justice in current day avenues.

Another socially inclusive museum model is the Community-Based Exhibition model, or CBE, developed at the Wing Luke Museum of the Asian Pacific American Experience.[61] The CBE model acknowledges several core ideals of the socially inclusive museum: 1) museums are "purveyors of public knowledge and interpretation and are powerful institutions;" 2) museums should ask "Who gets presented? How are they presented and under what terms?" and 3) that within museums there are "many voices and personalities to take into consideration."[62] In particular, the Wing Luke Museum has actively engaged their community as transmitters and creators of culture, and in doing so empowered their community through museum participation.[63]

Other museum models of social justice and progressive community action are difficult to find within the United States, but may be further explored through the International Coalition of Sites of Conscience (ICSC).[64] The ICSC lists an international directory of museums and cultural groups that self-align with this mission statement, "We are sites,

---

59. "Our History and Vision – Museum of Tolerance, Los Angeles, CA," Accessed May 26, 2015, http://www.museumoftolerance.com/site/c. tmL6KfNVLtH/b.4866027/k.88E8/Our_History_and_Vision.htm.

60. Ibid.

61. Chinn, *Community–Based Exhibition Model*, 3-26.

62. Ibid., 13.

63. Ibid.

64. "Sites of Conscience," *Sites of Conscience*, March 2015, http://www.site-sofconscience.org/.

individuals, and initiatives activating the power of places of memory to engage the public in connecting past and present in order to envision and shape a more just and humane future."[65] Museum professionals seeking to engage their communities as agents of social change should be encouraged to familiarize themselves with the work of the ICSC.

What are Other Advantages of Social Inclusion Theory Use within Museums?

There are several other inherent advantages in the use of social inclusion theory to understand the impact of museums on marginalized or divided segments of societies. The primary advantage of social inclusion theory is that it extends museological dialogue beyond traditional discussions of diversity and multiculturalism. In addressing the socially inclusive /exclusive dilemma of museum cultural heritage exhibition development, Lavine wisely remarked, "There is no institutional stance adequate to another culture's art."[66] As museums grapple with social inclusivity, the multilayered concept of social inclusion may seem to be in direct conflict with traditional museum practices that emphasize the authority of the museum: social inclusion asserts the importance of including more than the institutionalized representations of marginalized communities, actively engaging those communities in the co-creation of community heritage exhibits.[67] In 2001, Newman and McLean reported the results of research performed to study the role of museums in identity creation, with the specific goal of providing suggestions to the UK government concerning social inclusion policy. Newman and McLean employed a "circuit of culture" model based on Burgess and Johnson's five cultural processes, "identity, representation,

---

65. Ibid.

66. Ivan Karp and Steven Lavine, *Exhibiting Cultures: The Poetics and Politics of Museum Display.* Edited by Rockefeller Foundation (Washington, DC: Smithsonian Institution Press, 1991), 163.

67. Newman and McLean, "The Impact of Museums," 64.

production, consumption, and regulation."[68] An interesting description of the socially excluded emerged as a result: their "identity formations were characterized by an inability to manage aspects of the social world in the ways they would wish."[69] Newman and McLean surmise that there is extensive confusion concerning the museum's role in combating social exclusion, even amongst museum practitioners.[70] This confusion may be the result of traditional museum practice in which the institutional voice asserts the community heritage. Traditional approaches to community representation include diversity, in which differences are celebrated, and multiculturalism, in which the museum professional is tasked with the curation of differences and similarities between cultures.[71] Social inclusion supports the role of community self-curation, as opposed to institutional curation, and amplifies the role of museum professionals as facilitators in information provision.

Sandell and Nightingale explored the changing social role of museums and the interwoven natures of equality, diversity and social justice in their book, *Museums, Equality and Social Justice*.[72] They acknowledged that the traditional museum "often operated in ways which exclude, marginalize and oppress," and proposed that "There is growing support (and evidence) for the idea that museums can contribute towards more just, equitable and fair societies."[73] Museums, as evidenced by the Wing Luke exemplar, can empower communities to transmit and foster culture.[74]

How does social inclusion theory move beyond traditional discussions of diversity and multiculturalism, and enter the realm of social justice and equality? Social inclusion is the platform upon which social change is built, embedded in the community, and empowered by co-curation.

---

68. Ibid., 50.

69. Ibid., 64.

70. Ibid.

71. Sandell and Nightingale, *Museums, Equality, and Social Justice*, 3.

72. Ibid.

73. Ibid.

74. Chinn, *Community–Based Exhibition Model*, 13.

Although museums have historically engaged in multicultural and diversity initiatives, these activities have not promoted a strong social justice element. It is the proposition of this chapter that without a foundation of inclusion, any social change initiated by museum professionals will lack fortitude.

The second key advantage of social inclusion theory is the awareness it generates concerning marginalization and division within society. Social inclusion theory, birthed from the presence of social exclusion, directs the attention of citizens to the social problems at hand. The term *social inclusion* developed as a reactionary term to *social exclusion*, and is mainly conceptualized as the counterpart or "assumed corollary"[75] to exclusion. At a foundational level, social inclusion positively reassures society of two key assertions: yes, there is a problem in the society; and yes, there is a solution.

Although this advantage may appear to be little more than rhetoric, it has provoked much research throughout Western Europe and the UK, and therefore should not be discounted.[76] In museum research, there is the opportunity through social inclusion theory to realize that, "Contrary to conventional museum wisdom and discipline-based dogma, research and social action are not incompatible but are necessary allies."[77] Social inclusion theory provokes the study of exclusion on a multidimensional level: cultural, economic, political, and social.[78] Social inclusion theory allows for the recognition that there is no one solution to societal problems of division and marginalization. The multidimensional nature of

---

75. Rawal, "Social Inclusion and Exclusion," 171.

76. Rawal, "Social Inclusion and Exclusion," 171-172; Tlili, "Behind the Policy Mantra," 123-124; R. Labonte, "Social Inclusion/Exclusion: Dancing the Dialectic," *Health Promotion International* 19, no. 1 (March 1, 2004): 115–21; Dodd et al., *A Catalyst for Change*, 2; Dodd and Sandell, *Including Museums*, 3; "The GLLAM Report," 5-6; Sandell, "Museums as Agents," 415; Sandell and Nightingale, *Museums, Equality, and Social Justice*, 1-8; Sandell, "Social Inclusion," 45.

77. Janes, *Museums in a Troubled World*, 126.

78. Sandell, "Museums as Agents," 405.

exclusion, once revealed by social inclusion theory, may then be tackled by multidisciplinary teams.

Are There Disadvantages of Social Inclusion Theory Application within Museums?

Although social inclusion theory has influenced both museum research and practice, it is not without its limitations. The under-development of social inclusion terminology in museum literature is problematic, and research utilizing social inclusion theory for museum evaluation is performed only sporadically. Yet these limitations may also be viewed as unique opportunities: emergent social inclusion terminology may offer researchers the opportunity to work with museum practitioners to design a standard vocabulary. A standardized social inclusion vocabulary is an important step in the production of valuable museum assessment tools. The demands of policy makers to produce measurable social change may be countered by industry definitions of social inclusion and museum professional associations. Social inclusion theory may serve as a framework to guide the production of a standardized vocabulary for the articulation of both the social role of the museum, and the significance of evaluating that role effectively.

Although social inclusion theory-based museum evaluation is a recent research trend, it has yielded significant insights into the evaluation of museum impact. Lynda Kelly, drawing upon a social inclusion theoretical base, notes in her Australian museum research that there is no one template for measuring museum impact, no one set of indicators, and no precise path for mapping the relationship between museums, individuals, and communities.[79] Researchers attempting museum impact evaluation generally agree that such assessments should connect back to the communities involved. The long-term impact of museums should be considered, not only at the level of the visitor, but also at the level

---

79. Lynda Kelly, "Measuring the Impact of Museums on Their Communities – Australian Museum," In *New Roles and Missions of Museums* (Taipei, Taiwan: International Council on Museums, 2006), 2.

of the local community. Thus, understanding the long-term socially inclusive impact of museums enables a better understanding of how to serve and enrich communities, of which museums are a part. Again, social inclusion theory provides a foundation for museums to better understand their communities, and then illuminates pathways for social justice through progressive community action.

A Socially Inclusive Example Application of LIS Theory for Museums: Gatekeeping.

Proponents of socially inclusive museums, such as the progressive bloggers of www.incluseum.org, assert that museum professionals should ask several questions of themselves: Who is your museum for? How is your museum socially inclusive?[80] Whose voice is heard within a museum exhibit? Who decides the cultural information to be presented to the public? How will that cultural information be packaged to be most impactful in the creation of identity? These questions center on the concept of *curatorial voice*, a concept central to museology. Curatorial voice is an inherent element of an exhibit and functions as a socially inclusive/exclusive gatekeeping mechanism for cultural information. Curatorial voice is the message received by museumgoers throughout the exhibit, a message that may relay intent or museum authority.[81] Yet who speaks curatorial voice? And what mechanisms do they use to craft that voice? Museum Informatics applies LIS gatekeeper theory to our understanding of information gatekeeping mechanisms and sheds light on the crafting of the socially inclusive curatorial voice.

Simply, gatekeeper theory describes the processes and players associated with the transfer of information within a given context. In the journey from one individual to another, information is conceptualized as

---

80. "The Incluseum," *The Incluseum*, 2014, www.incluseum.com.

81. Gaea Leinhardt, Kevin Crowley, and Karen Knutson, eds., *Learning Conversations in Museums* (Mahwah, NJ: Lawrence Erlbaum, 2002), 45-46.

passing through a gate.[82] The presence of a gatekeeper, such as a librarian or a museum curator, promotes a monitored situation in which the gatekeeper utilizes mechanisms, such as information selection, deletion, and hoarding, upon the intended recipients, such as museum visitors. These information recipients are "the gated" ones, and may vary in the level of control they have over the information within the context.[83] This information transfer theater, complete with gatekeeping actors and multidimensional relationships, is the basis of gatekeeper theory. Each gatekeeper has a rationale, such as preservation of culture, for the approach taken in exercising gatekeeping mechanisms, and much research has been done into these rationales.[84] Museums are also an information transfer theater, complete with actors and multidimensional relationships. It follows logically, then, that there is an application for gatekeeper theory within a museum context for the purposes of examining the social inclusivity of curatorial voice.

Any application of gatekeeper theory to the museum context must account for the reality that museums are as unique as the communities in which they exist. Their gatekeeping mechanisms most likely vary considerably from one museum to the next, reflecting this uniqueness. However, generalizable characteristics of these gatekeeping mechanisms exist; e.g., curatorial voice is altered by the mechanism of object selection on the part of curators, or curatorial voice is altered by the mechanism of text choice on the part of exhibit label designers.

It is important to note that curatorial voice may also exist in the community gatekeepers who utilize their joint roles of museum volunteer and community leader for exercising mechanisms of connection. As Agada suggests, community gatekeepers act in this capacity "as information intermediaries who move between cultures, linking their community

82. Karine Barzilai–Nahon, "Toward a Theory of Network Gatekeeping: A Framework for Exploring Information Control," *Journal of the American Society for Information Science and Technology* 59, no. 9(2008):1493–1512.

83. Ibid., 1496.

84. Karine Barzilai–Nahon, "Gatekeeping: A Critical Review," *Annual Review of Information Science and Technology* 43 (2009): 433–78.

members with alternatives or solutions."[85] Whether the curatorial voice resides in the museum professional or in the community, certain general characteristics apply: curatorial voice can be directly expressed to the gated, re-interpreted for the gated, or blocked completely from the gated. For the purposes of re-imagining curatorial voice with gatekeeper theory, the gated should refer to the intended audience of the museum, the museum visitor(s).

In order to explore the socially inclusive application of gatekeeping theory within a museum context, the author initiated a qualitative research study. Beginning in 2014, a series of curatorial interviews explored the gatekeeping role of curators within museums. This research, titled "Curators of Conflict: the Gatekeeping Mechanisms of Curatorial Voice," began with an in-depth review of LIS gatekeeping theory literature.[86] As a result of this literature review, a *Curatorial Voice Gatekeeping Mechanisms Chart* has been developed. In a pilot test, curators of a small regional museum in the southeastern United States reviewed this chart and participated in semi-structured interviews. During the pilot study, the curators reflected upon their crafting of curatorial voice in a recent exhibit. The pilot study participants described the gatekeeping mechanisms employed in creation of community curatorial voice in an exhibit entitled "The Identity Project."[87] The results of the pilot study informed the revision of the gatekeeping mechanisms chart, and the chart is currently being vetted by a group of professional curators throughout the United States. This chart provides a strong theoretical background for museum curators to articulate the gatekeeping mechanisms used to craft socially inclusive curatorial voices within their museum exhibits.

---

85. Agada, "Inner-City Gatekeepers," 75.

86. Laura Coleman, "Curators of Conflict: The Gatekeeping Mechanisms of Curatorial Voice " (presentation, Tallahassee, FL, September 22, 2014), http://www.lauraedythe.com.

87. Ibid., Amber O'Connell, "The Identity Project," *Tallahassee Museum*, accessed August 5, 2015, http://tallahasseemuseum.org/blog/event/identity–project/.

This *Curatorial Voice Gatekeeping Mechanisms Chart* builds on the work of LIS researchers, Barzilai-Nahon and Metoyer-Duran, to illuminate the cultural information connection for museum professionals.[88] Inspired by Barzilai-Nahon's suggestion that "preservation of culture" is one of the dominant rationales for the execution of gatekeeping mechanisms, curators have been asked to utilize this chart to articulate the ways in which they craft curatorial voice.[89] This chart, developed in collaboration with museum curators during the pilot study, depicts the application of gatekeeper theory to the actions of crafting curatorial voice. Limited to a description of gatekeeping mechanisms, this chart does not outline the different types of possible curatorial gatekeeper roles, merely the gatekeeping mechanisms employed by curators in the crafting of curatorial voice.

The *Curatorial Voice Gatekeeping Mechanisms Chart* is by no means exhaustive, and the definitions are under continuous scrutiny by the curators involved in the current research study, *The Socially Inclusive Role of Curatorial Voice: A Qualitative Comparative Study of the Use of Gatekeeping Mechanisms and the Co-Creation of Identity in Museums.*[90] Ultimately, this chart will evolve to reflect both curatorial practice and gatekeeper theory. As it reads in this chapter, this *Curatorial Voice Gatekeeping Mechanisms Chart* accounts for prior LIS gatekeeper models that have extracted the core attributes of gatekeepers for a given situation.

This chart also implements the 2008 work of Karine Barzili-Nahon who proposed a Network Gatekeeper Theory (NGT), in which traditional models of gatekeeping are recast for the modern networked

---

88. Cheryl Metoyer–Duran, "Information–Seeking Behavior of Gatekeepers in Ethnolinguistic Communities: Overview of a Taxonomy," *Library and Information Science Research* 13, no. 4 (1991): 319–46; Barzilai–Nahon, "Gatekeeping: A Critical Review," 433-478; Barzilai–Nahon, "Toward a Theory," 1493-1512.

89. Coleman, "Curators of Conflict."

90. Laura Coleman, "The Socially Inclusive Role of Curatorial Voice: A Qualitative Comparative Study of the Use of Gatekeeping Mechanisms and the Co–Creation of Identity in Museums," Florida State University, forthcoming.

world.[91] In this model, the process of gatekeeping involves not only the selection of information, but also an entire spectrum of information control processes.[92] These gatekeeping processes, which are applicable to the role of curatorial voice, include "selection, addition, withholding, display, channeling, shaping, manipulation, repetition, timing, localization, integration, disregard, and deletion."[93] Practical application of NGT is found at multiple points in the curation processes; for example, when an exhibit curator selects the objects for display only after an original selection process was made by the museum to collect certain items for preservation.

The rationale for gatekeeping may be practical, because museums have the ability to physically display only a small portion of their collection, and it is inevitable that certain objects must be withheld from exhibit display. The act of choosing objects to be withheld is a gatekeeping process. Channeling of the intended message through the shaping of the exhibit story is an essential gatekeeping process performed by curators and docents. Repetition of important themes and timing of presentation of objects is an inherent part of the storytelling role of curators and is also a gatekeeping process. The curators involved in the study, *Curators of Conflict*, related anecdotally to these processes, and appeared keenly aware of the mechanisms needed to craft curatorial voice.[94] Despite the negativity often associated with terms such as "manipulation," the curators were observed by the researcher to be relieved to be in possession of the *Curatorial Voice Gatekeeping Mechanisms Chart*. The generation of this chart is one small way in which LIS research, through museum informatics, can assist museum professionals in meeting their goals of crafting a socially inclusive curatorial voice.

---

91. Barzilai–Nahon, "Toward a Theory," 1495-1506.

92. Ibid., 1495-1506.

93. Karen E. Fisher, Sanda Erdelez, and Lynne McKechnie, eds. *Theories of Information Behavior*, ASIST Monograph Series, (Medford, N.J: Published for the American Society for Information Science and Technology by Information Today, 2005), 249.

94. Coleman, "Curators of Conflict."

Table 1. Curatorial Voice Gatekeeping Mechanisms Chart[95]
(for Definition sources, see below)[96]

Term	Definition	Application to Curatorial Voice
Selection	"Making a choice or choosing from alternatives"	Do curators select objects and text from the available items?
Addition	"Joining or uniting information"	Do curators pair items and text to convey a message?
Withholding	"Refraining from granting, giving, or allowing information"	Is it the case that curators cannot/do not place all items on display?
Display	"Presenting information in a particular visual form designed to catch the eye"	Do curators work with museum staff and exhibit designers to create a visual message?
Channeling	"Conveying or directing information into or through a channel"	Do curators work with museum staff and exhibit designers to place items and text in a particular pathway?
Shaping	"Forming, especially giving a particular form of information"	Do curators work with museum staff and exhibit designers to shape the message into particular forms? Perhaps digital formats, accessible formats, or educational formats?
Manipulation	"Changing information by artful or unfair means to serve the gatekeeper's purpose"	Do curators work with museum staff and exhibit designers to change the meaning of items?

95. Ibid.

96. Metoyer–Duran, "Information–Seeking Behavior," 319-346; Barzilai–Nahon, "Gatekeeping: A Critical Review," 17; Barzilai–Nahon, "Toward a Theory," 1498; Karine Nahon, "Fuzziness of Inclusion/Exclusion in Networks," *International Journal of Communication* 5 (2011): 756–72.

Repetition	"Saying, showing, writing, restating; making; doing, or performing again"	Do curators work with museum staff and exhibit designers to create a message that includes repetition of thematic content?
Timing	"Selecting the precise moment for beginning, doing, or completing an information process"	Do curators work with museum staff and exhibit designers to time the presentation of items within an exhibit?
Localization	"Process of modifying and adapting information, products, and services to distinct target audiences in specific locations in a way that takes into account their cultural characteristics"	Do curators work with museum staff and exhibit designers to localize the presentation of items or text for target audiences?
Integration	"Forming, coordinating, or blending into a new functioning or unified whole"	Do curators work with museum staff and exhibit designers to integrate the exhibit into the greater whole of society?
Disregard	"Paying no attention to information, treating it as unworthy of regard or notice"	Do curators work with museum staff and exhibit designers to disregard irrelevant items or text?
Deletion	"Eliminating information especially by blotting out, cutting out, or erasing"	Do curators work with museum staff or exhibit designers to cut out particular items or text from an exhibit?

Future Research Suggestions and Conclusions

Where do we go from here?

Interestingly enough, these gatekeeping processes may be visible not only in the physical museum, but also in the digital museum. As digital museums are in their infancy, this chart does not yet reflect the application of gatekeeper theory to the crafting of curatorial voice in digital exhibits. As museums struggle to recreate themselves in the digital realm, an understanding of network gatekeeping processes of curatorial voice will be necessary. Nahon proposes that the widespread use of technology has granted researchers the opportunity to see the transformation of the transient elites, the dynamics of power, and the "duality of dependency and control."[97] If Nahon is correct, the technology that distributes curatorial voice amongst the masses also grants researchers a new vantage point in the discovery of networks and power. The usage of NGT allows for the justification of analysis at the community level rather than the individual level, yet reveals an additional dimension of needed research in the field of museum informatics: the study of gatekeeping in digital exhibits.

The curator participants in *Curators of Conflict* utilized the *Curatorial Voice Gatekeeping Mechanisms Chart* to reflect upon past usages of gatekeeping mechanisms in the crafting of curatorial voice. As digital museums are a relatively new phenomenon, an opportunity exists to utilize the analysis of curatorial voice gatekeeping mechanisms in the *planning stages* of digital museums.

Museum professionals reading this chapter should be challenged to take the *Curatorial Voice Gatekeeping Mechanisms Chart* to their collections, to their exhibitions, and to view their work anew through the lens of gatekeeping theory. The curators involved in the generation of this chart were observed by the researcher to be deeply committed to the creation of an authentic curatorial voice. This commitment to authentic curatorial voice is jeopardized by a scenario in which museum professionals are burdened with a multitude of objects to care for and a vast array of stakeholders to please with their exhibits. The intention of this research is to lessen that burden and to assist curators in the articulation and construction of curatorial voice. The expressed purpose of providing this curatorial voice mechanisms chart is to aid museum professionals in the exploration of the socially inclusive role of museums.

---

97. Nahon, "Fuzziness of Inclusion/Exclusion," 765.

Despite the existence of several socially inclusive museum exemplars, such as The Museum of Tolerance and the Wing Luke, museum professionals must not rely entirely on these models. Instead, they must perform self-reflection on their own gatekeeping mechanisms and examine the ways in which their museum is culturally inclusive. Additionally, museum professionals should begin to consider the ways in which cultural inclusion lays the foundation for social justice initiatives with their community.

Museum researchers should be challenged by this chapter to investigate notions that are inherently understood by museum professionals and society. The role of museums has expanded dramatically within society over the past several decades. Despite the widening role of museums and museum professionals, a similar expansion of professional guidance such as standardized terminology, policies, and evaluation methodologies has not followed these changes within museums. Museum professional associations, such as the American Alliance of Museums (AAM), have struggled to provide professional guidance to museums. This lack of expansion is especially evident in the recently developed AAM "Diversity and Inclusion Policy," a vague paragraph that outlines little of the needed terminology.[98] Professional guidance would assist museum professionals with the articulation and construction of curatorial voice, with the expressed purpose of aiding museum professionals in the exploration of the socially inclusive role of museums.

The extent to which the lack of terminology, standards, and evaluative tools for museum researchers has hindered social inclusivity of museums is unknown, yet it is understood that such guidance, if it existed, would assist curators in their articulation of museum societal roles. Who is better equipped to develop the needed terminology than LIS researchers? LIS researchers bring an unparalleled philosophical fervor to the importance of expanding social inclusion, community involvement, and social justice for libraries. Museum informatics proposes that LIS

---

98. "Diversity and Inclusion Policy."

researchers could bring that same fervor to museums, assisting museum professionals in reaching their socially inclusive goals.

Conclusion

Museums wield tremendous power to change society, to uphold society, and to affirm society, contributing to both individual and collective identities. Despite the call for museums to act more strongly as champions of social justice, museums have not yet assumed that role as agents for social change.[99] This chapter asserts that before they can assume this social justice role, museums must first strengthen their role as socially inclusive institutions through their collections, exhibits, and policies. Museum professionals, committed to serving humanity and history, should use the *Curatorial Voice Gatekeeping Mechanisms Chart* provided in this chapter to reflect upon their role in the crafting of curatorial voice.[100] Ultimately, museum professionals should be able to identify and articulate their socially inclusive role in the generation of curatorial voice, and in so doing, take responsibility for their own place in history. Once museums provide a socially inclusive institution in which equity of access to cultural information is the cornerstone, only then can they begin to ponder the possibility of implementing social justice through progressive community actions. Museums and museum professionals have the opportunity to become the agents of social change, but only through the socially inclusive provision of access to identity-related information for their communities.

Bibliography

Agada, John. "Inner-City Gatekeepers: An Exploratory Survey of Their Information Use Environment." *Journal of the American Society for Information Science* 50, no. 1 (1999): 74–85. http://search.proquest.com/docview/231475609?accountid=4840.

---

99. Sandell, "Museums as Agents," 415.
100. Coleman, "Curators of Conflict."

American Library Association. "Core Values of Librarianship."
    American Library Association, 2004. http://www.ala.org/advo-
    cacy/intfreedom/statementspols/corevalues.

Barzilai-Nahon, Karine. "Gatekeeping: A Critical Review." *Annual
    Review of Information Science and Technology* 43 (2009): 433–78.
    doi:10.1002/aris.2009.1440430117.

———. "Toward a Theory of Network Gatekeeping: A Framework
    for Exploring Information Control." *Journal of the American
    Society for Information Science and Technology* 59, no. 9 (2008):
    1493–1512. doi:10.1002/asi.20857.

Bates, M.J. "Toward an Integrated Model of Information Seeking and
    Searching." *The New Review of Information Behaviour Research*
    3 (2002): 1–15. https://pages.gseis.ucla.edu/faculty/bates/
    articles/info_SeekSearch-i-030329.html.

Bennett, Tony. *The Birth of the Museum: History, Theory, Politics. (Culture :
    Policies and Politics)*. London; New York: Routledge, 1995.

Bernhard, Stefan. "Beyond Constructivism: The Political Sociol-
    ogy of an EU Policy Field." *International Political Sociology*
    5, no. 4 (December 1, 2011): 426–45. doi:10.1111/j.1749–
    5687.2011.00143.x.

Caidi, Nadia, and Danielle Allard. "Social Inclusion of Newcomers
    to Canada: An Information Problem?" *Library & Informa-
    tion Science Research* 27, no. 3 (2005): 302–24. doi:10.1016/j.
    lisr.2005.04.003.

Chatman, E.A. "A Theory of Life in the Round." *Journal of
    the American Society for Information Science & Technol-
    ogy* 50, no. 3 (1999): 207–17. doi: 10.1002/(SICI)1097–
    4571(1999)50:3<207::AID-ASI3>3.0.CO;2-8.

———. "The Impoverished Life-World of Outsiders." *Journal
    of the American Society for Information Science & Technol-
    ogy* 47, no. 3 (1996): 193–206. doi: 10.1002/(SICI)1097–
    4571(199603)47:3<193::AID-ASI3>3.0.CO;2-T.

———. "The Information World of Retired Women. " *New Directions in Information Management* no. 29. New York: Greenwood Press, 1992.

Chinn, Cassie. *Community-Based Exhibition Model.* Seattle, Washington: Wing Luke Asian Museum, 2006. https://www162.safesecureweb.com/wingluke/pages/process/introduction.html.

Coleman, Laura. "The Socially Inclusive Role of Curatorial Voice: A Qualitative Comparative Study of the Use of Gatekeeping Mechanisms and the Co-Creation of Identity in Museums." Florida State University, forthcoming.

Coleman, Laura-Edythe. "Curators of Conflict: The Gatekeeping Mechanisms of Curatorial Voice." Presentation, Tallahassee, FL, September 22, 2014. http://www.lauraedythe.com.

"Diversity and Inclusion Policy." 2014. http://www.aam-us.org/about-us/who-we-are/strategic-plan/diversity-and-inclusion-policy.

Dodd, Jocelyn, Helen O'Riain, Eilean Hooper-Greenhill, Richard Sandell, Heritage Lottery Fund, and Great Britain. *A Catalyst for Change: The Social Impact of the Open Museum.* RCMG Leicester, 2002.

Dodd, Jocelyn, and Richard Sandell. *Including Museums: Perspectives on Museums, Galleries and Social Inclusion.* Leicester, UK: Research Centre for Museums and Galleries, 2001.

Falk, John H. *Learning from Museums: Visitor Experiences and the Making of Meaning.* American Association for State and Local History Book Series. Walnut Creek, CA: AltaMira Press, 2000.

Fisher, Karen E., Sanda Erdelez, and Lynne McKechnie, eds. *Theories of Information Behavior.* ASIST Monograph Series. Medford, N.J.: Published for the American Society for Information Science and Technology by Information Today, 2005.

Froehlich, T.J. "Ethical Considerations of Information Professionals." *Annual Review of Information Science and Technology* 27 (1992): 291–394. http://garfield.library.upenn.edu/histcomp/annualreviews/ann-rev-inform-sci-tech/node/324. html.

Hendry, J.D. "Social Inclusion and the Information Poor." *Library Review* 49, no. 7 (2000): 331–36. doi:10.1108/00242530010344192.

Hjorland, B. "Social and Cultural Awareness and Responsibility in Library, Information and Documentation Studies." In *Aware and Responsible*, edited by B. Rayward, J. Hansson, and V. Suominen, 71–91. Lanham, MD: Scarecrow Press, 2003.

Hodgetts, Darrin, Ottilie Stolte, Kerry Chamberlain, Alan Radley, Linda Nikora, Eci Nabalarua, and Shiloh Groot. "A Trip to the Library: Homelessness and Social Inclusion." *Social & Cultural Geography* 9, no. 8 (December 2008): 933–53. doi:10.1080/14649360802441432.

ICOM. *The ICOM Code of Professional Ethics*. Available at http://icom. museum/the-vision/code-of-ethics/code_ethics2013_eng-2. pdf, Seoul, Korea, 2013.

Janes, Robert R. *Museums in a Troubled World: Renewal, Irrelevance or Collapse?* London; New York: Routledge, 2009.

Karp, Ivan, and Steven Lavine. *Exhibiting Cultures: The Poetics and Politics of Museum Display*. Edited by Rockefeller Foundation. Washington, DC: Smithsonian Institution Press, 1991.

Kelly, Lynda. "Measuring the Impact of Museums on Their Communities —Australian Museum." In *New Roles and Missions of Museums*. Taipei, Taiwan: International Council on Museums, 2006. http://australianmuseum.net.au/document/Measuring-the-impact-of-museums-on-their-communities.

Labonte, R. "Social Inclusion/Exclusion: Dancing the Dialectic."
     Health Promotion International 19, no. 1 (March 1, 2004):
     115–21. doi:10.1093/heapro/dah112.

Leinhardt, Gaea, Kevin Crowley, and Karen Knutson, eds. *Learning
     Conversations in Museums*. Mahwah, NJ: Lawrence Erlbaum,
     2002.

Marty, Paul. *Museum Informatics: People, Information, and Technology in
     Museums*. [S.l.]: Routledge, 2009.

———. "The Changing Nature of Information Work in Museums."
     *Journal of the American Society for Information Science and Technolo-
     gy* 58, no. 1 (January 1, 2007): 97–107. doi:10.1002/asi.20443.

Mehra, Bharat, Kendra S. Albright, and Kevin Rioux. "A Practical
     Framework for Social Justice Research in the Information
     Professions." *Proceedings of the American Society for Informa-
     tion Science and Technology* 43, no. 1 (October 10, 2007): 1–10.
     doi:10.1002/meet.14504301275.

Mehra, Bharat, Kevin Rioux, and Kendra Albright. "Social Justice in
     Library and Information Science." In *Encyclopedia of Library
     and Information Sciences*, 3rd ed., 4820–36. New York, N.Y:
     Taylor and Francis, 2009.

Metoyer-Duran, Cheryl. "Information-Seeking Behavior of Gate-
     keepers in Ethnolinguistic Communities: Overview of a
     Taxonomy." *Library and Information Science Research* 13, no. 4
     (1991): 319–46.

"Museum Definition- ICOM." 2007. http://icom.museum/the-
     vision/museum-definition/.

"Museum Next." *Museum Next*. 2014. http://www.museumnext.com.

"Museums and Social Inclusion: The GLLAM Report." Group for
     Large Local Authority Museums. Leicester, UK: Research
     Centre for Museums and Galleries, 2000.

Nahon, Karine. "Fuzziness of Inclusion/Exclusion in Networks."
    International Journal of Communication 5 (2011): 756–72. http://
    ijoc.org/index.php/ijoc/article/view/1119/552.

Newman, Andrew, and Fiona McLean. "The Impact of Museums
    upon Identity." *International Journal of Heritage Studies* 12, no. 1
    (January 2006): 49–68. doi:10.1080/13527250500384514.

O'Connell, Amber. "The Identity Project." *Tallahassee Museum.* Ac-
    cessed August 5, 2015. http://tallahasseemuseum.org/blog/
    event/identity-project/.

"Our History and Vision–Museum of Tolerance | Los Angeles, CA."
    Accessed May 26, 2015. http://www.museumoftolerance.
    com/site/c.tmL6KfNVLtH/b.4866027/k.88E8/Our_His-
    tory_and_Vision.htm.

Rawal, Nabin. "Social Inclusion and Exclusion: A Review." *Dhaulagiri
    Journal of Sociology and Anthropology* 2, (October 2, 2008):161–
    80. doi:10.3126/dsaj.v2i0.1362.

Rioux, Kevin. "Metatheory in Library and Information Science: A
    Nascent Social Justice Approach." *Journal of Education For
    Library & Information Science* 51, no. 1 (2010): 9–17.

Sandell, Richard. "Museums as Agents of Social Inclusion." *Mu-
    seum Management and Curatorship* 17, no. 4 (1998): 401–18.
    doi:10.1080/09647779800401704.

———. , ed. *Museums, Society, Inequality.* Museum Meanings. London;
    New York: Routledge, 2002.

———. "Social Inclusion, the Museum and the Dynamics of Sec-
    toral Change." *Museums and Society* 1, no. 1 (2003): 45–62.
    http://www2.le.ac.uk/departments/museumstudies/muse-
    umsociety/volumes/volume1/volume1.

Sandell, Richard, and Eithne Nightingale, eds. *Museums, Equality, and
    Social Justice.* Museum Meanings. Abingdon, Oxon; New
    York, NY: Routledge, 2012.

Schroeder, Robert, and Christopher V. Hollister. "Librarians' Views
on Critical Theories and Critical Practices." *Behavioral &
Social Sciences Librarian* 33, no. 2 (April 3, 2014): 91–119. doi:1
0.1080/01639269.2014.912104.

Shera, Jesse H. *Introduction to Library Service: Basic Elements of Library
Service.* Littleton, CO: Libraries Unlimited, 1976.

Silver, Hilary. "Social Exclusion and Social Solidarity: Three Paradigms." *International Labour Review* 133, no. 5,6 (1994):
531–531. https://login.proxy.lib.fsu.edu/login?url=http://
search.proquest.com/docview/224008056?accountid=4840.

Simon, Nina. *The Participatory Museum.* Santa Cruz, CA: Museum 2.0,
2010.

"Sites of Conscience." *Sites of Conscience,* March 2015. http://www.
sitesofconscience.org/.

Stauffer, S. "'She Speaks as One Having Authority': Mary E.
Downey's Use of Libraries as a Means to Public Power."
Libraries and Culture 40, no. 1 (2005): 38–62.

"The Incluseum." *The Incluseum,* 2014. http://www.incluseum.com.

"The Inclusive Museum." *The Inclusive Museum,* 2014. http://onmuse-
ums.com/the-conference.

Tlili, A. "Behind the Policy Mantra of the Inclusive Museum: Receptions of Social Exclusion and Inclusion in Museums and
Science Centres." *Cultural Sociology* 2, no. 1 (March 1, 2008):
123–47. doi:10.1177/1749975507086277.

Weil, Stephen E. *Making Museums Matter.* Washington, DC: Smithsonian Institution Press, 2002.

Chapter 7

Questioning "Positive Development": Toward Centering YA Library Practice on the Lived Realities of Youth

Jeanie Austin

Young adult librarianship was founded on the idea of "youth development" as a guiding principle. At the present moment, the Young Adult Library Services Association (YALSA), a division of the American Library Association, utilizes just such a narrative of development to describe the role of YA librarians in youths' lives. Named the 40 Developmental Assets for Adolescence, and developed by the Search Institute,[1] this document shows that YALSA considers youth development to be one of the touchstones of YA library services. These "assets" concern the following areas:

- Support
- Empowerment
- Boundaries and Expectations
- Constructive Use of Time
- Commitment to Learning
- Positive Values
- Social Competencies
- Positive Identity

1. Search Institute, "40 Developmental Assets for Adolescents," accessed November 11, 2014, http://www.search-institute.org/content/40-developmental-assets-adolescents-ages-12-18.

At face value, the 40 Developmental Assets seem to be straightforward and transparently positive. They are associated with what is broadly discussed in various social science fields with positive development, the process of becoming a better, more attenuated social and political actor (given the premise of present society as either *close to* or *capable of becoming* a desirably functioning society of relative equals).[2] The underlying premise of a functioning society is apparent in the ways in which the Search Institute self-describes as "a leader and partner for organizations around the world in discovering what kids need to succeed. Our research, resources, and expertise help our partners in organizations, schools, and community coalitions solve critical challenges in the lives of young people."[3] In this description, challenges exist in the *lives* of youth – an amorphous positioning that is open to interpretation. It is not clear whether or not the challenges that the Search Institute seeks to address are present in individual youth, within family structures, or at the (inter)national level. Not present here is any straightforward acknowledgement of how social and political factors (including manifestations of systemic oppression or the social and political positioning of youth and specific groups of youth) shape the lives of and possibilities available to youth in the United States.

While the Search Institute's 40 Developmental Assets sit under the auspices of positive development, to which is ascribed the quality of being a divergence from deficit-based models of youth (i.e. positive development focuses on what youth can become rather than their ascribed personal failures), they do not clearly carry a message of social change that recognizes the positions of youth. The Assets follow a larger trend of positive developmental models, described by Sukarieh and Tannock as utilizing "concepts of 'competence,' 'character,' 'caring,' 'prepared' and 'productive' adulthood and so on [as though they were] self-evident, unproblematic and easily measurable terms, rather than

2. Mayssoun Sukarieh and Stuart Tannock, *Youth Rising? The Politics of Youth in the Global Economy* (New York: Routledge, 2015): 1-8.

3. Search Institute, "About Search Institute," accessed July 16, 2015, http://www.search-institute.org/about.

being controversial and politicized social and cultural constructs."[4] Emphasizing this point, Sukarieh and Tannock later state that "[a]lthouth the new youth development movement claims to have shifted away from an individualist model of earlier periods to an ecological model that addresses the environmental contexts of youth development, these contexts almost never include broad social, economic and political issues and conflicts."[5] The implementation and widespread adoption by YA librarians of the Search Institute's 40 Developmental Assets, then, may even work to the detriment of youth by failing to give room for youth activism and response to social and political oppression.

A deeper examination of the premise of a relatively functioning society that underlies the 40 Developmental Assets will reveal that the assets do not necessarily consider the lived realities of many youth who face individual and institutionalized racism, sexism, homophobia, and a myriad of other constraints and confrontations in their day-to-day lives. Many of the assets are related to ideas of youth becoming law abiding and productive citizen-adults (within a fairly well-functioning society), an option that is not readily available for many young people, despite the language of plurality that is utilized in discourses of American democracy. For example, Kwon, in a brief description of how youth are "imagined as crucial to a nation's future," states that "youth of color are not often imagined as future agents of democracy, but as objects already under suspicion and state surveillance and regulation."[6] Theorists within critical pedagogy have emphasized how disparities continue within a dominant culture that has historically privileged Whiteness, heterosexuality, and being male[7]. As illustrated in this chapter, a common

---

4. Mayssoun Sukarieh and Stuart Tannock, "The Positivity Imperative: A Critical Look at the 'New' Youth Development Movement," *Journal of Youth Studies* 14 (2011): 679.

5. Sukarieh and Tannock, "Positivity Imperative," 684.

6. Soo Ah Kwon, *Uncivil Youth: Race, Activism, and Affirmative Governmentality* (Durham, NC: Duke University Press, 2013), 7.

7. Gloria Ladson-Billings and William Tate, "Toward a Critical Race Theory of Education," *Teachers College Record* 97 (1995): 47 – 68; Cris Mayo, "The Tolerance that Dare Not Speak Its Name," in *Democratic Dialogue in Education:*

conception of *positive development* may be implicitly tied to values that position straight White males as those most likely to be granted access to becoming "fully developed."

Thus, the narrative of positive development stands to be interrogated by YA librarians. This involves a shift away from recreating discourses that privilege the already privileged, and questioning the constructs that underpin what can, in society, or within a profession, often be taken on first encounter as immutably true and unquestionable. The previously mentioned 40 Developmental Assets, a backbone of much YA library literature and practice, stand to be unsettled and disturbed, interrogated for their value to YA librarians who seek to engage in social justice and social change through resisting, among other forces, the ageism that centers adults as knowers and youth as forming, but not yet complete, adults.

Queer theory presents a viable tool for examining how adults are positioned in shaping the positive development of children and youth. Queer theory, while inherently indefinable, is about "resisting categorization, for itself and for its subjects."[8] It works to destabilize what are accepted as existing truths to show the abnormality that waits beneath the ways in which normality has been constructed.[9] Aligning with Stockton's assertion that the child exists in a queered (oddly positioned in regard to sexuality, weird) existence, unknowable to the adult,[10] this chapter proposes that youth, socially and politically, are not accessible to the adult through a strict paradigm of development and understanding, asserting

---

Troubling Speech, Disturbing Silence, ed. Megan Boler (New York, NY: Peter Lang, 2004): 33-47; Michelle Fine, "Sexuality, Schooling, and Adolescent Females: The Missing Discourse of Desire," *Harvard Educational Review* 58 (1988): 29-54.

8. Robert Lecky and Kim Brooks, "Introduction," in *Queer Theory: Law, Culture, Empire*, eds. Robert Lecky and Kim Brooks (New York: Routledge, 2010), 1.

9. Michel Foucault, *Abnormal: Lectures at the College de France 1974-1975* (New York, NY: Verso, 2003).

10. Kathryn Bond Stockton, *The Queer Child: Or Growing Sideways in the 20th Century* (Durham, NC: Duke University Press, 2009), 1-59.

that the model of positive development utilized by YA librarians may actually create an impediment in the work of YA librarians who propose to engage *with* youth in projects that seek to destabilize existing power structures and create more equitable societies and ways of being (i.e., to work toward social justice, social inclusion, and/or social change).

Queer theory is also a useful theoretical lens for interrogating how the 40 Developmental Assets, and ideas of positive youth development in general, recreate existing forms of privilege as it seeks to denaturalize information and ideas that, on the surface, appear to be transparent and normal. Working within the context of the public library, this chapter moves through the concepts of childhood and youth[11] and explores how youth development and the historical conceptualizations of development have surrounded adolescence, within and outside of the profession. The chapter will then turn to the practices undertaken by youth and by YA librarians to focus specifically on youth and their lived realities.

Foundations for the following analysis can be found in the space of overlap between critical social theory and queer theory. Drawing from both of these traditions adds to an understanding of the positioning of youth in a modern context (an important step in discussing conceptions of youth in YA library practice). As this chapter is concerned with youth, the critical theory utilized draws heavily from the foundations of critical pedagogy – a form of education that seeks to destabilize power structures in the classroom and other learning environments, to promote understandings of social phenomenon and relationships to power, and to destabilize the ways in which power is reified through the education process.[12] Based in Gramsci's analysis of hegemony (the ways in which normalized behavior and social expectations work to

---

11. Childhood and youth are utilized interchangeably in this chapter, as much of the research related to youth in queer theory utilizes the term "childhood," broadly defined.

12. Henry Giroux, "Critical Theory and Educational Practice," in *The Critical Pedagogy Reader*, eds. Antonia Darder, Marta P. Baltodano, and Rodolfo D. Torres (New York: Routledge, 2009), 27-51.

further power) and Foucault's descriptions of power as distributed and dynamic, and following the traditions of the Frankfurt School, critical pedagogy utilizes critical social theory to untangle and push against hegemonic systems of power.[13]

Critical social theory and critical pedagogy are not without their criticisms. These have arisen, over time, in relation to the ways in which class structures were often privileged over other areas of oppression and resistance. Among these critiques were the inaccessibility of the language of critical social theory, the overarching Whiteness of critical theorists, the lack of complexity relating to identity categories as presented within critical theory, and a noticeable lack of analysis given to homosexuality.[14] The work of many authors, theorists, and practitioners to levy and address these critiques is astounding, inspiring, and beyond the scope of this chapter to document completely. As this chapter is concerned with both critical social theory and queer theory, however, it is useful to turn to examples of the overlap between these two theoretical positions. Cohen and Hames-Garcia have called for queer theory to take an approach that recognizes the structures of power, oppression, and resistance as beyond the scope of occurring in clear lines between homosexuality and heterosexuality.[15] Cohen argues for queer theory to pull from concepts of intersectionality, stating that "if there is any truly radical potential to be found in the idea of queerness and the practice of queer politics, it would be located in its ability to create a space in opposition to dominant norms, a space where transformational political work can begin," gesturing toward the critical analyses of power

---

13. Antonia Darder, Marta P. Baltodano, and Rodolfo D. Torres, "Critical Pedagogy: An Introduction," in The Critical Pedagogy Reader, eds. Antonia Darder, Marta P. Baltodano, and Rodolfo D. Torres (New York: Routledge, 2009), 1-20.

14. Darder, Baltodano, and Torres, "Critical Pedagogy," 14-18.

15. Cathy J. Cohen, "Punks, Bulldaggers, and Welfare Queens: The Radical Potential of Queer Politics?" *GLQ* 3 (1997): 437 – 485; Michael Hames-Garcia, "Can Queer Theory Be Critical Theory?" in *New Critical Theory: Essays on Liberation*, eds. William S. Wilkerson and Jeffrey Paris (Boston: Rowman and Littlefield, 2001), 201 – 222.

found in more contemporary critical theory.[16] Cohen calls for a more complex approach to queer political action, one that seeks to undo "bounded categories" while also acknowledging lived oppressions and subject positions.[17]

The tie between critical social theory and queer theory is prominent in Hames-Garcia's call for a "critical queer theory."[18] Borne out of the analysis of power, Hames-Garcia draws from Marcuse to illustrate how the dominance and prominence of White individuals and initiatives in queer theory have worked to negate other understandings of oppression, suggesting that queer theory can interact with critical race and critical social theory to "look beyond and glimpse what kind of world, what practice is being prevented from coming to being."[19] Critical queer theory can work to recognize and question systems of power as they relate to both sexuality and the process through which youth are made queer (Other) by and to adults.

Although the context for this examination is public libraries, it may translate to other contexts, with limitations. As opposed to school environments, public libraries and librarians are often not as constrained by the goals of facilitating the creation of employable adults or an engaged citizenry. School libraries, for instance, are often positioned within institutions that ascribe to specific narratives of youth development and educational attainment. Public libraries are not completely removed from this framing, but they are less likely to be bound to clear guidelines for the development of youth into productive adults. This is not to state that public libraries do not frequently align with ideas of productive citizenship, or that school librarians do not skillfully navigate the contexts of the U.S. education system. Instead, it is an acknowledgment that YA

---

16. Cohen, "Punks, Bulldaggers, and Welfare Queens: The Radical Potential of Queer Politics?" 438.

17. Ibid., 481.

18. Hames-Garcia, "Can Queer Theory Be Critical Theory?" 216.

19. Ibid., 219

librarians in public library contexts may have more opportunities to challenge developmental narratives in their personal practice.

Youth (ages 13-21) and children (those younger than 13)[20] are often viewed, in Gordon's terms, as "citizens-in-the making"—thus, youth and children have limited levels of social and political power in traditional adult realms.[21] Gordon examines how "age is an axis of inequality,"[22] illustrating the ways in which youth activism can change how stratification exists within society. Youth activism and political resistance can be acts of social justice—acts that seek to move toward creating a new set of relations in which hierarchies of age, race, sex, sexuality, and class status are no longer relevant. Activism and resistance typically have the goal of creating an equal society. While youth may not necessarily be engaged in struggles that address all of the divisions and privileges currently present in society, Gordon believes that youth activism counters adult conceptions of youth as future adults, unsettling adult ideas of youth through political and social engagement, resistance, and collectivity. This is relevant to YA librarianship, as developmental models re-institute ideas of youth as future adults, rather than necessarily providing library services to youth as individuals—where and how they are situated in the moment of encounter.

To provide services to youth at the point of encounter(s) is to address youth and their *present* selves and interests. Providing services that are not based (or heavily based) in developmental models involves listening and responding to youth input *in tandem* with youth. Examples for this type

---

20. Age frames for these categories are constructed loosely, with recognition that age itself is constructed and that age-based restrictions (and possibilities) vary from location to location, country to country, and context to context. Sukarieh and Tannock discuss the varying definitions of age as related to social circumstances, including an expansion of adolescence as an age category downward into childhood and upward into what was previously adulthood as features of a neoliberal society (Mayssoun Sukarieh and Stuart Tannock, "The Positivity Imperative: A Critical Look at the 'New' Youth Development Movement," *Journal of Youth Studies* 14 [2011]: 682-683).

21. Hava Rachel Gordon, *We Fight to Win: Inequality and the Politics of Youth Activism* (New Brunswick, NJ: Rutgers University Press, 2010), 8.

22. Gordon, *We Fight to Win*, 6.

of process can be found in Participatory Action Research, which involves a methodology in which participants and researcher(s) come together to solve a problem or address an issue, work cooperatively—with an awareness of the informed knowledge that *all* participants bring to the process—and address power relations within the group (for example, a researcher may write a paper at the end of the experience, but will ask participants to review the document and make any changes that seem appropriate).[23] Keeping this in mind, working *with*, rather than *for* youth means that YA librarians will not view themselves as experts on the developmentally 'best' choices that youth can make, which runs counter to developmental narratives that continue to shape the lives of youth in the United States and, increasingly, in global contexts.

This chapter seeks to better understand how narratives of youth development, including positive youth development, inform the field and practice of YA librarianship. It begins with an overview of how adult definitions of youth shape library practice and youth activism. This overview is informed by an understanding that adult ideologies—conceptions, definitions, and dominant accounts—of youth and of specific groups of youth shape the experiences of youth in powerful and complex forms. By disturbing the surface of adult perceptions of youth through examples of youths' conceptions of themselves within these structures, this chapter seeks to decenter adult conceptions of youth and to unsettle the underlying philosophy found in the 40 Developmental Assets—that adults are authoritative knowers of how youth development should occur. This process informs an argument for youth-centered YA library services. This is a form of community action and an act of social justice with and by youth—drawing from various forms of youth activism to create new ways of working *with* youth from the communities served by public libraries. Working *with* youth, rather than providing services *to* youth, involves listening to the voices of youth, their feedback, their

---

23. Alice McIntyre, *Participatory Action Research* (Thousand Oaks, CA: Sage Publications, Inc., 2008); Tara M. Brown and Louie F. Rodriguez, "Issue Editor's Notes," *Youth in Participatory Action Research. New Directions for Youth Development* 123 (2009): 1 – 9.

recommendations, and their desires, without an eye turned critically to whether or not their suggestions are linked to developmental processes or assets. Working *with* youth, as YA librarians, involves facilitating access to information, programs, and media that they desire and value, giving space for youth to not only speak but to also be heard, taking actions with and for youth when appropriate.

In order to better work *with* youth, it is useful to understand how young people (as a group) have been and continue to be constructed within society. Moving between the historical construction of children and youth as a group through the critical lens of denaturalizing ideologies and queer theory provides context for understanding the ways in which developmental assets – the idea that there can and should be a standard form of development into adulthood – reinstate privileged forms of belonging to the world of adults and of becoming-adult, which may be to the detriment of many youth.

To denaturalize adult conceptions of youth requires an understanding of how power operates to create these categories. This calls for an analysis of how youth have been positioned throughout history and in the current context, as well as an understanding of how youth navigate their current positions to address their own life needs and desires.[24]

Individual youth share various positions in relation to power – the prominent targeting of youth of color by police for imprisonment and death stands in deep contrast to the life chances currently afforded to White youth.[25] Yet the construction of youth as a category works against youth on a global scale.[26] Following Dean Spade's work on a critical trans politics, which utilizes the tradition of critical theory and practice by women of color, this chapter seeks to understand how youth have come

---

24. Henry Giroux, *Youth in a Suspect Society: Democracy or Disposability?* (New York: Palgrave Macmillan, 2009), 1-26; Sunaina Maira, "Cool Nostalgia: Indian American Youth Culture and the Politics of Authenticity," in *Contemporary Youth Research*, eds. Helena Helve and Gunilla Holm (Burlington, VT: Ashgate Publishing, 2005), 197-208.

25. Lisa Marie Cacho, *Social Death: Racialized Rightlessness and the Criminalization of the Unprotected* (New York: NYU Press, 2012), 35-60.

26. Giroux, *Youth in a Suspect Society*, 1-26.

to inhabit locations of "subjection" in the contemporary period, as well as the meaning of social change for "youth" in subject positions.[27] It is largely concerned with how ageism has limited the scope of possibilities for youth, including through models of positive development.

Considering the positions of youth, recognizing and resisting the structures of power that surround adult conceptions of youth is an act toward social change. Creating ways of understanding youth that push against understanding youth as a category of "becoming" works to resist the ways in which distributed power works to further inscribe youth and to describe some youth as "good" (or potentially good) and other youth as "bad" (or potentially bad). Beyond and within this are youths' own conceptions of projects for social change—the idea that the world in which they live is not the only possible world, that they have power to help push for a world, society, and distribution of power that enhances their own chances of survival and thriving, as well as those of others and of the Earth. These notions of social change and youth power are evident in accounts of youth activism described below. Framing these actions and beliefs within the context of the historical construction of youth helps to create deeper understanding of how power has functioned and shifted to shape the current state of youth actions for social change, as well as how positive youth development models, such as the 40 Developmental Assets, continue to work against youth power.

Conceptualizing Youth: Dominant Adult Conceptions of the Young

The category of youth is viewed and discussed as a creation of adults, a feared and hoped-for entity, a desired object, and as a cleaver between what is viewed as the innocence of subservient childhood and adulthood, with its social and political dominance.[28] Contradictions related to how

---

27. Dean Spade, *Normal Life: Administrative Violence, Critical Trans Politics, and the Limits of the Law* (Brooklyn, NY: South End Press, 2011), 19 – 28, 25.

28. Kwon, *Uncivil Youth*, 27-44; Stockton, *Queer Child*, 1-50.

youth are defined and perceived rest in the world of the adult and of media, forces that tend to group youth into cohesive forms, systematically including or precluding (certain groups of) youth participation in spaces.[29] Utilizing queer theory in a way that questions or dismantles the premises on which information about youth is produced, assessed, and normalized opens the doors for youth librarianship to reevaluate interaction and services to youth. As stated above, the queer theory position being taken in this chapter is one that refuses ideas of normality (including normal development), and works to destabilize ideas of achievable norms by asserting that these have been processes of social control.[30] Narratives of normal development, and of the role of adults and institutions in curating young people's development, create a fear of (and possibility for) abnormal children and youth. It is this fear of aberration, of the wolf at the door, which may refuse domestication and is moved by (what is perceived as) instinct, that drives contemporary constructions of children and youth, and guides youth (forcibly) through multiple systems.[31]

In evaluating Stockton's[32] idea that all children are queer(ed), the question becomes, "what does it mean for youth to be queer or queered?" Here, there are multiple definitions. There are youth who self-identify as queer—Lesbian, Gay, Bisexual, Transgender, Queer, and gender non-conforming youth. Then there are children who are made queer and strange by adult conceptions, social expectations, and dominant values. K. B. Stockton's *The Queer Child, or Growing Sideways in the Twentieth Century* expounds upon this latter point, exploring the ways that concepts of children's innocence, sexuality and sexual expression, psychology, money, and the concept of gay adults as childish, have worked to make childhood a period strange to adults during the current historical period. Stockton

---

29. Cacho, *Social Death*, 35 – 60; Kwon, *Uncivil Youth*, 27-44; Stockton, *Queer Child*, 1-50.

30. Michel Foucault, *Abnormal: Lectures at the College de France 1974-1975* (New York, NY: Verso, 2003).

31. Kwon, *Uncivil Youth*, 27-44.

32. Stockton, *Queer Child*, 1.

asserts that children (and, we can extrapolate, youth) are made strange to adults through the paradigms that adults have created, including the idea of proper development.[33] Meiners describes adult conceptions of youth as centered in adult "anxieties."[34] In an interrogation of the construction of sex offender as a category, Meiners asks "How do we acknowledge and discuss that we continually reproduce constructs of the child that are filled with our own anxieties about sexuality and race and gender?"[35] Meiners utilizes the "racial contract" defined by Mills and the "sexual contract" defined by Pateman to illustrate the historical roots of these cultural anxieties.[36] In a similar vein, many researchers and practitioners have called for frank discourse around racialized representations in books for children and youth and of the material power held by librarians and publishers.[37] The pressures that surround youths' positions in relation to moral issues of sex, sexuality, race and racism, appropriate family structures, and other hot button topics,[38] suggest that YA librarians are required to continuously interrogate these fears and the bases of these fears, to reconceptualize youth.[39]

---

33. Ibid., 37-38.

34. Erica Meiners, *Right to be Hostile: Schools, Prisons, and the Making of Public Enemies* (New York: Routledge, 2007), 137.

35. Meiners, *Right to be Hostile*, 137.

36. Ibid., 19, 44.

37. Rudine Sims Bishop, *Shadow and Substance: Afro-American Experience in Contemporary Children's Fiction* (Urbana, IL: NCTE, 1982); Mingshui Cai, *Multicultural Literature for Children and Young Adults: Reflections on Critical Issues* (Westport, CT: Greenwood Press, 2002), xiii-34; Michael Cart, *Young Adult Literature: From Romance to Realism* (Chicago: ALA, 2010), 75-202; Violet J. Harris, "The Complexity of Debates About Multicultural Literature and Cultural Understanding," in *Stories Matter: The Complexity of Cultural Authenticity in Children's Literature*, eds. Dana L. Fox and Kathy G. Short (Urbana, IL: NCTE, 2003), 116-134; Sandra Hughes-Hassell and Ernie Cox, "Inside Board Books: Representations of People of Color," *Library Quarterly* 8 (2010): 211-230.

38. Janet R. Jakobsen and Ann Pellegrini, *Love the Sin: Sexual Regulation and the Limits of Religious Tolerance* (Boston, MA: Beacon Press, 2003), 16, 93 – 94.

39. While other issues related to dominant, normative moralities (including physical health, appropriate relationship styles, family structures) exist in the public as well as in librarianship and publishing, they are less openly discussed and debated within the profession of librarianship.

This is true even when youth have been presented in terms of empowerment, civic participation, and youth voice – features of a neoliberal shift in the conceptualization of youth.[40] As Sukarieh and Tannock state, "[y]outh as a social category has always been double-sided, encompassing both negative and positive stereotypes."[41] Models of youth positive development are couched in, and work to reveal the ways in which, adult and institutionalized anxieties about youth failing to become functioning members of a generally static system of social and political power.[42] While youth studies have focused on many aspects of youth, including youth subculture, youth relationships, youth as consumers, and youths' relationships with their families, there has been an increasingly intensified focus on individual youth and individualized group practice in the field.[43] A critical approach to youth studies, as proposed by Sukarieh and Tannock, examines the positioning of youth *as a category* across time and space in a global context, one that recognizes the limitations and opportunities made available for youth as social and political actors.[44] In order to better understand the positioning of youth, as a category, it is necessary to understand the histories and conceptions of youth that have informed both the long-standing tradition of deficit models of youth as well as the more recently embraced models of positive development.

Childhood has been constructed as a space *Other than adult*, a time of presumed "innocence" that stands in contrast to (and subject to) the state of adulthood, which is informed, knowledgeable, and almost universally culpable.[45] Narratives of children's innocence are popularly utilized to leverage and avoid political aims.[46] Individual children, though,

---

40. Sukarieh and Tannock, *Youth Rising?* 12-32.

41. Ibid., 7.

42. Ibid., 19.

43. Ibid., 5-8.

44. Ibid., 13-32.

45. Stockton, *Queer Child*, 30-33.

46. Edelman, in Stockton, *Queer Child*, 12-13; Patrick McCreery, "Save Our Children/Let Us Marry: Gay Activists Appropriate the Rhetoric of Child Protectionism," *Radical History Review* 100 (2008): 186-207.

are not immediately included in this category, leaving childhood as a shifting category of access, entitlement, and varying levels of policing. Children who are racialized, or make sexualized identity claims, fall out of the purview of childhood innocence and are more subject to State surveillance and intervention.[47]

G. Stanley Hall's *Adolescence: Its Psychology and Its Relations to Physiology, Anthropology, Sex, Crime, Religion, and Education* (originally published in 1904), contorted ideas of racial development theories that were used to promote imperialism among the populace of colonizing countries and applied them to childhood as stages of life development that could be passed through in order for children to reach an ideal (White, middle-class, male) adulthood.[48] Highly influential on then emerging theories of adolescent development, Hall's work sets a framework in which some youth are unable to reach a full form of humanity in the public sphere– they are positioned as developmentally deviant, non-normative, and therefore suspect.

Whether or not one is willing to accept the idea that childhood and the individual child are necessarily queer ("strange", at least to adults), it is obvious that children experience the same social policing and legal regulation that has been placed upon LGBTQ and other non-normative, socially "deviant" individuals. As Kelleher states, "[t]he child and the homosexual, each historically objects of social discipline, control, aggression, and (too often) outright violence, are recast or, more to the point, are ideologically re-inscribed as the agents of social aggression and violence."[49] A shared history of surveillance, control, regulation, and enforced behavior join childhood and queerness at the hip, even if they do not (necessarily) create the child-queer as a social figure. Kelleher

---

47. Stockton, *Queer Child*, 30-33.

48. Granville Stanley Hall, Adolescence (New York: Appleton, 1904), v-xx; Nancy Lesko, "Denaturalizing Adolescence: The Politics of Contemporary Representations," *Youth & Society*, 28 (1996): 139-161.

49. Paul Kelleher, "How to Do Things with Perversion: Psychoanalysis and the 'Child in Danger'" in *Curiouser: On the Queerness of Children*, eds. Steven Bruhm and Natasha Hurley (Minneapolis: University of Minnesota Press, 2004), 167-168.

describes increasingly tightening "conceptual relations among perversion, childhood, and criminality."[50] Stockton's descriptions of "fallen" children redeemed through punishment in popular film,[51] as well as the racialized and sexualized tensions between a "good" childhood and the deviant-child, constructed at the categorical level, circumscribe the ways in which adult fears of abnormality work to move children into structures of proper social development. These narratives of children and youth as a future project, Gordon's "citizens-in-the-making,"[52] shape childhood experience through adult access to power and social, political, and economic realms. Conceptualizations of proper development underlie the structures that children and youth encounter or are under legal compulsion to attend (for instance, schooling is compulsory in the United States, and schooling requires its own set of behavioral modes – to fail to adhere to these behaviors can move children and youth from one institution to another – from the school, for instance, to incarceration).[53] Still, the continued so-called deviance of children and youth illustrates that narratives of development, and the control and policing of development, do not indefinitely confine or define childhood, despite their best efforts. Children and youth remain abnormal, strange, and queer to the world of adulthood.

The 'queerness' of youth does not somehow act as a means by which YA librarianship can disregard the concept of youth, because concepts, however they may have been created, continue to reverberate forward through time. This is present even in Hine's oft-cited work on teenagers, in which G. Stanley Hall's formative work on adolescence is named

---

50. Kelleher, "How to Do Things with Perversion," 153.

51. Stockton, *Queer Child*, 32-33.

52. Hava Rachel Gordon, *We Fight to Win: Inequality and the Politics of Youth Activism* (New Brunswick, NJ: Rutgers University Press, 2010), 8-10.

53. Jeanie Austin, "Critical Issues in Juvenile Detention Center Libraries," *Journal of Research on Libraries and Young Adults*, last modified July 26, 2012, http://www.yalsa.ala.org/jrlya/2012/07/critical-issues-in-juvenile-detention-center-libraries/.

as "mystical Darwinism with a racist tinge."[54] Hine continues this tinge through the language used to describe youth, stating that, "the American teenager is a noble savage in blue jeans, the future in your face."[55] In this way, the teenager is not allowed a present tense, and is described in models that continue the early roots of recapitulation theory.[56]

Racialized conceptions of youth, and of Whiteness as a normative position of value, continue to haunt the ways in which youth development is assessed in American society, possibly informing the present set of positive developmental values utilized by a majority of YA librarians. One of the ways in which new models for recognizing youth as other-than-adult can be created lies in the possibility of recognizing youth voice as something socially constructed and also as able to be transformative in the context of working toward social change. This is made clear in the ways in which youth describe their own activism, activities, and lives.[57]

Youth in the Streets: Young People's Community Action

Community action, activism, and resistance on the part of youth occurs in relation to, and interaction with, adult conceptions of children and youth. Taft includes information related to girls' activism and adult conceptions of youth across the Americas (specifically located in San Francisco, Mexico City, Caracas, Vancouver, and Buenos Aires) in *Rebel*

54. Thomas Hine, *The Rise and Fall of the American Teenager* (New York: Perennial, 2000), 160.

55. Hine, *Rise and Fall*, 10.

56. Recapitulation theory informed the work of G. Stanley Hall. This theory proposed that all human development occurred in parallel to the conceived patterns of the development of civilizations, with African (Black) civilizations being positioned at the lower end of development and White, European civilizations positioned at the apex.

57. Jessica K. Taft, *Rebel Girls: Youth Activism and Social Change Across the Americas* (New York City: New York University, 2011); Mary L. Gray, *Out in the Country: Youth, Media, and Queer Visibility in Rural America* (New York, NY: New York University Press, 2009).

Girls, a study of young women in various activist communities.[58] The youth interviewed do not present a cohesive account of youth activism in relation to adults. Rather, they set forth complicated and individualized understandings of adults and youth activism—understandings that can help to inform the practice of YA librarians working for social justice or social change.

Central to the statements of girls in Taft's study are ideas of youth as being uniquely positioned to respond to the issues that most affect their lives. As Taft writes, "[t]eenage activists directly assert their authority to organize around 'youth issues' like educational policy and school privatization, student bus fares, juvenile justice system reforms, teenagers' reproductive rights and sexual education, child abuse and youth rights, and curfews and police harassment, precisely because these are topics that impact their lives but are not, in their view, part of the political concern of most adults."[59] While youth in the study make arguments both for a difference in age and a difference in "historical moment" (generations) as defining their activism as divergent from that of adults, they almost consistently emphasized a difference between their social positions and the social positions of adults as shaping which social justice issues were addressed by activist movements and how they were addressed.[60] Acting in relation to a feeling of a "world in crisis," youth did not exclusively concern themselves with youth issues.[61] Participants in the study named aspects of adult constructions of youth as both valuable and detrimental to their activist practice – including the idea of youth as not yet fully formed (becoming adult) as creating a possibility for youth to take more risks and speak more openly, since they were not expected to be authoritative knowers. In all sites except Venezuela, youth also expressed that adults *were largely disillusioned or unresponsive to the needs of youth*.[62] Youth expressed their relationship to adults and

---

58. Taft, *Rebel Girls*, 56-66.

59. Ibid., 56.

60. Ibid., 57.

61. Ibid., 66.

62. Emphasis added by author.

adult activism as shaping "their political action and practice," utilizing constraints, such as the distance between the worlds inhabited by adults and those inhabited by youth, to create instances of possibility—in this case through the utilization of peer networks.[63]

Youth also noted the difference in legal ramifications between their own civil disobedience and that of adults, citing the possibility of expunged legal records and the reduced likelihood of legal consequences as creating space for them to engage in acts deemed illegal by the State. As Taft shows, however, the idea and practice of reduced consequences does not hold true for all youth – being protected by and from the law is an aspect of activist practice for youth who are White and who have access to financial resources.[64] Cacho, in an examination of the ways in which the law shapes and values specific lives (through the same identity categories that have historically informed developmental theories and ideas of valued citizenship), stresses and reiterates this point in a discussion of who has access to human and legal rights, and how they have them, which are focuses often undertaken by activist communities.[65]

LGBTQ and gender non-conforming identified youth have engaged in their own forms of activism in both urban and rural contexts. At times, they have drawn upon existing legacies to inform their resistance, countering that there must necessarily be a distance between adults and youth in activist practice. Shepard ties the legacy of Sylvia Rivera, who fought police in the Stonewall Riots and struggled for the inclusion of trans people in the gay and lesbian resistance, to a more recent resistance among queer youth and adults to the gentrification of the New York City West Side piers.[66] One of the groups of youth mentioned in Shepard's discussion of this resistance to erasure is FIERCE, which describes itself as "...an LGBTQ youth of color-led organization. We

---

63. Ibid., 59.

64. Ibid., 56-66.

65. Cacho, *Social Death*.

66. Benjamin Shepard, "Sylvia and Sylvia's Children: A Battle for a Queer Public Space," in That's Revolting!: Queer Strategies for Resisting Assimilation, ed. Mattilda Bernstein Sycamore (Brooklyn, NY: Soft Skull Press, 2004), 123-140.

build the leadership, political consciousness, and organizing skills of LGBTQ youth. In New York City, we organize local grassroots campaigns to fight police harassment and violence and increased access to safe public space for LGBTQ youth."[67]

The work of FIERCE draws from multiple identity positions to address real issues in the lives of LGBTQ youth. In other cases, LGBTQ and gender non-conforming identified youth have reworked (queered) the resources and power structures in which they find themselves. This is the focus of Gray's work on queer youth in rural areas in Appalachia.[68] Youth who navigated constraints related to community access and family acceptance utilized media, including the Internet, to create community and shape and reshape their identities and identifications.[69] Youth worked with respecting adults to advocate together in the self-described interests of youth, even when these acts went unheard in traditional political contexts.[70] Youth in Gray's book also created new and meaningful ways to leverage their own positions as "consumer citizens"[71] to claim their own space through drag shows in a local Wal-Mart.

The youth practices described above illustrate that youth are innovative, reflective, resourceful, aware, and willing to work with adults who will meet them with a recognition of youths' knowledge of their own unique social positions. Even in instances where youth are engaged with adults in more mainstream social movements—including the recent global uprisings, the Occupy movement, and the less recent but still notable WTO protests in Seattle in 1999—they are made strange to adults through their positioning in narratives of youth and resistance.[72] Contemporary discussions of youth resistance simultaneously celebrate and condemn the idea of youth agency—creating images of youth as

67. FIERCE, "What We Do," last accessed April 13, 2015, http://www.fiercenyc.org/what-we-do.

68. Gray, *Out in the Country*, 22-28.

69. Ibid., 121-126.

70. Ibid., 40-47.

71. Ibid., 98.

72. Sukarieh and Tannock, *Youth Rising?*, 101-112.

innately rebellious creators of the progressive future and as a threat to the status quo.[73] The neoliberal positioning and framing of youth as social actors and creators of social change works to "obscure broader divisions of class, race, ethnic, regional and ideological struggle," regardless of the ways in which youth (and adults) promote these narratives in their own movements and actions.[74] Sukarieh and Tannock counter arguments of youth activism as clearly demarcated from that of adults, stating that "[w]hat we can say with certainty is that, in all cases, the power of autonomy of the young will inevitably be circumscribed, due to their marginal position in social, political and economic structures of power; and their ideas and actions, potent as these may sometimes be, will be developed and carried out in conjunction with other groups, classes and movements in society as a whole."[75]

Youth activism, uprising, and resistance is clearly not separate from adult worlds and social issues, yet it continues to be positioned in mainstream descriptions as occurring without reference to the long histories that precede specific youth movements, precedents for actions and rebellions, and cooperation with various groups. Adult fears about youth as separate from adulthood are evident in descriptions that place youth as both responsible for the future (a progressive positioning), and simultaneously as threats to the standing order of things. In addition to this, as illustrated in accounts of youth activism and resistance reviewed above, the practices of youth are in tension with adult ideas of youth as "becoming adult"—youth describe adults as minimizing youth knowledge about their lived situations and viewing their actions and passions as passing phases. On a smaller scale, these tensions play out in the library setting. The power structures that shape the lives of youth, their opportunities, and their forms of resistance, continue to exist once youth enter the library doors. YA Librarians seeking to work *with* youth can draw from the requests of youth to be heard and can even organize *with* them to

73. Ibid., 111-112.
74. Ibid., 108.
75. Ibid., 112.

provide useful information and skills for the projects they undertake. This stands in opposition to the 40 Developmental Assets, in which YA librarians are primarily facilitators of youths' entrée into normative adulthood.

In the Library: Youth as Concept, Youth as Practice

YA librarians, and other information professionals working with youth, are made aware of the ways in which individual youth very much exist in a present that is lived, even as adult expectations and their own hopes and fears involve manifestations of the future. As "all literacy is local," the lives of individual youth are localized as well.[76] They may be limited by their position in relation to global forces and neoliberal politics, but the practices of youth agency in addressing power and retaining culture are well documented.[77] Local, national, and global issues and trends have impacts for youths' lives as they are lived – defining their opportunities and constraints in particular ways due to the adult ideas that surround and often limit their possibilities. YA librarians should have a working comprehension of these issues, how they (potentially) affect youth, and how youth utilize their own agency and negotiate power through traditional and new technologies (this is seen through the exploration of personal identities and youth culture described by Rothbauer[78] and in Jenkins' descriptions of the power structures surrounding the creation of Harry Potter fan-fiction[79]).

---

76. Anthony Bernier, "Not Broken by Someone Else's Schedule: On Joy and Young Adult Information Seeking," in *Youth Information Seeking Behavior II: Context, Theories, Models and Issues*, eds. Mary K. Chelton and Colleen Cool (Lanham, MD: Scarecrow Press, 2007), xix.

77. Henry A. Giroux, "Expendable Futures: Youth and Democracy at Risk," in *Youth in a Suspect Society: Democracy or Disposability?* (New York: Palgrave Macmillan, 2009), 1-26; Maira, "Cool Nostalgia," 197-208.

78. Paulette Rothbauer, "Chapter 3: Young Adults and Reading," in *Reading Matters: What the Research Reveals about Reading, Libraries, and Community*, eds. Catherine Sheldrick Ross, Lynne (E.F.) McKechnie, and Paulette M. Rothbauer (Westport, CT: Libraries Unlimited, 2006), 101-132.

79. Henry Jenkins, "Why Heather Can Write: Media Literacy and the Harry

YA librarians should be skeptically aware of how youth are defined and the research that surrounds them, noting the ways in which that research perpetuates existing ideas of youth as a threat to the world of adulthood and existing social orders (after all, social change and social justice will involve an interruption in the existing social order). Maybe our history can critically inform us here—as Braverman shows, this lack of insight (disturbing adult ideas of youth) is one of the faults of librarianship in the 1960s, in which a divisional line between youth social movements and YA librarianship became an apparent fault on the end of the libraries.[80] Meiners speaks to a similar possibility – that the angry responses of youth (especially youth of color) to their lived realities of surveillance and potential imprisonment are responses only made illegitimate through power structures that refuse to acknowledge youth agency as an informed knowledge.[81]

YA librarians have the opportunity to acknowledge that agency, to support it, and to share knowledge with youth. Rolon-Dow's work with after-school youth illustrates this concept.[82] Building on existing literacies and knowledges of youth, Rolon-Dow supported youth in describing microaggressions (manifestations of racism in their lives). Rolon-Dow shows that the uses of multiple modalities (literacies / media) "can be particularly helpful as students try to narrate and illustrate the covert and coded forms that racism takes in contemporary contexts."[83] YA librarians can facilitate knowledge through relationships with individual youth and groups of youth, which makes more room for youth to share and hone their skills. In doing this, YA librarians must recognize that

---

Potter Wars," in *Convergence Culture: Where Old and New Media Collide* (New York: NYU Press, 2006), 169-205.

80. Miriam Braverman, *Youth, Society and the Public Library* (Chicago: ALA, 1979).

81. Meiners, *Right to be Hostile*, 28.

82. Rosalie Rolon-Dow, "Race(ing) Stories: Digital Storytelling as a Tool for Critical Race Scholarship," *Race, Ethnicity and Education* 14, no. 2 (2011): 159-173.

83. Rolon-Dow, "Race(ing) Stories," 171.

youth already possess myriad skills that come into play as they navigate their worlds.

Swygart-Hobaugh's account of a freshman college course emphasizes this possibility.[84] YA librarians hold specific knowledge regarding information as politically, economically, and socially situated, and on how to evaluate information given its positioning within these contexts. Research into youth agency and information-seeking behavior reveals the complex modes by which information pertinent to their lives is accessed and evaluated by young people and the way that they are positioned by power.[85] YA librarians should recognize youths' appreciation for peer knowledge and resources, as well as their methods of accessing information, including Everyday Life Information Seeking (ELIS)[86] behaviors, and modes of engagement around technologies.[87] YA librarians that are seeking to engage *with* youth (rather than serving youth or furthering 'normal' youth development) should be responsive to youth information needs[88] as they are described by youth, including their social, emotional, reflective, physical, creative, cognitive, and sexual information needs—needs that youth may be reluctant to address with adults.[89]

---

84. Amanda J. Swygart-Hobaugh, "Information-Power to the People: Students and Librarians Dialoging About Power, Social Justice, and Information," in *Information Literacy and Social Justice: Radical Professional Praxis*, eds. Lua Gregory and Shana Higgins (Sacramento, CA: Library Juice Press, 2013), 219-243.

85. Elaine Meyers, "Youth Development and Evaluation: Lessons from 'Public Libraries as Partners in Youth Development,'" in *Urban Teens in the Library: Research and Practice*, eds. Denise E. Agosto and Sandra Hughes-Hassell (Chicago: American Library Association, 2010), 129-142.

86. Reijo Savolainen, "Everday Life Information Seeking: Information Seeking in the Context of 'Way of Life,'" *Library and Information Science Research* 17 (1995): 259-294.

87. Sandra Hughes-Hassell and Denise E. Agosto, "Modeling the Everyday Life Information Needs of Urban Teenagers," in *Youth Information Seeking Behavior II: Context, Theories, Models and Issues*, eds. Mary K. Chelton and Colleen Cool (Lanham, MD: Scarecrow Press, 2007), 27-61; Mizuko Ito et al., *Hanging Out, Messing Around, and Geeking Out: Kids Living and Learning with New Media* (Cambridge, MA: MIT Press, 2010).

88. Needs, in this context, is used to describe those things that youth have described as making their lives possible.

89. Hughes-Hassell and Agosto, "Modeling the Everyday Life Information Needs of Urban Teenagers," 27-61.

Given that specific groups of youth are more heavily targeted by power (such as youth of color, queer youth, young women, poor and immigrant youth, and other groups), YA librarians need to be aware of issues that affect these groups and their life-worlds.[90] YA librarians must not treat youth as victims of their circumstances but provide opportunities based on those circumstances, while acknowledging that they may live within power structures that can be constrictive of their agency, or provide opportunities depending on their circumstances. Maybe the motivation for this type of engagement can be found in Mehra and Braquet's study of young adult's coming out experiences, in which "accurate and supportive information would have made their experiences related to sexual identity and orientation easier and less painful," both personally and socially.[91] YA librarians have an opportunity to provide this information, supporting youth as they move through turbulent structures that work to shape them into normative adulthood.

YA librarians need to meet with youth, individually and as a concept, where and as they are, with respect that is not built out of the ideas that youth are victims or creators of their social and political positioning. At the same time, they must be informed about both the power structures that shape youth as an experience and a category.[92] Doing this may even provide an entrance into communities of interest with youth, through a variety of new media experiences, passive or active (including collection development and programs in which youth choose music or video games). It may provide spaces for encounter between the life-worlds of

---

90. Meiners, *Right to be Hostile*, 1-25.

91. Bharat Mehra and Donna Braquet, "Process of Information Seeking During 'Queer' Youth Coming-out Experiences," in *Youth Information Seeking Behavior II: Context, Theories, Models and Issues*, eds. Mary K. Chelton and Colleen Cool (Lanham, MD: Scarecrow Press, 2007), 99.

92. Noble et al., show that such an awareness is a transformative interruption in much the same way that Library and Information Science (LIS) curriculum is constructed and how library services are discussed within LIS education (Safiya, et al., "Changing Course: Collaborative Reflections of Teaching/ Taking 'Race, Gender, and Sexuality in the Information Professions,'" *Journal of Education for Library & Information Science* 55 (2014): 212-222.

YA librarians and adolescents based on relationships of shared interest and knowledge, including around technologies.[93]

YA librarians' knowledge of youths' actual practices should not mirror the pragmatic foundations of the profession as described by Braverman, but can reenact these in forms that are critically concerned with the life-worlds of individual youth.[94] Knowledge of online and offline practices, ways of knowing, and systems of sometimes immediate and intense oppression that categorically target youth are requisite for librarians who seek to approach youth as individuals, strange to adults and to one another, and as a grouping created through the very power structures that rearrange its part, at once made real and marginalized, and also "a figment of our collective imagination."[95]

Conclusion: Tying the Threads

This chapter began with a discussion of the 40 Developmental Assets, but that is just one place to begin examining how narratives of positive development limit the scope of YA library practice. These guiding principles for YA library services offer a brief glance into how positive developmental models continue to inform the profession but fall short of a practice that centers youth knowledge and positions within society. At the surface, these values seem to break from early developmental models (and ideologies) that limited the life chances of youth who were described as unable to become fully developed—youth who are racialized, perceived to be (or who actually are) sexually deviant, poor, or women. Upon troubling the waters, though, it becomes apparent that the 40 Developmental Assets continue a legacy that informed early models of adolescence and development into adulthood. A queer theoretical lens reveals that the assumptions that shape these values—that youth

---

93. Ito, et al., *Hanging Out.*

94. Braverman, *Youth, Society and the Public Library.*

95. Hine, *Rise and Fall of the American Teenager*, 304; Michael Zuckerman, "The Paradox of American Adolescence," *Journal of the History of Childhood and Youth* 4, no. 1 (2011): 11-25.

have access to certain resources and are positioned with relative equality to one another in their access to positive adult development—are false, and may lead the profession of YA librarianship into echoing other structures that limit the ways in which youth live their lives.

This happens through structures within the library as well as through individual encounters. If youth are not able to achieve positive development and become productive citizen-adults, even under the guidance of professionals, then neoliberal ideologies of self-efficacy point to the failure of assuming this status as a fault within individual youth.[96] Certain youth, such as those who engage in behaviors that resist development into productive citizen-adults, may then be perceived as less worthy of engagement and access to information that aligns with their interests and desires. Recognizing this requires that YA librarians interested in engaging in activism and supporting youth resistance must be able to unsettle narratives that separate the good kids from the bad, those worthy of effort and those who have (by force of social position, option availability, or through contextualized personal choice) have limited access to (or desire for) the possibility of becoming positively developed citizen-adults.

Queer theory positions that view youth as necessarily queer to adults provide one point of access into unsettling adult knowledge of youth, youth behavior, and adult assumptions of what youth ought to become. If adults are unable to understand youth through social positioning, then what provides adults with the authority to make assumptions about youth choices and decisions? This authority comes from positions of power accorded by the state through age and dominant ideology. The distance between adults and youth suggests, as youth involved in activist projects state, and the principles of Participatory Action Research affirm, that adults seeking to work *with* youth must begin from a place of recognition of differences between youth and adults without essentializing these differences. Youth as a grouping are made strange to adults through various systems of power, but this does not mean that youth and adults

---

96. Sukarieh and Tannock, "Positivity Imperative," 682.

(including YA librarians) are always and inherently so separate as to be completely indiscernible to one another.

The accounts of youth activism in this chapter are but a taste of the various projects and individual acts of resistance in which youth engage. The projects described are disparate, but they share a common theme—youth involved in activist projects in a variety of contexts have called to be heard by adults in their struggles. YA librarians have a unique opportunity to listen to and work *with* youth as they state their goals and desires. The first step in this process is to discern how youth are valued and evaluated. If it is by their success (or lack thereof) in working toward or achieving positive development, then the efforts of individual youth to make change in their worlds and to resist a world in which normative development may not be available to them may only be viewed as bad behavior. Questioning "positive development" as a professional value of YA librarianship may open doors for new connections, new interactions, new acts for social change that work *with* youth and against ageism. To do this is an act of social justice and social change as it destabilizes the ways in which adults approach youth, as a concept and as individuals. It may be a strange terrain we enter together, one without the borders and boundaries of becoming "adult" as a definite goal, but if YA librarians turn toward youth as knowers of their own lives and reflect critically on the ways in which youth are constructed within society, we may go with those youth, queered, familiar with strangeness and estrangement, as our companions and guides.

Bibliography

Austin, Jeanie. "Critical Issues in Juvenile Detention Center Libraries." *Journal of Research on Libraries and Young Adults.* Last modified on July 26, 2012. http://www.yalsa.ala.org/jrlya/2012/07/critical-issues-in-juvenile-detention-center-libraries/.

Bernier, Anthony. "Not Broken by Someone Else's Schedule: On Joy and Young Adult Information Seeking." In *Youth Information*

Seeking Behavior II: Context, Theories, Models and Issues, edited by Mary K. Chelton and Colleen Cool, xiii-xxviii. Lanham, MD: Scarecrow Press, 2007.

Bishop, Rudine S. *Shadow and Substance: Afro-American Experience in Contemporary Children's Fiction.* Urbana, IL: NCTE, 1982.

Braverman, Miriam .*Youth, Society and the Public Library.* Chicago, IL: ALA, 1979.

Brown, Tara M. and Louie F. Rodriguez. "Issue Editor's Notes." *Youth in Participatory Action Research. New Directions for Youth Development* 123 (2009): 1-9.

Cacho, Lisa Marie. *Social Death: Racialized Rightlessness and the Criminalization of the Unprotected.* New York: NYU Press, 2012.

Cai, Mingshui. *Multicultural Literature for Children and Young Adults: Reflections on Critical Issues.* Westport, Conn.: Greenwood Press, 2002.

Cart, Michael. *Young Adult Literature: From Romance to Realism.* Chicago, IL: ALA, 2010.

Cohen, Cathy J. "Punks, Bulldaggers, and Welfare Queens: The Radical Potential of Queer Politics?" *GLQ* 3 (1997): 437-485.

Darder, Antonia, Marta P. Baltodano, and Rodolfo D. Torres, "Critical Pedagogy: An Introduction." In *The Critical Pedagogy Reader*, edited by Antonia Darder, Marta P. Baltodano, and Rodolfo D. Torres, 1-20. New York: Routledge, 2009.

FIERCE. "What We Do." Accessed April 13, 2015. http://www.fiercenyc.org/what-we-do.

Fine, Michelle. "Sexuality, Schooling, and Adolescent Females: The Missing Discourse of Desire." *Harvard Educational Review* 58 (1988): 29-54.

Foucault, Michel. *Abnormal: Lectures at the College de France 1974-1975.* New York: Verso, 2003.

Giroux, Henry. "Critical Theory and Educational Practice." In *The Critical Pedagogy Reader*, edited by Antonia Darder, Marta P. Baltodano, and Rodolfo D. Torres, 27-51. New York: Routledge, 2009.

————.. *Youth in a Suspect Society: Democracy or Disposability?* New York: Palgrave Macmillan, 2009.

Gordon, Hava Rachel. *We Fight to Win: Inequality and the Politics of Youth Activism*. New Brunswick, NJ: Rutgers University Press, 2010.

Gray, Mary L. *Out in the Country: Youth, Media, and Queer Visibility in Rural America*. New York, NY: New York University Press, 2009.

Hall, Granville Stanley. *Adolescence*. New York: Appleton, 1904.

Hames-Garcia, Michael . "Can Queer Theory Be Critical Theory?" In *New Critical Theory: Essays on Liberation*, edited by William S. Wilkerson and Jeffrey Paris, 201-222. Boston: Rowman and Littlefield, 2001.

Harris, Violet J. "The Complexity of Debates About Multicultural Literature and Cultural Understanding." In **Stories Matter:** *The Complexity of Cultural Authenticity in Children's Literature*, edited by Dana L. Fox and Kathy G. Short, 116-134. Urbana, IL: NCTE, 2003.

Hine, Thomas. *The Rise and Fall of the American Teenager*. New York: Perennial, 2000.

Hughes-Hassell, Sandra and Ernie Cox. "Inside Board Books: Representations of People of Color." *Library Quarterly* 8 (2010): 211-230.

Hughes-Hassell, Sandra and Denise E. Agosto. "Modeling the Everyday Life Information Needs of Urban Teenagers." In *Youth Information Seeking Behavior II: Context, Theories, Models and Issues,* edited by Mary K. Chelton and Colleen Cool, 27-61. Lanham, MD: Scarecrow Press, 2007.

Ito, Mizuko, Sanja Baumer, Matteo Bittanti, danah boyd, Rachel Cody, Becky Herr-Stephenson, Heather A. Horst, Patricia G. Lange, Dilan Mahendran, Katynka Z. Martinez, C. J. Pascoe, Dan Perkel, Laura Robinson, Christo Sims, and Lisa Tripp. *Hanging Out, Messing Around, and Geeking Out: Kids Living and Learning with New Media.* Cambridge, MA: MIT Press, 2010.

Jakobsen, Janet R. and Ann Pellegrini. *Love the Sin: Sexual Regulation and the Limits of Religious Tolerance.* Boston, MA: Beacon Press, 2003.

Jenkins, Henry. "Why Heather Can Write: Media Literacy and the Harry Potter Wars." In *Convergence Culture: Where Old and New Media Collide*, 169-205. New York: NYU Press, 2006.

Kelleher, Paul. "How to Do Things with Perversion: Psychoanalysis and the 'Child in Danger.'" In *Curiouser: On the Queerness of Children*, edited by Steven Bruhm and Natasha Hurley, 151-171. Minneapolis: University of Minnesota Press, 2004.

Kwon, Soo Ah . *Uncivil Youth: Race, Activism, and Affirmative Governmentality.* Durham, NC: Duke University Press, 2013.

Ladson-Billings, Gloria and William Tate. "Toward a Critical Race Theory of Education." *Teachers College Record* 97 (1995): 47-68.

Lecky, Robert and Kim Brooks. Introduction to *Queer Theory: Law, Culture, Empire*, edited by Robert Lecky and Kim Brooks, 1-18. New York: Routledge, 2010.

Lesko, Nancy. "Denaturalizing Adolescence: The Politics of Contemporary Representations." *Youth & Society* 28 (1996): 139-161.

Maira, Sunaina. "Cool Nostalgia: Indian American Youth Culture and the Politics of Authenticity." In *Contemporary Youth Research*, edited by Helena Helve and Gunilla Holm, 197-208. Burlington, VT: Ashgate Publishing, 2005.

Mayo, Cris. "The Tolerance that Dare Not Speak Its Name." In *Democratic Dialogue in Education: Troubling Speech, Disturbing Silence*, edited by Megan Boler, 33-47. New York: Peter Lang, 2004.

McCreery, Patrick. "Save Our Children/Let Us Marry: Gay Activists Appropriate the Rhetoric of Child Protectionism." *Radical History Review* 100 (2008): 186-207.

McIntyre, Alice *Participatory Action Research*. Thousand Oaks, CA: Sage Publications, Inc., 2008.

Mehra, Bharat and Donna Braquet, "Process of Information Seeking During 'Queer' Youth Coming-out Experiences." In *Youth Information Seeking Behavior II: Context, Theories, Models and Issues*, edited by Mary K. Chelton and Colleen Cool, 93-131. Lanham, MD: Scarecrow Press, 2007.

Meiners, Erica. *Right to be Hostile: Schools, Prisons, and the Making of Public Enemies*. New York: Routledge, 2007.

Meyers, Elaine. "Youth Development and Evaluation: Lessons from 'Public Libraries as Partners in Youth Development.'" In *Urban Teens in the Library: Research and Practice*, edited by Denise E. Agosto and Sandra Hughes-Hassell, 129-142. Chicago: American Library Association, 2010.

Noble, Safiya, Miriam Sweeney, Jeanie Austin, Lucas McKeever and Elizabeth Sullivan. "Changing Course: Collaborative Reflections of Teaching/Taking 'Race, Gender, and Sexuality in the Information Professions.'" *Journal of Education for Library & Information Science* 55 (2014): 212-222.

Rolon-Dow, Rosalie. "Race(ing) Stories: Digital Storytelling as a Tool for Critical Race Scholarship." *Race, Ethnicity and Education* 14, no. 2 (2011): 159-173.

Rothbauer, Paulette . "Chapter 3: Young Adults and Reading." In *Reading Matters: What the Research Reveals about Reading, Libraries, and Community*, edited by Catherine Sheldrick Ross, Lynne (E.F.) McKechnie, and Paulette M. Rothbauer, 101-132. Westport, CT: Libraries Unlimited, 2006.

Savolainen, Reijo. "Everday Life Information Seeking: Information Seeking in the Context of 'Way of Life.'" *Library and Information Science Research* 17 (1995): 259-294.

Search Institute. "About Search Institute." Accessed July 16, 2015. http://www.search-institute.org/about.

————. "40 Developmental Assets for Adolescents." Accessed November 11, 2014. http://www.search-institute.org/content/40-developmental-assets-adolescents-ages-12-18.

Shepard, Benjamin. "Sylvia and Sylvia's Children: A Battle for a Queer Public Space." In *That's Revolting!: Queer Strategies for Resisting Assimilation*, edited by Mattilda Bernstein Sycamore, 123-140. Brooklyn, NY: Soft Skull Press, 2004.

Spade, Dean. *Normal Life: Administrative Violence, Critical Trans Politics, and the Limits of the Law*. Brooklyn, NY: South End Press, 2011.

Stockton, Kathryn Bond. *The Queer Child: Or Growing Sideways in the 20th Century*. Durham, NC: Duke University Press, 2009.

Sukarieh, Mayssoun and Stuart Tannock. "The Positivity Imperative: A Critical Look at the 'New' Youth Development Movement." *Journal of Youth Studies* 14 (2011): 675- 691.

————. *Youth Rising? The Politics of Youth in the Global Economy*. New York: Routledge, 2015.

Swygart-Hobaugh, Amanda J. "Information-Power to the People: Students and Librarians Dialoging About Power, Social Justice, and Information." In *Information Literacy and Social Justice: Radical Professional Praxis*, edited Lua Gregory and Shana Higgins, 219-243. Sacramento, CA: Library Juice Press, 2013.

Taft, Jessica K. *Rebel Girls: Youth Activism and Social Change Across the Americas*. New York City: New York University, 2011.

Zuckerman, Michael. "The Paradox of American Adolescence." *The Journal of the History of Childhood and Youth* 4, no. 1 (2011): 11-25.

Chapter 8

Using Unstructured Research as a Data Gathering Methodology for Community-Based Actions in Support of Social Justice in Public Libraries

Kaurri C. Williams-Cockfield

Introduction

This chapter examines the use of small world[1] and information grounds[2] theory to gather data on the information needs of rural public library users. The experientially-based library leadership model reviewed in this chapter was developed through participant observation, semi-formal interview experiences, and appreciative inquiry techniques for the revitalization of three rural libraries over a twelve-year time frame. This model specifically addresses the role of a public library leader as an advocate for change, a builder of community, and an advocate of social justice. The essential question addressed is: how does a library leader develop, implement, and advocate for progressive library services in a community that has no collective construct of a need for change?

---

1. Elfreda A. Chatman, "A Theory of Life in the Round," *Journal of the American Society for Information Science* 50, no. 3 (March 1999): 209.

2. Reijo Savolainen, "Small World and Information Grounds as Contexts of Information Seeking and Sharing," *Library and Information Science Research* 31 (2009): 41.

The first three sections of the chapter review the context of the public library and its role in supporting social justice in a service community, including access to information and the transitioning public library role, defining healthy communities, and describing the characteristics of transformational leadership. The second three sections make the case for the use of unstructured research methodologies in a rural public library setting based on Chapman's small world theory[3] and Pettigrew's information grounds theory[4] as applied to three case study libraries, identifying the steps in a change model for library leadership and discussing community-based actions implemented in support of social justice in a service community. The summation reflects on the leadership role as the catalyst for community action for placing the library in a position to impact social justice issues in the service community and provides guidance on processes for use of unstructured research.

The Public Library – Social Justice Connection

Access to Information

The public library and its connection to social justice issues is immediately understandable when examining access impediments to information, as access is characterized by physical, intellectual and social aspects.[5] Physical access is primary, and centers on a library user's ability to physically access information. "Factors that impact physical access include technology, economics, geography, and disability."[6] Intellectual and social access refer respectively to understanding information and its

---

3. Chatman, "A Theory of Life in the Round," 209.

4. K.E. Pettigrew, "Waiting for Chiropody: Contextual Results from an Ethnographic Study of the Information Behavior among Attendees at Community Clinics," *Information Processing & Management* 35 (1999): 811.

5. Gary Burnett, Paul T. Jaeger, and Kim M. Thompson, "Normative Behavior and Information: The Social Aspects of Information Access," *Library & Information Science Research* (2008): 56.

6. Ibid., 57.

value within a particular small world.[7] By comparing these three aspects of information access to the precepts of social justice, which is based on equal rights and liberties within a society,[8] the public library connection to the community becomes evident. Public libraries, by virtue of mission, support and defend the freedom of thought, speech, and assembly to address critical societal problems. A cursory identification of disenfranchised individuals within a community illustrates the "links between income equity and happiness, physical health, mental health, drug abuse, education, imprisonment, obesity, social mobility, trust and community life, violence, teenage births and child well-being."[9] The transitioning role of the public library into an institution that advocates for social justice has its foundations in the provision of user-centered services (needs-based and community-led services).[10]

The Transitioning Public Library Role

Traditionally, the role of public libraries has been to provide services in support of a "few key themes: collective buying agent, economic stimulus, center of learning, safety net, steward of cultural heritage, cradle of democracy, and symbol of community aspirations."[11] Technology advances and the demand for increased science, technology, engineering and math (STEM) skills have had a profound impact on how libraries provide services. This new role requires that libraries and librarians become facilitators of knowledge by working to build smarter communities.[12]

---

7. Ibid., 58.

8. John Rawls, "Justice as Fairness," *Philosophy & Public Affairs* 14, no. 3 (Summer 1985): 234.

9. John Pateman, "Public Libraries, Social Class and Social Justice," *Information, Society and Justice* (2011): 58.

10. Ibid., 63.

11. David Lankes, "Expect More: Demanding Better Libraries for Today's Complex World," R. *David Lankes*, 2012, accessed January 24, 2015, http://www.DavidLankes.org.

12. Ibid., 43.

Lankes, in his research on the new role of librarians, ascertains that libraries facilitate knowledge in a community through: 1) Provision of access to information and people so exchange from both occurs; 2) Training on the use of information access/sharing tools as well as job skills; 3) A physically and intellectually safe environment; 4) The building on motivation to learn by inviting the community to take an active role in the development/provision of library services.[13] Essentially, the public library is a "culturally competent organization" in that it fosters the access and success of a diverse user base, promotes a positive, welcoming, and affirming environment, and offers/infuses a diverse perspective through the holistic work of the organization.[14]

Healthy Communities vs. Rural Communities

A healthy community is defined as a community "where people come together to make their community better for themselves, their family, their friends, their neighbors and others by creating an ongoing dialog, generating leadership opportunities for all, embracing diversity, connecting people and resources, fostering a sense of community and by shaping its future."[15] Essentially, a healthy community is "safe, economically secure, and environmentally sound, as all residents have equal access to high quality educational and employment opportunities, transportation and housing options, prevention and healthcare services, and healthy food and physical activity opportunities."[16] Rural communities typify "small world lives"[17] with common limiting characteristics such as low population density, limited availability of support services, a high number

---

13. Ibid., 43, 47, 48, 52, 57.

14. Kumea Shorter-Gooden, "The Culturally Competent Organization," *Library Quarterly* (2013): 207.

15. "Healthy Communities," 2013, *Health Resources in Action: Advancing Public Health and Medical Research*, http://www.hria.org/community-health/healthy-communities/.

16. Ibid., 24.

17. Chatman, "A Theory of Life in the Round," 209.

of disenfranchised populations, social isolation, and a high occurrence of social, mental, and physical issues.[18] However, there are also a number of significant attributes found in a rural society, including a deep sense of community with a religious underpinning, a strong work ethic, gratitude and fortitude, and a sense of independence.[19] Lankes' research identifies conversation as being "key to the public library role as it implies both talking and listening with the outcome being a conversation where ideas are exchanged and both parties are shaped by the conversations."[20] Rural community characteristics create an environment especially suited for library-led change made possible through the use of unstructured research methodologies (i.e., the close connections that exist between residents and the ongoing community conversation).

Characteristics of the Transformational Library Leader

The role of the library leader, as a transformational leader,[21] is central to the use of public library services in building healthy communities.[22] A library leader is the professional tasked with applying critical appraisal to library services in a holistic manner and for implementing a change process that combines user-centered input with knowledge gained from participation in the community conversation.[23] Essentially, a library leader serves as the guide for facilitating knowledge creation within a community, and in doing so, sets the foundation for implementing social change.

---

18. Gail Kouame, "Charting Consumer Health: Reflections on Rural Communities," *Journal of Hospital Librarianship* (2010): 166.

19. Ibid., 166.

20. Lankes, "Expect More," 62.

21. Michael A. Germano, "Library Leadership that Creates and Sustains Innovation," *Library Leadership & Management* (August 2013): 7.

22. Bharat Mehra and Ramesh Srinivasan, "The Library-Community Convergence Framework for Community Action: Libraries as Catalysts of Social Change," *Libris* 57 (2007): 130.

23. Lindsay Glynn, "A Critical Appraisal Tool for Library and Information Research," *Library Hi Tech* 24, no. 3 (2006): 398.

Successful change processes in public libraries occur from the bottom up, with empowerment of staff as the foundation. "Empowerment is a long-term process that results from encouragement, motivation and the removal of barriers from job performance, trust and patience."[24] The empowerment of staff can be accomplished through the establishment of two-way communication between leadership and all staff, the provision of ongoing training on the direction (why) of library services as well as the mechanics (how) of library services.

This same empowerment can be applied to library boards and friends groups. A library leader prepares, empowers, and encourages staff, boards, and friends to participate in and advocate for library service development and provision.

Participation of a library leader in local and state government and community organizations comes next. A library leader, along with empowered staff and board members, can embed the public library into the fabric of the community by participation in and coordination with a myriad of community groups, including the chamber of commerce, schools and colleges, health care and social service organizations, community service and economic development groups, and workforce development entities. Empowering community participation through collaboration with these groups lays the groundwork for building healthy communities.

The Case for Unstructured Research Methodologies in a Rural Public Library Setting

Public libraries have historically operated under less-than-ideal situations, making the use of structured research impractical for implementing holistic change.[25] Inadequate fiscal and human resources often restrict

---

24. Gisela von Dran, "Human Resources and Leadership Strategies for Libraries in Transition," *Library Administration & Management* 19, no. 4 (Fall 2005): 181.

25. Harry Kogetsidis, "Critical Systems Thinking: A Creative Approach to Organizational Change," *Journal of Transnational Management* (2012), 194.

public libraries from investing the time required to conduct structured research.[26] These same restrictions impede the realization of benefits from structured research by preventing the effective implementation of findings into library operations.

Additionally, time is often a factor due to increasing demands for change from library users. A library leader, as a transformational manager,[27] serves in a key position within the community and has a unique vantage point for the use of unstructured research methods within the context of both a professional and political role. Additionally, as a transformational manager, a library leader cultivates a sustainable culture of innovation by developing services that are both wanted and needed by library users.

This atmosphere of innovation results in a library where change is embedded in the culture, thereby permitting a flexible and timely response to community needs, especially where services intersect with social justice.[28] Applying Chatman's concept of small worlds,[29] the public library job context affords a library leader access to three distinct groups of community participants. The first group includes the library staff, library board (or other governing department tasked with library oversight), and library support groups (friends or foundation members). The second group includes local government representatives and elected officials, including peer level departments within the government construct. The third group is composed of community organizations, including service clubs and business associations (Chamber), and peer information professionals. These three groups are accessible to a library leader during the course of library operations and represent distinct social constructs, or information grounds,[30] where individuals come together

26. Germano, "Library Leadership that Creates and Sustains Innovation," 2.

27. Ibid., 7.

28. Ibid., 12.

29. Chatman, "A Theory of Life in the Round," 213.

30. Reijo Savolainen, "Small World and Information Grounds as Contexts of Information Seeking and Sharing," *Library and Information Science Research* 31 (2009): 40.

for "a singular purpose resulting in the creation of a social atmosphere that fosters information sharing."[31] Additionally, these groups represent a balanced slice of the community given their differing mission/role in the community, socio-economic levels, age, education and life experiences.

Small World Theory

Small world theory, as a theory for understanding information seeking/sharing behaviors as impacted by social norms, has been discussed across socio/political research [32] over the past fifty years. It is Chatman's research,[33] however, that connects small world theory specifically to information access/use behaviors. Her application of small world theory[34] is a construct for information seeking in daily life of people living in an environment that precludes interaction with the outside world due to physical, social, or world view isolation. Chatman theorizes that small worlds are held together by "a common assessment of information worthy of attention, social norms that allow members to approach or ignore information, and behaviors that are deemed by other inhabitants to be appropriate for this world."[35] Her theory progressed into the theory of normative behavior, "which draws on four major concepts: social norms, worldview, social types, and information behavior."[36] Essentially, these four concepts represent behaviors that are the most appropriate within a unique small world, and explain how a small world can be

31. K.E. Pettigrew, "Waiting for Chiropody: Contextual Results from an Ethnographic Study of the Information Behavior among Attendees at Community Clinics," *Information Processing & Management* 35 (1999): 811.

32. Gary Burnett and Paul T. Jaeger, "Small Worlds, Life Worlds, and Information: the Ramifications of the Information Behaviour of Social Groups in Public Policy and the Public Sphere," Information Research 13, no. 2 (June 2008): 12-13.

33. Savolainen, "Small World and Information Grounds," 40.

34. Ibid., 40.

35. Leena Maija Huotari and Elfreda Chatman, "Using Everyday Life Information Seeking to Explain Organizational Behavior," *Library & Information Science Research* (2001): 352.

36. Savolainen, "Small World and Information Grounds," 40.

defined by socioeconomic factors such as income, education, geography, location, profession, cultural norms and mores, language, religion, health, and incarceration. In the context of this research, small world theory is used to explain the distinct qualities of rural communities and how these qualities can be utilized by a library leader to build a service construct that addresses community needs through library offerings.

Information Grounds Theory

Pettigrew, whose work focused on social settings and their impact on information flow,[37] defines an information ground as "an environment temporarily created by the behavior of people who have come together to perform a given task, but from which emerges a social atmosphere that fosters the spontaneous and serendipitous sharing of information."[38] Information grounds can be defined by a series of commonalities including activities, identity based on shared circumstance, characteristics (mental, physical, and emotional), and interests.[39]

Fisher, (also known as Pettigrew), identified "seven key concepts" to describe an information ground. She determined that an information ground can occur anywhere people gather, regardless of the purpose, and that the social types involved will assume different roles in the information flow. Social interaction is the primary activity in an information ground, with information flow being secondary, and both the formal and informal information flow occurs in many directions. Information ground participants' individual perspectives and physical factors play a key role in creating context, and the information shared at an information ground can be used to benefit the physical, social, affective, and cognitive dimensions.[40]

---

37. K.E. Fisher and Charles M. Naumer, "Information Grounds: Theoretical Basis and Empirical Findings on Information Flow in Social Settings," in *New Directions in Human Information Behavior*, ed. A. Spink and C. Cole (Springer, 2006), 97.

38. Pettigrew, "Waiting for Chiropody," 7.

39. Fisher and Naumer, "Information Grounds," 104-105.

40. Ibid., 98-99.

Fisher et al. continued to conduct empirical research using the information ground model in other situations in an effort to determine what types of spaces serve as information grounds, why a particular information ground space is a good place to acquire information, and what types of information are gathered at an information ground space.[41] Findings indicated that information grounds are valued because the information exchange occurs in a social setting with shared common interests, trust, and diversity.[42] The other significant findings were related to the importance of place and levels of familiarity, comfort, and convenience.[43] Information ground theory applies to this research in the context of gathering information through social interactions, where a library leader participates in activities that occur across a community's diverse information grounds as an active participant in informal community conversations.

Unstructured Research Methodology Applications

The use of unstructured research methodology permits timely and informal data gathering opportunities on the information needs of rural public library users by a library leader, thereby circumventing the funding and human resource limitations present in each case study library. Evidence and data collection techniques used to gather input on library services from the three identified community groups (library groups, local government/elected officials, and community organizations) included direct observation, interviews (scheduled meetings and opportunistic informal interviews), participant observation of both staff and library users, SWOT (strengths, weaknesses, opportunities and threats) analysis of data findings, and lastly, the application of findings to strategic directions.[44]

41. Ibid., 100.

42. Ibid., 10.

43. Ibid., 104.

44. Jessica Iacono, Ann Brown, and Clive Holtham, "Research Methods

The data gathering process was guided by the library leader who, as a participant researcher, made use of available avenues (formal and informal conversations) for public input to share positive existing/potential library impacts on the community (appreciative inquiry)[45] as well as to apply questioning techniques to gather feedback on the direction of library service development from both individual and group perspectives.[46] These responses were then applied to strategic directions development.

Application of the unstructured research methods discussed in this chapter occurred in three separate rural public library settings where the author served as the library director/participant researcher.[47] Library A, the Sevier County Public Library System (Sevierville, TN), serves a rural area of East Tennessee complete with the socio/economic issues typically found in rural communities (low population density, limited availability of support services, a high number of disenfranchised populations, social isolation, social, mental, and physical issues.)[48] The author served as the system director for eight years, during which four individual libraries came together to form a true library system with centralized operations and a new organizational structure. The total system square footage was expanded from 16,000 square feet to 49,000 square feet, with a new $12 million main library. Staffing grew from sixteen to twenty-four FTE employees including three MLIS-credentialed librarians, and the operational budget was increased by fifty percent. These accomplishments were possible because of the relationships built between the library and the community through staff participation in community activities. Other outcomes included the establishment of a foundation

---

- A Case Example of Participant Observation," *Electronic Journal of Business Research Methods* (2009): 41.

45. Maureen Sullivan, "The Promise of Appreciative Inquiry in Library Organizations," *Library Trends* (2004): 223.

46. Ibid., 223.

47. Iacono, Brown, and Holtham, "Research Methods," 42.

48. Gail Kouame, "Charting Consumer Health: Reflections on Rural Communities," *Journal of Hospital Librarianship* (2010): 166.

and improvement of library products. But, most importantly, a common dialog was established among the staff and boards that was used to promote the value of the library to the community through outreach to individuals, groups, and local government.

Library B, the Cayman Islands Public Library Service (CIPLS), is headquartered on Grand Cayman in the Cayman Islands. The author served as the director of the public library service for two years, which is the standard expatriate contract with the Cayman Islands Government. The Cayman Islands constitute a rural community due to geographic isolation. There are a range of socio/economic issues arising from the isolation of the island, including the presence of a multicultural expatriate workforce competing with Caymanians for jobs and an educational system not equipped to produce a native workforce that can compete in the international job market that exists in the country.

The CIPLS is comprised of four small district libraries and one main library. All resources except digital have to be shipped into the country. Digital resource acquisition is complicated because the country currently has no copyright law. The CIPLS should serve as a pivotal institution for addressing existing social issues, but information access is impacted by lack of resources, absence of professional library staff, low technology skill sets, and no community construct of the value of public libraries beyond access to books. Given the two year time constraint, efforts were focused on creating a foundation for expansion of library services and on the development of policy and strategic directions. Outcomes included a new public library law draft, intensive staff training on how libraries impact communities, increased technology access, improvement in the efficiency of library operations and programming, and building connections with the community and other government offices. The improved community and government relationships with the library service made the adoption of the first strategic plan for the public library service possible. This plan laid out a foundation for addressing social issues in the country.[49]

---

49. Kaurri Cockfield-Williams, "Building Civic Capacity Using a Holistic

Library C, the Blount County Public Library (BCPL), is located in Maryville, TN, which is considered rural, but is a bedroom community of Knoxville, TN. The author has served as the director for just over a year. BCPL is a single library of 60,000 square feet that serves the entire county, but sits in the heart of downtown. The library building is thirteen years old, was built as a book-centric facility, and has outdated technology for both staff and the public. The library holds a place of honor in the community and serves as a true destination space. The library is open seven days a week for a total of seventy hours and hosts approximately forty programs, meetings, and classes each week. This high level of service to the community makes existing modes of communication ineffective, but has established the library's standing in the community as a valuable and revered institution. Building relationships with local government, industry, education, and community service organizations has been opportune. However, the communication and technology issues, specifically information distribution, training, and collaboration for both the staff and the community, are impeding service growth. Outcomes to date include the development and adoption of a one year business plan designed to address communication and technology issues, raise additional revenues, and position the library at the center of workforce development in the county. Phase one of the business plan is in the implementation phase with a go-live date of May 31, 2015.

A Change Model for Library Leadership

Relating library service offerings to the tenets of social justice bring to light commonalities in public library settings, especially in rural societies. The three libraries in this study are all considered rural public libraries with similar socio/economic issues, yet each case study library had a focus of change unique to its situation. All three library boards specifically recruited a library leader to improve library services within

Approach to Public Library Service: a Participant Researcher's Perspective on Social Justice in the Cayman Islands Public Library Service," *Qualitative and Quantitative Methods in Libraries* (October 31, 2013): 35-37.

a short time frame, given the critical nature of each library situation. A review of the three case study libraries through analysis of library products (collections, services, programs)[50] revealed situational similarities as follows: 1) inefficient available space/space use within facilities; 2) predominately non-professional, untrained staff; 3) print-centric dated collections; 4) high percentage of service offerings focused on children; 5) outdated technology access for staff and public; 6) ineffective community connection between libraries and community-at-large; 7) weaknesses arising from ineffective funding levels; and 7) absence of transformational leadership. Additionally, each of the three libraries were impacted by community perceptions of the continuing value of public libraries by local funding bodies.

The focus of change for each of the libraries was community driven but required a library leader to direct the change process from concept through implementation. The critical need for Library A was new, expanded library facilities. Library B required a defined role within the community and effective operational guidelines. Library C, the most advanced of the three libraries, needed a technology upgrade for staff and public access and was in a position to move forward with advanced technologies. In each case, the library leader conducted a series of actions designed to gather community input, impact public perceptions, generate excitement and understanding of the value of public libraries within the community, improve the library products, and direct the implementation of ongoing change as the status quo. Time was the delimiting factor in each situation. Library A required two years for improvement of library products before substantial fundraising for new facilities could occur. Library B was limited by expatriate contract time limits (two years) for foreigners working in the Cayman Islands. Library C, which is situated within a growing advanced industries economy, started the actual implementation of advanced technologies one year into the new director's tenure with an estimated time frame of three years for completion.

---

50. Darlene E. Weingand, *Future-Driven Library Marketing* (Chicago: American Library Association, 1998), 80.

Outcomes for all three libraries necessitated the implementation of a change process that educated staff, library boards, and library support groups to a level where participation in the planning process was effective and where advocacy for the library within the community occurred from a positive and informed perspective. Accomplishing outcomes was dependent on these three groups embracing the change process and feeling empowered to participate. In each situation, a series of actions were implemented to improve library products.

Community-Based Actions

When examining the methods undertaken by the library leader in these three case study libraries, it is necessary to consider situational commonalities that serve as preliminary factors in the community action change process. The first consideration is the professional training and experience of the library leader. Critical appraisal of both the library and community are influenced by a leader's construct of the public library. The second consideration is the recognition by library governance and staff that the library, as a public institution, should move beyond the status quo. In all three situations, library governance and library staff understood that change needed to happen and that a transformational library leader was needed to expand library services and increase library use by the community. The third consideration is that before actually being hired, the library leader should identify existing social issues in the community, assess library services, and begin the input process from the three key groups during the interview phase, as the interview process is a key point of user-based input on library service directions and on library perceptions within the community.

During each interview process for the three case study libraries, the library leader asked a series of questions of the library board to identify board members' understanding of the public library role in the community, as well as their individual visions for library growth. Inherent in the third consideration is the understanding that a library leader will conduct a complete demographic and economic analysis of both the library and service community prior being hired, so critical appraisal[51] of the situation can begin prior to actual tenure. These three considerations lay the groundwork for a library leader to quickly establish a change dynamic in the staff and in library governance.

In the three case study situations, actions were undertaken by the library leader within the first three months of tenure to gather and assess perspectives on the library from all three groups of community participants. The first group, which encompassed staff, library governance and library advocacy groups, were informally interviewed in a variety of informal and social settings. The library leader met one-on-one with every staff member (one to two hour sessions) to conduct informal SWOT analyses of the library and to discuss job satisfaction and career goals. Once these staff sessions were completed, the SWOT analysis responses were shared anonymously with staff and board members. The job satisfaction and career goal responses were held in confidence between individual staff members and the library leader, but were applied to library organizational structure development. This one-on-one interview process allowed the library leader to gather input from the staff, both as members of the community and as library employees. Additionally, these informal meetings initiated the building of a trust relationship between the staff and the library leader.

The final information input from the staff occurred during an intensive training workshop (thirty-five hours) provided to all staff in each case study library. This training workshop covered information access and application software use in specific library applications, but was delivered within a construct developed to raise awareness of how a public library can contribute to building healthy communities. The library leader implemented a similar process with library governance and support groups, but used the informal social dialog that occurs before and after already scheduled meeting times to gather data by asking the same types of questions asked of the staff during the SWOT analysis

---

51. Virginia Wilson, "EBL 101: An Introduction to Critical Appraisal," *Evidence Based Library and Information Practice* 5, no. 1 (2010): 155.

segment in the one-on-one meetings. Additionally, the library leader made use of the structured meeting time to ask similar questions of the groups as a whole.

The second group, which included local government officials and department heads, was informally interviewed in social settings interspersed with small informal meetings. The application of appreciative inquiry[52] questioning techniques and the possibilities of library service, i.e., how the library could truly impact community issues were the primary focus of these conversations. Background research on the economic and community focus for government officials is a crucial element for building connections between their priorities and library services, as well as for changing their perspective of the public library's impact on the community. Actions taken by the library leader to gain access to this group included attending local government meetings to stay current on issues/situations across all government departments, volunteering for community events supported by government officials or where government officials were in attendance, and meeting informally with individual government officials and department heads to discuss how the library could help solve/support government and constituent issues. These actions placed the library leader outside the library so conversations could occur with government officials in their comfort zone, which provided non-threatening social opportunities for influence of individual perceptions of the role of the public library, both as partner and change-agent. Interfacing with local government officials and departments was ongoing in all three case study libraries and eventually became a formal part of the library leader's job responsibilities.

The third group, which encompassed community organizations, service clubs, and business organizations, were accessed through active participation, with data being gathered during the informal conversations that occurred during social time before and after scheduled meetings, during shared community service activities, and during actual social events within the community. There was no formal plan for gathering

52. Sullivan, "The Promise of Appreciative Inquiry," 219.

input, but when the conversation allowed, appreciative inquiry-type questions structured around determining what was "good" about the library and on how the library positively impacted individuals and the community were worked into the social exchange. The intent of these conversations was to build community connections and establish the value of the public library as a contributor/partner with other key institutions and organizations in their mission.

In all three case study situations, connections were made between the library and organizations resulting in library contributions to workforce development, economic development, cultural access and preservation, discovery learning and recreation, as well as other forms of social inequity existing within the case study communities. The library leader served on the adult education foundation board in the two Tennessee locations and served as a member of the local literacy organization in the Cayman Islands.

Other key actions for building community relationships and participating in the community conversation included participation in community leadership development groups (Leadership Sevier, Leadership Blount), as well as participation in community service groups (Lions Club, Rotary Club and Kiwanis Club). Additionally, the library leader asked to become part of community committees established to address social issues such as homelessness, drug abuse, child abuse, domestic violence, rehabilitation, etc., including the United Way, local family resource centers, and drug court offender reentry programs. The library leader also invited these groups and organizations to establish permanent library connections by holding meetings and events in library facilities.

Essentially, the focus of these actions centered on building and amplifying community services in situations where local, service-group programs crossed paths with strategic library initiatives. Becoming part of the community conversation through outreach and service in an informal construct presented ongoing opportunity for the library leader to influence community perceptions of the value of the public library within the different information grounds. Successful application of these actions varied in each of the case study libraries as implementations changed according to attributes found within the culture (small world) of each community. All these action sets progressed at the same time as the opportunities for relationship building between the library leader and the community occurred daily inside and outside of the library.

Each of the case study libraries serves a "small world" community within which a variety of information grounds exist. This research presents a flexible plan for using informal research techniques as an effective data-gathering model for user-centered input on library services and as a way to impact community perceptions of the value of a public library.

Considerations and Conclusions

The experientially-based library leadership model discussed in this chapter provides a road map for the facilitation of knowledge transfer across the community to identify, amplify, and address social justice issues, and to design, implement, and measure solutions. Additionally, experientially-based library leadership directly impacts both the perception of the public library in the community as an agent of change, and the implementation of library programs and services in support of social justice. A library leader, through the application of unstructured research methodologies, is able to quickly position the library as a community-action institution through: 1) Comprehension of the unique small world construct found in a library service community; 2) Participation in local government and the community on all levels generally and in the information grounds specifically; and 3) Application of professional knowledge and experience to the community-at-large for building connections between library services and user-centered input.

The methodologies utilized in this research required ongoing data recording, careful attention to opportunities for asking questions in social and informal settings, and focusing these conversations around community concerns. Data recording is crucial in unstructured research and typically occurred through the use of some type of technology. Data recording for Library A was limited to desktop computing for recording and analysis, so informal note taking was completed using pen and paper and recorded/reconstructed after the fact from the library leader's memory. Data recording for the other two case study libraries occurred in real time, or immediately after useful dialog occurred through the use of mobile technology. All informal discussions occurring through government and community participation stayed focused on the community and its needs. These conversations were never used to discuss library needs or funding as the community focus is vital to changing perceptions of the public library role within the community.

Bibliography

Burnett, Gary, and Paul T. Jaeger. "Small Worlds, Life Worlds, and Information: the Ramifications of the Information Behaviour of Social Groups in Public Policy and the Public Sphere." *Information Research* 13, no. 2 (June 2008): 1-17.

Burnett, Gary, Paul T. Jaeger, and Kim M. Thompson. "Normative Behavior and Information: The Social Aspects of Information Access." *Library & Information Science Research*, (2008): 56-66.

Chatman, Elfreda A. "A Theory of Life in the Round." *Journal of the American Society for Information Science* 50, no. 3 (March 1999): 207-217.

Counts, Scott, and Karen E. Fisher. "Mobile Social Networking as Information Ground: A Case Study." *Library & Information Science Research* (2010): 98-115.

Fisher, K.E., and Charles M. Naumer. "Information Grounds: Theoretical Basis and Empirical Findings on Information Flow in Social Settings." In *New Directions in Human Information Behavior*, edited by A. Spink and C. Cole, 93-111. Springer, 2006.

Fisher, Karen E., Sandra Erdelez, and Lynn (E.F.) McKechnie, eds. *Theories of Information Behavior.* American Society for Information Science & Technology, 2005.

Germano, Michael A. "Library Leadership that Creates and Sustains Innovation." *Library Leadership & Management*, (August 2013): 1-14.

Glynn, Lindsay. "A Critical Appraisal Tool for Library and Information Research." *Library Hi Tech* 24, no. 3 (2006): 387-399.

"Healthy Communities." 2013.*Health Resources in Action: Advancing Public Health and Medical Research*, http://www.hria.org/community-health/healthy-communities/.

Huotari, Maija-Leena and Elfreda Chatman. "Using Everyday Life Information Seeking to Explain Organizational Behavior." *Library & Information Science Research* (2001): 351-366.

Iacono, Jessica, Ann Brown, and Clive Holtham. "Research Methods - A Case Example of Participant Observation." *Electronic Journal of Business Research Methods*. 2009. accessed March 16, 2013, http://www.ejbrm.com/volume7/issue1/p39,

Kogetsidis, Harry. "Critical Systems Thinking: A Creative Approach to Organizational Change." *Journal of Transnational Management* (2012): 189-204.

Kouame, Gail. "Charting Consumer Health: Reflections on Rural Communities." *Journal of Hospital Librarianship* (2010): 165-169.

Lankes, David. "Expect More: Demanding Better Libraries for Today's Complex World." *R. David Lankes*. 2012. Accessed January 24, 2015, http://www.DavidLankes.org.

Mehra, Bharat, and Ramesh Srinivasan. "The Library-Community Convergence Framework for Community Action: Libraries as Catalysts of Social Change." *Libris* 57 (2007): 123-139.

Pateman, John. "Public Libraries, Social Class and Social Justice." *Information, Society and Justice* (2011): 57-70.

Pettigrew, K. E. "Waiting for Chiropody: Contextual Results from an Ethnographic Study of the Information Behavior among

Attendees at Community Clinics." *Information Processing & Management* 35 (1999): 801-817.

Rawls, John. "Justice as Fairness." *Philosophy & Public Affairs* (Iowa State University Department of Economics) 14, no. 3 (Summer 1985): 223-251.

Savolainen, Reijo. "Small World and Information Grounds as Contexts of Information Seeking and Sharing." *Library and Information Science Research* 31 (2009): 38-45.

Shorter-Gooden, Kumea. "The Culturally Competent Organization." *Library Quarterly* (2013): 207-211.

Simons, Marcy, and Mandy L. Havert. "Using Appreciative Inquiry to Support a Culture Shift in Transition." *Technical Services Quarterly* 29, no. 3 (2012): 207-216. doi:10.1080/07317131.2012.681285.

Sullivan, Maureen. "The Promise of Appreciative Inquiry in Library Organizations." *Library Trends* (2004): 218-229.

von Dran, Gisela. "Human Resources and Leadership Strategies for Libraries in Transition." *Library Administration & Management* 19, no. 4 (Fall 2005): 177-184.

Weingand, Darlene E. *Future-Driven Library Marketing.* Chicago: American Library Association, 1998.

Williams-Cockfield, Kaurri. "Building Civic Capacity Using a Holistic Approach to Public Library Service: a Participant Researcher's Perspective on Social Justice in the Cayman Islands Public Library Service." *Qualitative and Quantitative Methods in Libraries* (2014): 31-38.

Wilson, Virginia. "EBL 101: An Introduction to Critical Appraisal." *Evidence Based Library and Information Practice* 5, no. 1 (2010): 155-157.

Chapter 9

A CRITICAL ASSESSMENT OF INFORMATION PRACTICES IN A HIGH SCHOOL ENVIRONMENT: THE STUDENT PERSPECTIVE

Punit Dadlani

Abstract

This chapter develops a framework for a critical assessment of information practices involving social justice through the analysis of a week-long
online discussion in a high school project. It is based on exploratory analysis that looks at:1) What collaborative groups of high school students
construct as "social justice," in particular around ideas of control of
the project environment, voice, and what constitutes fair contributions
to the distribution of work; 2) How these collective ideas are framed
in the discussion by students in terms of power and institutional ideology; and 3) How these collective ideas are enacted through information
exchange and use. Findings suggest interventions that can be taken by
teachers and librarians to enhance project environments and pedagogical
strategy to better support social justice ideals constructed by collaborative student work groups. Together, these questions form a map of the
information practices in collaborative work that underpin group-specific
notions of social justice through both practice and critical theory lenses.
Accordingly, this research also introduces novel methods for assessing
social justice concepts in context through the use of practical and critical theory.

Introduction

Social justice concepts continue to be a central concern in libraries and other information settings, but have seldom been invoked directly as theories or metatheories that guide LIS research.[1] As a result, research on social justice concepts is not clearly connected across studies. Accordingly, the accumulation of findings into "unit theories,"[2] or other coherent groupings, has been difficult to identify, leaving LIS researchers with challenges in achieving methodological portability/continuity, especially in terms of social justice findings and research designs. Furthermore, because "social justice" may refer to a wide array of concepts, frameworks, and theories, researchers face the challenge of building research projects that indicate what in particular about social justice is of interest and how it will be operationalized in context.[3]

Because social justice concepts are tied so closely to context, researchers are challenged to find innovative ways to directly focus on and engage them in practical situations. Indeed, context itself has been defined in many different ways in LIS research,[4] but researchers agree that examining contextual factors is important as it can enrich findings with relevant social and temporal dimensions of study.[5] Thus, studying

---

1. Bharat Mehra, Kendra S. Albright, and Kevin Rioux, "A Practical Framework for Social Justice Research in the Information Professions," *Proceedings of the American Society for Information Science and Technology* 43, no. 1 (2006): 1–10; Kevin Rioux, "Metatheory in Library and Information Science: A Nascent Social Justice Approach," *Journal of Education for Library and Information Science* (2010): 9–17.

2. Rioux, "Metatheory in Library and Information Science."

3. Punit Dadlani and Ross J. Todd, "Collaboration, Social Justice and School Libraries: Taking a Micro-View," *Library Quarterly* 86, no. 1 (2016).

4. Sanna Talja, Heidi Keso, and Tarja Pietiläinen, "The Production of 'context'in Information Seeking Research: A Metatheoretical View," *Information Processing & Management* 35, no. 6 (1999): 751–63; Brenda Dervin, "Given a Context by Any Other Name: Methodological Tools for Taming the Unruly Beast," *Information Seeking in Context* 13 (1997): 38; Christina Courtright, "Context in Information Behavior Research," *Annual Review of Information Science and Technology* 41, no. 1 (2007): 273–306.

5. Paul Solomon, "Discovering Information in Context," *ARIS Annual Review of Information Science and Technology* 36, no. 1 (2002): 229–64.

ideas closely tied to context requires researchers to search for new and creative methods that engage a middle ground that can help illuminate such concepts in context, as opposed to neatly disentangling them from it.[6] In this way, the research presented here does not attempt to objectify social justice concepts, but instead points out how they can be examined in a situation in context. Accordingly, social justice concepts can be investigated in a situation, or a space of action within which practices may take place within a context[7] as this creates some permeable parameters, like a high school project in a digital environment, around which social justice concepts can be discussed more concretely.

Despite its relevance, one area that deserves more attention for research on social justice concepts is the study of school libraries. School environments have embedded power relations that have been theorized to arise from the interaction between students and teachers.[8] Despite a number of education studies that examine power relations in classrooms,[9] there are very few studies that examine school libraries directly other than from a literacy[10] or theoretical standpoint.[11]

---

6. Brenda Dervin, "Given a Context by Any Other Name."

7. Diane H. Sonnenwald, "Evolving Perspectives of Human Information Behavior: Contexts, Situations, Social Networks and Information Horizons," in *Exploring the Contexts of Information Behavior: Proceedings of the Second International Conference in Information Needs* (Taylor Graham, 1999), http://eprints.rclis.org/archive/00006960; Colleen Cool, "The Concept of Situation in Information Science," *Annual Review of Information Science and Technology* 35 (2001): 5–42.

8. Mary Manke, *Classroom Power Relations: Understanding Student-Teacher Interaction* (Routledge, 1997).

9. Stephen J Ball, "Education Policy, Power Relations and Teachers' Work," *British Journal of Educational Studies* 41, no. 2 (1993): 106–21; Antonia Darder, *Culture and Power in the Classroom: A Critical Foundation for Bicultural Education* (Greenwood Publishing Group, 1991); Jennifer M. Gore, "Foucault's Poststructuralism and Observational Education Research: A Study of Power Relations," in *After Postmodernism: Education, Politics and Identity* (Routledge, 1995), 98–111; Jennifer M. Gore, "Disciplining Bodies: On the Continuity of Power Relations in Pedagogy," *Learning, Space and Identity* (2001): 167–81.

10. Teresa L. McCarty, *Language, Literacy, and Power in Schooling* (Routledge, 2006); Cushla Kapitzke, "Information Literacy: A Review and Post Structural Critique," *Australian Journal of Language and Literacy* 26, no. 1 (2003): 53.

11. John M. Budd, "The Library, Praxis, and Symbolic Power," *Library Quarterly* (2003): 19–32.

Additionally, school libraries tend to espouse several social justice values, such as equal access to information, services, and ideas, and diversity and intellectual freedom, though few studies[12] exist that focus on these concepts. Thus, there is fruitful opportunity for studying social justice in the context of school libraries.

In light of the need for more studies of social justice concepts in school libraries and the embeddedness of social justice concepts in context, LIS researchers need to rely on methods for research that take both a situational perspective that acknowledges the details of action that reflect social justice concepts, and an analytical perspective that can reveal assumptions that are taken for granted and that influence how social justice concepts are framed. As information settings, school libraries provide an opportunity for researchers to follow how social justice concepts influence and are influenced by information seeking and use. In other words, since school libraries are motivated by several social justice values, the resources/services they provide are meant to reflect these ideals, which in turn could be reflected in the way students use the setting. The point is, there is a need to provide a voice for students insofar as which social justice concepts they enact through their collective use of the school library. Social justice concepts in school libraries, in other words, should be driven not only by librarians and teachers, but through an understanding of how information practices are used to enact social justice concepts. This additive process should involve iterative investigation between not only the use of information resources but also their development, as the structure of the information resources may have an impact on how social justice ideals are constructed in context.[13]

---

12. Dadlani and Todd, "Collaboration, Social Justice and School Libraries: Taking a Micro-View"; P. Dadlani and Ross Todd, "Information Technology Services and School Libraries: A Continuum of Social Justice," *Qualitative and Quantitative Methods in Libraries Journal, Special Issue* 2014 (2014): 39–48; Punit Dadlani and Ross J. Todd, "Social Justice as Strategy: School Libraries and Information Technology," *Library Trends* 63, no. 3 (2016).

13. For example, see: Dadlani and Todd, "Collaboration, Social Justice and School Libraries: Taking a Micro-View."

Because social justice concepts are dynamic and intertwined with context, practice theory is particularly useful for studying them, since it can be used to focus on how, in the course of ongoing action, they play a role in social interaction. For example, Dadlani and Todd[14] showed how social justice ideals were co-constructed, re-constructed, and sustained during collaboration between project groups of high school students in a school library. One finding from the study was that students structured and organized group work around collectively defined epistemic boundaries for what counts as fair or equitable collaborative work practices. Thus, practice theory, with its particular focus on socially embedded routines and actions, is useful for exploring social justice concepts, especially given the LIS interest in information practices (discussed below).

Critical theory approaches can help LIS researchers to investigate social justice concepts by engaging embedded ideologies, power dynamics and institutionalized social practices that underpin information services, infrastructure, policy, and design.[15] While critical theory has been used in LIS scholarly work,[16] studies relating the concept to school libraries are scarcer and tend to focus on information literacy.[17] Additionally, critical theory focuses on creating social transformation toward more equity and justice,[18] and is thus methodologically geared towards the

---

14. Ibid.

15. Gloria J. Leckie, Lisa M. Given, and John Buschman, *Critical Theory for Library and Information Science: Exploring the Social from across the Disciplines* (ABC-CLIO, 2010).

16. John M. Budd and Douglas Raber, "Discourse Analysis: Method and Application in the Study of Information," *Information Processing & Management* 32, no. 2 (1996): 217–26; Bernd Frohmann, "The Power of Images: A Discourse Analysis of the Cognitive Viewpoint," *Journal of Documentation* 48, no. 4 (1992): 365–86; Sanna Talja, "Analyzing Qualitative Interview Data: The Discourse Analytic Method," *Library & Information Science Research* 21, no. 4 (1999): 459–77.

17. Lauren Smith, "Towards a Model of Critical Information Literacy Instruction for the Development of Political Agency," *Journal of Information Literacy* 7, no. 2 (2013): 15–32; Kapitzke, "Information Literacy"; Troy A. Swanson, "A Radical Step: Implementing a Critical Information Literacy Model," *portal: Libraries and the Academy* 4, no. 2 (2004): 259–73.

18. Yvonna S. Lincoln, Susan A. Lynham, and Egon G. Guba, "Paradigmatic

study of social justice ideas. Accordingly, there is an opportunity for the production of novel studies that integrate critical theory, school libraries and social justice concepts.

Thus, what follows is an example of how LIS research might benefit by using practice theory and critical theory to investigate how social justice concepts are constructed by a collaborative work group in a school library and enacted through their communicative and informational action. By focusing attention on normativity, ideology, and power relations through practical and critical theory lenses, I illuminate social justice concepts as they appear in context. Accordingly, this chapter analyzes data from a study that explores particular social justice concepts related to control, voice, and work contributions/distributions that arise during the collaborative, text-based discussions between students undertaking a high school project over the course of one week in a school library. First, we analyze the data using an inductive and emergent process[19] informed by the work of Dadlani and Todd[20] to reveal the student-group constructed guidelines (later referred to as social justice ideals) for how social justice concepts ought to be understood and applied in a collaborative project environment. Then, using critical and social practice lenses, I build a framework for critically assessing information practices involving social justice issues related to control of the project environment, the expression of dissent, and individual/group contributions.

This chapter is particularly relevant because it develops a novel methodological approach, in this case an inductive approach informed by practical and critical theory, for examining social justice concepts in an information context. The combination of practical and critical theories can benefit researchers of social justice concepts because: 1) it enables analysis that is focused on critiquing implicit ideologies as observed

Controversies, Contradictions, and Emerging Confluences, Revisited," *The Sage Handbook of Qualitative Research* 4 (2011): 97–128.

19. Kathy Charmaz, "Grounded Theory as an Emergent Method," *Handbook of Emergent Methods* (2008): 155–70.

20. Dadlani and Todd, "Information Technology Services and School Libraries."

in actual action, and 2) it illustrates how actual project or pedagogical decisions in practice shape and are shaped by often hidden ideological notions that have social justice implications. In this way, the intersection of these theories connects situational (micro) and societal (macro) thinking around social justice concepts. Further, this proposal uses extant research to pose relevant and integral implications for examining social justice concepts in future LIS research and practice related to information technology, collaborative learning, pedagogical strategies, and policy. Accordingly, these implications can inform the design of information services, information technology infrastructure, and school environments by providing ideas, methods, and techniques for eliciting, evaluating, and implementing notions of social justice in different types of information settings. Thus, a major goal of this exploratory research is to introduce a novel method for evaluating social justice concepts in context.

Importance to Pedagogy/Projects

This research is particularly important to the construction of project environments, and pedagogy more generally, for a few reasons. First, as Coates[21] claims, the social justice paradigm can be particularly important to pedagogy if it can articulate for individuals the difference between social justice that is deserved (merits) from social justice that is adopted for the greater good (benefits). Thus, pursuing a pedagogical approach that supports students learning to navigate between these two notions has the potential to teach students that social justice ideas are products of multiple, overlapping cultural centers.[22] Importantly, designing pedagogical approaches that allow the most effective collaborative group environment can lead to increased mutual respect between group

---

21. Rodney D. Coates, "Social Justice and Pedagogy," *American Behavioral Scientist* 51, no. 4 (2007): 587.

22. Ibid.

members due to the flexibility provided for learners to self-organize.[23] Closely evaluating how a pedagogical approach can maximize such conditions can therefore lead to better learning outcomes, as well as in situ opportunities for social justice education.

Another important finding from the educational literature is that positive collaborative learning outcomes have been associated with groups that monitor, challenge, and consequently negotiate each others contributions to group work.[24] Thus, an understanding of how social justice ideals are formed by collaborative groups can be seen as an important area that potentially contributes to positive learning outcomes, and may deserve more direct attention in pedagogical practice. The research presented here gives one methodological example of how an assessment of such social justice ideals could be approached. From an online learning perspective, given the evidence that collaboration in online environments can have similar components to that of face-to-face learning (Curtis and Lawson 2001), online collaborative learning environments experience similar processes around group contributions when compared to face-to-face scenarios. Importantly, a major goal of this research is to suggest methodology to assess social justice ideals, and in this sense, the research presented here applies to both face-to-face and online learning situations.

Theoretical Influence: Critical Theory

While "critical theory" most generally refers to the work of the Frankfurt School, including thinkers such as Horkheimer, Adorno,

23. Allison M. Ryan and Helen Patrick, "The Classroom Social Environment and Changes in Adolescents' Motivation and Engagement during Middle School," *American Educational Research Journal* 38, no. 2 (2001): 437–60; Martin R. Fellenz, "Toward Fairness in Assessing Student Groupwork: A Protocol for Peer Evaluation of Individual Contributions," *Journal of Management Education* 30, no. 4 (2006): 570–91.

24. David W. Johnson and Roger T. Johnson, "Cooperation and the Use of Technology," in *Handbook of Research for Educational Communications and Technology*, ed. David H. Jonassen (Macmillan, 1996), 1017–44.

Marcuse, and more recently to the work of Habermas,[25] there are multiple approaches that are considered part of the critical theory canon including, for example, forms of psychoanalysis, postcolonialism, and studies of culture, power, and gender.[26] Despite the wide variety of these approaches, several ideas are common to critical approaches. Alvesson and Deetz[27] identify four key ideas that critical approaches propose, including: 1) that knowledge claims are tied to social communities with embedded power relations rather than a value-free environment with rational actors; 2) a replacement of individualist accounts of experience for constructionist ones based on intersubjectivity in situated, social environments; 3) attention to history as an essential part of context, and 4) the focus on individuals as complex, dynamic, and knowing subjects rather than as autonomous, rational persons. Arising largely in response to positivism,[28] a major goal of critical theory is to closely scrutinize and suggest interventions to the taken-for-granted ideologies that shape society.[29] Critical theory approaches largely understand that the basis and logic for action are preconfigured through embedded ideologies in society.[30]

---

25. Max Horkheimer and Theodor W. Adorno, *Dialectic of Enlightenment* (London; New York: Verso, 1997); Max Horkheimer, *Critical Theory* (New York: Continuum 1982); Herbert Marcuse, "One Dimensional Man," *Studies in the Ideology of Advanced Industrial Society*, 1964; Jürgen Habermas and Thomas McCarthy, *The Theory of Communicative Action: Lifeworld and System: A Critique of Functionalist Reason*, Vol. 2 (Boston: Beacon Press, 1985).

26. Leckie, Given, and Buschman, *Critical Theory for Library and Information Science*; Joe L. Kincheloe and Peter McLaren, "Rethinking Critical Theory and Qualitative Research," in *Ethnography and Schools: Qualitative Approaches to the Study of Education*, ed. Yali Zou and Enrique T. Trueba (Lanham, MD: Rowman and Littlefield, 2002): 87–138.

27. Mats Alvesson and Stanley Deetz, "Critical Theory and Postmodernism: Approaches to Organizational Studies," in *Studying Organization: Theory and Method*, ed. Stewart R Clegg and Cynthia Hardy (SAGE, 1999), 185-211.

28. Ben Agger, "Critical Theory, Poststructuralism, Postmodernism: Their Sociological Relevance," *Annual Review of Sociology* 17, no. 1 (1991): 105–31.

29. Leckie, Given, and Buschman, Critical Theory for Library and Information Science.

30. Edward Granter, *Critical Social Theory and the End of Work* (Ashgate Publishing, Ltd., 2012).

Critical theory, however, is not singularly defined,[31] as there are myriad interpretations of it.[32] Consequently, researchers applying critical theory have taken multiple self-reflective approaches that critique the often implicit, dominant ideologies present in the research situation of focus, and then intervene in some way on the practice examined.[33] Critical research projects tend to embrace a transformative paradigm in which a major goal is to create the possibility for change towards the greater good in situations studied.[34] The use of multiple methods/perspectives is seen as a key to creating a more complete picture of the social world studied.[35] Critical approaches to research generally involve a mix of situated, reflexive and dialectic methods to study the conditions under which people live. Common techniques include: historical analysis, observation, and interviewing, but also a vast number of other qualitative or quantitative techniques.[36] In other words, critical research, through no single, unified method, provides a social critique that highlights implicit ideology, power relations, etc., in the social situations examined and empowers those disadvantaged in that situation through action or

31. Kincheloe and McLaren, "Rethinking Critical Theory and Qualitative Research."

32. David Held, Introduction to *Critical Theory: Horkheimer to Habermas* (Berkeley, CA: University of California Press, 1980).

33. Brian D. Steffy and Andrew J. Grimes, "A Critical Theory of Organization Science," *Academy of Management Review* 11, no. 2 (1986): 322–36.

34. Noella Mackenzie and Sally Knipe, "Research Dilemmas: Paradigms, Methods and Methodology," Issues in Educational Research 16, no. 2 (2006): 193–205.

35. Bridget Somekh and Cathy Lewin, *Research Methods in the Social Sciences* (Sage, 2005).

36. J. M. Budd, "Critical Theory," in *The Sage Encyclopedia of Qualitative Research Methods*, ed. L. M. Given (Thousand Oaks, CA: SAGE Publications: 2008), 175-180.

implications for action.[37] Thus, critical theory should not be understood as a particular set of techniques, but rather as a reflexive orientation towards understanding social situations that foregrounds concerns of power, ideology, and domination.[38]

In particular, the research discussed in this chapter draws from a qualitative technique employed by critical theorists known as ideology critique. Ideology critique is a common technique from critical theory that focuses on the unearthing of beliefs and claims used to justify actions that have taken on an unquestioned status in society.[39] Frieson[40] elaborates that ideology critique at its most basic form first identifies claims that are presented as obvious and unquestioned, scrutinizes these ideas based on alternative conceptions, reveals that there are multiple ways of viewing the claim in question, and finally elaborates some kind of intervention or alternate theory for understanding the situation. These four major points will be used as a guide for elaborating the critical aspects of the framework discussed later in this chapter.

Theoretical Influence: Practice Theory

Generally, practice theory is used across several social science disciplines, including organizational studies, sociology, anthropology, and

---

37. Joseph G. Ponterotto, "Qualitative Research in Counseling Psychology: A Primer on Research Paradigms and Philosophy of Science," *Journal of Counseling Psychology* 52, no. 2 (2005): 126.

38. Ojelanki K. Ngwenyama, In *The Critical Social Theory Approach to Information Systems: Problems and Challenges*, ed. Hans-Erik Nissen, Heinz-Karl Klein, and Rudy A. Hirschheim (Amsterdam: North-Holland, 1991), 267-280.

39. Norm Friesen, "Critical Theory: Ideology Critique and the Myths of E-Learning," *Ubiquity* 2008, no. June (2008): 2.

40. Ibid.

science and technology studies.[41] Feldman and Orlikowski[42] discuss three common ideas across practice theory approaches: (1) actions are seen as consequential of producing physical structure in life, (2) phenomena exist through a process of mutual constitution, and (3) the basic constitutive elements are all interrelated rather than dichotomized. Though a single formulation of practice theory does not exist, practice theorists see human action as creating some sort of enduring social infrastructure, which is constituted through complex interrelations between various elements that exist only in embedded relationships with one another.[43] Some elements of practice theory may be seen in other approaches such as institutionalism,[44] but practice theory differs from these in its more micro and action-oriented focus on how individuals make decisions and solve problems in the course of ongoing action.[45]

Methodologically, practice theorists draw upon a wide variety of qualitative techniques that use thick description to reveal how groups gain the competence that makes it possible to follow rules and norms, and

---

41. Wanda J. Orlikowski, "Using Technology and Constituting Structures: A Practice Lens for Studying Technology in Organizations," *Organization Science* 11, no. 4 (2000): 404–28; Anthony Giddens, *The Constitution of Society: Outline of the Theory of Structuration* (University of California Press, 1984) ; Theodore R. Schatzki, *Social Practices: A Wittgensteinian Approach to Human Activity and the Social* (Cambridge University Press, 1996).; Andreas Reckwitz, "Toward a Theory of Social Practices: A Development in Culturalist Theorizing," *European Journal of Social Theory* 5, no. 2 (2002): 243–63; Jean Lave, *Cognition in Practice: Mind, Mathematics and Culture in Everyday Life* (Cambridge University Press, 1988); Bruno Latour, *Science in Action: How to Follow Scientists and Engineers through Society* (Harvard university press, 1987).

42. Martha S. Feldman and Wanda J. Orlikowski, "Theorizing Practice and Practicing Theory," Organization Science 22, no. 5 (2011): 1240–53.

43. Reckwitz, "Toward a Theory of Social Practices: A Development in Culturalist Theorizing"; Feldman and Orlikowski, "Theorizing Practice and Practicing Theory."

44. Richard Whittington, "Putting Giddens into Action: Social Systems and Managerial Agency," *Journal of Management Studies* 29, no. 6 (1992): 693–712.

45. Feldman and Orlikowski, "Theorizing Practice and Practicing Theory"; Sanna Talja, "Jean Lave's Practice Theory," in *Critical Theory for Library and Information Science: Exploring the Social from across the Disciplines*, eds. Gloria J. Leckie, Lisa M. Given, and John E. Buschman (Santa Barbara, CA: ABC-CLIO 2010), 205–220.

articulate meaning in action.[46] Thus, practice theorists use methods and techniques that examine the pre-existing understanding of individuals as they shape and are shaped by their interactions in social situations. The patterns of rules and norms examined might be seen as an ephemeral reflection of practice, but social interaction can be seen as the generative force that mixes an unarticulated background understanding with rules and norms to generate action.[47] Accordingly, rather than offering a set of operationalized constructs for research, practice theory is a lens for seeing and analyzing social action.[48] Thus, methods and techniques structured through these theoretical considerations could be considered practice-theoretic.

Within LIS, practice theory has influenced some scholars to differentiate the concept of information practice, seen as a more sociological, context-embedded, and constitutive approach to information, from information behavior, seen as a user-centered, cognitive, and more objectified approach.[49] Studies of information practices are common in LIS, and specifically the everyday-life information-seeking literature, such as studies of the information practices of vault inspectors,[50] midwives,[51]

---

46. Clifford Geertz, *The Interpretation of Cultures: Selected Essays* (New York: Basic Books, 1973).; Joseph Rouse, "Practice Theory," Handbook of the Philosophy of Science, no. 15 (2007), http://wesscholar.wesleyan.edu/cgi/viewcontent.cgi?article=1028&context=div1facpubs.

47. Ludwig Wittgenstein, *Philosophical Investigations.* (New York: Macmillan, 1968).

48. Reckwitz, "Toward a Theory of Social Practices: A Development in Culturalist Theorizing," 257.

49. Sanna Talja, Kimmo Tuominen, and Reijo Savolainen, "' Isms' in Information Science: Constructivism, Collectivism and Constructionism," *Journal of Documentation* 61, no. 1 (2005): 79–101; Reijo Savolainen, "Information Behavior and Information Practice: Reviewing the' Umbrella Concepts' of Information-Seeking Studies," *Library Quarterly* 77, no. 2 (2007): 109–32.

50. Tiffany C Veinot, "'The Eyes of the Power Company': Workplace Information Practices of a Vault Inspector," *Library Quarterly* 77, no. 2 (2007): 157-79.

51. Pamela J. McKenzie, "Mapping Textually Mediated Information Practice in Clinical Midwifery Care," in *New Directions in Human Information Behavior* (Springer, 2006): 73–92, http://link.springer.com/content/pdf/10.1007/1-4020-3670-1_5.pdf.

and nurses,[52] as well as the framing of information literacy as information practice[53] and theorizing about information practices generally.[54] Taken together, the activities around social justice ideas discussed in this research may be considered "fair" information practices, as they reflect routinized, collective, and intersubjectively agreed upon actions that affirm roles, structures, and forms of interaction[55] in support of particular social justice ideals. As will be explained, social justice is not a singular concept to the students studied, but a container for a myriad of differentiable, collectively constructed ideals about fairness in the process of collaborative work.

The research presented here examines practice from an empirical approach,[56] in which the focus of study is the interactive discussion about collaborative work practices undertaken by high school students related to social justice concepts. In particular, practices are defined as those routinized and interconnected forms of physical and mental behaviors, things and their use, including the necessary background understanding and know-how for their application and configuration.[57] A practice theory lens will be brought to bear on the data by identifying the collective routines performed, the rationales for their performance, and the background understandings applied or surfaced through the project environment. The framework will be discussed below, but it is important to note that there is overlap between the practice theory and critical theory as drawn from in this research due to the overlap

---

52. Jenny Johannisson and Olof Sundin, "Putting Discourse to Work: Information Practices and the Professional Project of Nurses," *Library Quarterly* 77, no. 2 (2007).

53. Annemaree Lloyd, "Framing Information Literacy as Information Practice: Site Ontology and Practice Theory," *Journal of Documentation* 66, no. 2 (2010): 245–58.

54. Pamela J. McKenzie, "A Model of Information Practices in Accounts of Everyday-Life Information Seeking," *Journal of Documentation* 59, no. 1 (2003): 19–40; Savolainen, "Information Behavior and Information Practice."

55. Lloyd, "Framing Information Literacy as Information Practice."

56. Feldman and Orlikowski, "Theorizing Practice and Practicing Theory."

57. Reckwitz, "Toward a Theory of Social Practices: A Development in Culturalist Theorizing," 249.

between the general concerns of these perspectives more generally. This overlap is reflected in the framework, and serves to deepen and integrate the analysis.

Critical Theory and Practice Theory: Intersection

Practice theory can generally be seen as compatible with and complementary to critical approaches for several reasons. First, critical theory has been described as bringing together technical (instrumentalities), practical (social ways of being), and emancipatory (embedded ideologies) knowledge interests[58] to provide a holistic approach to inquiry and intervention.[59] This means, from a critical perspective, that practice theory can shed light on how routinized social action shapes and is shaped by the context in which it takes place, including through uncovered ideological, power, and normative forces of the practices. Second, practice theory can be seen as a useful heuristic device that explores the embedded understanding and knowing that takes place in action,[60] often across space and time.[61] Practice theory, in other words, also focuses on the interconnection between practices across time, taking into account socio-historical changes in context. This idea is of importance in critical theory, which focuses on realities that are socially and historically constituted.[62] Lastly, practice theory, like critical theory, is focused on human matters and sees power, conflict, and politics as constitutive of social reality,[63] and is therefore useful for delineating components of practice that are of interest to critical research. In terms of the edu-

---

58. Jürgen Habermas, *Toward a Rational Society: Student Protest, Science, and Politics* (Boston: Beacon Press, 1971).

59. Ngwenyama, *The Critical Social Theory Approach to Information Systems.*

60. Reckwitz, "Toward a Theory of Social Practices: A Development in Culturalist Theorizing."

61. Davide Nicolini, *Practice Theory, Work, and Organization: An Introduction* (Oxford, UK: Oxford University Press, 2013).

62. Ponterotto, "Qualitative Research in Counseling Psychology."

63. Nicolini, *Practice Theory, Work, and Organization*, 6.

cational environment, classrooms are known to have embedded power relations,[64] since students adopt classroom practices, like technology, based on how their teachers construct them.[65] School environments have also been shown to reflect social justice values and are thus a fruitful ground for studying the intersection of these topics.[66]

Research Purpose

In order to make proper use of these theories, studies of social justice concepts in LIS need to be more contoured and operationalized so that actions taken related to social justice, a mostly non-tangible macro-concept, can be observed systematically. As noted by Mehra et al.,[67] there are several integral frameworks and theories in the philosophical discipline that are especially relevant to LIS research. Thus, this chapter uses data from a previous study[68] designed around philosophical theory to understand:

1. What social justice ideals around contributions, expressions of dissent, and control are developed by students in the course of the project?

2. How are the social justice ideals developed by students impacted by power relations and ideology?

---

64. Derek Edwards and Neil Mercer, *Common Knowledge* (London: Methuen, 1987).

65. E. Cutrim Schmid, "Investigating the Use of Interactive Whiteboard Technology in the English Language Classroom through the Lens of a Critical Theory of Technology," *Computer Assisted Language Learning* 19, no. 1 (2006): 47–62.

66. Dadlani and Todd, "Information Technology Services and School Libraries"; Dadlani and Todd, "Social Justice as Strategy: School Libraries and Information Technology"; Dadlani and Todd, "Collaboration, Social Justice and School Libraries: Taking a Micro-View."

67. Mehra, Albright, and Rioux, "A Practical Framework for Social Justice Research in the Information Professions."

68. Dadlani and Todd, "Collaboration, Social Justice and School Libraries: Taking a Micro-View."

3. How do the students enact these social justice ideals through the project environment?

Together, these points show what information practices used in supporting these ideals might look like. This is accomplished through an analysis of a week long collaborative digital project undertaken by high school students in a school library in New Jersey. Using both practical and critical theory lenses, this research produces a framework that can be used as an heuristic to identify information practices related to social justice concepts and suggest interventions to better support those practices.

Sample

Dadlani and Todd[69] examined perceptions of social justice amongst a group of high school students undertaking a group research task in a New Jersey high school library. The sample examined consisted of forty-two ninth grade students undertaking an accelerated Language Arts curriculum. The school was selected based on previous research[70] that showed the school demonstrated high proficiency with instruction and learning, particularly in digital environments. The school chosen was considered above average, since it ranked in the top ten percent of New Jersey schools and was in an affluent community, where only eleven percent of residents were considered "Asset Limited, Income Constrained Employed," compared to the national average of thirty-seven percent.[71] Two sections of students were divided by the teacher into thirteen groups and assigned a research task for which they had to determine if each of their assigned novels had literary merit.

---

69. Ibid.

70. Ross J. Todd, C. Gordon, and Y. Lu, "Report on Findings and Recommendations of the New Jersey School Library Study Phase 1: One Common Goal: Student Learning," New Brunswick, NJ: CISSL, 2011.

71. United Way of Northern New Jersey, *ALICE: Study of Financial Hardship in New Jersey*, Morristown, New Jersey: Halpin, 2012.

Data Collection

The students were required to produce an interactive presentation on their findings at the conclusion of the eight day project. The main method of data collection was a Google Docs environment in which students were required to interact with one another each day. Students were required to reflect about their experience in the collaborative project, including challenges, successes, and questions, and by posting a public statement in the Google Docs environment. Students were also required to respond to at least two posts from other students on each day. This approach was useful for instigating conversation and cross-team collaboration/learning as the project unfolded. Also, at the onset and close of the project, students were asked to identify in open-ended form "How do you feel about working in group projects," and on the final day, "How do you feel about working in digital environments," in order to juxtapose their perceptions of the project with the collaborative action that took place during discussion. Together, these data points led to a rich discussion about the students' ongoing collaborative experience in the digital environment. For more details about the data collection aspect of the study, please see Dadlani and Todd.[72]

Data Analysis

Several interesting findings have arisen from this exploratory study around the idea of student/teacher control of the project environment, having a voice, and equal or equitable contributions that seem worth looking at deeper because of their possibly negative impact on the project experience. Thus, this research uses new analysis of the online discussion data from Dadlani and Todd[73] to produce a critical assessment of information practices related to social justice concepts.

---

72. Dadlani and Todd, "Collaboration, Social Justice and School Libraries: Taking a Micro-View."

73. Ibid.

Charmaz[74] identifies several qualitative methodological ideas that are particularly well suited to the study of social justice concepts, such as the use of inductive logic, emergent strategies, and comparative inquiry. Accordingly, an inductive process of coding, informed by Dadlani and Todd,[75] was first used to highlight patterns in the discussion. First, both sets of data were analyzed etically to identify statements that talk about the categories of interest: control of the project process, the expression of dissent, and individual/group contributions. These ideas were chosen because they were spoken of frequently by students and caused controversy during the project process as observed in Dadlani and Todd.[76] Then, the statements were coded using an emergent approach where the statements were grouped together within categories based on other, often more specific ideas that emerged from the statements emically (see **Table 1**). The themes name particular social justice ideals with a summative term that each set of group statements reflected. For example, under the "Individual/Group Contributions" category, there were the themes equal contributions, even/balanced contributions, and divided contributions, reflecting three separate ideas about fair individual and group contributions/distributions of work. This coding process was iteratively repeated and refined until all themes reflected a stable fit, with clear and cohesive ideas in the statements under each of them.

After completing the coding process, the next step of analysis involved returning to the longer discussions in which the themes identified arose. In particular, through an adaptation of Friesen,[77] which supplies four core objectives of ideological critique, the longer discussions were analyzed to identify: (1) how the social justice ideals put forth by the groups were framed (framing) (2) how elements of individuals' preconceived

---

74. Kathy Charmaz, "Grounded Theory Methods in Social Justice Research," The Sage Handbook of Qualitative Research 4 (2011): 359–80.

75. Dadlani and Todd, "Information Technology Services and School Libraries."

76. Dadlani and Todd, "Collaboration, Social Justice and School Libraries: Taking a Micro-View."

77. Friesen, "Critical Theory."

Table 1: Coding Categories

Individual/Group Contributions statements that reflect fair systems of work distribution and individual contribution	Equal – equal in amount of something Even/Balanced - overall balance or harmony Divided - divided by some rationale
Control of Project Process statements that reflect struggles over control of the project tools, process and collaboration in order to enable success	Research choice – multiple techniques Self expression – allowance of multiple modes of discussion
Having a Voice statements that reflect creating an environment that give voice and enable dialogue	Inclusive Decision Making – take into account all views Safe Environment – foster a non-threatening environment Dissent Channels –create space for expressing dissent

notions about social justice impact the collaborative groups' social justice ideals (normativity), and (3) what actions became part of the routines in response to the ideological framing (information tasks). Finally, these findings are then assessed to produce interventions to the project environment and pedagogical approach that address the barriers suggested by students. Table 2 was compiled and details a critical assessment of information practices involving social justice ideals for the collaborative work project.

In **Table 2**, Social Justice Ideals refer to the particular social justice ideals that arose out of the students interactions. The ideals are summations of what the statements in the coding sub-categories reflect in terms of fairness in the collaborative workspace for each of the three main categories. Framing and Normativity refers to the way the particular social justice ideal is ideologically framed in light of the project. The routine actions that reflect the ideology espoused by students were identified along with an interpretation of the overriding ideology. The particular information tasks identified shape and are shaped by collective notions of the particular social justice ideal. Finally, the interventions suggested address ways of enhancing the project environment and, consequently, the pedagogical approach to better support the social justice ideals indicated.

Limitations

This study provides a framework for doing a critical assessment of information practices related to social justice concepts, but the framework is only part of what a researcher might use. First, the research presented here does not include a situated component, but instead looks at textual data. While the text data does not provide the embodied or other physical components of the situation studied, it still serves as a useful heuristic for developing these missing components. Second, the research presented here is based on inductive reasoning and should not be seen as generalizable to broader situations. Instead, the framework itself may be applied in other situations as an heuristic for evaluating information practices. Third, although the practices are understood through their textual representations by students rather than through face-to-face interaction, this textual data entails asynchronous interactions between students and teachers over the course of a week, thus providing a rich source of connected discussion that shows how they claim to perform these practices. Future research may benefit from using mixed method approaches that triangulate this data with more situated action.

Though both critical theory and practical theory do not have particular methods through which they are applied, as conceptual lenses both sensitize research to the underlying, unquestioned nature of action. In this sense, inductive frameworks built around these theories offer a breakdown of seemingly passive conceptual scaffolding as active components in understanding actions. Also, the coding process undertaken was undertaken by a single researcher rather than through an intercoder reliability process. While intercoder reliability can be used to confirm

Table 2. Critical Assessment

Social Justice Ideal	Framing and Normativity
Description of the social justice ideal	How is the social justice ideal framed? What are the institutional ideologies it entails, if any?
A fair distribution of work within the group and/or fair contributions to work. The three perspectives endorsed are: 1. A system of division of labor where tasks are split 2. Equal distributions/contributions to and by each individual 3. Even or balanced distributions/ contributions to and by each individual	Fairness = equality or even-ness. Embraces an egalitarian and utilitarian model of thinking in which "equality" is the basis for a just distribution and distributions are seen as a matter of efficiency Communicative actions: (1) Non-confrontational comments and constructive criticism to non-contributors (2) Open communication of issues (3) Active Participation (4) Appealing to other groups through discussion system Adopts the "Homo Economicus" as it follows an economic model of thinking whereby maximizing efficiency in terms of the output of the process is key. Yet, within that thinking is the nuanced belief of being "even" rather than "equal"

Information Tasks	Project/Pedagogical Interventions (5)
What are the situations in which this arises? What are the information tasks that "deal" with it?	How could the environment or situation be intervened on to make things support the constructed social justice ideas?
Arises at the beginning of the process as students attempt to organize their groups and becomes more seamless as the project continues. In particular, when students are: deciding how to search for information, gathering information, and when they decide how to use/apply the information to create the final product. Tasks used: (1) Using online tools to document task ownership (2) Creating online repository for posting contributions (3) Prioritizing task interests by individual	(1) Provide tools that allow students to track accountability (2) Separate classroom session for group project training or discussion

Social Justice Ideal	Framing and Normativity
Group members should have the freedom to structure their work environment, use techniques unrestrictedly based on their particular strengths, and should be able to choose the means by which they collaborate. Main points are: 1. Unrestricted use of techniques/tools 2. The ability to use multiple modes of self expression	Restrictions marginalize individuals with particular skillsets and remove a "natural" aspect of research that excludes certain approaches that might be more suitable to the needs of the group. Communicative Actions: 1. Appealing to other groups through the discussion system 2. Bringing new tools/modes of communication to bear where not restricted Adopts an attitude of activism (almost insubordination) and pragmatism by expressing dissent collectively, learning from other groups and repurposing the environment to their purposes.
Groups should foster a safe environment in which expressions of dissent are not marginalized. The main details are: 1. A system for discussion that takes into account all opinions before making decisions 2. Fostering a safe, non-threatening environment for posing alternative ideas 3. Expressing dissent even in the face of diversity (Student A example)	Expressions of dissent from minority opinions are overpowered by passionate members or a general atmosphere of tension. Group members ought to feel safe rather than vulnerable about having a different opinion. The group decision process can be oppressive, rather than democratic, if voices are excluded Communicative Actions: 1. Supportive communicative techniques 2. Presenting ideas with evidence to have more constructive discussions 3. Collaborative rather than combative discussion Adopts an attitude of sensitivity through communication and creates a system to make all opinions more accountable through evidence.

Information Tasks	Project/Pedagogical Interventions (5)
This arises most heavily at the onset of the project but maintains some force till the end. Students shared their similar experiences and how they dealt with them through the system. In particular, this occurred during the information gathering and analysis phases of the project: 1. Using external, "non-standard" tools as supplements to the environment 2. Posting comments that instigate discussion that corroborates each other's experience	(1) Providing a wider variety of online tools for communication and data representation (2) More tailored explanation of project environment and process (3) Anonymous discussion space for process related issues
This arises midway through the project, when discussion has become more critical to completing the project. Particularly when the students decide how to apply the information they have found. 1. Using tools to document, analyze, and return to differing opinions 2. Reducing the use of technological tools for discussion purposes 3. Using the discussion system as a place to get support for dissenting opinions within and across groups	1. Anonymous discussion space for process related issues 2. Provide tools specifically for brainstorming, comparing information and ideas, and gaining agreement (voting)

the validity of constructs studied,[78] the iterative process of coding used should serve to recontextualize, reinterpret, and redefine the concepts studied to yield a plausible interpretation clearly supported by the data provided.[79] Additionally, a main purpose of this research is to introduce methods for assessing social justice concepts in context, and thus the framework presented is independently important to the interpretation of this particular group project.

Findings

Contributions

In analyzing the data for students talking about fair contributions, three perspectives emerged from the data that fit along a similar spectrum. Overwhelmingly, students were concerned about the fairness of work distribution and/or work contributions to/by their group members, as sixty-six percent of the statements identified pertained to this topic. The terms that frequently arose in these discussions included: division, tasks, split, equal, even, balanced and efficiency.

At one end of the spectrum, students felt that a systematic division of labor was at least a prerequisite for doing work, because it is efficient and removes the burden of all work on a single individual. This student elaborates about the need to create a way of splitting the project tasks to increase the group's output efficiency by eliminating duplicated tasks:

> **Student 1:** I feel that we should have a way to split the workload among the three of us. It would certainly be inefficient if we are all doing the exact same thing. Today, Student 2 and I were on the same webpage at the same moment and were looking at the same material. While this may help to reinforce our understanding of the material as a group, I feel that we are all capable of finding good sources on our own.

---

78. Karen S. Kurasaki, "Intercoder Reliability for Validating Conclusions Drawn from Open-Ended Interview Data," *Field Methods* 12, no. 3 (2000): 179–94.

79. Klaus Krippendorff, *Content Analysis: An Introduction to Its Methodology* (Sage, 2012).

In this example, a student similarly describes the need to split tasks to maximize efficiency through collective effort:

> **Student 1:** After working with my group today we finally saw how we are going to set up our project and we split the research by people to maximize our efficiency. We haven't actually started any research yet but this planning is bound to save us a lot of time in the long run. By working together today we managed to clear up a lot of confusions we had about the project.

These students speak about what they appreciate about group work; in doing so they highlight that one requirement for splitting up work fairly should be that everyone contributes and that work doesn't fall to one group member:

> **Student 1:** I feel that it (group work) can be helpful when everyone splits up the work. However, it can be frustrating if one member either does not work as hard or his/her work is not sufficient and is lacking. **Student 2:** I like working in groups because work can be divided, but sometimes one person ends up doing all of the work.

Moving along the spectrum, other students felt that a fair system of work requires equal distribution of work and/or equal contributions from each group member. This concept of equality discussed by the students is ambiguous. In some cases, they refer to "equal" strictly, as in the exact same "work" or contribution to the project from each individual.

> **Student 1:** I felt that working in a group project was very fun. I enjoyed it a lot. The best part about working in a group, which is why I prefer it over individual projects, is that the workload can be divided among the group members. For individual projects, one must do all the work by himself, but for group projects, each member needed only to do a third of the actual work, making it a lot less stressful for us.

Other times they refer to equal in terms of the amount of work distributed or contributed, though what the amount refers to in terms of measurement seems ambiguous:

Student 1: I also really like your idea of breaking up the assignment into three parts and pursuing it individually. I was just uncertain if you mean each person was going to do one part or all three people were going to do each part and mix your ideas in the end. In my opinion, the latter may be very effective considering everyone has their own unique ideas to contribute. I also think a good idea may be to break up sources and make sure everyone contributes the same amount individually

Finally, most students settled on the idea that, rather than a strictly equal distribution or equal contributions, group members ought to use even distributions or contributions, in which the tasks are not clearly equal in amount, but together provide a balance based on some principle. These two separate statements make this point clear:

Student 1: It sounds like Student 2 and I both have similar groups in the sense that each member seems to contribute an equal amount. We each do different types of tasks but no one task is more important than the other, which is why we have been able to make an enormous amount of progress in our research in only five days in the library.
Student 2: I feel like each individual has something different to contribute. What one person may lack in researching capability, they would make up with their analysis and vice-versa. This creates quite a good balance in our overall strength as a group. My group narrowed the literary merit down to three individual topics. However, during my research today, I came across an article that connected all three of our ideas, which was quite exciting for me. I was able to make a formal thesis from this connection.

Several communicative actions comprised the fair work practice that the students described, including the use of non-confrontational language when dealing with non-contributing members, open communication, active participation, and the use of the Google Docs system to inquire with other groups. One student explains these norms clearly by referencing the flexibility that is necessary to build group consensus and ideas:

Student 1: It's okay to pass judgement (about other's ideas) as long as it's meant well and kind and constructive. You tell someone what they could do better or ask to not use a certain stat because of certain reasons. Criticism allows us to mature and see things about ourselves that we normally can't see.

Student 2: Even now, my group's thesis is far from being complete, and very different than it was early last week. Flexibility is essential to the research process. As we encounter more evidence that can sometimes contradict our ideas, we have to adapt. I also agree that criticism is a necessary part of group work. This is the way that we can improve our work and learn to take advice.

Interestingly, the students used several information tasks to structure these systems. For example, some groups chose to use information technology to document task ownership, prioritize tasks, analyze conflicting points of view, and record contributions. Students saw information technology as a means to keep track of the group's ideas and circumvent project limitations. One student explains:

Student 1: Yesterday, I felt that this project was more difficult that it first appeared to be, and that it will take a lot of effort to do it well. I still feel the same right now, but with a little more confidence, since my group and I have made some headway. My group and I have decided to use Facebook and a separate Google Doc to share ideas and to record comment and ideas, since the chat log on the docs disappear each time the page is closed. I ideally envision that we get all the sources we need (H and I) for the project within the next three days, which does not seem entirely impossible if we split the workload. This way, we will have plenty of time to work out the second L. If the best-laid plans do go awry, then we will communicate via Facebook to complete the research.

The day previous to this comment, this same group showed concern about individual voices being "drowned out" in majority opinions, to which the students responded by using the Google Docs environment in their own way to organize their work and extend its use beyond the recording of reflections and comments to bolstering systematic collaboration.

There is some evidence that a strictly equal distribution of work is not what all students actually think is the fairest ideal for collaboration. One student, for example, clarifies what he means by equal contributions, stating that equal does not mean everyone should perform the exact same actions, but rather should accept project tasks in more or less equal chunks. Relatedly, at one point in the discussion, the teacher intervenes on a student who comments that their group will not have enough time to finish the assignment by stating that they can come up with a solution as long as there is an equal distribution of work.

> **Student 1:** It seems that we are in a small bit of trouble. I don't know about you or P1F16maoe, but I might not have much time this week to do any work. However, I can assure you that I will have plenty of time next week. I feel like we really have to get our game on to get this done on time.
> **Teacher:** Understandable. But can you and your group delegate, with the understanding that equal distribution of work will be done.

In this case, the teacher as authority figure portrays the value of "equal distribution" as something normative within which the group should operate. Yet, as we have seen from previous examples, the students portray an equal distribution in different ways. The notion of equality that students seem to favor implies a balance or evenness to tasks, rather than a strict notion of exactly the same thing per task. Accordingly, the common notion of strict egalitarianism is supplanted by a utilitarian model of thinking in which "equality" implies balance, which students imply as the basis for a fair system of distribution/contribution. Furthermore, systems for work are frequently mentioned in terms of maximizing efficiencies. Yet, there are tensions among the students (and generally) in complying with this ideology of the "economic man," which the students allude to in the pre and post responses, such as the difficulties in splitting work, the domination of work groups by single individuals, and the inability to effectively integrate ideas from the minority.

Control and Expression of Dissent

Students made multiple comments about social justice ideas related to the control of their project environment that were connected to their ability to express dissent; thus, this section is jointly presented. Approximately fifteen percent of the statements identified concerned expression of dissent and about nineteen percent concerned control of the project process. Frequently used terms in the combination of these statements are: voice, marginalized, control, and restrictions. In terms of control, the students presented issues during discussion about the project environment related to their inability (due to the project's guidelines) to use techniques/tools and modes of communication that would enable their success. This student expresses his reservations as well as his assimilation into the "obligatory process":

> **Student 1:** Lastly, though, I am not fond of the restrictions that appear to be on our process. I'm not sure, but I feel as though the ANTHILL is in place more as an obligatory process rather as an aid, and this just confuses me even though I am good at researching.
> **Student 1** (separate comment): I'm not concerned about our group (as we are partners) finding research, as the book *The Hobbit* is very often read and acclaimed. However, I do feel your anxiety about the ANTHILL packet, and I truly hope we have to deal with it no more after tonight: I found it only confusing and destructive of the natural processes of my brain. It should become more clear, however, as we now are becoming familiarized with the format and obligations of our project, even though in a chaotic way.

Students had specific ideas about how the project environment should be structured to avoid marginalizing minority opinion or those otherwise expressing dissent, such as structuring a system of collaboration that necessarily includes all involved and fosters non-threatening discussion. The following lengthier exchange between the teacher and students during the project illustrates these issues:

> **Student A:** I believe that the search process that we spoke about today in the library was unhelpful and mostly a waste of time. I felt this because I believe that the process is merely multiple (ISP, SIK, SINK, ANThill) contrived methods of doing things that I would consider common sense. These things are all things we have learned from doing independent research in the past and we would do them naturally to move along the research process. The various acronyms/initialisms also confused the basic ideas that composed the research process. This was due to the sheer amount of them and also due to the fact that they didn't directly correlate with the ideas they related to.
> **Teacher:** Student A, Student A, Student A. Just when you typed such beauty before, here you type spoiled mashed potatoes. Every experience in life is different. You will always be Student A, you come in all forms on any given day, but no matter what names people call you, you will

never be redundant because you have knowledge to offer. You may be redundant too, but someone out there has yet to learn from you. This is not a place to critique the research method. You are aware that mostly everything you are being given is directly from the author of the methodology, right? You have reached your quota of comments. You have been thrown off Research Island.

Student 1: (responding to Student A) Though I do feel that the acronyms are not very helpful (being a mathematics and computer science person, straightforward instructions are much more helpful), I do not fully agree with Student A's idea that the breakdown is useless, for the breakdown allows for a much easier understanding of the research project, especially for people without any headway.

Student A: I am sorry. I may have been too critical, as pointed out by Student 1. I understand that my response was negative. However, I do not feel that it is invalid because it was made to express my true opinions about the process. I wanted to point out the flaws that I felt the process had, just as others have. I understand that my tone may have not been appropriate, especially for a comment here specifically. But I feel that some of my points were valid in that they were honest and corresponded to many people's opinions.

Student 2: (responding to Student A) Student A, I appreciate the honesty. I want to add that negative criticism can be helpful in finding flaws in this "research process," for nobody and nothing is perfect. I also would like to say that Student A's comment has been very worthy of debate, and thus I have chosen to comment on it. Without contrast, there is no beauty in anything. We need color in language and the literary world, as well as in the area of criticism. We need variation, and we need different ideas. Therefore, I would like to praise those who have stated their ideas straight out and flatly, for it is those people who have spent a lot of time and effort in order to have their ideas heard. Usually, these are the ideas that allow us to be exposed to different viewpoints, and ultimately, allow us to become more open-minded.

Librarian: I think constructive criticism is thought provoking and well worth it. I agree that a lot of "stuff" was given to you that took time that you thought you would be clicking away at the keyboards looking for information. I have to disagree that knowing the history and basis of something is not relevant.

The students make an argument that they do not have sufficient control of the research and project environment and that this hinders their ability to succeed. At points, there are clear indications that the students feel forced into the framework of research. This becomes particularly apparent when one student (Student A) uses the discussion system to voice a complaint about the research packet used. The teachers involved in the project monitor the discussion and occasionally respond to student comments. In this particular case, the teacher becomes an enforcement figure and uses the situation to publicly rebuke the student, thereby setting the precedent that only particular types of criticism (here inferred as constructive) will be accepted and that the research method as given to the students is not a matter for negotiation. Here, the traditional student-teacher ideology allows the teacher and librarian to exercise power over the students. Here power is asymmetric, with the teacher and librarian maintaining control over the students through the enforcement of the project process.

This particular situation can be seen as oppressive in that, although the students are asked to discuss their challenges for the particular day of research, the research framework itself is excluded from consideration for discussion. The teacher, for example, lets Student A know that his previous compliance with the project method (also referred to as the research packet) was an exemplar of what is expected from students ("such beauty before") while his current complaints amount to "spoiled mash potatoes." The teacher then claims that the discussion system is not an appropriate channel for such criticism, but does not offer any sort of alternative in her statement, thus denying students the ability to exercise any influence on the process. Finally, she appeals to the ideology of "authorship" and cognitive authority as a way to legitimize the content of the methodology, stating that the author of the methodology is, in fact, the person involved in the project and providing the methodology.

It is also clear that other students feel similarly—others in the same discussion thread commend Student A for openly expressing dissent as "it is those people who have spent a lot of time and effort to have their ideas heard." The librarian authoring the framework then claims that constructive criticism is fair because it is "thought provoking and well worth it," which resonates with the social notion that the fair way to give criticism is to do it in a constructive manner. Thus, the librarian surfaces the idea of constructive criticism into the project environment through its association as an embedded process in other aspects or ideologies of everyday life. The idea was already accessible to students from other experience; the librarian, in a sense, used it to delegitimize the appropriateness of the student's complaint, similar to the way an equal distribution was legitimized in the earlier example through a teacher comment.

In essence, the idea that the students should only provide constructive criticism is subject to perspective. On the one hand, constructive criticism may make the project environment a safer place, where one need not worry about being disparaged. At the same time, criticism of other sorts may sometimes be warranted to start the process of acknowledging a problem or bring attention to a matter. Clearly, the students want to voice an opinion about the research process, as evidenced by the several students who responded to Student A, but the teacher wants to maintain a particular ideology.

In the above example, many of the communicative actions taken by the students related to these social justice ideals are also evident, such as appealing to the group on controversial matters like the project process and supportive communication through student corroboration of ideas (when others supported Student A). The concept of constructive criticism is also shown as a problematic but adopted practice of the students. At other points, students used tools like Google Docs and Facebook in unexpected ways to circumvent restrictions on the process. This exchange between students and the librarian illustrates these particular actions:

> **Student 1:** It's a good thing to be opening up your perspective to the viewpoints of others, as the flow of ideas and being open to what others think is important. I'm actually intrigued by some of the topics we're researching, such as the historical accuracy of the Da Vinci Code. Scheduling meeting times will definitely be necessary, but I feel our group will have no trouble communicating due to the convenience of Facebook.
> **Librarian:** How about the convenience of the research packet/google doc? It really is ok to put your ideas there, challenge each other, encourage, disagree, plan, etc., right in the Google Doc and you can do it from anywhere and anytime and then you don't have to redo some of the conversation from FB to the google doc....just a thought.
> **Student 2:** There is no chat feature on mobile Google Docs, nor is there

a comment feature, so there is no form of communication.
Student 3: I definitely agree with what Student 2 is saying and what the other groups are doing. I believe that the more we can collaborate, the more the ideas will spark. Working at a computer is not enough. Talking face to face with others will really give us the ability to finds paths in which to drive our research

In this conversation, one student talks about the leveraging of outside tools such as Facebook for communication because, as the second student implies, the convenience of the chat features in Facebook are preferred by the students to the Google Doc environment, despite the inconvenience of moving conversation from Facebook to the Google Docs after each use. In fact, students even preferred avoiding information tools completely in favor of face-to-face conversation, due to how it enables the students, even though doing so goes against the point of using the research packet for the project process. In this case, power shifts to the students who assert their own control over the environment by re-purposing the information tools.

Project and Pedagogical Conclusions

Perhaps one lesson to be learned from this situation is that allowing students to express dissent to other students actually had an empowering effect, where other students may have stated their true feelings about the research process when they otherwise may not have. In terms of collaborative learning, such expressions may have also led to more mutual respect and positive interdependence, considered enablers of collaborative learning[80] between the students, as several students clearly stated that the complaint was worth discussion and built on Student A's comments. With good reason, the teacher and librarian want to keep a certain research structure in place, as that is part of what is being taught. But, without a clearly articulated channel or space for students to voice their concern with the process, it is difficult to tell if students

---

80. Ryan and Patrick, "The Classroom Social Environment and Changes in Adolescents' Motivation and Engagement during Middle School"; Johnson and Johnson, "Cooperation and the Use of Technology."

understand its value or actually learn from it. One takeaway from this finding might be to create a separate and anonymous discussion thread for dialogue between the students and the teacher/librarian specifically about the process.

With regard to contributions, it seems that students usefully transformed tools they were given to the purposes they needed them for, such as using Google Docs to track issues of accountability. However, perhaps one tangible intervention that might help students maintain their sense of fairness with regards to contributions would be to provide tools that aid in that specific purpose. The very appearance of these tools may lead students to their use for those purposes. Also, discussing aspects of the research and project process in a separate space may allow for a more congenial construction of mutual understanding and power relations between students and teachers.

It is also clear from the data that the students struggle with reconciling their own conceptions of fairness with those that are more normative to their group members, as well as in terms of the project environment. There appears to be a process of adjustment that occurs, where group members find a balance, sometimes driven by efficiency, other times by individual interests, after which the practices of the group become more specific and collectively understood. As one student explains:

Student 1: This kind of project is new to me because in the past I primarily chose to do individual projects because they're much easier to have full control over, however as we were given an assignment, I am liking it because it's easier to split up the amount of work, as well as get a large variety of ideas, many of which I could not have thought of without them. However, since I was used to individual projects, whenever something I did not agree with in our group arose, I tended to get more angry than I should have, however after working in a coalition with my group, I have become more adjusted. Fortunately, I did not say any derogatory statements and rather had a debate over which decision to choose. I have managed to suspend judgement because as the work progressed and we as a group progressed, I managed to see the wisdom in the words of my partners and stopped arguing for this reason.

This adjustment seems to be one that occurs through remediation of beliefs within the groups, across the groups and finally between the students and teachers. Each of the groups struggled initially with coming to terms with their own processes for pursuing the project, including their ideals about social justice. When students commented on other group members' posts, they often asked questions about how the groups handled certain situations or provided their own group ideas. Finally, as shown in the example of Student A, students used the Google Docs system to voice concern to the teacher and librarian over the process itself. At various times during this process, students were impacted by ideology explicitly, as in the directive to use an equal distribution of work that was previously discussed. In this way, there was a mutual process through which student ideals about social justice were shaped.

Therefore, the project process clearly has ideological stances embedded in it that are reinforced through the teacher and librarian. But at the same time, the technology used by the students is more open-ended, as it allows them to adapt some portion of the project process to their specific ideas of fairness, such as creating their own Google Docs to track their points of view, or using Facebook as an external alternative form of communication to the Google Docs comment feature.

Part of the advantage of using the critical assessment framework discussed here is that it gives a sense of the information tasks that were used collectively by students to construct social justice ideals. While the students came into this project with particular preconceived notions about social justice in terms of group work, there is a process through which that understanding is mediated to yield a set of routine actions that students follow. Parts of these actions, such as building a system for fair contribution and work distribution, revealed the contested nature of "equal" work as being about division of tangible labor (an amount of tasks) but also division of conceptual labor (types of tasks), maximizing efficiency (output) but also balancing individual strengths. From a critical perspective, there are multiple conflicting ideologies that are reconciled when the students take action. These ideologies were embedded in the groups of students as well as in the project process itself. The teacher and librarian acted as arbiters of the project process, signaling particular ideologies that were at times resisted by students through their dissent and at other times circumvented through the repurposing of information tools.

Social justice concepts, in this case the social justice ideals of the students around control, expression of dissent, and contributions/ distributions, were identified through discussion processes between students. Accordingly, a primary factor used to identify these statements were the terms used by students. Future researchers of social justice concepts would also benefit from thinking about the vocabularies that reflect the particular expression of social justice they are pursuing. Such vocabularies may be easy to identify in context, such as "equal," but deeper comparison across individuals serves to make such terms more ambiguous, as in the different ideas of equality of work distribution and contribution described here. Thus, future researchers can benefit from focusing on more specific social justice concepts to build unit theories across research on a particular social justice concept.

The framework provided here acts as an heuristic that highlights the connection between informational and communicative action as it relates to social justice concepts in the group project. However, future researchers may use a similar assessment process with collaborative work groups in other contexts related to different areas of focus (i.e., ideas other than control and expressions of dissent or work distribution/contributions). This assessment framework may also be useful for discovering areas of informational or communicative action that require deeper qualitative engagement, thereby acting as a roadmap of research opportunities. In conclusion, research on social justice concepts in the LIS field will benefit from integration with critical and practical theory perspectives because of their joint focus on context and analytical view of action. Creative uses of methodology should pave the way for these relevant and integral perspectives.

Bibliography

Adorno, Theodor W., and Max Horkheimer. *Dialectic of Enlightenment*. London: Verso, 1997.

Agger, Ben. "Critical Theory, Poststructuralism, Postmodernism: Their Sociological Relevance." *Annual Review of Sociology* 17, no. 1 (1991): 105-131.

Alvesson, Mats, and Stanley Deetz. "Critical Theory and Postmodernism: Approaches to Organizational Studies." In *Studying Organization: Theory and Method*, edited by Stewart R Clegg and Cynthia Hardy , 185-211. Thousand Oaks, CA: SAGE, 1999.

Ball, Stephen J. "Education Policy, Power Relations and Teachers' Work." *British Journal of Educational Studies* 41, no. 2 (1993): 106-121.

Budd, John M. "Critical Theory." In *The SAGE Encyclopedia of Qualitative Research Methods*, edited by Lisa M. Given, 175-80. Thousand Oaks, CA: SAGE, 2008.

———. "The Library, Praxis, and Symbolic Power." *Library Quarterly* 73, no. 1 (2003): 19-32.

Budd, John M., and Douglas Raber. "Discourse Analysis: Method and Application in the Study of Information." *Information Processing & Management* 32, no. 2 (1996): 217-226.

Charmaz, Kathy. "Grounded Theory Methods in Social Justice Research." *The SAGE Handbook of Qualitative Research* 4 (2011): 359-380.

Charmaz, Kathy. "Grounded Theory as an Emergent Method." *Handbook of Emergent Methods* (2008): 155-170.

Coates, Rodney D. "Social Justice and Pedagogy." *American Behavioral Scientist* 51, no. 4 (2007): 579-591.

Cook, Deborah. "Adorno, Ideology and Ideology Critique." *Philosophy & Social Criticism* 27, no. 1 (2001): 1-20.

Cool, Colleen. "The Concept of Situation in Information Science." *Annual Review of Information Science and Technology (ARIST)* 35 (2001): 5-42.

Courtright, Christina. "Context in Information Behavior Research." *Annual Review of Information Science and Technology* 41, no. 1 (2007): 273-306.

Curtis, David D., and Michael J. Lawson. "Exploring Collaborative Online Learning." *Journal of Asynchronous Learning Networks* 5, no. 1 (2001): 21-34.

Dadlani, Punit, and Ross J. Todd. "Information Technology Services and School Libraries: A Continuum of Social Justice." *Qualitative and Quantitative Methods in Libraries Journal*, Special Issue (2014): 39-48.

Dadlani, Punit, and Ross J. Todd. "Social Justice as Strategy: School Libraries and Information Technology." *Library Trends* 63, no. 3 (2016a): Forthcoming.

———. "Collaboration, Social Justice and School Libraries: Taking a Micro-view." *Library Quarterly* 86, no. 1, (2016b): Forthcoming.

Darder, Antonia. *Culture and Power in the Classroom: A Critical Foundation for Bicultural Education.* Connecticut: Berger & Garvey, 1991.

Dervin, Brenda. "Given a Context by any Other Name: Methodological Tools for Taming the Unruly Beast." *Information Seeking in Context* 13 (1997): 38.

Edwards, Derek, and Neil Mercer. *Common Knowledge.* London: Methuen, 1987.

Feldman, Martha S., and Wanda J. Orlikowski. "Theorizing Practice and Practicing Theory." *Organization Science* 22, no. 5 (2011): 1240-1253.

Fellenz, Martin R. "Toward Fairness in Assessing Student Group-work: A Protocol for Peer Evaluation of Individual Con-tributions." *Journal of Management Education* 30, no. 4 (2006): 570-591.

Friesen, Norm. "Critical Theory: Ideology Critique and the Myths of E-Learning." *Ubiquity* no. 2, (June, 2008).

Frohmann, Bernd. "The Power of Images: A Discourse Analysis of the Cognitive Viewpoint." *Journal of Documentation* 48, no. 4 (1992): 365-386.

Giddens, Anthony. *The Constitution of Society: Outline of the Theory of Structuration.* Los Angeles: University of California Press, 1984.

Gore, Jennifer M. "Disciplining Bodies: On the Continuity of Power Relations in Pedagogy." *Learning, Space and Identity* (2001): 167-181.

————. "Foucault's Poststructuralism and Observational Education Research: A Study of Power Relations." In *After Postmodern-ism: Education, Politics and Identity,* edited by Richard Smith and Philip Wexler, 98-111. Routledge, 1995:

Granter, Edward. *Critical Social Theory and the End of Work.* London: Ashgate Publishing, 2012.

Habermas, Jurgen. *Knowledge and Human Interests.* Boston: Beacon Press, 1971.

————. *The Theory of Communicative Action: Reason and the Rationaliza-tion of Society.* Boston: Beacon Press, 1985.

Held, David. *Introduction to Critical Theory: Horkheimer to Habermas.* Berkeley, CA: University of California Press, 1980.

Horkheimer, Max. *Critical Theory.* New York: Continuum, 1982.

Johannisson, Jenny, and Olof Sundin. "Putting Discourse to Work: Information Practices and the Professional Project of Nurses." *Library Quarterly* 77, no. 2 (2007).

Johnson, David W., and Roger T. Johnson. "Cooperation and the Use of Technology." In *Handbook of Research for Educational Communications and Technology*, edited by David H. Jonassen, 1017-1044. Routledge, 1996.

Kapitzke, Cushla. "Information Literacy: A Positivist Epistemology and a Politics of Outformation." *Educational Theory* 53, no. 1 (2003): 37-53.

———. "Information Literacy: A Review and Post Structural Critique." *Australian Journal of Language and Literacy* 26, no. 1 (2003): 53.

Kincheloe, Joe L., and Peter McLaren. "Rethinking Critical Theory and Qualitative Research." In *Ethnography and Schools: Qualitative Approaches to the Study of Education*, edited by Yali Zou and Enrique T. Trueba, 87-138. Lanham, MD: Rowman and Littlefield, 2002.

Klemm, M., S. Sanderson, and G. Luffman. "Mission Statements: Selling Corporate Values to Employees." *Long Range Planning* 24, no. 3 (1991): 73-78.

Krippendorff, Klaus. *Content Analysis: An Introduction to its Methodology*. Sage, 2012.

Kurasaki, Karen S. "Intercoder Reliability for Validating Conclusions Drawn from Open-Ended Interview Data." *Field Methods* 12, no. 3 (2000): 179-194.

Latour, Bruno. *Science in Action: How to Follow Scientists and Engineers through Society*. Cambridge, MA: Harvard University Press, 1987.

Lave, Jean. *Cognition in Practice: Mind, Mathematics and Culture in Everyday Life*. Cambridge, UK: Cambridge University Press, 1988.

Leckie, Gloria J., Lisa M. Given, and John Buschman. *Critical Theory for Library and Information Science: Exploring the Social from Across the Disciplines.* ABC-CLIO, 2010.

Lincoln, Yvonna S., Susan A. Lynham, and Egon G. Guba. "Paradigmatic Controversies, Contradictions, and Emerging Confluences, Revisited." *The Sage Handbook of Qualitative Research* 4 (2011): 97-128.

Lloyd, Annemaree. "Framing Information Literacy as Information Practice: Site Ontology and Practice Theory." *Journal of Documentation* 66, no. 2 (2010): 245-258.

Mackenzie, Noella, and Sally Knipe. "Research Dilemmas: Paradigms, Methods and Methodology." *Issues in Educational Research* 16, no. 2 (2006): 193-205.

Manke, M. *Classroom Power Relations: Understanding Student-Teacher Interaction.* Routledge, 1997.

Marcuse, Herbert. *One-Dimensional Man; Studies in the Ideology of Advanced Industrial Society.* Boston: Beacon Press, 1964.

McCarty, Teresa L., ed. *Language, Literacy, and Power in Schooling.* Routledge, 2006.

McKenzie, Pamela J. "Mapping Textually Mediated Information Practice in Clinical Midwifery Care." In *New Directions in Human Information Behavior*, 73-92. Netherlands: Springer, 2006.

———. "A Model of Information Practices in Accounts of Everyday-life Information Seeking." *Journal of Documentation* 59, no. 1 (2003): 19-40.

Mehra, Bharat, Kendra S. Albright, and Kevin Rioux. "A Practical Framework for Social Justice Research in the Information Professions." *Proceedings of the American Society for Information Science and Technology* 43, no. 1 (2006): 1-10.

Ngwenyama, Ojelanki K. "The Critical Social Theory Approach to Information Systems: Problems and Challenges."In *Information Systems Research: Contemporary Approaches and Emergent Traditions*, edited by Hans-Erik Nissen, Heinz-Karl Klein, and Rudy A. Hirschheim, 267-280. Amsterdam: North-Holland, 1991

Nicolini, Davide. *Practice Theory, Work, and Organization: An Introduction.* Oxford University Press, 2013.

NJASL. "About the New Jersey Association of School Libraries." http://www.njasl.org/page-1863043.

Orlikowski, Wanda J. "Using Technology and Constituting Structures: A Practice Lens for Studying Technology in Organizations." *Organization Science* 11, no. 4 (2000): 404-428.

Pearce, John A., and Fred David. "Corporate Mission Statements: The Bottom Line." *The Academy of Management Executive* 1, no. 2 (1987): 109-115.

Pettigrew, Andrew M. "Context and Action in the Transformation of the Firm." *Journal of Management Studies* 24, no. 6 (1987): 649-670.

———. "Contextualist Research and the Study of Organizational Change Processes." *Research Methods in Information Systems* (1985): 53-78.

Ponterotto, Joseph G. "Qualitative Research in Counseling Psychology: A Primer on Research Paradigms and Philosophy of Science." *Journal of Counseling Psychology* 52, no. 2 (2005): 126.

Reckwitz, Andreas. "Toward a Theory of Social Practices: A Development in Culturalist Theorizing." *European Journal of Social Theory* 5, no. 2 (2002): 243-263.

Rioux, Kevin. "Metatheory in Library and Information Science: A Nascent Social Justice Approach." *Journal of Education for Library and Information Science* (2010): 9-17.

Rouse, Joseph. "Practice Theory." *Handbook of the Philosophy of Science* 15 (2007).

Savolainen, Reijo. "Information Behavior and Information Practice: Reviewing the 'Umbrella Concepts' of Information Seeking Studies." *Library Quarterly* 77, no. 2 (2007).

Schatzki, Theodore R. *Social Practices: A Wittgensteinian Approach to Human Activity and the Social*. Cambridge, UK: Cambridge University Press, 1996.

Schmid, E. Cutrim. "Investigating the Use of Interactive Whiteboard Technology in the English Language Classroom Through the Lens of a Critical Theory of Technology." *Computer Assisted Language Learning* 19, no. 1 (2006): 47-62.

Smith, Lauren. "Towards a Model of Critical Information Literacy Instruction for the Development of Political Agency." *Journal of Information Literacy* 7, no. 2 (2013): 15-32.

Solomon, Paul. "Discovering Information in Context." *Annual Review of Information Science and Technology* 36 (2002): 229-264.

Somekh, Bridget, and Cathy Lewin. *Research Methods in the Social Sciences*. Sage, 2005.

Sonnenwald, Diane H. "Evolving Perspectives of Human Information Behavior: Contexts, Situations, Social Networks, and Information Horizons." In *Exploring the Contexts of Information Behavior: Proceedings of the Second International Conference in Information Needs*, 176-190. Taylor Graham, 1999.

Steffy, Brian D., and Andrew J. Grimes. "A Critical Theory of Organization Science." *Academy of Management Review* 11, no. 2 (1986): 322-336.

Swanson, Troy A. "A Radical Step: Implementing a Critical Information Literacy Model." *portal: Libraries and the Academy* 4, no. 2 (2004): 259-273.

Talja, Sanna. "Jean Lave's Practice Theory." In *Critical Theory for Library and Information Science: Exploring the Social from Across the Disciplines*, edited by Gloria J. Leckie, Lisa M. Given, and John E. Buschman, 205-220. Santa Barbara, CA: ABC-CLIO, 2010.

———. "Analyzing Qualitative Interview Data: The Discourse Analytic Method." *Library & Information Science Research* 21, no. 4 (1999): 459-477.

Talja, S., Keso, H., & Pietiläinen, T. "The Production of 'Context' in Information Seeking Research: A Metatheoretical View." *Information Processing & Management* 35, no. 6 (1999): 751-763.

Talja, Sanna, Kimmo Tuominen, and Reijo Savolainen. "'Isms' in Information Science: Constructivism, Collectivism and Constructionism." *Journal of Documentation* 61, no. 1 (2005): 79-101.

Todd, Ross J., C. Gordon, and Y. Lu. "Report on Findings and Recommendations of the New Jersey School Library Study Phase 1: One Common Goal: Student Learning." New Brunswick, NJ: CISSL, 2011.

United Way of Northern New Jersey. *ALICE: Study of Financial Hardship in New Jersey*. Morristown, NJ: Halpin, 2012.

Veinot, Tiffany C. "'The Eyes of the Power Company': Workplace Information Practices of a Vault Inspector." *Library Quarterly* 77, no. 2 (2007).

Whittington, Richard. "Putting Giddens into Action: Social Systems and Managerial Agency." *Journal of Management Studies* 29, no. 6 (1992): 693-712.

Wittgenstein, L. *Philosophical Investigations*. New York: Macmillan, 1958.

About the Contributors

Jeanie Austin is a doctoral candidate at the Graduate School of Library and Information Science at the University of Illinois at Urbana-Champaign. Their research and interests focus on the incorporation of critical praxis in LIS, especially regarding the gendered, racialized, and ability-centric systems that affect youth. They are also interested in the provision of library services to incarcerated youth, and the complex political, social, and publishing processes surrounding that work.

Clara M. Chu is Director of the Mortenson Center for International Library Programs, and Mortenson Distinguished Professor at the University of Illinois at Urbana-Champaign. She specializes in the sociocultural study of information use, practices, and systems that impact access and representation in multicultural communities. Having published, presented, and consulted internationally in English and Spanish, Chu is a leading voice on multicultural library and information issues. Active in professional associations, she has served as the 2014/15 President of the Association for Library and Information Science Education (ALISE) and on the 2013-15 Governing Board of the International Federation of Library Associations and Institutions (IFLA).

Laura-Edythe Coleman is a museum informaticist and a doctoral candidate in information science at Florida State University. As a museum informaticist, her focus is on the point of convergence for museums, information, people, and technology. Knowing that societies need museums for creating and sustaining cultural memory, she strives to help communities co-create heritage collections with museums. Coleman's particular focus is cultural institutions that are embedded in communities reconciling civil conflict.

Nicole A. Cooke is an Assistant Professor at the Graduate School of Library and Information Science, University of Illinois, Urbana-Champaign. Her research and teaching interests include diversity and social justice in librarianship, information behavior (particularly in online contexts), online teaching and learning, and critical information literacy. She has published articles in *Library Quarterly, Library and Information Science Research, InterActions: UCLA Journal of Education and Information*, and the *New Review of Academic Librarianship*. She also co-authored *Instructional Strategies and Techniques for Information Professionals* (Chandos Press, 2012).

Jonathan Cope is a Reference/Instruction Librarian at the College of Staten Island, City University of New York (CUNY). His research focuses on the ways in which library and information literacy work is situated within specific social, cultural, economic, and disciplinary contexts. In his free time he enjoys plucking at his guitar and mandolin, reading science fiction, and running.

Punit Dadlani is a Ph.D. candidate in the School of Communication & Information at Rutgers University, and is the Barham Scholar with the Center for International Scholarship in School Libraries (CiSSL), funded by the Carole & Norman Barham Family Foundation. His primary research interests focus on information behavior and practices, social justice, and organizational communication. His current research explores how information-intensive organizations like school and public libraries integrate technology into their practices, and how social justice concepts are understood, embedded, and enacted through information services in organizations.

Gabriel Gomez is a Professor in the Information Studies Department, College of Education, Chicago State University. Since earning his Ph.D. in Radio/TV/Film at Northwestern University, he has been teaching and researching in a multidisciplinary mode, covering everything from topics in LGBT representation to matters in distance and multicultural education. He has also recently tackled issues regarding evolving student attitudes toward copyright and plagiarism, and the effects of big data on libraries. Currently he is co-executive director of the Legacy Project Education Initiative, a collaborative grassroots effort to promote LGBT history through the Legacy Walk (a permanent outdoor exhibit) and formal K-12 education.

Wendy Highby is the Social Sciences Reference Librarian at the Michener Library at the University of Northern Colorado. She received a bachelor's degree from the University of Colorado at Denver, and a master's degree in library science from Emporia State University. Formerly a paralegal, she became a librarian in mid-life. She grew up in Oaks, Oklahoma and Safford, Arizona, developing a deep connection to nature by learning to swim in Ozark creeks and hiking on Mount Graham ("Big Seated Mountain"). She co-founded Weld Air and Water, a grassroots environmental group in Greeley, Colorado, and writes poetry and satirical song parodies.

Zachary Loeb is a writer, activist, librarian, and terrible accordion player. He was involved with the Occupy Wall Street People's Library and has since been active in organizing other activist libraries. He earned an M.S.I.S. from the University at Texas-Austin, an M.A. from NYU's Media, Culture, and Communication Department, and in the Fall of 2016 began working towards a Ph.D. in the History and Sociology of Science at the University of Pennsylvania. Zachary is interested in questions raised by the Science and Technology in Society field, including: ideologies that develop in relation to technology, critiques of technology, and ethical issues raised by technology. Zachary writes regularly about technology and libraries at the blog LibrarianShipwreck using the moniker The Luddbrarian.

Bharat Mehra is Associate Professor in the School of Information Sciences at the University of Tennessee. His research furthers diversity and intercultural communication, social justice in library and information science, critical and cross-cultural studies, and community informatics or the use of information and communication technologies to empower minority and underserved populations to make meaningful changes in their everyday lives.

Joseph D. Minarik has been a social worker for more than two decades in communities and within organizations that promote racial justice and systems-level change. Currently, he coordinates, teaches, and trains others to teach at the Program on Intergroup Relations at the University of Illinois at Urbana-Champaign (UIUC). His research interests include exploring ways to help learners understand and resist privileging and contemporary oppression. His doctoral work in social work focuses on developing policy advocacy training for human service nonprofit administrators and leaders. He is also championing the use of Universal Design for Learning at UIUC.

Kevin Rioux is Associate Professor of Library and Information Science at St. John's University, New York. In his teaching and research, he uses social justice metatheory, information behavior frameworks, and integrated human development models to explore issues related to information access and information technologies as tools of social and economic development in both local and international contexts.

Kaurri C. Williams-Cockfield has over twenty-five years of progressively responsible work experience in both U.S. and international library settings. She currently serves as the Director of the Blount County Public Library in Maryville, Tennessee. Her research areas include public libraries, social justice and sustainable communities, and school media center impacts on student test outcomes. K.C. holds an M.L.I.S. from the University of Southern Mississippi. She has been an adjunct instructor for the School of Information Sciences at the University of Tennessee, Knoxville since 2011.

INDEX